AT THE SERVICE
OF THE CHURCH

AT THE SERVICE OF THE CHURCH

Henri de Lubac Reflects on the Circumstances that Occasioned His Writings

Translated by
Anne Elizabeth Englund

COMMUNIO BOOKS

IGNATIUS PRESS   SAN FRANCISCO

Title of the French original:
Mémoire sur l'occasion de mes écrits
© 1989 Culture et Verité
Namur, Belgium

Cover from a letter written by Henri de Lubac
Cover design by Roxanne Mei Lum

© 1993 Ignatius Press, San Francisco
ISBN 0-89870-414-6
Library of Congress catalogue number 92-71933
Printed in the United States of America

CONTENTS

Foreword 7
Preface 9

I. MEMOIR

CHAPTER ONE 15
  The Very Beginnings 15
  Mentors and Colleagues 18
  First Articles 24

CHAPTER TWO 27
  Catholicisme, Corpus mysticum, Bouddhisme 27
  Surnaturel, Atheisme, God 34

CHAPTER THREE 44
  Before the Second World War 44
  The War Years 48
  Témoignage chrétien 50
  Affrontements mystiques 57

CHAPTER FOUR 60
  From 1946 to 1950 60
  From 1950 to 1953 71

CHAPTER FIVE 80
  From 1953 to 1958 80
  From 1958 to 1959 88
  Sources chrétiennes 94

CHAPTER SIX 97
  Montcheuil and Valensin 97
  Teilhard de Chardin 103

Christian Mysticism 112
Victor Fontoynont 114

CHAPTER SEVEN 116
Before and after the Council 116
The Twins 123
Les Eglises particulières 132
Claudel et Péguy, Pic 137

CHAPTER EIGHT 140
A Glance at My Work (1975) 140
Hans Urs von Balthasar 150

CHAPTER NINE 153
From 1975 to 1981 153
Daniélou, Fessard, Bouillard 160
Again 168
Wojtyla 171

II. APPENDICES

APPENDIX I 177

APPENDIX II 190

APPENDIX III 225

APPENDIX IV 245

APPENDIX V 310

APPENDIX VI 320

APPENDIX VII 340

APPENDIX VIII 360

APPENDIX IX 376

INDEX OF PERSONS 405

FOREWORD

(by the publisher of the French edition)

In 1976, Father Hans Urs von Balthasar wanted to offer his "mentor and friend", Father Henri de Lubac, on the occasion of his eightieth birthday, a little book that would bring out "the organic work of a life".[1] He had finished it when, as he wrote in the preface, "Father de Lubac and a few other friends placed in my hand a large manuscript (provided, as one might expect, with numerous notes), in which he explains the genesis, meaning and fate of his books and situates them within the course of the various stages of his life, his studies, his meetings, his friendships as well as his legendary exiles and banishments. These pages are so alive, so useful for a precise understanding of his intentions, that I cannot keep from gathering a few flowers from them to add to my own vase".[2]

Twelve years later, Father von Balthasar, convinced of the importance of this manuscript and having overcome a final hesitation on the part of its author, had decided to publish it in a German translation that would coincide with its publication in French. Father von Balthasar's death prevented the accomplishment of this amicable plan.

In 1981, Cardinal de Lubac added a final chapter to the 1975 manuscript that Father von Balthasar had known. For the purposes of publication, the author read through the text a final time with the publisher.

G. Chantraine

---

[1] Hans Urs von Balthasar, "Une Oeuvre organique", in Hans Urs von Balthasar and G. Chantraine, *Le Cardinal Henri de Lubac. L'Homme et son oeuvre*, Sycomore series (Paris: Lethielleux, 1983). [English translation: *The Theology of Henri de Lubac* (San Francisco: Ignatius Press, 1991).]

[2] Op. cit., 45–46.

PREFACE

These Notes were compiled or collated as a result of several discreet but earnest requests addressed to me. They concern the period that runs from August 26, 1946, to October 28, 1951. Up to February 4, 1949, and then after July 22, 1950, I had the help of a notebook of memoranda, which most often I had only to transcribe or summarize. For the period between those two dates, I could refer only to the texts that I had here at hand.

I hope that in general I have been accurate. A few mistakes may have slipped in nonetheless. Of course, when I quote the remarks or writings of others, I do not for all that vouch for their contents.

Even for the period covered by my memoranda, there are gaps, due mainly to the fact that I was often too busy to note down everything or to fatigue or illness. I also had to exclude a few letters as being too personal or too confidential. On the other hand, matters were not written down according to their respective importance but according to my direct knowledge about them; some are of no interest; but sometimes what seemed almost insignificant at the time subsequently assumed great importance in the light of later events.

It is not without embarrassment, or even more than that, that I transcribe some of the texts in which I am too central a figure. But I have not wanted, through some subjective consideration, to omit anything that might help to shed some light on the matters concerned. Because of the circumstances, from beginning to end, the point of view is strictly personal: this is not an historical sketch but merely one particular document that should be compared with and completed by others. Such as it is, and notwithstanding the several omissions I have pointed out, it remains strictly confidential.

I have added, in an Appendix, a number of auxiliary documents, which I have listed farther on.

PARIS, OCTOBER 29, 1951.

I have often been asked why I was interested in one particular subject or another. People have been surprised at the real or apparent diversity in my "focuses of interest". They have questioned me about my books, about the circumstances surrounding their origin or their publication, about the difficulties to which several of them gave rise, and so forth. . . . Some of those who posed these questions to me are no longer with us; others, scattered around the world, have since taken up more serious concerns. Yet perhaps the recollections I am undertaking to set down will still be of interest to some of them as well as to younger friends whom God has given me in my old age. I expect to spend a few free days at it. Many of the names, incidents and dates escape me. I do not have any of my publications at hand. I have no notes at my disposal. I am not doing any research. Which is to say that my accounts, which are always fragmentary, might also at times lack precision; they will be nothing but a written conversation. But that is not so important, after all, since the subject himself has little importance.

EEGENHOVEN, DECEMBER 1973

~

First written in 1973, during a time of convalescence, far from any books or papers, this text contained inaccuracies and even a few errors. I revised and edited it in 1975 and then again in 1978. If it were worth the trouble, it should be revised again and completed in the light that the course of the years has thrown on earlier events (at least for those not content with official sources and printed texts).

What I have written is a memoir, not memoirs, as several have recommended and at times urged me to write. The reader will find here (with the exception of an occasional reference made in passing) neither personal secrets nor colorful recollections, neither detailed accounts nor judgments about contemporaries nor reflections about the spiritual life in the Church and about the apostolate; a fortiori, a picture of neither history nor people. I am incapable of that, and I have always had something else to do.

"As men draw towards their end," wrote Newman at the beginning of his *Apologia*, "they care less for disclosures." I have not, however, followed that inclination. "As sensitive then", he added, "as I have always been to the imputations which have been heaped upon me. . . ." In my case, the sensitivity, without disappearing, has in the end lost its edge.

PARIS, 1980

N.B. In order to situate the subjects of this Memoir in a broader context and a more precise (or at times perhaps more accurate) chronology, it would be good to refer, among other things:

1. to a collection of correspondence, most of which is dated from July 24, 1942, to around 1970; and

2. to a group of eight notebooks containing a Journal kept from 1946 to 1968.

[*Bracketed numbers within the text refer to documents located in the Appendices in the back of the book. The number of the appropriate Appendix precedes the colon; the number of the document follows the colon.*]

PART ONE

MEMOIR

CHAPTER ONE

Apart from a few earlier, insignificant lines, my first article, entitled "Apologétique et Théologie" appeared in 1930 in the *Nouvelle revue théologique* published by the Jesuits of Louvain.[1] This was my opening lecture at the Theology Faculty of Lyons (October 1929), in the chair of fundamental theology, where I succeeded Father Albert Valensin. The latter had not reached retirement age, but he had asked to be discharged from his teaching duties in order to give himself entirely to the ministry of priestly retreats. Our Provincial, Father Jean-Baptiste Costa de Beauregard, had to find a replacement for him *ex impromptu*. I was then completing my "third year" at Paray le Monial, where Father Auguste Bulot was the instructor. I was at that time without any preparation (in the years that followed, I more than once asked for a "repeal" of at least six months to a year—always in vain). Suffering after my return from the war from earaches and headaches that caused frequent bouts of dizziness, I had not even been able to follow with regularity the courses during my four years of theology (Ore Place, Hastings, 1924–1926; Fourvière, Lyons, 1926–1928); it was Father Charles Nicolet who, in 1928, had helped me prepare for the final examination (the "points"); he was more clever than I (he would soon prove to be an eminent philosopher as well as deeply spiritual): he failed his examination, and I passed. I had occasion to reminisce about these four years of theology, and particularly about the first two, those at Ore Place, when I was invited, on April 25, 1956, to the celebration of Father Emile Delaye's fifty years of religious life:

> It is said that those who did not live before the 1914 war—before the Revolution, before the Flood . . . —did not know the sweetness of living. There is much illusion in that. What I believe I can say with greater truth is that anyone who did not live at Ore Place did not know in all its fullness the happiness of being a "scholastic". There we were really rather far from the world, away for a while from nearly all the responsibilities of the apostolate; alone among ourselves, as if in a big ship sailing, without a radio, in the middle of the ocean. But what an intense life within that ship, and what a marvelous crossing! At the helm, under the very good and peaceful direction of Father

[1] Father Karl H. Neufeld, whom I had known as a scholastic at Fourvière, surprised me by reprinting this article, translated by him into German, in 1976, in *Zeitschrift für Katolische Theologie*, in celebration of my eightieth birthday. And a request came to me at that time from America to reprint it in English. [Cf. "Apologetics and Theology", in Henri de Lubac, *Theological Fragments* (San Francisco: Ignatius Press, 1989), 91–104.]

Riondel, a prefect who was still young and as welcoming and encouraging as he could be. And not lacking in bold wisdom! What a joy it was to plough the waters of the high sea with him, to explore in every sense the infinite spaces of dogmatics, to lose oneself, without getting lost, in the depths of mystery! Two names will for me always remain associated with the memory of those happy years: Father Joseph Huby, whom we still mourn; and Father Emile Delaye, whom we are celebrating. Two alert and trustworthy guides, whom we felt to be so well matched; both of whom helped us so much, and in so many ways, in clear weather as well as in stormy, to follow the course without danger of shipwreck, and also without giving in to the call of some premature port. —My Father, the opportunity today to say thank you once again is a joy from that distant past that rises, intact, in my heart.

So, in September 1929, I arrived on the Lyons peninsula, at the residence on rue d'Auvergne. It was an old shack that was demolished shortly afterward. In the loft where I was lodged, which was lit by a little skylight, I had not a single book. The Fourvière library was scarcely accessible: it had no room at that time where one could work, and none of the books could be checked out; the library of the Catholic Faculties was miserable: two dusty rooms in an old, shaky main building, where they had a little bit of everything. Fortunately I discovered a treasure in the attic of Saint Joseph's day school, in the beautiful, old-fashioned quarters located over the chapel: a library, particularly of literature, which had long been neglected but which contained several tiers of theology well furnished with old books. A few young theologian friends came from Fourvière to help me get settled, and, not without fear, I set to work. My October lecture was well received by my audience: a group of about fifteen, all candidates for the licentiate or doctoral degrees (our Faculty at that time gave courses only in preparation for those degrees). One of them came to tell me a few days later, however, that it was too academic and that it was not easy to draw any precise ideas from it. He was soon reassured. The following lectures were much less prepared in form; they were more spoken than read. I believe that, on the whole, relations between the professor and his students, both in and out of class, were simple, cordial and very lively.

I sent my first article to Father Laberthonnière. He sent a very pleasant reply, declaring himself to be in agreement with me but reproaching me for having quoted Saint Thomas, against whom his animosity was becoming more and more intransigent [1:1]. I answered him with a rather mischievous letter, which, I am told, was later to amuse those who found it among his papers after his death. I had also, of course, sent a courtesy copy of my article to the Rector of the Faculties, Msgr. Fleury Lavallée. The Rector's acknowledgment was very flattering. When I showed it to Father Auguste Valensin, Albert's younger brother, who taught philosophy (with marvelous success) at the Faculty of Letters and who lived like I did on rue d'Auvergne, he explained to me that it was not necessary to set great store by those kinds of compliments; they were common practice and without any meaning. I had even then ceased to be very naïve; but that warning from an elder was nonetheless useful.

Msgr. Lavallée was for me an object of veneration but also somewhat of fear. His simplicity, which was at once serious and smiling, but with a cold smile, was intimidating. He was not talkative, and in his presence I was mute. He was a model of the priestly life. He was called the "foremost priest in France". I do believe he was the last in our house to abandon the rabat for the roman collar. Despite a certain stiffness, his thin silhouette was always associated in my mind with that of Cardinal Couillé, the archbishop from whose hands I had formerly (around 1906) received Confirmation in the archbishop's drawing room, which had been transformed into a chapel (and has since become the reading room of the municipal library). Ever since my youth, the old cardinal, a slender little man, quite amiable and very popular, was surrounded by a halo for me because of the memory of Msgr. Dupanloup, whose associate he had been. Cardinal Couillé was an invalid from that time on and only appeared carried on a "sedia" like the pope in Rome. As for Msgr. Lavallée, I saw him for the first time a few years later, one year before I entered the Jesuits. It was in November 1912, at the solemn session opening the school term of the Catholic Faculties, where I had come to enroll for a year of law. This kind of session was at that time in fact very solemn. In the morning, at the cathedral, the nave of which was filled to overflowing, the Lyonese liturgy displayed all its pomp and ceremony perfumed with incense; despite the recent "Separation", all public authorities of the city and State were still represented; the faculty was well fitted out in robes with varicolored ornaments; the students were numerous; the bishop "patrons" (a group of about thirty) presided in liturgical dress; one of them proclaimed a lengthy discourse. (In following years, as affluence diminished, they withdrew to the Ainay basilica.) In the afternoon, they gathered again in the large hall in the Europe Hotel on rue Bellecour. The main "attraction" of the session was the Rector's speech.

On that day, listening for the first time to Msgr. Lavallée speak, I had been filled with admiration. It was an anti-modernist discourse. Only just having come from a philosophy class whose professor was less than mediocre (he was an old, retired missionary, who dictated to us summaries from Lahr's manual that he had made in little notebooks), I did not understand very distinctly the ideas presented.[2] Nevertheless the discourse seemed to

[2] The stout Cardinal Dubillard, Archbishop of Chambéry, who was presiding, declared

me to be of profound and sublime seriousness, and above all the music of the long, well-constructed phrases enchanted me. (I have since reread this speech, which was in fact solid and written in finely crafted Latin: Msgr. Lavallée was a Latin professor.) Our Rector excelled also in homilies. In the early years of my professorship, before he retired, I relished every year the one he gave in the crypt of Saint Irenaeus Church, where we were gathered at the end of June for the feast of the great bishop of Lyons. Msgr. Lavallée spoke in a measured, almost hushed voice. One felt in his tone of voice, combined with great nobility of expression and, as it were, suffused by the light of one or two fine symbols, a firmness of faith that was more impressive than the most heated exhortations. Yet what always made me feel a bit ill-at-ease in my relations with him, besides his habitual reserve and despite his kindness, was his reputation for extreme traditionalism[3] and the perception (shared by all of us at the Theology Faculty) of a doctrinal prudence that was not always perfectly informed. Yet he was not an "integrist", particularly, in fact, because of his perfect honesty and unpretentiousness; he was well able to defend his professors on occasion; it was in that way that he always protected Father Auguste Valensin, whose teaching was criticized more than once, and that he maintained, very warmly, complete confidence in him right to the end. But finally, he was a member of the Faculty of Letters, and, while Theology had long had a reputation for liberalism within the Catholic Faculties of Lyons, Letters had had the opposite reputation. The latter had been well earned during the period when the chair of French literature was held by Msgr. Théodore Delmont, who was a well-known integrist closely associated with the terrible Abbé Barbier in the *Critique du Libéralisme*.[4] But at the time I arrived as a professor, these were already age-worn reputations.

During the 1930s, I also gave to the *Nouvelle revue théologique* an article entitled "Sur la philosophie chrétienne" (1936) [1:2] as well as a brief Note on "Le Motif de la création dans *l'Etre et les êtres*" by Maurice Blondel (1938).[5] During my years of philosophy (1920–1923) on Jersey, I had read

---

quite candidly in his final address that he himself had not understood everything very well.

[3] He was to give an amusing sign of this around 1938. M. Bollaërt, prefect of Rhône, former under-secretary of fine arts, offered to restore the cathedral but imposed his own plans for it. He envisaged moving back the main altar, which was at that time in the transept crossing. Msgr. Lavallée considered it necessary to reject everything rather than violate in that way the tradition of the Lyons church. M. Bollaërt then proved with documentary evidence that this tradition dated from . . . 1793! Msgr. Lavallée lost no time in acquiescing to the restorative alteration.

[4] Msgr. Delmont: *Modernisme et modernistes* (Paris: Lethielleux, 1910). See also the *Critique du Libéralisme* of September 1, 1913.

[5] Reproduced in *Théologies d'occasion* (DDB, 1984), 425–32. This was essentially a reply to

with enthusiasm Maurice Blondel's *Action, Lettre* (on apologetics) and various other studies. Through a praiseworthy exception, some of our masters at that time, who were quite strict in what they excluded from our
reading,[6] allowed us, though without encouraging us, to study the thought
of the philosopher from Aix. Father Robert Hamel (d. 1974) and I read
him together. I had heard a lot about him from Father Auguste Valensin. I
had visited him for the first time in 1922, on a trip made to the property
of "La Félicité" (an agricultural school on the outskirts of Aix) in order to
care for my earaches. (As the doctor on Jersey had spoken of trepanation,
Father Gabriel Picarda, our Rector, had judged it more prudent to send
me off right away to my home province in France. It was only much later,
in 1954, that a final operation freed me from continual spells of dizziness
and a threat of meningitis.) An unpublished portrait of Blondel, sketched
by Antoine Denat,[7] recalling a visit made to the philosopher in 1935, corresponds rather well to my own impressions at that time:

> In his presence I understood from the outset what it meant to consider the
> teaching profession as a kind of priesthood. . . . In Maurice Blondel's patient
> voice and sustained eloquence there were at that time inflections of goodness,
> charity and urbanity, in the broad sense of that word, that I have rarely found
> in so developed and refined a degree in men of the Church. In the conversation
> of this so-called great "combatant" of ideas, there was not the least trace of that
> bitterness that, visible in Maritain, at times showed through in the Kantian
> ardor of M. Lachièze-Rey. I left Maurice Blondel not only enlightened but
> calmed, and, reading his long works, which are more spoken than written, I
> found once again that immense patience, at once gentle and persistent, which
> ended in triumphing over all: *Labor improbus omnia vincit.* . . . —Once again
> the meek have inherited the earth.

Among the contemporaries studied during my formation, I owe a particular debt to Blondel, Maréchal and Rousselot. I did not have the opportunity to know Father Pierre Rousselot personally. He was killed at
Eparges, near Verdun, in the spring of 1915, at the very place were I was to
be one year later. On the other hand, from 1919 on, I had access to all his
papers, which had been entrusted at that time to Father Auguste Valensin
in Lyons. Most have remained unpublished. When he left for the war in
August 1914, Rousselot was in a state of complete intellectual ferment.
What has been written about him since has been incomplete, sometimes

---

the criticism of the work presented by Pierre Guérin in the *Revue d'histoire et de philosophie
religieuses* (1937), 191–99.

[6] For example: Gilson's *Saint Thomas*, labeled "modern philosophy", was locked up in a
cupboard that was opened only on holidays.

[7] Now a professor of French literature in Melbourne, Australia. (He has since died.)

inaccurate or too superficial. One of the principal subjects that needs to be studied is that of his relations with Blondel and with Laberthonnière;[8] as opposed as the latter was to the Thomist positions of Rousselot, he recognized his exceptional value and was grateful to him for having seen him to be, not at all a modernist, but an Augustinian [1:3]; and, on the other hand, several passages from Rousselot's latest unpublished writings show that the exchanges with Laberthonnière had borne fruit in his reflection. An attempt has been made at least three times to collect Rousselot's scattered and unpublished writings: first by Father Joseph Huby, his most faithful disciple [1:4], a second time by me. Each time, "Rome" stood in the way. As far as I have been able to discover, the Society's opposition expressed above all that of Msgr. Pietro Parente, who had power in the Holy Office; he was not the only one but the most determined.[9] The third attempt was made shortly after the last Council. The project could have been carried out without difficulty at that time. The staff of our "Théologie" series seemed favorably disposed toward it. But none of the men there had an interest in it any longer; I ran into indifference. In Germany, however, Father Kunz [1:4], now professor and rector at the theologate of Frankfurt, has published an important thesis, backed by the Gregorian, on Rousselot's doctrine; a young American Jesuit is now following his example. Father Hans Urs von Balthasar had already published a German translation of "Les Yeux de la Foi [The eyes of faith]" in one of his series at Johannes Verlag (Einsiedeln).

This long and dramatic "Rousselot affair" [1:5], launched in the summer of 1920, is one of the principal examples of the impossibility encountered, all during the first half of the twentieth century, of any adaptation or in-depth updating of doctrine and classical teaching in the Church. Attempts, however, were not lacking. One of the finest, and in large part successful even though still incomplete and prematurely interrupted, was that of Father Léonce de Grandmaison, in our Lyons-Paris scholasticate of

---

[8] Some indications of this will be found in the edition of the Blondel-Valensin correspondence. See also Laberthonnière's discussion of Rousselot's theses on the understanding of faith (*Annales de philosophie chrétienne*, vols. 159 and 165 [February 1913], particularly 547–48, on the Thomist and Augustinian theories of faith). It is equally indispensable to know Rousselot's thought in order to understand the problematics of Father Teilhard de Chardin's *Écrits du temps de la guerre*.

[9] The General, Father Janssens, gave, I believe, as the reason for his refusal the fact that he did not want to seem to disavow the decisions of his predecessor. —On March 15, 1948, Father Huby shared with me the *miramur* [admonitory notice] he had just received from the Father General for his Bulletin, which had appeared in the *Recherches de science religieuse*, in which he criticized a work as having been inspired by Rousselot's doctrine; he said to me, on the other hand, that this *miramur* had come in the wake of an objection from Msgr. Parente.

Fourvière, Canterbury and Ore Place (1899–1908). His successors have only been half able to follow his lead.

During the summer of 1930, while staying in Louvain, where I had gone to have contact with the faculty, I had the opportunity to talk at length, on several occasions, with Father Joseph Maréchal. He was living in the suburbs, at Eegenhoven, in this house (since burned and rebuilt) where I am writing today. There was at that time only one Belgian province in the Society: Louvain (rue des Récollets) was the theologate, Eegenhoven the philosophate. What was very remarkable about Father Maréchal was the fact that, unlike so many intellectuals, he was not at all enclosed in his own theories, although these were very systematized. He had a mind that was broader than his ideas. It is well known, moreover, that the occasionally rather complicated Scholastic form of his large "Cahiers" [Notebooks] on the "Point of Departure of Metaphysics" is in large part due to the prudential demands of his editors. Much criticized,[10] he was energetically and victoriously defended in Rome by Father J. Janssens, our future general. During that summer of 1930, Father Janssens was professor of canon law and rector in Louvain itself. I saw there, among others, Father Joseph de Ghellinck, who showed me his rich library; Father Edgard Hocedez, who had taught me "De Verbo incarnato" at Ore Place; Father Léopold Malevez (who died a few months ago), who had just completed his years of theology, and so on. It was especially Father Pierre Charles whom I had come to consult for my twofold assignment of teaching fundamental theology and (as we shall see) the history of religions. He was well known in my province, for he had done part of his theology in Ore Place, where he had a particularly close friendship with Auguste Valensin and Pierre Teilhard de Chardin. On Jersey, I had recopied some of his manuscript notes (notably his Ontology, which was so antipathetic to his friend Teilhard), which were still circulating in our houses of studies. He had published some very remarkable articles in the *Revue de philosophie*; his prestige was heightened in our eyes by the semi-disgrace into which he had fallen, like Father Huby, following the "Yeux de la foi" affair.[11] His conversation was a rolling fire. The discussions he granted me were as amusing as they were instructive.

[10] Just as he was criticized one day in front of us on Jersey, in 1923, with almost angry vivacity by Father Pedro Descoqs, in the days following the publication of his first "Cahier", which I had brought from Paris and which Father Descoqs had spent the night reading and assailing.

[11] A little story (or legend) relates that in 1920, when Father Bulot, named visitator of the scholasticates of the Society, came to Louvain, Father Charles, who had had him as rector at Ore Place, went to look for him at the station. "What do you think of the *Eyes of Faith*?", Charles had asked. Bulot's reply: "I am coming here precisely to put them out."

The dean of our Lyons Theology Faculty when I arrived there was
Emmanuel Podechard, a Sulpician whose specialty was the Old Testament.[12] His book on *Ecclésiaste* [Ecclesiastes] in Lagrange's series of "Etudes
bibliques" is justly famous. The translation of the final page filled Abbé
Monchanin with enthusiasm. I recall one day when, in a little group of
priests who had the habit of gathering around him, Abbé Monchanin
read it to us, bringing out the beauty of word and rhythm, which were
marvelously in harmony with this finale of disillusionment. (Abbé Monchanin had disappointed the dean, who had wanted him as a professor at
the Faculty, by giving up the preparation for his doctorate in order to go
evangelize and support the workers of Ricamarie, a parish on the outskirts
of Saint-Etienne.) This pious and gentle priest, chaplain of the Visitation,
was a scholar of rigorous strictness. "I admire Father Lagrange", he told
me one day. "Without giving way on the basic issues, he knows how
to get around all difficulties. The path is closed from the Old Testament
side: he turns to the New. He finds some phrases to agree with him when
it's necessary. As for me, I don't know how to do that." (If I remember
correctly, I had just quoted an amusing passage to him with respect to the
appearance of the second Isaiah: "The voice raised at that time seemed
to come from the tomb. One reads in the second part of the book of
Isaiah. . . .") But in his calm, positive mind, M. Podechard welcomed
neither a recalcitrant disposition nor adventurous philosophy. He was the
most submissive of the Church's children. Now and then I went to pay
him a little visit at his chaplain's residence. Once it was he who came to
my garret, where an attack of dizziness had confined me. That year, he
came to give a course on the Servant of Yahweh. As he was explaining to
me the great lines with both liveliness and a deep religious sense, I said
to him that he really should make a book out of it and publish it. "That
is impossible", he replied. "And why?" "It is based on critical positions
that are not admissible today. You see, my Father, with respect to biblical
questions, the Church and I are not in agreement; so one of us must be
silent, and it is only natural that it be I."

Among the professors, there was, for dogma, Father Hugueny, O.P.,
who had been in Jerusalem, then in Baghdad. Already elderly, he was very
cheerful, very good-natured; people often made fun of him, he was famous
for his absent-mindedness. He became quite attached to me. Later, at Saint
Maximin, I prayed at his graveside, where he rested beside Father Lagrange.
Canon Félix Vernet, from the diocese of Valence, taught ecclesiastical history; he had both good sense and critical sense; his conversation had a

---

[12] Cf. G. Jouassard: "In memoriam, M. le Doyen Emmanuel Podechard, 1866–1951", in
the *Bulletin des Facultés catholiques de Lyon*, 13 (1952), 1–19. Engraved on his tombstone were
these words from Psalm 16:11, which he loved to repeat: "You will show me the path of life."

friendly mischievousness about it; one felt him to be strongly attached to the tradition of the Church but without any need for either illusions or complacency. Canon Léon Vaganay, from Lyons, was the great specialist in textual criticism; he relished it with all the love of a keen amateur just as he practiced it with the skill of a master. When the war years came and there was no way to obtain the Nestlé New Testament, he heard his colleagues groaning about it and said to them, smiling: "Oh, that does not bother me; at the beginning of the first class, I dictate to the students a half verse from Mark, and with that we have material for the whole year".[13] For Holy Scripture we also had Abbé Joseph Chaine. (Our Faculty was particularly well supplied in this field, attracting students at times from great distances.) A guileless soul, with a gentle and ingenious charity, Abbé Chaine was to die shortly after the war, still a young man, following the privations he had imposed on himself in order to provide more for the poor than for himself. He belonged to the so-called "liberal" branch of the large Chaine family, the nephew of a lawyer who had played a rather active role in modernizing Lyons circles;[14] with an innocent boldness in his criticism, he seemed at times not to understand fully the grandeur of certain biblical texts, but he had a profound sense of the Gospel inside and out. Patristics was the domain of Abbé (later Msgr.) Georges Jouassard, also from Lyons, who later became my dean; he combined, in the history of dogma, rigorous criticism, following the tradition of his predecessor, M. Tixeront, with a very lively and sympathetic presentation of the Fathers. Rather sharp of manner, as if he bore in mind his role as an officer during the war of 1914–1918, he was well aware, through his old mentor, Bishop Catherinet, editor of L'Ami du clergé, as well as through his connections in Rome, of more or less underground doctrinal battles, of rivalries for influence and threatening storms. He became annoyed once or twice at seeing that I was seemingly unconscious of the danger; but he was always very loyal to me and even, in difficult times, increasingly friendly. Father Martin Jugie, A.A., who taught oriental theology, divided his time between Lyons and Rome; strict in his scholarship and readily polemical, he was personally good, without any malice; I can still hear him saying to me one day, about a book he was holding in his hand: "When I read a book, I love to look for heresies in it"; he never seemed to engage in this

[13] 1882–1969. "This man who sometimes confessed that the Jesus of Mauriac seemed to him closer to the Jesus of history" than the one found in many scholarly works, "was consistent in conveying to the end that discreet joy and simple evangelical goodness that the received text cannot translate nor the critical apparatus record but of which the life of a man can furnish the most faithful variant" (Maurice Joujon).

[14] But who, prompted by the old Abbé Rambaud, had first firmly taken the defense of Alfred Dreyfus, in company with his friends Abbé Bergerette and Pierre Jay.

sport at my expense. When Rome took him full-time, he was replaced by his confrère, Father Salaville, a man whose gentleness and modesty were equal to his knowledge and to the shrewdness of his judgment. After the death of Abbé Chaine, his position was held by Albert Gélin, a Sulpician, who, like him, was to die prematurely, leaving a corpus of work that was already considerable and of high quality. I also saw the arrival of a young colleague, Abbé Jean Villot, whom Cardinal Gerlier had brought with him to Lyons; first a professor of moral theology, he soon became vice rector, then director of the "Propagation of the Faith", before succeeding Bishop Chappoulie as secretary of the French episcopate, then returning to Lyons as coadjutor of Cardinal Gerlier, then succeeding him as archbishop and finally ending up in Rome as Secretary of State. Our faculty also included, soon after my arrival, the mild, peaceful Father Mellet, O.P., who breathed spirituality as much as he taught it. I had had him first, right at the beginning, as a student. For I have counted students from at least forty dioceses (some have become bishops) and from all sorts of religious institutes, even Dominicans (once the Dominican studium of the Lyons province, returned from Holland to Saint-Alban-Leysse, near Chambéry, was filled with my former students, who invited me twice to give lectures there and to share their monastic life for a few days)—but never a single Jesuit.

The article on Christian Philosophy that I mentioned above also had its origins in my teaching. It was a kind of review of the three different positions held on that subject, which was then at the forefront of intellectual discussions (following a resounding article by Emile Bréhier), by Jacques Maritain, Etienne Gilson and Maurice Blondel. In it, I tried to show, without "concordism", that these three positions did not contradict each other but were responding to three different situations engendering three different problems. For Maritain, there was no Christian philosophy, properly speaking, but rather the Christian who philosophized received from his faith extrinsic confirmations for his rational reflection. According to Gilson, who was more attentive to history, Christian revelation was, through one whole part of itself, the generator of reason, and consequently there could be a philosophy drawing its origin from Christianity, but it ceased to be Christian in order to become rational at the moment when it became truly a philosophy (unless it still wished to call itself Christian in considering its origins, on which it was still dependent through some of its problems and concepts, as the rationalist atheism of Léon Brunschwicg paradoxically did). Finally, for Blondel, who rejected the expression (he spoke, in another sense, of "Catholic philosophy"), philosophy was not yet Christian since it was hollowing out the empty space that Christian revelation was to fill. I ended by outlining the idea of a subsequent stage of

philosophy, enlightened by Christian faith, after the manner of the reflection of the Fathers of the Church and of certain studies by Gabriel Marcel
[1:6]. (About which the excellent Abbé Charles Journet, since Cardinal,
who was too kindly disposed at that time to suspect a beginning of heresy
in any Jesuit, made a big mistake in interpretation, in his journal *Nova et
vetera*, by judging me to be a fideist.) For a long time I did not want this
article, or the one on "Apologetics and Theology" or several other more
recent ones, included in collections of my work because they seemed to
me to have something, not too rational, but too scholarly or too academic
about them, something too abstract, too distanced from human reality,
from its conflicts, its tragedy (or to use a word that has since made its
fortune, something a bit too existentialist).

The *Nouvelle revue théologique*, which nearly always welcomed my work,
had already taken from me, in 1934, the "Remarques sur l'histoire du mot
surnaturel" [Remarks on the history of the word supernatural], which I
was to complete subsequently [1:7]. Among the letters this article earned
me, I note one from Aimé Forest, because it expresses the opinion of a
good expert on Saint Thomas about a problem that was to arouse some
impassioned discussions a dozen years later:

> I am very struck in particular by a text of Saint Thomas that you quote
> on p. 357, "Sola autem natura rationalis habet immediatum ordinem ad
> Deum. . . ." [But only a rational nature is immediately ordered toward
> God. . . .] It seems to me that this text gives much strength to your the-
> sis by justifying the necessity of a rediscovery of finality and spirit, necessary
> in fact when one thinks, or tries to think, of the meaning of our real destiny.
> I am also very interested in the argument by which you show that a certain
> concept of the supernatural opposed to "philosophy" in fact takes its stand on
> the ground of this abstract doctrine and implies the same attitude of separation
> and isolation. Moreover, it seems to me that the idea that the integral reality
> is one, being unified by the first intention of God, is that which P. Motte
> brought out in his report on Christian philosophy. An Aristotelian mentality
> is perhaps at a distance from this point of view, but it can lead to it if the
> very analysis of nature, from which one starts, guides the mind to recognize
> creative freedom as the foundation of this nature. This is on the whole the
> criticism that Saint Thomas endlessly makes of necessitarianism or of the
> ancient naturalism that reappeared in Arab doctrines, but the metaphysical
> point of view he adopted certainly went beyond that of Aristotle [1:8].

In 1932, I had published another study: "Le Pouvoir de l'Eglise en
matière temporelle" [The authority of the Church in temporal matters].
It was Canon Jean Rivière, professor at Strasbourg and friend of our Lyons
Faculty, who got it accepted by the *Revue des sciences religieuses*. Rivière had
taught first at Toulouse, and he still had a devotion to Monsignor Bat-

iffol.[15] He had little liking for religious but made a few exceptions, and his sympathy in my regard was all the more meritorious as our minds had little in common. The genesis of my article, and the eager acceptance which many gave it, is explained by a theological situation following the condemnation of *l'Action française*. It is in some ways a final liquidation of the Bellarmine theory, understood literally, called "indirect authority". More immediately, it was a criticism of, or an effort to straighten out, to move from the side of the conscience, the position first adopted by Jacques Maritain in *Primauté du spirituel* and more precisely sustained by his friend Abbé Charles Journet in *La Juridiction de l'Eglise dans la cité*.[16] I am led to believe that, without arousing any rebuttals, my brief study bore fruit. But, since it was too superficial historically and fortunately soon surpassed, I have preferred that it, like the others I have mentioned in this section, not be included in collections, although this request has occasionally been made [1:9].

[15] Antoine Denat wrote of him: "One had to hear him debate to know him. A formidable dialectician, and often bristling with texts, his memory served him well. As he had kept intact both his youth and his southern accent, all this ended up in mumbling and stammering in his discussions. . . . He had none of Msgr. Batiffol's irony; he rushed into theological disputes with the fervor of a young seminarian who discovers for the first time the infinite depth of theology. I suspect Pascal of such 'rubella' when he wrote the *Provinciales*."

[16] Cf. Jacques Maritain, *Primauté du spirituel* (Paris: Plan, 1927) and *Du régime temporel et de la liberté* (1933), where he explains, on p. 80, that in a more modern conception of Christianity, one no longer burns heretics, because one prefers mercy to justice. In *La Juridiction de l'Eglise sur la cité*, C. Journet does not see the middle term between a temporal jurisdiction and mere counsels; he judges that "in cases of interference, the Church possesses the right of the State, sometimes eminently without the authority to exercise it, sometimes indirectly and formally when she can proceed to exercise it"; she has the right to command the temporal authority to decree the pain of death, although she neither decrees nor executes the sentence herself . . . (cf. 80, 94–97, 108–9); she can "depose princes". . . . To me this work seems totally lacking in historical perspective.

CHAPTER TWO

My first book was *Catholicisme* [Catholicism] (1938). It is made up of bits and pieces that were first written independently, then stitched together, so to speak, into three parts, without any preconceived plan. The first part sums up the main outlines of something I taught at the Faculty. These were two lectures given at the offices of the *Chronique sociale*, to which I had been introduced by Father Albert Valensin, for the Catholic group interested in social issues over which Joseph Vialatoux and Colonel André Roullet had charge; these lectures appeared first in a pamphlet from Editions de la Chronique under the title: "Le Caractère social du Dogme chrétien" [The social character of Christian dogma] (1936). The second part of the work gathers together various texts given in lectures, some of which had already been published here and there; one of them is a report requested of me by Msgr. Olichon for a congress of the *Union missionaire du clergé* at Strasbourg (1933), over which the bishop, Msgr. Ruch, presided (who proved to be only half-satisfied with my remarks); Abbé Bruno de Solages had been asked to give a closely related report: it was from this meeting, which was our first, if I am not mistaken, that a trusting friendship dates, a friendship that has never ceased and the benefit of which I have more than once experienced in a particular way. The third part of the book, more spiritual and "personalist" in nature, had seemed to me necessary for the overall balance of the book. In general, one might say that the work tries to show the simultaneously social, historical and interior character of Christianity, this threefold mark conferring on it that character of universality and totality best expressed by the word "catholicism". This was very close to the idea of Gerbet (not to mention other antecedents), who wrote in 1829 in his celebrated book *Considérations sur le dogme générateur de la piété catholique*: "Everything is social in Catholicism", it gives rise to "a parallel development of the interior life and the social life, combining the two in such a way that there is a continual action and reaction between them."

Catholicisme was assuredly responding to the "mood of the times". Emmanuel Mounier liked to use it as a doctrinal basis for his "personalist and communitarian revolution" (many have since completely forgotten the first of the two adjectives!). So the work was often quoted. But frequently, references were made only to the first part of the book, which might have contributed to a distortion of its meaning. As a result, some,

27

believing the title to be "Le Catholicisme", supposed the book was intended to be a treatise on the Catholic Church. They began to reproach me for omissions that, if this had been the case, would have in fact been regrettable: not a single chapter on the papacy! (I recall a certain storm of abuse from a vicar general and professor of dogma in a diocesan seminary where I was visiting; the dear man, who wished me no ill, was nevertheless very upset: he attributed the worst intentions to me and foresaw the worst misfortunes for me.) The idea that such a misunderstanding could take place from the grouping together of rather disparate pieces under a common label had never for an instant entered my mind [2:1]. I owe the publication of the book to Father Yves Congar, O.P., who had just then launched the ecclesiological series "Unam sanctam" at Editions du Cerf. Having read several of the pieces that had already appeared, he gave me the idea for it and extracted, so to speak, the accomplishment of it from me during a visit made to Fourvière in 1935 or 1936. But the work narrowly missed being buried before having seen the light of day. I had sent the manuscript of it to good Father Duchamp, my rector at Fourvière (where I had just been installed after five or six years spent at rue d'Auvergne). The latter, timid by nature, took fright; instead of transmitting it for review to the Father Provincial (Christophe de Bonneville), he put it away in his cupboard. As I was surprised not to receive anything from the Provincial in the passing months, the reason was discovered, and soon the reviews, which were favorable, reached me.

The origin of *Corpus mysticum*, which, except for some slight alterations, was also composed before the war of 1939–1945, was different. The administration of our Faculty was reduced to a minimum. The cumbersome structures, numerous meetings, liaison committees, masses of duplicated paper, which are the rule everywhere today, had not yet been invented. Relations were quite simply human, and the necessary discipline was not contested by anyone. Even when our Faculty, in order to satisfy the requirements of the constitution *Scientiarum Dominus* by Pius XI, had to add the teaching of the first years of the theological cycle to its licentiate and doctoral program, the organization remained very simple. The faculty got together once a trimester; the first two trimesters at the rector's home, in the little apartment on rue d'Enghien near the Ainay basilica, where he lived with his sister; the third trimester, at the university seminary, behind the church of Saint Just. The basic essentials of these meetings consisted of a good meal, followed by good recreation; many jokes were exchanged there—sometimes a bit too narrowly ecclesiastical for my taste. Then, before breaking up, we quickly reviewed the list of students, and, if necessary, the dean gave a few opinions. All everyday matters were handled during the course of the year directly between the dean and each professor, most often (for we were scattered all over) by means of little notes that we would find in our pigeon-hole when we came to teach a class. One day, I found a note worded about like this: "M. l'Abbé X will defend his doctoral thesis on Florus of Lyons on such and such a day, at such and such an hour, in such and such a classroom. You will be second (or third) examiner". This Florus, the important Lyonese archdeacon of the ninth century, about whom I should have known at least a little, was completely unknown to me. So I really had to read him, read his contemporaries, who had, like him, dealt with the Eucharist, sound out something of what came before and after. It was in this way that my attention was drawn to the words "corpus mysticum" and similar expressions. Later, after an illness, I was sent to convalesce in Aix in Provence (where, in the company of Father Victor Fontoynont, of whom I will speak later, I met Blondel several times again, sometimes in his little hotel on rue Roux-Alphéran, sometimes at our residence on rue de l'Opéra). In those happy times, when neither the dispersions of the days of Combism[1] nor the ravages of the First World War had taken their full effect, the smallest "residences" still had a good basic library, not always well maintained by some rather sleepy little communities, to tell the truth, but still giving witness to the real love of study that animated the Fathers of that "ignorant" and "stupid" nineteenth century. Aix had all of Migne and several other editions of ancient writers. There was nothing more pleasant, to complete one's recuperation and to forget as much as possible the daily increasing threat of Hitler, than to plunge into these old books. On my return to Lyons, before the end of 1938, *Corpus mysticum* was almost finished; the foreword of the book, written a little later, is dated June 8, 1939. The war was to delay its publication. While waiting, Father Lebreton, editor of *Recherches de science religieuse*, was very happy to publish it in slices, in his journal, in 1939 and 1940, although the misfortunes of those times would make copies of it scarce [2:2]. That did not keep a recent historian from informing me that the author of C.M. "became the echo of the mentality that prevailed around the end of the war".[2] What things, and sometimes more incriminating things, have I learned about myself like this!

This book is a naïve book. What gave me, or at least did not take from me, the courage to undertake and complete it was the fact that the literature on the subject, and consequently many of its difficulties, was almost

---

[1] This term refers to Emile Combe, a French politician who was adamantly anti-clerical and who pushed for separation of Church and state.

[2] Cobman E. O'Neill, in *Bilan de la théologie du XXe siècle*, 467. Already in 1951, an article in *Theological Studies* cited me among theologians who supposedly wanted, after the war, to present Catholicism in an attractive form, in terms of something "vital" and "existential". That is all quite imaginary. But the article was nonetheless not without good will.

entirely unknown to me. What, despite its lacunae, originally attracted me
to it, in contrast to other readers, was the fact that I was not encumbered
by any of the categories and classical dichotomies into which I would
necessarily have fallen if I had read the historians,[3] who were nearly all
German (I do not know German, although I learned a little in my youth).
Corpus mysticum thus enjoyed a certain success [2:3]. Even Abbé A. Michel,
the best known representative of the most classical, indeed the most "textbook", Scholasticism, hailed "this magnificent study" in *L'Ami du clergé*!
The other reviews were generally as favorable, as much from the point
of view of the freshness of the book's conclusions as of its historical and
doctrinal correctness. This was the case in the *Bulletin de théologie ancienne
et médiévale*, from the pen of Dom Cappuyns (M. C.; [October 1946], 97–
98); so too in one of the first issues of *Dieu vivant*, on the part of Father
M. D. Chenu, who usually received my work with generosity. Father Congar, however, expressed several reservations in a moderate way. The *Revue
thomiste* did likewise, with greater emphasis, in the course of a long article,
which was, contrary to the intentions of its authors, Fathers Nicolas and
Labourdette, at the origin of a large-scale campaign that I will discuss later
on [2:4].

For some time, a project had been developing at Fourviére, under the
impulse principally of Fathers Victor Fontoynont, Henri Rondet, Pierre
Chaillet and Henri Bouillard. A series would be founded that would accommodate essentially the works by professors of the house. It was known
by the title "Théologie" [Theology], and Father Bouillard, professor of
fundamental theology, had written the prospectus. It was at this time
shortly after June 1940. Father Gustave Desbuquois, publisher of *L'Action
populaire*, which had taken refuge from Paris (Vanves) in Lyons, offered
us the firm of Editions Spes for the publication. If my memory is correct,
two volumes were printed: Father Bouillard's thesis, *Conversion et grâce chez
saint Thomas d'Aquin* (a master's thesis, undertaken at Fourvière because
of the circumstances, under the chairmanship of Father Charles Boyer,
then dean of theology at the Gregorian, who, at that time, had found
nothing to criticize in it) [2:5]; and *Corpus mysticum*. Now it happened
shortly afterward that the management of Editions Spes, which remained
in Paris, raised difficulties. During this time, the publisher Fernand Aubier
was planning with Father Jean Daniélou a patristics series, the first volume
of which would be the thesis undertaken at the Sorbonne by Daniélou
on Saint Gregory of Nyssa. He agreed to enlarge his project and bought
our two volumes, which were already printed. Thus, before the end of

---

[3] In like manner, Father Teilhard de Chardin once complained about professional theologians "tyrannized by their philosophical categories".

the Second World War, the "Théologie" series was launched, under the official direction of the rector of Fourvière and with Father Bouillard as the first and very diligent secretary. Five or six years later, two of its first three volumes as well as one other were to meet with some misfortune, and the secretary had to be changed, without, however, this seriously hindering the forward progress of the series, which was in the hands of Father Donatien Mollat and then of Father Jacques Guillet. A little celebration in Paris marked the publication of the fiftieth volume, which was *Mystère du Temps* by Canon Jean Mouroux. In a speech, Father Bouillard defined the twofold aspiration that had been at the origin of the enterprise: "to go to the sources of Christian doctrine, to find in it the truth of our life." This is also what is said in the foreword of the fiftieth volume: "Theology, which is a work of the reason, cannot without danger ignore the very movement of human thought; but its true refreshment comes from submersion in the Word of God, such as it is taught in the Church, ripened in a time-honored spiritual experience, developed by those great Doctors who were at once geniuses and saints. When a theologian works, it is to this school that he returns." The Théologie series was still to run an honorable course. It was at a later time, when it might have played a fortunate and efficacious role in the renewal of the Church, that diverse influences, about which I prefer to remain silent, came to condemn it to a slow death. A wind of destruction had blown.

I had scarcely begun my teaching of fundamental theology some six months before (a doctoral course, the particular subject of which was normally to change every year): then one fine day in the spring of 1930, our dean said something like this to me: "My Father [he was very kind to me, but to say "My dear Father" would have seemed to him an unwarranted familiarity], there is a serious lack in our Faculty. The history of religions is taught everywhere in the universities; even in teachers' colleges, future teachers receive some notions about it; a whole literature informs the public at large about it; it is intolerable that young priests who are doctors in theology should remain ignorant of this discipline, and it is necessary that they be able to consider the problems involved in it in a Christian light. But we see no specialist to hire, and besides, our Faculties do not have the means to found a new chair. The discipline closest to the history of religions is yours; would you agree to undertake a supplementary course beginning this next October?" I had the weakness to accept. Without preparation, without books, without knowledge of any language, European or Asiatic, without any spare time beforehand, and with the prospect of another supplementary course to provide in the transformed program of the Faculty, it was an impossibility; especially since it would be necessary for me to change the subject matter every year, for I would have the same students several years in a row. Finally, it had to go well. The history of religions is what for a long time required by far the most work from me and for the most meager results. For me at least, the preparation for this teaching, which was as absorbing as it was secondary, brought a precious benefit: it confirmed my conviction, with ever more convincing clarity, of the extraordinary unicity of the Christian Event in the complex immensity offered to our gaze by the spiritual history of our humanity. I derived from this spectacle an admiration, certainly not better founded but more reflective and more filled with wonder, for what I like to call the "Christian Newness" [la Nouveauté chrétienne].

I considered successively in this new course the theories on the origin of religion, the one recently formulated by Henri Bergson on its "two sources", Christianity and the mystery cults (a work by Alfred Loisy was popularizing that theme at the time), Buddhism, comparative mysticism, the positivist religion of Auguste Comte. . . . I had always had a certain attraction for the study of Buddhism, as I consider it something like the greatest human feat, because of its originality and its multiform expansion across time and space as well as because of its spiritual depth. My acquaintance at that time with Abbé Jules Monchanin, who was then vicar at Saint-Maurice de Monplaisir, spurred me on in this path. It was at the suggestion of my colleague, Father Jean Zupan, with whom I had studied and then lived, who was destined for a career of heroic apostolic work, that I had gone to see him. Even at that time, he was reading Sanskrit at sight; he took as lively an interest in Buddhist metaphysics and mystics as in the Buddhist expansion in central Asia and China; but in what great thing did he not take an interest [2:6]? When, from 1950 on, I had some spare time in Paris, I drew from my course notes the initial material for three books on Buddhism. The Bibliothèque nationale and the library of the Musée Guimet allowed me to complete my documentation. In 1950, I was recommended to the Curator of the Musée Guimet, Philippe Stern, by Bishop Bruno de Solages, who, having become in January 1932 the rector of the Institut catholique of Toulouse,[4] had sheltered him as well as other Jews close to him during the nazi occupation, while waiting himself to be deported.[5] This specialist in Khmer art, who also had a devotion to

---

[4] Cf. "Cimetier, Mgr. Bruno de Solages", in La Vie catholique (February 20, 1933).

[5] Sketch by Antoine Denat (1935): "Bruno de Solages is a bundle of nerves tuned and refined by centuries of Christian aristocracy. Unlike those who know everything and understand nothing, he knows everything and understands everything. . . . He used to work himself into a state of concentrated rage if anyone spoke ill of Briand in his presence. His health has all the fragility of a thoroughbred, and his pallor accentuates the flash of his purple belt. His hair, turning grey, looks powdered. The fine smile of a man of the world, a glance that attracts, a Christian scent. He gives himself to his task with the sincerity of one descended

Piero della Francesca, was a very fine artist; he was besides a very obliging man. Toward the end of the afternoon, we sometimes left the Museum together; one day, he asked me to accompany him to his home, where his wife, who was a photographer, wanted to take my photograph as she had taken that of Bruno de Solages. I really had to let her do this. . . .

So that was the origin of those three Buddhist books, *Aspects du bouddhisme* (1951), *La Rencontre du bouddhisme et de l'Occident* (1952) and *Amida* (1955). I was surprised to find that in India, Japan, and so forth, even in Paris itself, they were not poorly received by men often more competent than I. The first is directly comparative; the other two are also in their own way. A fourth book failed to see the light of day: it was a comprehensive exposition, summing up the courses taught at Lyons, followed by a copious selection of texts; a publisher, whose name I do not remember, had asked me for it; occupied with other duties, I gave up trying to edit it for publication. *Amida* was criticized, from a point of view that might be called confessional, by Frithjof Schuon, a brilliant and very personal representative of Guénonian gnosis and, contrary to Guénon, a great admirer of Buddhism; after having criticized my "dogmatism" and my "religious exclusivism", he reproached me, quite wrongly, for ridiculing the "upaya" Buddhists.[6] The two previous works had been the object of a more delicate criticism on the part of Gabriel Germain,[7] with whom I was later to come into contact with respect to Teilhard and Péguy. *Aspects* earned

---

from a line formerly opposed to the sincerity of someone like Jaurès, and there is something in him like an ulterior motive of reparation in all his social ideas, while his philosophical ideas look to the future, as is right. One can also know Bruno de Solages by contemplating him in a kind of duplicate since Abbé Mauriès is another, more plebeian 'Christianus'. . . . The tandem Mauriès-Solages: a bundle of 1935 ideas; but ideas that are inserted into history, that break through boundaries. ['Christianus' was the pseudonym used on the notes that Solages and Mauriès, his former philosophy professor, wrote in turns for *Vie intellectuelle*.] In private, Msgr. de Solages is gentleness incarnate; there is at once a dialogue, whereas one had feared the magnificent rector and aristocrat. But it would take too many pages here to explain about this old provincial nobility, which is still closer to the earth and to men than are some Parisian workers." The Society of Jesus, particularly in France, owes Msgr. de Solages a double debt of gratitude for his two resounding interventions, one in November 1947, on "La Pensée chrétienne face à l'Evolution" [Christian thought with respect to evolution] (an address at the annual opening of the Institut catholique of Toulouse, published in the *Bulletin de litt. ecclés.*), which was a defense of Father Teilhard de Chardin; the other: "Pour l'honneur de la théologie: les contresens du R. P. Garrigou-Lagrange" [For the honor of theology: the misinterpretations of Father Garrigou-Lagrange], which, in the same *Bulletin*, answered a truly rash article appearing in *Angelicum*, 23:126–45, and took the defense of Fathers Teilhard de Chardin, G. Fessard, H. Bouillard and myself, in a controversy in which what was at stake went well beyond many of our individual works.

[6] "Orthodoxie et originalité du bouddhisme", *France-Asie*, February–June 1959.

[7] "Lettre sincère aux chrétiens sincères", *France-Asie*, 155.

me a visit, in 1951, from Jacques-Albert Cuttat, then envoy of Switzerland to Bogotá; a visit that began a deep and lasting friendship.[8] I had hoped to be able to see a second edition of *Rencontre*, in view of which for several years I amassed numerous notes, drawn both from the old literature of missionaries and travelers as well as from more recent authors; but the book sold too slowly to permit this. As for *Amida*, a subject to which I was lovingly attached, establishing its onomastic table was a headache for me. Through this oriental approach, I hoped to bring back to an examination of higher spiritual problems at least a few members of a generation that was turning away from them. I wrote in the foreword:

> A malady of languor is undermining a certain number of Christian consciences in our day. It unfortunately allows them only indifference or scorn with regard to their own spiritual tradition. Will the one who, by chance, finds himself overtaken by this illness not find his interest in themes he thought to be hackneyed renewed by discovering them again in their Buddhist transformation? Will he not in that way begin to have a better sense of the price of certain interior processes? Will this detour through the Far East not revive his taste by piquing his curiosity?

This appeal was scarcely heard. . . . But *Amida* put me in cordial communication with Msgr. Paolo Marella, who arrived in Paris as nuncio just at the time when the book appeared; longtime apostolic delegate to Tokyo, he had formed a rich library on the religions of the Far East that he had me visit one day in Rome. Much later, I was given the opportunity to return to the subject of Amidism in a report to the Secretariate for Non-Christians (over which Cardinal Marella presided), published in 1971 in its Bulletin [2:7].

When I was a student in theology, three free "academies" were in operation within the scholasticate: one for pedagogy, one for social sciences and one for theology. I was part of the latter, which was called with more or less amicable derision "La Pensée" [Thought]. There were a dozen of us in it. Members were recruited by cooptation. We gathered each Sunday, under the benevolent and discreet patronage of Father Joseph Huby, to debate a subject chosen and prepared by one of us. This was how the first sketch was born of what would become in 1946 the book entitled *Surnaturel, études historiques*. From then on, the subject was much in discussion.

---

[8] An amusing detail. At the opening of the book, I said that the French were ordinarily as ignorant about religions as about geography, and in particular they often confused Buddhism and Hinduism. Now I soon received a letter from a rather important personage to whom I had sent a copy of the book: "How I thank you", he said to me, "for this magnificent work on Hinduism!" Threefold information (or rather confirmation) drawn from this simple line: my correspondent knew how to flatter, he had not opened the book, he confused Buddhism with Hinduism.

It had just been treated by Father Guy de Broglie in some articles that attracted considerable attention and which I considered to be something like a form of passage from the theses in our manuals to the rediscovery of traditional thought. It was at the center of the reflection of the masters about whom I have spoken: Rousselot, Blondel, Maréchal; we discovered it at the heart of all great Christian thought, whether that of Saint Augustine, Saint Thomas[9] or Saint Bonaventure (for these were our classics par excellence); we noted that it was likewise at the bottom of discussions with modern unbelief, that it formed the crux of the problem of Christian humanism. Father Huby, following the line of reflection inaugurated for us by Rousselot, had warmly urged me to verify whether the doctrine of Saint Thomas on this important point was indeed what was claimed by the Thomist school around the sixteenth century, codified in the seventeenth and asserted with greater emphasis than ever in the twentieth. My first exposition on the subject, made at Ore Place, was expanded during the two following years with the assistance of several friends, particularly Fathers Charles Nicolet and Armand de la Croix-Laval.[10] Then I put it almost completely aside during the first ten years of my teaching.[11] In June 1940, leaving in haste with a group of companions for La Louvesc, after having evaded the Germans who were approaching Lyons, I carried along a bag with a parcel of notes in it, among which was the notebook for *Surnaturel.* I spent several days up there putting a little order into it. Soon there was the return from our exodus (when Lyons was south of the famous "line of demarcation"), and I gave no more thought to it. But when, in 1943, being hunted by the Gestapo, I had to flee once more, I again carried along my notebook. Hidden away in Vals, which I could not leave and where I could not engage in any correspondence, I thus had something to occupy my retreat. Taking advantage of the resources offered by the Vals library, the manuscript swelled. When I came back to Lyons soon after the departure of the German army, it was ready to be delivered to the printer [2:8].

I forgot to say that the first three chapters, concerning Baius and Jansenius, had been written long before and had appeared, in 1931, in the *Recherches de science religieuse.* I had been able to refine them further, after

[9] Saint Thomas is the only author (along with the Gospels) whom I regularly put on index cards throughout my years of study. The authorities on Jersey had put me down as a "Thomist", and even a "neo-Thomist", which, for those faithful members of the Suarezian rear-guard, made me doubly heretical with regard to the "doctrines of the Society".

[10] I had even made a plan, which was much too broad, for "Etudes sur le Surnaturel chrétien" [Studies on the Christian supernatural].

[11] In 1939, however, a sketch of what would be the second part of the book had appeared in the *Bulletin de littérature ecclésiastique* of Toulouse.

a first draft made in theology, thanks to the library of the college on rue Sainte-Hélène, whose fine shelves of theology I have already mentioned. (It was there that I read, certainly not the whole forty or so large volumes of the works of the great Arnauld, but many pages by him, his confederates and assailants.) To my astonishment, *Recherches* published the two articles as soon as I offered them, after a very flattering review by Father Adhémar d'Alès. I learned much later that my pieces had arrived just at the right moment and that I had been welcomed as a providential savior: those in the more "orthodox" theological circles were preoccupied precisely with finding a study that would counterbalance some others, which had appeared somewhere or other, according to which Baius and Jansenius were the legitimate sons of the great Saint Augustine. A short time later, and my articles, reproduced unchanged in *Surnaturel*, would draw thunderbolts down upon me. So turns the wheel of Fortune. . . . The entire work aroused the opposition of numerous Scholastics. Forgetting their domestic quarrels, they joined forces against it. They made it say what it did not say, indeed quite the contrary of what it said; they opposed it with misinterpreted texts and sophistic reasoning. But at the same time, they happened to perceive, better perhaps than I had, what was at stake in the dispute. This is because I believe I showed, particularly in the second part, the composition of which is rather strict, that since the various schools of modern Scholasticism had abandoned the traditional systematic (and already a bit compromised) synthesis in the work of Saint Thomas, they could only wear themselves out in sterile combats, each being both right and wrong, against the others, while withdrawing from living thought into an artificial world, leaving the field open to all the ups and downs of a "separated philosophy".

The work thus constituted a sort of attempt to reestablish contact between Catholic theology and contemporary thought, or at least to eliminate one basic obstacle to that contact [2:9]—not with a view to any "adaptation" whatsoever to that thought, but rather with a view to engaging in dialogue with it—which, as always when it is a question of serious ideas, could only be a confrontation, a combat.[12] To the degree to which I was aware of this, I really expected to see a number of Scholastic eyebrows pucker, and one such review, while very flattering, was of necessity to help me see it better.[13] Yet I did not foresee so strong and so generalized

[12] I was able to note with truth: "I am accused in Rome of confusing nature with the supernatural: I spend my time fighting against this confusion, which is everywhere today, even where Rome does not see it".

[13] Dom Illtyd Trethowan wrote in *The Downside Review* (January 1947), 71–72: ". . . This is not the place to show how revolutionary these conclusions are. All we want to do is to suggest that theologians undertake a very close study of this book. If Father de L. is right in

an obstinacy in identifying these anemic and belated systems, often based on obvious misinterpretations, with the very Tradition of the Church, so that to touch them was to appear to be sacrilegious.

Surnaturel was printed in Lyons, for Aubier, in 1945–1946. Paper was lacking. One part of the edition was done on big bulking paper, another on smooth paper, so that the first lot of copies was twice as thick as the second. There were in all seven hundred copies. One of the first reviews, entirely sympathetic, was that of the bibliographical journal *Erasmus*, which had just been founded; it came from Msgr. Gérard Philips of Louvain, the future secretary (with Father Sébastien Tromp) of the Doctrinal Commission at Vatican II. Having appeared in the summer of 1946, the book did not reach Rome until September. I was myself in Rome at that time, for the General Congregation in August (I believe) that elected Father Janssens. I recall the day when the book, newly arrived, was displayed in the recreation room of the Curia. If I note this detail, it is because it has often been said that *Surnaturel*, by scandalizing certain theologians in Rome, had triggered a whole process against me that was to end, four years later, in the encyclical *Humani generis* (1950). In reality, the process had been set off much earlier [2:10]. It had already been said in Rome (I am speaking here only of what concerns me) that my election to the General Congregation was a provocation; many complaints (often the most fantastic) had already made their appearance or had been expressed in secret (I knew something of this later); the Holy Father had already been alerted, and the magic words "new theology" had been launched. The innocent series "Sources chrétiennes" was presented as a machine mounted against dogmatic theology, and so forth. A certain number of the Fathers at the General Congregation (Germans, Spaniards, Poles . . .) had questioned me right from the beginning, some with anxiety, about this organized opposition. *Surnaturel* had nothing to do with it at first. It merely came along at a propitious time, allowing the bill of indictment to grow. I will say a few words farther on about these prehistoric battles, which continued over fifteen years and in which I played scarcely more than a passive role. They brought me much evidence of sympathy. Among the numerous letters received with respect to *Surnaturel* or the writings that appeared in its wake, I will recall here only those from Etienne Gilson, which were as delectable as they were approving;[14] still more delectable or pungent were

---

saying that modern theologians have moved a long way away from the teaching of the Fathers and Saint Augustine on this large question, that they have misunderstood the condemnation of Baius, that they have left Saint Thomas in favor of his commentators, that they have not been able to see the true signification of his doctrine because they have lost their 'spiritual eye', then they must set to work and put their house back in order. . . ."

[14] I will have occasion to quote from some below.

the remarks he was to make about an important philosophical-theological personage of the period during the course of conversations we had, beginning in 1959, in a nook of the library at the Institut [2:11].

Two other books, which appeared before *Surnaturel* but were prepared in much less time, were the fruit of the war and occupation years. One was *Proudhon et le christianisme* (1945). I had chosen this theme, in 1941–1942, for my course in fundamental theology because I saw in Proudhon one of the most vigorous representatives of the doctrine of immanence opposed to the Christian faith and at the same time a very significant human and historical case (I have always had a lively interest in the history of religious thought in the nineteenth century). Now, at that particular time, a number of Parisian intellectuals were living "in retreat" in Lyons. Among them was Emmanuel Mounier, with whom I had already formed a friendship that was soon to become closer. A great worker and, in addition, if one can say so, an honest conspirator, Mounier nevertheless had a little spare time. He was coming at that time, alone or with Madame Mounier, to attend my course. Albert Béguin, who often came to Lyons, joined them. Sometimes, too, as far as I remember, André Rousseaux. Béguin was thinking about his "Cahiers du Rhône"; Urs von Balthasar was a living bond for us. Mounier, guided like Péguy by the tiny little hope, was already making plans for the future liberation. In resuming the publication of *Esprit* in Paris, he wanted to increase the size of his journal with several series of works. He made me promise to give him my course on Proudhon to launch one of his series. I did so as soon as the moment arrived, which is to say, too soon, for some parts of the work had been drafted too hastily and the whole had not had sufficient time to ripen. Despite the intimidation brought to bear at that time on a number of minds by Marxist intellectuals, the book was nevertheless well received.[15] It provided me with the occasion to correspond with several readers who were unbelievers. One of them had been surprised that a Catholic had been able to speak of the anticlerical Proudhon with freedom and sympathy; he wondered if such an attitude would be approved by the Church; he brought up some facts ascertained in his youth, at the time of the reaction against modernism. I have discovered a copy of one of my replies:

> . . . My first letter did not dispel your surprise about the freedom of spirit you found in my book. But I believe that you will find as much in a good number of my coreligionists and colleagues. As a professor of theology for

---

[15] I have just read, on p. 168 of a work that appeared in 1949: "Father de Lubac, in his *Catholicisme de Proudhon* (sic), perhaps the best book written on Proudhon since that of Sainte-Beuve. . . ." Alain Sergent and Claude Harmel, *Histoire de l'Anarchie*, Le portulan. In 1947, the *Revue de métaphysique et de morale* (vol. 52, pp. 91–92) had given the work a very favorable review.

over seventeen years, I have not had the feeling of being such an exception. It is within our faith that we draw this freedom of spirit, and in a very sincere submission to our Church. For the faith, fully lived—as much, at least, as human weakness permits—does not appear to us to be a constraint but a liberation. Unquestionably, it entails sacrifices. There are also the demands of Catholic discipline. Unquestionably, again, the men of the Church are not all saints and luminaries, far from it. Who should be surprised by that? During certain times of crisis (as during the modernist crisis), there was moreover some noticeable stiffening, which in some places became a narrowing, and this at times caused scandals. . . . Nothing that has to do with man can escape such troubles. But we know that through these very troubles themselves, the essential thing is assured us. And when, by chance, it is necessary, those who continue to be guided by the light coming from Christ know how to be patient then without disregarding the truth. The Church, which from the outside can at times seem to impose on her faithful a quasi-tyrannical conformity, is on the contrary, for those who strive to live by her spirit—the very Spirit of Christ—like an immense maternal womb, in which all that is authentically human is in the final analysis received with the same love, whatever might be the differences and eccentricities. From this stems the extreme diversity, to which history gives witness, of doctrinal currents, theological schools, attitudes assumed in the face of social or other kinds of problems; from this comes the ever-increasing variety of forms of spiritual life. This is what can be observed in the strictest and most traditional Catholicism . . . (summer 1946).

It is well known that Abbé Pierre Haubtmann—younger brother of Father Georges, who was always a great support to me in difficult times and whose encouraging sympathy often spurred me on—took up the study of Proudhon on a much more extensive scale [2:12]. His work in Rome at the time of the Council and then his rectorship at the Institut Catholique in Paris slowed down his publications. Because of his accidental death, the greatest part of his studies on Proudhon are still unpublished.[16] I reviewed a little volume he had devoted to "Marx et Proudhon, leurs rapports personnels, 1844–1847" [Marx and Proudhon, their personal relations, 1844–1847]:

We know about the meeting of Marx and Proudhon in Paris under the July Monarchy; we know about the quarrel that soon arose between them, following an exchange of letters, and how Marx wrote in 1846, in reply to Proudhon's *Philosophie de la misère*, the *Misère de la philosophie*, which is an anti-Proudhonian pamphlet. This episode has an historical interest and above

---

[16] Today, this work has appeared: *P. J. Proudhon, sa vie et sa pensée (1809–1849)* (Beauchesne, 1982), then the rest in two volumes: *P. J. Proudhon, sa vie et sa pensée (1849–1855)*, vol. 1; *(1855–1865)*, vol. 2 (DDB, 1988).

all, perhaps, a symbolic value of the first order. Numerous historians have recounted it. Now Abbé Pierre Haubtmann completely reopens the study of it. First, through the new documents he brings forward, drawn from the family archives of Madame Henneguy, Proudhon's older daughter; then through a minute examination and methodical explanation of contemporary sources. The extreme intensity of Marx' work is well explained by the fact that the latter must have, with good reason, felt himself to be the target when he read Proudhon's work: it was only because they did not read closely enough that "too many inattentive commentators" failed to see in *Philosophie de la misère* the criticisms it contains with respect to Marx and that it thereby "remained for them a sealed book". We should also note the extreme psychological plausibility of the hypothesis formulated toward the end of the volume to explain why Proudhon neglected to reply in turn to Marx . . . [2:13].

Le Drame de l'humanisme athée (1944) was a composite work, similar to *Catholicisme*. Some people have asked me how much time it took me to compose it; my reply was: "About an hour." That was hardly an exaggeration. In fact, scarcely more than that was necessary in order to select and reassemble the different, independently written pieces and to find a common title for them. Father Gustave Desbuquois was responsible for the initiative behind it. Several chapters of it had appeared, in 1942 and 1943, in the journal *Cité nouvelle*, the substitute for *Etudes* in the southern zone, which he edited in Lyons and which had some trouble surviving.[17] Annoyed that Editions Spes had not confirmed, in Paris, the offer he had made us in Lyons for the Theology series, desiring also to dispel the shadow of slight disagreement that had arisen among us over his politics of presence (in my opinion a little overdone) in Vichy, Father Desbuquois spontaneously offered to have a book by me taken by Editions Spes on his return to Paris. It was necessary to act quickly. I put together in a first part several disparate articles coming principally from semi-clandestine conferences with an anti-nazi point; the second part, more homogeneous, was made from a Faculty course on Auguste Comte,[18] which had been written well enough; the third, from some articles on Dostoyevsky that were ardent but, I must admit, rather superficial. Father Desbuquois made haste. There was also very soon a German edition. When the English edition appeared, an American reviewer, who had undoubtedly not opened the book, reproached me with indignation for having placed Dostoyevsky

[17] I had also published several pieces in it from my course on Proudhon as well as a fragment of what would become *De la connaissance de Dieu*; another piece of the future *Drame* had been given to Béguin for his *Cahiers du Rhône*.

[18] I remembered Comte and his idea of the Catholic Church when I wrote, in 1965, a preface for the collective work on the Church of Vatican II, edited by Father Barauna, O.F.M.

among the atheists:[19] he might just as well have reproached me about Péguy, to whom the first chapter refers.

Just as with certain passages of *Catholicisme, Drame*, particularly in the part devoted to Auguste Comte, did not at all please the followers of Maurras. Yet I knew that, in his prison, Charles Maurras had read me, pen in hand, and that in several places he had noted that what I saw was correct. It is true that the correspondent who gave me these details, with quotations in support, was not able to quote other places for me where I was perhaps struck down. The book went into several editions. It earned me, after a few years, not so much opposition or refutation as the contempt shown by a whole new school that had become triumphant within the very heart of the Church and more particularly of the Society of Jesus. It attributed to me, in order better to overcome it, a fine simplism. One had to be an "idealist", they said (euphemistically), to dare criticize someone like Feuerbach, Marx or Nietzsche, who must, on the contrary, be our masters in thought; to do so must mean that one has understood nothing of the great enlightener, Hegel, who disencumbered us forever from the twofold fantasy of objectivity and transcendence, Nietzsche having brought his work to a conclusion by dissipating the mist of "other-worlds". Such is the basis for today's new catechism, expanded by the apostles of a "renewal" that has no inhibitions about attacking the Christian faith at the roots; such is the lesson recited with as much docility as brilliance by a whole covey of young student masters, sometimes full of talent.

Three short works also date from nearly this same time of the "liberation". One of them was due to Stanislas Fumet, like *Proudhon* had been to Mounier. In his free time in Lyons, Fumet dreamed too of creating in Paris a series, and even a publishing house, in the wake of *Temps présent*. He snatched *Paradoxes* (1946) from me, most of which dates from before the war; this was the first, I believe, of his series of "Cailloux blancs". An excellent writer and shrewd critic, Fumet was the least commercial of men. It took no time at all, of course, for his house to go bankrupt. After various transfers, my little book ended by falling into the basement of Editions du Seuil, from which it had some trouble getting out. Yet there was a subsequent *Nouveaux Paradoxes*, then an edition that joined these two works into a single, somewhat augmented volume.

The second small book was *De la connaissance de Dieu* (1945). Some fragments of it had already appeared in publications I no longer remember. Father Pierre Chaillet, a great and heroic friend, also wanted something of mine for "Editions du Témoignage chrétien", which he wanted to create

---

[19] The English publisher had wrapped the book in a jacket on which four heads were pictured, at four angles: those of Marx, Comte, Nietzsche and Dostoyevsky. Whence the hurried reviewer's mistake.

as early as the liberation, a venture separate from the weekly and under different management. During the years preceding the war, the same enthusiasm for the Moehlerian vision of the Church, the same ardent love for Catholic unity and Catholic tradition had united us closely. The text that I delivered to him was, on the whole, older than that of *Paradoxes*. The reflections that comprise it were for the most part old ones. In 1915–1917, during the war, I had among my companions a future primary-school teacher, a student in a teachers' college. He was not a Christian, and, without being a militant atheist, he did not believe in God. We talked. We debated. We were young and simple: twenty years old. . . . I had not yet ever read a serious book of philosophy. It was from our conversations that my first slightly serious personal reflections date. This was the source of the plan, which had not yet taken shape, of what would later be this little book. But another matrix was needed: on Jersey, in 1920–1923, the philosophy courses, particularly those of Father Pedro Descoqs, during which I sometimes scribbled some rather nonconformist notes. . . . They were inspired more by Saint Thomas than by my Suarezian master, whose combative teaching was a perpetual invitation to react. The little book also contains the echo of other conversations with unbelieving friends. And then, here and there in my reading I gathered some beautiful texts. . . . During the German occupation, I got around to assembling my little collection, adding to it a few thoughts suggested to me by the preparation of a course on the theories concerning the "origin of religion". And all with the idea of offering it to a few friends who had little faith.

How, when the little book appeared, serious men could think they caught the scent in it of a weapon against the faith of Holy Church, an attempt by neo-modernism, a desire to combat underhandedly the teaching of Saint Thomas, I still do not know. Without pretending to systematize anything, I took my material from the purest Catholic tradition, which I loved more and more every day, with no other end but to open the treasure of it to a few brothers, both known and unknown, without any intention of laying the foundations of a learned treatise, and even less, if possible, of trying to pick a quarrel with anyone. There was a second edition of it, somewhat augmented. It was not to bring me good fortune. The numerous testimonies about the graces of light occasioned by these pages have brought me a superabundant consolation for the trouble they caused.[20]

The third little book, published by Editions du Seuil, reproduced two

---

[20] See below, pp. 73 and 80–81. One of the characteristics that had particularly satisfied Father Lachièze-Rey in this book was that it had emphasized "that truth of the philosophical tradition that the idea of God can come only from God himself" (Letter of January 10, 1946). The same judgment was given by Father Scheuer, S.J. (Louvain), who was to express it in very vivid terms in 1950.

lectures on the *Fondement théologique des missions*, given to the Catholic Faculties at Lyons in December 1940. They were considered by the audience, just after our defeat, to be a profession of universalism and a protest against Hitlerian racism, which they very well were in part and which made the authorities of our Faculties a bit nervous, and not only for my personal safety. It is, in brief, merely an elementary exposition of what the title indicates.

For the year 1944, I must note, simply by way of bibliographical curiosity, an article that appeared in the last issue of *Cité nouvelle*. It is entitled: "La Malfaisance de Rousseau". Father André Ravier had defended an important doctoral thesis on "Education according to Jean-Jacques Rousseau". The work had been the object of repeated denunciations, coming from *l'Action française* circles. In order to put an end to the matter without having to condemn it, Rome had finally demanded a compensatory article. It was more or less necessary to find fault with the work. Chosen for this task, which they knew I would acquit as benignly as possible, I managed besides in a way to criticize more strongly the doctrines held or at least tolerated by some of those who had denounced it. The trick was a bit risky. But it happened that this swan-song of *Cité nouvelle* left the presses just at the moment of the Vichy debacle and the disorganization of the mail, so very few copies arrived at their destination. And besides, people had to be busy with other things. . . . The article therefore remained practically unknown, and that was precisely what we were hoping for.[21]

---

[21] A few years later, Rome had to recognize that the discredit cast on Father Ravier's work stemmed from political passions, and the author was authorized to republish it as he wished, without having to submit it for a new review.

CHAPTER THREE

My years of teaching in Lyons can be divided into three very different periods: first of all, before the Second World War, then during the years of the war and occupation, and finally the years that followed, from 1945 to 1950. A fourth period should be added to these, that of my nearly total professorial unemployment, from 1950 to 1960.

My first beginnings were rough, especially since several not very absorbing but at times unproductive ministries were added onto a still-improvised intellectual work in the difficult circumstances I have already described. Yet what reasons for joy! Often excellent students with a real taste for their task, confident in their young master; I watched them, too, outside of class, alone or in small groups; the awareness of the priestly responsibilities that awaited them, far from working against their intellectual fervor, only fanned its flames.[1] Great freedom in the choice of subjects for the courses and in the manner of treating them, thanks to the dean's benevolence. On the outside, I was taking part in the first launching of a "Catholic action" filled with spiritual vigor, and I had contact with it in various ways, particularly through several Sunday recollection days of the J.O.C. [Young Worker's Catholic Association], newly installed in the Châtelard house. A little group of students from the *Ecole normale d'instituteurs* [college for primary-school teachers] was meeting in my room on rue d'Auvergne, brought from the Red Cross by Tournissou (who recently became a priest at over 60 years of age, in company with his friend Georges Belleville, and is today parish priest at Saint-Denis, an untiring catechist). With Catholic and other interested students from the Cagne [those preparing for entrance exams for the higher-level teacher's college] from the Parc Lycée, I went to the Trappist monastery at Dombes, where I met with them once or twice in the narrow room of the *Chronique sociale*, which had welcomed so many different meetings; it had been organized by Fernand Guimet, whose premature death still grieves me [3:1] and who leaves us this masterful work: *Existence et eternité* (1974). Through Emile Janier, who was to die at Tlemcen, I had a connection with the *Equipes sociales* of Robert Garric, recruited in Lyons to give out elementary education and proofs of friendship to the North Africans in the region; in order to print some

[1] One of them has become, since 1972, the Rector of our Catholic Faculties in Lyons. The war of 1939, captivity, then the needs of his diocese prevented Msgr. Paul Chevallier from finishing the preparation of a thesis on Luther whose importance could have been capital. I owe much to his friendship.

sound orientational material for the *Equipes*, we had Louis Massignon, whom all of us venerated, come to us. During the summer, there were the "priests' months" at Valence, Montauban, Dax . . . ; the atmosphere, at once religious and intellectual, was very lively; they began with a retreat of eight days, after which generally came three weeks of courses on subjects relating to theology, moral theology, apologetics, and so forth. . . , given by a balanced team of several members; that obliged me to bring the questions treated during the year at the Faculty into line, so to speak, with current reality; at Dax, our director for the month was Monsieur Gounot, a Lazarist, whom I was later to meet again at Tunis, when he took me in for a while in order to protect me.[2]

In Lyons itself, at the university seminary of Saint-Just, hospitality was always warm. Three generations of superiors lived peacefully together there at that time: M. Choublier, a venerable old man (Robert Flacelière's uncle), was ending his days there. M. Cimetier, still alert, was teaching canon law; when he died, the famous prayer taken from the *Divine milieu* was found on his desk, copied out in his own hand. M. Girard, superior in office, a builder, overflowed with cordial activity. The director of the university seminary, who had come from the diocesan seminary of Francheville to our Faculty, was M. Louis Richard: he was theology incarnate, the doctrinal consultant for the *Chronique sociale*, the model of the priest according to Saint-Sulpice—as different as can be from the robot model that some have formed. I often visited him, consulted him. The discerning friendship of M. Georges Villepelet (d. 1975), director of the seminary, having succeeded M. Girard as superior, was an even greater support to me; when, in order to conform to the new norms set according to the decree "*Scientiarum Dominus*" of Pius XI, it was necessary for me to teach first-year students the whole ensemble of treatises on Revelation and the Church, Villepelet offered me very effective assistance; afterward, in all things, our understanding remained perfect. During those same years of the 1930s, the saintly Abbé Paul Couturier enlisted me to preach during the Weeks of Unity, then a new thing: my first initiation to an "ecumenical" activity that was going to place me in contact with two young Swiss pastors, Roger Schutz and Max Thurian, when they were laying the foundations for their Taizé monastery. It was also from the 1930s that close bonds were formed with Abbé Monchanin, whom I mentioned above,[3] as well as with his friend Abbé Edouard Duperray, then vicar at Saint-Alban, who was coming to found a center for Chinese students, then very numerous in Lyons. I knew several of these students well: Vincent Ou (d. 1972) and

---

[2] Despite a few common traits, I would not dare to compare these "priests' months" to some of the meetings that are today called "continuing education".

[3] The Monchanin papers are preserved at the municipal library of Lyons.

François Houang, the one a Confucian and the other Buddhist, the one a mathematician and the other a philosopher, who converted in Lyons, one after the other, both becoming priests of the Oratory; yet another, who was working at night in a glassworks factory in order to learn about French literature during the day: he had taken a course from Joseph Segond, an unbelieving psychologist, on Pascal; "It was there", he told me, "that I first knew Christianity and understood that the problem of the Christian faith was being set to me, personally". I was present at his baptism in Fribourg, where he had gone to finish his studies, in the chapel of the Foyer Saint-Justin, founded by Abbé Charrière, future bishop of Fribourg. Having returned to China and become a professor at the National University of Peking, he published a *Pascal* as his first book, in a gesture of gratitude. We exchanged a few more letters. After Mao came to power, I had no further news of him.

In Lyons, we had small priestly gatherings around Abbés Monchanin and Duperray and their friend Abbé Maillet (d. 1973), Pastor at the Immaculée Conception; they communicated to us something of their missionary zeal, nourished by their contemplation of the mystery of Christ and the Church. On rue d'Auvergne, having Father Auguste Valensin so close was invaluable to me; he forced me to tighten up my thought and to express it clearly; we read together the letters received from Blondel and Teilhard. Father Jean Zupan had me take (a very small) part in his charitable activity, particularly with the unemployed, whose number was growing; he was soon to leave Lyons, appointed, in virtue of the fourth vow of profession that he would soon pronounce, to go and found a small Eastern-Rite seminary in Sofia.[4] At Fourvière, Father Victor Fontoynont, who had succeeded Father Delaye as prefect of studies, was a wise and encouraging advisor, who was not afraid to point out my weaknesses to me; I had visited him a lot during my "regency [*régence*]" at Mongré (1923– 1924), where he was then teaching philosophy; I submitted everything I wrote to him; I dedicated *Corpus mysticum* to him, but I should have done so for many other publications as well! Some good companions from the scholasticate came down to see me during the first years: Gaston Fessard, René d'Ouince, Henri Rondet, Raymond Jouve, Alfred de Soras, Yves de

[4] Lacking all resources, exposed to hostilities of all kinds, religious as well as political, ignorant, above all, of the Bulgarian language, he nonetheless accomplished his mission. Then the war, the nazi persecution, succeeded by the communist persecution, destroyed everything. After a long time spent in a work camp, he was able, thanks to a passport delivered by our ambassador, to return to France in 1950 and then to take up again an extremely fruitful apostolic and social activity in Nice. He died in 1968. Recently a French traveller, questioned secretly in Sofia by a high-level communist, saw this man weep as he recalled the memory of Father Zupan. I have published some of his letters in *Trois Jésuites nous parlent* (Lethielleux, 1980) [*Three Jesuits Speak* (San Francisco: Ignatius Press, 1988)].

Montcheuil, Emile Rideau (who was preparing his thesis on Bergson). . . . Then, at the end of five or six years, when I had gone back up on the hill, I found there a new generation full of life, with Henri Mogenet, Donatien Mollat, Pierre Ganne, François Varillon, Jean Daniélou, and so forth. . ., and the very dear and faithful Hans Urs von Balthasar, whose brilliance was already shining forth. It was at that time, during fifteen days of rest at Annecy during the Easter season, that Balthasar read the entire works of Gregory of Nyssa and composed the outline for the work that would later appear through Beauchesne, written directly in French; it was also at that time that he gave a discourse, for a "Disputatio menstrualis", the *Mysterion d'Origène* that Editions du Cerf would publish. The first of the numerous works of the future Cardinal Daniélou was also prepared at that time, the *Signe du Temple* (which appeared in 1942, through Gallimard).[5]

Troubles were certainly not lacking in these years before the war. One would have had to be deaf and blind not to have made out much lack of understanding, distrust and even opposition within the Church. The condemnation of *l'Action française* had stirred deep unrest. A certain Scholastic conservatism, which claimed in all good faith to be tradition itself, was alarmed at any appearance of novelty. A kind of so-called "Thomist" dictatorship, which was more a matter of government than intellectuality, strove to stifle any effort toward freer thought. A network made up of several professors and their former students, which was spread throughout the world, distrusted anything that came into existence outside itself. So, already, as in the period of "integrism", denunciations began to pour out once again. I will note here, in what concerns me, only one serious warning, dating from 1935: following my summer conferences during the month-long course for priests at Dax, Canon Lahitton, who was in close contact with Father Pègues, O.P., of Saint-Maximim, was charged (or had himself charged?) by Msgr. Ruffini, then secretary of the Congregation

[5] I gave the following review of it in 1942: "In our opinion, there is nothing precisely like this little volume in the religious literature of our time. Yet it would be a mistake nonetheless to seek to find in it some sort of unprecedented originality. Its entire novelty derives, on the contrary, not only from a profoundly traditional spirit but also from a profoundly traditional structure. Father Daniélou does not just quote the Fathers of the Church, he goes back to one of their favorite themes, he enters into their method and, so to speak, espouses their rhythm. This gives better proof than all dissertations put together that the thought of the first Christian centuries is still living and that if we do not live by it all the more, the fault is in ourselves. There is a lot of talk today, particularly following the last works of Claudel, of the spiritual interpretation of Scripture. Here is an admirable example of it, in the great, robust manner of the ancients. The Temple where Yahweh resided is taken to be the symbol of the Presence of God in the universe, in the Mosaic Law, in Christ, in the Church, in history, in the Christian soul and finally in Heaven. In this way, the whole Christian mystery, according to each of its fundamental aspects, unfolds before our eyes, in a series of brief chapters loaded with doctrinal and spiritual substance."

of Seminaries and Universities, to make an inquiry. I was energetically
defended by the Bishop of Dax, Msgr. Mathieu, by the organizer of the
occasion, Msgr. de Solages, by his responsible Superior, M. Gounot, and
by Father F. Cavallera, who had all attended my classes. Msgr. Saliège,
Archbishop of Toulouse, joined them. All begged me not to abandon the
course as a result of this. But the affair threatened to go rather far; so,
on May 31, 1936, M. Gounot had to come see my Provincial, Father
Christophe de Bonneville, in Lyons and to address a long defense to Father Demaux-Lagrange, then secretary of the Society in Rome.[6]

Above all, from the time Hitler rose to power, we sensed with ever-
increasing anguish the "mounting dangers". The social, national and international atmosphere was weighed down with a heaviness that kept growing to the point of being intolerable. But despite everything, including a
more or less insidious integrism always in the background, to which I have
just referred, there was in the Church, under Pius XI, a spirit of joyful
hope, a lively interest in work, without any questioning of fidelity.

In the following period, both in 1940–1942 and under the total occupation in 1942–1944, Lyons was quite different. Just as earlier, in the sixteenth century, it had been the "intellectual capital" of France, it became
in 1940, as is often said, the "capital of the Resistance". It was also, at
least during the first two years, almost the capital itself. What Parisians
"in retreat"![7] Stanislas Fumet, André Frossard, Gabriel Marcel, Wladimir
d'Ormesson, Robert d'Harcourt came to Fourvière, where I met them in
the city. They gathered around Paulus Lenz-Médoc, who was protected
by his diplomatic Vatican passport, in the little room where he lived in
Villeurbanne.[8] One day Paul Petit arrived, the translator of Meister Eckhart and Kierkegaard, the bibliographer and correspondent of Claudel, one
of the first authors of anti-nazi tracts, who was to be arrested, deported
to Cologne and executed with an axe on August 24, 1944;[9] another day,

---

[6] See this letter in Appendix III, along with three others, addressed to me by him, by Msgr.
Mathieu, Bishop of Dax, and by Father Cavallera [3:2].

[7] We might also recall that, in less tragic conditions, Lyons was at the beginning of the
nineteenth century the city where autochthonal Lyonese and exiled Parisians met.

[8] He gave German lessons at our university seminary. Having not long before fought courageously against the rise of nazism, he had then been imprisoned and had finally found asylum
in France. In 1940, he had fled Paris. After the war, he had me come to give some conferences
at Gemen, in the Munster diocese, where he organized international youth meetings every
summer.

[9] ". . . Paul Petit was a knight. With the help of a deep knowledge of Germany and its
language, he was one of the very first to organize the Resistance in the Paris area. From the
beginning of 1941, having come to establish relations with the "unoccupied zone", he participated in several discussions that helped to refine the idea that would eventually take shape in
the *Cahiers du Témoignage chrétien*. He would have been its ardent disseminator if he had not

it was Jean Wahl, a survivor of the Drancy camp, and so forth. . . . Paul
Claudel came from Brangues on the hill to rekindle the zeal of our archbishop (Cardinal Gerlier), and, while I was visiting our library with him,
he asked me to hide certain manuscripts for him (which was very imprudent) [3:3]. I was sometimes called by the Chantiers de Jeunesse [youth work
camps], where a touching "Maréchalian" fervor usually reigned;[10] I gave
several lectures there, on "The Church in the Face of the World Crisis",
and similar subjects; I gave one, on "The Causes of the Diminished Sense
of the Sacred", to the gathering of Chantiers chaplains, organized in 1942 at
Sainte-Baume by Father Doncoeur and by Father Forestier, O.P. General
de la Porte du Theil presided at the Congress. My conference was not
exactly conformist. As with other texts, I have resisted several requests
since then to republish it; it remains buried in the papers of this gathering.
I also spoke several times to the Ecole des Cadres of Uriage, created and
directed by Commander Dunoyer de Seconsac, who was called "the old
chief"; Hubert Beuve-Méry filled the role of prefect of studies there; I
passed on to him some small unpublished works by Teilhard, for his spiritual enrichment. (We maintained our relations for a long time, outside
of all politics, under the aegis of the venerable Alfred Michelin.) It was to
Uriage, if I am not mistaken, that a pamphlet on La Vocation de la France
[The vocation of France] (1941) owed its birth; another most certainly
came from there: Explication chrétienne de notre temps [Christian explanation of our time] (1942). I was also induced to write at that time for the
Cahiers de notre jeunesse; it was in this Cahiers that I reviewed, in 1943, the
little, much-discussed work by Father Doncoeur: Péguy, la Révolution et le
Sacré; I think I succeeded, on that delicate occasion, to calm the minds
of many young friends without failing in what we owed to Father Don-

---

been arrested so soon. . . . An eminent expert in Claudel, very knowledgeable about Taoism,
attracted without any snobbishness to any profound mysticism, Paul Petit was especially well
known, outside diplomatic circles, for his translation of the Sermons and Treatises of Meister
Eckhart, which appeared when he was already a prisoner, and for that of the famous Post-
scriptum of Kierkegaard (from Danish). These works were not at all for him some literary or
speculative pastime. He committed his soul to it, just as he was to commit his life, as a believer,
as a magnificent Christian, as a seeker of God. . . ." The clandestine writings of Paul Petit
were published in 1947, with a poem by Paul Claudel and a foreword by Jacques Madaule (by
Gallimard).

[10] To give some idea, about one detail, of the atmosphere of the times, I will quote this
printed card I received (at the end of December 1941) from one of the chantiers where I had
spoken: "On the occasion of the new year, Commissioner X and the youth of the Chantier
de la Jeunesse 'le Fier' express to you their wish to see all Frenchmen understand at last the
sterility of their egoism and their materialism and to unite fraternally behind Marshal Pétain,
in a great and fruitful burst of enthusiasm for more spirituality, the indispensable condition of
the advent of better days." —Group 7, Rumilly, Haute-Savoie.

coeur, who later gave me a magnanimous welcome in Paris and Troussure [3:4].

When the German army invaded the southern zone (I still remember that morning of November 1942, when, from the d'Ainay basilica, where we were gathered for the opening Mass of the school year, we heard the tanks roll over the quay of the Saône), the refugees scattered, the suspects disappeared, all activity went underground. Each one had to hide from everyone, not only to avoid being compromised himself but in order not to compromise the other. The Jews, like Jules Isaac, Robert Aron (departed for Africa from the North), had disappeared. One day, however, I would meet André Chouraqui, then being hunted down, coming peacefully to the place Bellecour, to the Sacred Heart bookshop, in search of some mystical author. Emmanuel Mounier, who had returned to Lyons after his administrative internment at Vals-les-Bains and his hunger strike at the Aubenas hospital (alerted by a little note written in pencil and confided to a porter, in July 1942, I had gone to see him there [3:5]), was now preparing to flee into the Drôme mountains. On the day fixed for his departure, since he still had two hours before his scheduled rendez-vous, he came to spend them at the library at Fourvière, in order to work calmly on his *Traité du caractère*; I admired that marvelous self-possession.

The tension was constant. We lived in a fever increased by hunger, by the daily horror of the news, by the next day's uncertainty. And yet, work was carried on, became even more intense. It was at this time that the series *Sources chrétiennes* was begun, about which I will speak later on; that the *Revue du moyen âge latin* was founded, under the patronage of Henri Marrou and the direction of Abbé François Châtillon, the first issue of which could appear only in 1945.

As early as the winter of 1940–1941, the spiritual resistance to nazism was organized. In the years before the war, Father Chaillet had created a service to help the refugees of our region. On his return from Hungary to France, having been discharged, he had taken it up again under the most difficult conditions. Then, from Cardinal Gerlier, who always placed great confidence in him, he obtained protection for the Jewish children who were being demanded from the French administration by the nazis. He had sent me to Toulouse (what a journey!) to Cardinal Saliège to obtain his ringing intervention in favor of the persecuted Jews (I had feared that I would never be able to get to the end of our secret conversation that day, the Archbishop, who was paralyzed, was so incapable of articulating a single word, of writing a single word; patiently, he renewed his efforts until I finally guessed).[11] Thanks to the intrepid determination of Father

---

[11] After the liberation, I prepared the publication of a volume of selected "Témoignages"

Chaillet, the first "Cahier du Témoignage catholique" (which became *in extremis*, so as to permit the collaboration of Protestants, "du Témoignage chrétien" by sticking a butterfly on the cover) had been printed and distributed during the autumn of 1941. Its title was: "France, prends garde de perdre ton âme" [France, take care not to lose your soul]; it had been written entirely by Father Gaston Fessard, to whom I had furnished documentation; Father Fessard had already, in December 1940, published under his own name a premonitory article: "Custos, quid de nocte?" in *Temps nouveaux*, the ephemeral weekly that appeared in Saint-Etienne under the direction of Stanislas Fumet.[12] Actively pursued, Father Chaillet was going from one hiding place to another. The *Cahiers* came one after the other, at a good pace, just as the complete occupation of the territory continued to accelerate. I had secret rendez-vous with him, each time in a different place, each time with the fear of falling into some "trap", in order to take or deliver to him a new text. When I had to leave Lyons, it was with the unspoken understanding of Father Décisier, rector at Fourvière, with only a hint to ask permission or at least to warn him, without telling him where I was going or whom I was going to meet. Through Germaine Ribière or one of her messengers (particularly Adrien Nemoz), I supervised each of the *Cahiers* as closely as possible, to the point of checking the proofs when this was possible; we wanted not only that they be of high quality but that everything in them be of perfect Catholic loyalty. When, in 1947, in Berlin, I had a conversation with Msgr. von Preysing,[13] we embraced with emotion, stating that, from both sides, we had led the same combat, against the same adversary of Christ, with the same spiritual weapons [3:7]. One of our *Cahiers* had in fact quoted this declaration made by the Bishop of Berlin: "No doubt is possible for us: we are Christians, engaged in a hard battle. Against us is rising the religion of blood. The signs of the fight are flashing everywhere, everywhere from the scornful rejection of the doctrine of Christ to impassioned and overt hatred. A rolling fire of affirmations borrowed both from history and from the present is surging over us. The goal of the battle is clear: it is the suppression and expulsion

---

by Cardinal Saliège. I also reviewed the complete collection—published later—of his *Menus propos*, in seven volumes [3:6].

[12] After the liberation, when communist pressure was threatening, Father Fessard published, still under the imprint of Témoignage chrétien: *France, prends garde de perdre ta liberté* [France, take care not to lose your freedom]. In later times, to respond once again to the needs of the hour, he envisaged writing: "France, prends garde de perdre ta raison" [France, take care not to lose your reason] (this would finally become "Eglise de France, prends garde de perdre la Foi!" [Church of France, take care not to lose the Faith] [Julliard, 1979], published one year after his death).

[13] It was on Saturday, August 30.

of Christianity. A joyful clamor of victory is rising from the ranks of anti-Christianity. . . ." These tragic words, our *Cahier* added, were repeated many times by the bishops of Germany.

In order to show the spirit of the *Cahiers du Témoignage chrétien*, which were in no way a political undertaking, I will quote here one of their declarations. It is drawn from Cahier X–XI, *Collaboration et fidélité*, printed and distributed in November 1942:

> The *Cahiers* give witness for those Christians who are fully conscious of their present responsibilities; who, caught up in the tragedy of their times, perceive the immense danger of seeing stifled that Christian spirit that formed them, of seeing enchained that Christian freedom of spirit without which no power will be able to save the soul of France—or even its body. The danger of the progressive magic appeal achieved through nazi propaganda, which finds too many conscious or unconscious servants among us. The danger of daily lies and camouflages from the press, radio and cinema. The danger of silences imposed by a censorship dominated by the occupying or controlling power. Perhaps it will be said that the nazi error is not the only one and that there are other dangers. We do not argue with this. But the freedom of word and pen to denounce these other dangers remains intact. There are even many ways of combating them that only make them worse. Our *Cahiers* bear their witness where no voice can make itself heard publicly, where temptation is the most immediate or most all-embracing. —They keep strictly to the Christian level. They do not give any "political" orders, because it is not at all their business and because Christian fidelity, alone and directly, is not enough to determine political options. If, in the present state of confusion of minds and distress of consciences, faced with the spinelessness of too great a number from whom one would expect more dignity, they feel united to all those who are not resigned to letting France be debased, it is because patriotism is a virtue; it is because Christian fidelity and national honor are intimately connected. But the *Cahiers* are not for all that departing from the only field that is theirs. We affirm—and no one can seriously deny it—that any economic or political "collaboration" with the nazi power, in circumstances where collaboration signifies subjection, carries with it a closely related danger of subjection in the realm of culture. Now nazi "culture" is fundamentally anti-Christian, and neither the repeated declarations of the nazi leaders nor their renewed actions are in the least reassuring. We therefore want to show all Christians and also all those who, without being believers, are attached more than they think to the principles of a Christian civilization that, *on this level of the spirit*, the duty is to oppose and to organize resistance to nazism. The more strongly nazism brings its domination to bear over France, the more important it will be that this spiritual resistance become lucid and firm. We are simple Christians. We do not speak in the name of any authority. We are seeking honestly to inform consciences. We are reporting verified facts and authentic documents. We are recalling doctrinal directives that have come from the leaders of the

Church. Doing so, we are fulfilling the duty that any believer, engaged in temporal life, has to bear witness to his Faith, to protect it from corruption, to defend it when it is threatened. It would be a great error, the fruit of great cowardice, to put off doing so under any circumstances until one had received an official mission. The *Cahiers du Témoignage chrétien* are the testimony of numerous and varied Christians who, without ulterior political motives and without claiming in any way to involve the Hierarchy, are deeply committed as Christians.

The *Cahiers* enterprise gave rise to many instances of heroic self-sacrifice, much of which will always remain hidden.[14] Louis Cruvillier was the principal agent of our network, which until the end remained completely free of political or even national ties. Father Daniélou and Father de Montcheuil helped us a great deal, in the same spirit, with the distribution in the northern zone; along with them, Fathers Jacques Sommet and Michel Riquet (both of whom were deported), Father Gonzague Pierre, and so on. . . . Up until the eve of his death, Father de Montcheuil strove at the same time to caution the groups of students engaged in the Resistance against the Marxist influence, which was growing. One day, an emissary arrived at Fourvière to inform me that Father Chaillet had just been arrested, that he was being held at Gestapo headquarters, at the Hotel Terminus de Perrache; a few hours later, Father Chaillet came to reassure us, then left very quickly: he had not been recognized; ordered to stand with his chest against the wall, he had been able to swallow the compromising papers and cards before his turn for interrogation.[15]

But the vise was tightening. I remember the sudden raid by a German squad on a house on the outskirts of Avignon at the very moment when I was giving a presentation on nazism in a room on the first floor. It was only a coincidence. But other signs appeared. I received some suspicious visits at Fourvière. An agent provocateur came with his wife to beg me to show him a channel. An employee at the office of the Prefect had the Father Rector (who was Father Charles Chamussy at that time) warned that it was time for me to find some place of safety. At first I withdrew every evening to a little outbuilding (since demolished) of the boarding school run by the Dominicans, on the Choulans hill; then I stayed with

---

[14] The best published study on this subject is the article by François and Renée Bédarida, "Une Résistance spirituelle: aux origines du 'Témoignage chrétien', 1941–1942", in the *Revue d'histoire de la deuxième guerre mondiale* (January 1966), 3–31. Later, in March 1977, the work by Renée Bédarida (in collaboration with François Bédarida) was published: *Les Armes de l'Esprit. Témoignage chrétien (1941–1944)* (Les Editions ouvrières, 1977), 378 p. Renée Bédarida and Adrien Nemoz have published the whole series of the clandestine T.C. in facsimile (2 vols., 1979) [3:8].

[15] This was in February 1943. The details of this dramatic day have been written down elsewhere.

the curé in Tournon; finally, passing through Fourvière again, and having received a suitcase at a friend's, I left for Vals. A few days later, my colleague Louis Richard was arrested and deported; similarly, at Toulouse, Bruno de Solages, and so on. . . . In 1944, there was the tragedy of Vercors: Father de Montcheuil, having come from Paris to bring religious assistance to some students of the maquis, caring for the wounded in the cave of the Luire, was arrested, led to Grenoble and executed [3:9]. For a long time we hoped that he had been deported, that he would return. . . . His breviary was found. It contained a holy card that I still keep in mine, on the back of which, leaving to be shot at Polygone, he had said a final goodbye to me. . . .

In the months that followed the liberation, there were still other troubles. . . .

During the course of 1943, the *Cahiers* had been joined by a *Courrier français du Témoignage chrétien*, of more popular appeal but which claimed exactly the same inspiration. As attempts were sometimes made to portray us as guerrillas more or less in rebellion against the authority of the Church, the *Courrier* renewed the declarations of the *Cahiers*: We can read, for instance, in number 3, pp. 4 and 6:

> No one will be surprised that, in a country that numbers more than eighty dioceses, some differences occur. Despite a few discordant voices, we continue to think that the letter of the cardinals and archbishops in February and the declaration of the cardinals in May constitute in an unparalleled way the most authoritative and trustworthy documents and express the moral unanimity of the episcopate. . . . Careful observers are not fooled. The Church of France, in union with the universal Church, with all her soul rejects Hitlerism, with its cruelty, its tyranny and its lies. The French clergy is in profound sympathy with the people of France. It suffers with them, it hopes with them. Through an ever-growing number of its members, it is in the first ranks of those who are fighting against injustice and who are actively devoting themselves to their hunted brethren.

And again, in number 4, on page 4:

> The Church usually acts quietly. She does not like aggressive manifestations. She does not anticipate the hour of the *non possumus*. She detests polemics. She fears that her declarations might be exploited for means other than her own. She tolerates everything that can be tolerated. She binds herself to longstanding patience. As a constituted organism, she practices a loyalty that goes well beyond what is imposed on simple citizens. Until she has evidence to the contrary, she hopes for some ground of understanding. She encourages as far as possible the desire for reconciliation. But when it comes down to what is essential for her to say and do in order to prevent her mission from being betrayed, one can be sure that this will be said, this will be done. The

tragic events that have been transpiring in France over the past three years have shown this to us once more. The Church has not remained indifferent in the face of measures of persecution taken against the Jews or in the face of the progressive invasion of the Hitlerian poison into French souls or in the face of the forced requisitions and deportations. The texts that our *Cahiers* have published have repeatedly attested to this. Particularly on the subject of deportations, in the most restrained terms, the judgment has been pronounced: they are contrary to the law, they are unjust, no one is bound by conscience to submit to them.[16] Many things can be added to this minimum judgment: one cannot refuse to understand it. One cannot pretend that it has not been pronounced [3:10].

I have let myself digress at length. For a long time now, I have seldom thought of those terrible years. The younger generations naturally have no idea of them. Speaking in 1935 about the Dreyfus affair, which he had lived through, Léon Blum observed that he had been unable to interest his son in it: "My words were only words for him".[17] How much more serious still, and more difficult to evoke in their depth of substance, were the tragedies that occurred during the "occupation"! How is it possible to make those who did not live through those years have a sense of the spiritual stakes involved? As for the older generations themselves, how many other events, other combats come endlessly to claim all their powers of attention! Yet, now and then, the memory is rekindled: this happened again, two years ago, at the death of Father Chaillet, whose last twenty-five years, totally devoted to other forms of charity, were saddened at the sight of what had become of that "témoignage chrétien" that he had founded for the honor of the Church and the salvation of the French soul and whose effectiveness had been purchased at the price of blood [3:11]. This reminiscence, however, will not have been completely irrelevant if it permits me, in accordance with the purpose I have proposed to myself in these pages, to explain the part I took in the writing of the *Cahiers du témoignage chrétien* (more or less complete, more or less precise lists of authors have been published; the *Cahiers* enterprise, which was a work of the Church, was also a collective and anonymous work; it is good for it to retain something of that twofold character)—and then, in the years that followed, my part in the publication of the writings of Father Yves de Montcheuil.

The publication of these writings, which required my making a clean

---

[16] This referred to the deportation of young people for the S.T.O. (Service du travail obligatoire [obligatory work service]).

[17] *Souvenirs sur l'Affaire*, p. 13. In this book, Léon Blum himself no longer remembers Péguy, who was at that time militating with him every day; not once does he cite his name. It is true that other reasons besides the passage of time explain that silence.

copy of a number of pages (my close friendship with the author permitted, even compelled, me to do this: we had done this when he was alive), took me some time. I have spoken above about other books, prepared earlier, which appeared at that time. It was also necessary to publish a new edition of *Corpus mysticum* (1949): during these postwar years, minds that had long remained on nearly as strict a fast as bodies, threw themselves on the toughest food. In a new preface, I tried to define the spirit of this book, with respect to some sinister rumors that were circulating about it.

> In reacting [I said] against the "modern" sufficiency that makes our contemporaries believe they have more genius than their fathers for the sole reason that they were born after them, we intend to return to a more traditional estimation, which will benefit not only the patristic age and the high Middle Ages but the following centuries as well. In these immense realms, each can carve out his own choice of terrain. But no portion of the common inheritance may be systematically depreciated. One has spoken with good reason of the "change of scenery without which the effort at historical comprehension does not begin" (Paul Vignaux). The historian is obliged to make contrasts stand out for fear of saying nothing but banalities. May he not, for all that, close his eyes to the more fundamental continuities! For us, in the very history of human thought, and how much more in that of Christian thought, it is to these continuities that in the end our attention will always be drawn, it is in contemplating them that the historian will find his rest and his joy. Among so many varied riches that attract us, we will always ask to do what Plato's child did, that is, every time at least that the thing is strictly possible, not to make a choice. A unity too quickly asserted is without any stimulating value. Eclecticisms are without importance. But the methodical acceptance of what are at first perceived to be contrarieties is fruitful: it not only protects against partialities that are too swiftly formed; it not only opens one to an in-depth awareness of the unity: it is also one of the conditions necessary for the preparation of new departures.[18]

But neither these explanations nor the very favorable reviews received by the book [3:12] were to save poor *Corpus mysticum* from shipwreck.[19]

[18] I also like to recall these words by Father de Régnon on the variety of doctors and systems in the Catholic tradition: "The beauty of each must be shown in the light of the other."

[19] It was after the shipwreck that the critical review by Msgr. G. Philips, whose authority was already great and who was to play an eminent role, as we know, in the Council, appeared in *Ephemerides theologicae lovanienses* (1951, I–II, pp. 180–81). I permit myself to reproduce here the essence of that review:

"In order to understand well the meaning of Father de L.'s book, which is now appearing in its second edition, it seems to me that it would be necessary to begin by reading the Conclusion, pp. 279–94. . . .

"Please pardon this gross oversimplification, which neglects the details. Father de L. takes into account perfectly the danger inherent in making the history of a doctrine depend on

Father Chaillet also wanted to take from me, for the "Editions du témoignage chrétien", which was just barely managing to survive, a collection of four texts, which appeared in January 1950 under the title *Affrontements mystiques*. One of these texts, "Un Nouveau front religieux", was a protest against Hitlerian anti-Semitism; printed in 1941, destined for the journal *Chronique sociale*, it had been stopped by the Vichy censor; yet—I no longer have any reliable memory of how the thing could have been done—*Vie spirituelle* of June 1942 had published the first part of it, the part that no longer attained the most burning timeliness. The whole of the study had found a place in a collective volume entitled *Israël et la foi chrétienne*, published in Fribourg, Switzerland (1942), on the initiative of Abbé Joseph Chaine (who would have liked to make it a manifesto of our Lyons Theology Faculty), backed by Louis Richard and Father Joseph Bonsirven. I recently came across a copy of a letter from Father Victor Dillard, dated Vichy, December 12, 1941; since it is one of the rare written testimonies of that period of semi-freedom enjoyed at that time by the "unoccupied" zone, there might be some interest in quoting it:

> I am coming from a final try with the censor for your article "Defense of Christ and of the Bible" [that was the title chosen at first], and this time I am hopelessly beaten. I had made appeals at all levels . . . and I have come away rather pessimistic about these processes. I have the impression that we could have spoken about these questions several months ago, but the noose is tightening. "If we let this article go by," they said to me, "we would im-

---

the history of a word. So he has taken nearly laborious care to furnish us with an extremely extensive and scrupulously analyzed historical documentation. His spirit of exactitude spares us no detail, no matter how minimal, even if this does not make the reading any easier. Rarely, undoubtedly too rarely, he gives us an overall view to give us time to breathe. This makes the few passages of synthesis all the more invaluable. Thus, for example, p. 115. . . . Or again, p. 210. . . .

"Nevertheless, it is not a question, in the evolution of theological thought, of returning to or preferring the symbolic language of the ancients to the dialectical spirit of the Scholastics. Father de L., in the foreword of his second edition, vigorously defends himself against this accusation of extreme conservatism and anti-intellectualism. His apology gains us some fine pages (pp. 258ff.) not only on the true importance of Augustinian illumination but also on the 'positivism' of the ancients, which does not at all neglect intellectual analysis. The *fides quaerens intellectum* does not date from the time of Saint Anselm.

"The second part of the book . . . has the appearance rather of an appendix. This subsidiary question is treated with an historical precision that is, if possible, even more rigorous.

"The pale glimpse that we have sketched will nevertheless suffice, we hope, to make one admire how enriching Father de L.'s scientific investigation has been, not only for our erudition but also for our always infinitely respectful penetration into the very heart of revealed dogma. The Incarnation, continued in the Eucharist, finds its full flowering only in the supernatural efficiency of the Church. From beginning to end, the coming of the Son of God in the flesh must qualify as mystery, that is, as mysterious and as efficaciously salutary."

mediately have a reaction from the occupying power." For it is that which is obviously the cause. There could be even less doubt about it since all polemics are forbidden between the free zone and the occupied zone, and since your references to Montherlant, for example, could not get by. I objected that the question was serious, that it was the very freedom of the Church that was at stake. They replied that they had indeed taken this into account, but that they could do nothing about it, that some public declarations by the Cardinal himself on this question had been censored and that the pastoral letters from the bishops themselves could not escape censorship. I pointed out that they could nevertheless not keep us from speaking in the pulpit. But I wonder if we will be able to do that much longer. It would be good to keep the Cardinal informed, and, if it were possible to obtain an official declaration from him on the Jewish religious question, I believe that it could get by while things are still as they are. The future does not belong to us. I am all the more distressed because for over a year I have begged Father Desbuquois and others to take a position in *Cité nouvelle* or in *Renouveaux*. It seemed to me then that this was our duty. Now it is too late.

Another text from *Affrontements* dealt with the "Nietzsche mystique" in a much too cursory fashion, although its intention was to complete what had been said in one chapter of the *Drame de l'humanisme athée* [The drama of atheistic humanism]. Another simply reproduced a kind of meditation on "The Light of Christ", which had first appeared, in 1943, in a collection of little pamphlets published by the Fourvière house;[20] I have been told that Léon Brunschwicg, although he was an old man fleeing persecution from one hiding place to another and had had friendly conversations with his old comrade and adversary Blondel, had read it with attention and approval. The first and most important piece of the collection was an amplified version of a lecture on the Christian conception of man given in 1947 to the *Semaine sociale* in Paris. Rome had at first vetoed my participation in this *Semaine sociale* (as well as that of Father Chenu and even, if I remember correctly, that of Maurice Blondel);[21] then it let itself be swayed by the organizers, Charles Flory and Alfred Michelin, who made a special trip to Rome for the purpose; they obtained the desired authorization, on condition of a preliminary censorship exercised by the archbishop of Paris; Cardinal Suhard declared that he trusted my superior to do that and invited me shortly after to give a recollection day to his young priests. Would one believe it? Several readers, or presumably such, among whom were a Dominican philosopher, a Jesuit sociologist and a German

---

[20] The title of this collection was "Le Témoignage chrétien"; it was found rather often in churches. This resulted, at the time of the German occupation, in a few quid pro quos that at times constituted a saving alibi.

[21] It was on June 29, 1947, that I learned about this triple veto. The *Semaine sociale* was held from July 27 to August 2.

professor, a reputed jurist (father of a fervent follower of Blondel!), sub-sequently believed they saw in me, in this regard, the doctrinal inspiration for "Christian communists" [3:13]. It is true that none of the three was French and that during those years much unverified news, coming from France, was circulating abroad.[22] One listener, an Italian theologian and journalist, reproached me more objectively, if not more justly, for having set myself the task of criticizing Marxism from a Christian point of view, while it should have been refuted solely through the resources of natural philosophy. The fact was that my conference was an attempt at a Christian response to the Marxist conception of man, which Jean Lacroix had been charged with explaining in the preceding lecture.

This incident is characteristic of the conflict that was to set me in oppo-sition to one whole powerful school of theology, for which all Christian revelation constituted a "supernatural order" so apart that it was forbidden to have recourse to it in any of the great human debates of our time.[23] I have spoken of this earlier, with respect to my book *Surnaturel*. But al-ready, in this summer of 1947, we were in the third of the three periods I indicated, that of the years 1945–1950, which was to be crowned by the encyclical *Humani generis* and to put a quasi-definitive end to my teaching [3:14].[24]

---

[22] The work of Professor Hommes, "Das technische Eros" (?), dates, I believe, from around 1950. Father Georges Jarlot, who had consulted him at the Gregorian, wrote to me: "Roughly, very roughly, the poor character imagines that you are trying to baptize the problematic of historical materialism by transferring it into a theology in which the supernatural would be no more than an assumption of nature! He makes here a strange comparison with Hegel. . . . He has, like Gundlach and certain others, a concept of the relations between nature and the supernatural that is exactly contradictory to yours and, obviously, understands nothing of what you propose."

[23] See, in the Appendix, a passage from that lecture of 1947, expressing the distinction be-tween nature and the supernatural, which Father Garrigou-Lagrange and others still accused me for a long time of denying [3:15].

[24] For the period running from August 26, 1946, to September 23, 1954, I kept, more or less regularly, a kind of journal, containing 485 pages, to which are added some appended documents. I continued it until 1960.

CHAPTER FOUR

In August 1946, a General Congregation of the Order was convened at
Rome in order to elect a new Superior General. Because of the war, it was
impossible to convoke it immediately after the death of Father Wladimir
Ledochowski, and it was Father Norbert de Boynes who had then performed the function of Vicar General of the Society. I was among the
delegates to the Congregation. I remember having heard Father Janssens
say to us, on the terrace of the General Curia where we were taking our
usual evening recreation: In Rome, there is uneasiness as soon as they fail
to see the words they are used to in a piece of writing; but confidence is
easily placed in those who generally know how to use familiar expressions
to disseminate their new ideas. That was perhaps a day or two before his
election.[1] A few days later we were received by Pius XII, late in the morning, at Castelgandolfo. I was told (but I had no certain confirmation of it)
that Father de Boynes—who was a wise and experienced superior, kindly
disposed in everyday life, but with very conservative tendencies, not particularly competent in doctrinal matters and therefore especially fearful,
pushing to an extreme his respect for what one might call the "common
opinion"[2]—had prepared in advance for the Pope's address a little exhortation that consisted of a cautious reprimand directed at a few new tendencies; but neither he nor the new General expected the more severe
words with greater doctrinal range that were then pronounced, words that
were immediately attributed to other influences, notably to that of Father
Garrigou-Lagrange, O.P., of the Angelicum. Pius XII declared: "There has
been too much talk for some time about new theology"—which shows
besides that his personal information was rather vague, for none of the
members of what was called the "Fourvière school", as far as I know,
ever used that expression, and it was precisely Father Garrigou-Lagrange
who, picking up an old cliché, had launched it in a recent article with a
threatening tone: "The New Theology: Where Is It Going?" (Angelicum,
1946).[3]

For the period from September 9, 1946, to April 18, 1947, the reader can refer to the memorandum given in the Appendix [4:4].

[1] It took place on September 15.

[2] In addition, as a visitor in France during the years 1940–1942, he was alarmed to see
that the young men in the scholasticate did not seem very warm toward the authority of the
"Marshal", and he was particularly uneasy about me [4:1].

[3] The expression had already figured in an article by Msgr. Parente, aimed at the writings

The authorities of the Society thought at least they understood at first that the Pope's address, intended as a paternal admonition, would remain completely private. Pius XII had even sent his two assistants to have the doors carefully closed before beginning to speak. But hardly had we returned to Rome, when during dinner a messenger from Castelgondolfo came to tell the Father General that it was hoped he would not have anything against publishing it, and in fact the very next day the complete text of the address appeared on the front page of *l'Osservatore romano*. The passage on the "new theology" made news everywhere [4:3]. Then what whispering, what questioning, what uneasiness, echos of which reached me every day! What often absurd rumors, and accusations as well! At the end of the audience at Castelgondolfo, we had all filed before the Holy Father as the name of each was whispered to him by his respective assistants; he had said to me, in a friendly tone: "Ah! I know your doctrine very well". His words, indistinctly heard by those closest to us, repeated, distorted, exaggerated, were commented upon in every possible sense. Several came to ask me the meaning of them. For some, it was, without a doubt, a commendation; for others, it was a reproach, or at least a warning; for others, it was even the designation of the sacrificial victim. . . . In town, commentaries quickly made the rounds. At Saint-Louis-des-Français, Abbé Monchanin, who had come from India to accompany his bishop on his *ad limina* visit, heard me denounced in the middle of dinner as a heretic to be overcome. Yet, at the end of the General Congregation, Father Janssens took the initiative to call me. He had been obliged, he told me, to forego receiving many of the Fathers, Provincials and Superiors from distant missions who had asked him for an appointment before leaving Rome, but he insisted on seeing me in order to tell me this (and I report his remarks very faithfully): You have heard many rumors here; I am anxious to reassure you; in the misgivings that have been manifested, you are not in question; I speak to you in full knowledge of the case, after having been well informed by a good source: I have seen the secretary of the Holy Office[4] and the Holy Father himself. You can affirm it with certainty: know that you have the entire confidence of the Father General, and do not be concerned about anything [4:4].

---

of Fathers Chenu and Charlier, O.P., *Osservatore romano* of February 9–10, 1942. Cf. *La Croix* of February 26, 1942 [4:2].

[4] I too, during this stay in Rome, had seen Msgr. Ottaviani, then assistant at the Holy Office. I no longer remember what important Father had organized this interview for me (and similarly for Father d'Ouince, editor of *Etudes*), without having first spoken to me about it. I went to the meeting in all innocence. My interlocutor proved to be very friendly, gave me words of encouragement and even gave me a complimentary copy, with a beautiful inscription, of his *Traité de droit ecclésiastique*, in exchange for some volumes of *Sources chrétiennes*.

Nevertheless, shortly afterward critics abounded everywhere. "Refutations" of *Surnaturel* increased.[5] The most sinister news, apostasy included, circulated. Every country brought its own contribution to the campaign. Some *Semaines religieuses* warned the faithful against "wolves in sheep's clothing", and so on. . . . The Father General did not let himself be intimidated. Faithful to what he had said to me, to give me tangible proof of his confidence and in the hope that this gesture would be understood, he insisted—despite a report I made expressing the opposite view to the Provincials of France, asking that it be conveyed to him [4:5]—that the direction of the *Recherches de science religieuse* be confided to me.[6] From Lyons, this was not an easy task, and normal contributions slipped away. I did a few articles and notes as fillers for it. The article that appeared in 1949 on "Le Mystère du surnaturel" was not a repetition or refinement but rather a complement to the book. The Father General approved warmly of its publication, in accord with the opinion of the two special censors chosen by him [4:6]: one proposed only three slight corrections "ad opus perpoliendum" [to put a polish on the work]; the other judged that these new pages brought "very salutary clarifications for a better understanding of *Surnaturel*" and that, on condition that a "few slight alterations" (which he did not indicate) were made, their publication would be "truly useful and very desirable". The Father General likewise approved with equal warmth some statements written by Fathers Bouillard and J. M. Le Blond on the much-debated questions of that time. These were serene explanations concerning the principal points of doctrine criticized (and falsified) by our adversaries. One might have thought them sufficient to calm minds [4:7].

In my thinking, "Mystère du surnaturel" was not to appear as an independent article. It was first of all to constitute the second part of a little book, the first part of which was a series of precise responses (which I still have) to the objections made to *Surnaturel* [4:8]. Father René Arnou had in fact given me the insistent advice not to let any doctrinal attack pass without responding to it. But the Father General judged that another method would be better: he asked us to postpone any public discussion, so as to let passions subside on their own, and to send him privately justificatory memoranda, which he would use to defend us in high places.

---

[5] There was even—in a more peaceful tone than many others—an article by Father Karl Rahner, criticizing an article in German that was not mine and the very existence of which I was unaware. What Father Rahner argued in opposition to me, or rather thought he argued in opposition to me, corresponded rather closely, moreover, to what I myself was thinking, aside from a mixture of Heideggerian vocabulary that did not seem to me necessary or even opportune in a study of Scholastic tradition.

[6] I was notified of the decision on January 22, 1947.

This is what we did. The only actual discussion I had on the subject of my book was thus an "exchange of views" with Father Joseph de Blic, written in 1947 and published the same year in the *Mélanges de science religieuse* (Lille): "A propos de la conception médiévale de l'ordre surnaturel" [On the medieval concept of the supernatural order] (365–79).

The book had however given rise to (and would continue to do so in the 1950s) a considerable number of articles; I did not receive them all; the necessities of several moves made me throw away a good number of them; yet I still have a rather large packet of them. One of them, in a more moderate tone than many of the others but with very severe conclusions, was particularly disturbing because of the personality of its author and the place he occupied in the world of Rome. It elicited, as soon as it appeared, a letter to me from Father Joseph Huby (d. August 1948), which I am happy to quote here:

> Neuilly-sur-Seine, November 19, 1947. . . . I have read, as you might well imagine, the article from the Gregorianum.[7] I dreaded it, for I knew the obstinate Father Boyer. As I feared, his review is disagreeable and narrow-minded. He seems incapable of rising from the juridical level to that of religious intuition. Always this question of the rights of man over God, which is meaningless for anyone who has understood in what dependency creation places the creature with regard to God. If, in the system of "pure nature", one has to admit that man has rights over God and that his end is *owed* to him, this for me is sufficient reason to reject that system [4:9]. Find consolation in these failures to understand; you have opened perspectives that can no longer be closed.
>
> —I think there are still a good many equivocations in theological language and that in particular the word "nature" is taken in different senses that should be clearly defined. Anywhere certain theologians see the word "nature", they interpret it in opposition to "grace", which Saint Thomas himself calls *status naturae* the state in which the Patriarchs between Adam and the Mosaic revelation lived. It is rather clear that "nature" is not opposed there to "grace" but to "positive revelation". And what is the source of this metaphysical concept of "essence" or "nature"? Is it based on the study of real, existing man? But then by what right do they exclude the desire for the vision of God as constitutive of his being? Faith teaches us that this is not owed to him; everything in him is a gift from the divine liberality. *Quid habes quod non accepisti?* [What do you have that you have not received?]—But try to make these things understood by someone who has not grasped the fact that God is Love and that if he creates spirits it can only be in order to call them to participate in his life. . . [4:10].[8]

[7] C. Boyer, "Nature pure et surnaturel dans le *Surnaturel* du P. de Lubac", in *Gregorianum*, 28 (1947), 379–95.

[8] The article on "Le Mystère du surnaturel" earned me also many encouraging letters from

In 1948, I also published in *Recherches* a "Bulletin" that surveyed the principal current theories concerning the *development of dogma*, reviewing them one by one. I took Newman's principles as my basis. For the very conception of the "bulletin", I was inspired by those once published by Father de Grandmaison in the journal he founded, and I would have liked to be able to set up a team of specialists, whose respective reports would have consisted, not of a mere series of reviews, but a clarification, through the examination of a selected number of recent studies, of a real and central problem concerning their discipline.

Yet, despite the prudent policy of the Father General and the hopes he had placed in it, the attacks did not cease [4:12]. They were coming from all over the country. In 1949, when I had told the Father Assistant, B. de Gorostarzu, of their growing seriousness [4:13], he replied, in a tone at once affectionate and a bit irritated, something like this: Why do you keep worrying? We know very well here that the integrists are stirring things up; but do you think we are incapable of defending you? So be at peace. A little later—this was early in 1950—a secret letter arrived for me from the Father General: he had decided that beginning with the summer of 1950, I should leave *Recherches* and stop all teaching; for the moment, I was to say nothing about it to anyone and to keep working. Which I did.

In the spring of 1950, *Histoire et Esprit, l'intelligence de l'Ecriture d'après Origène* appeared in the "Theology" series. In the midst of the battle, this was an irenic book. I have been rather late in coming to Origen. When I returned from the war of 1914–1919, during the first semester of 1920, spent at Canterbury,[9] the *Confessions* of Saint Augustine and the three last

---

very wise and very competent men. Thus, M. Jean Mouroux: ". . . You preserve perfectly well the gratuity of the supernatural; and you demonstrate forcefully that this problem is addressed to me myself, who exists and who (in fact) am called. Theologically, I think it is unassailable, and I do not know if there is any other way to show that the supernatural is our entire good while being a pure gift." For his part, Father Louis Mariès, who had been placed very much on his guard about my book [4:11], wrote to me about the article: "Luminous, wise, (absolutely!) irenic; and well written and arranged besides. You explain and *justify perfectly* (at least for me) what the briefer summaries in *Surnaturel* caused your enemies to fear. But will they want to understand?" Among other testimonies, I will quote one more, excerpted from a letter from Father Daniélou: "Innsbruck, July 19. In Vienna, I saw von Ivanka, who was returning from Rome, where he gave a conference at the Oriental Institute. There was a question about you in the discussion and Father Hausherr defended you warmly. Ivanka himself approves of you completely. He very much liked your article on the mystery of the supernatural, in which he finds the idea, which is essential for him, that the spirit is of the order of mystery and cannot be treated as a reality of 'nature', at least in the modern sense of the word." (See pp. 123–24.)

[9] I did six months of my juniorate there before coming in September to Jersey for philosophy. It was at Canterbury, on Easter Sunday, that I pronounced my first vows, almost seven years after I entered the Society, in October 1913, at the novitiate of Saint Leonards-on-Sea (Sussex).

books of the *Adversus Haereses* by Saint Irenaeus had seduced me. (It was there too that I read in a state of wonder Father de Grandmaison's article "Jesus Christ" in the Dictionnaire d'Alès as well as Rousselot's thesis on the *Intellectualisme de saint Thomas*, which awakened me to metaphysical problems; I would have undoubtedly done better to apply myself more seriously to the study of Greek and Latin, a study for which we had an excellent guide, Father Debeauvais; but my mind, which had long lay fallow after the years of novitiate and the war, was ravenously hungry.) In philosophy, on Jersey, Saint Augustine and especially Saint Thomas had constituted my basic nourishment; numerous *excursus* had led me through Plotinus (about whom I did a rather overly enthusiastic paper, which earned me a few marks of uneasy sympathy from one of our professors, Father de la Vaissière). I had worked a bit on Bergson and Hamelin, read Blondel with Robert Hamel and Maine de Biran with Gaston Fessard.[10] During the year of my "regency", in 1923–1924 at Mongré, and in the course of vacations that followed in Montroland (near Dôle), I came into contact with Leibniz and Malebranche, supported by the fervor of Charles Nicolet. Among other authors of less breadth, Lachelier, recommended by Father Auguste Valensin for his style even more than for his ideas, was our delight.[11] Of course in those days, in the philosophy scholasticate, such reading was for the most part semi-forbidden fruit; thanks to indulgent masters and advisers, however, they were never clandestine. Any "modern" author was a priori suspect, or at least "guarded"; thus on Jersey, a recent work like that of Etienne Gilson on Saint Thomas Aquinas was shelved in a locked wall cupboard, which was opened only on holidays. Even in theology (1924–1928: two years at Hastings, two at Lyons-Fourvière), I read still rather little of the Greek Fathers; the numerous quotations that our dogma courses contained were ordinarily enough for us. It was only in my first years as a professor that I approached them in a more methodical and coherent manner—without ever, however, specializing in their study. One reason among others opposed such a study. Although at Mongré I had had in rhetoric a very good professor of Greek, Monsieur Mondésert,

[10] The first book written by Father Fessard (although it was published after *Pax nostra*) was to be devoted to *La Méthode de réflexion chez Maine de Biran* [The method of reflection in Maine de Biran] (1938). We had written a "Sketch" together on Jersey that attempted to bring out our basic philosophical ideas. The main outline of it was more his than mine. In complete independence, but in a profound communion of thought, intellectual and friendly exchanges have never ceased between us [4:14]. Not without difficulty, in 1945, I extracted a work on "Autorité et bien commun" [Authority and the common good] from him for the "Theology" series, a subject on which I myself wrote an article that, I believe, never appeared [4:15].

[11] I recall a brief stay in Paris, when we "typed out" the Lachelier courses for the Ecole normale, sometimes in a room on rue du Regard, sometimes in that of Father Teilhard de Chardin, rue du Vieux Colombier, on his typewriter, while he was working at the Museum.

I never had a firm grasp of this language; I could never read at one go a page of Greek without the aid of a dictionary. For Origen, whose greatness increasingly compelled my attention, I made an effort; but, if the part of his work that escaped the destruction ordered by Justinian (a crime for which the construction of Santa Sophia does not compensate) had survived entirely in Greek, I would have undoubtedly given up.

Be that as it may, this book on Origen, the material for which was gathered gradually over twenty years, was written with joy [4:16]. The writing was done during a period of rest, when I stayed, facing Mont-Blanc, in a little chalet attached to "Fleur-des-Neiges" (Saint Gervais). When it appeared, as it carried the *nihil obstat* of a censor of the Archbishop of Paris, the Father General was alerted: I was already, it was said, a semi-fugitive, I had escaped the supervision of the Society, I had arranged with a friend to publish surreptitiously, and so forth. . . . The Father General ordered my Provincial to make an inquiry into my personal relations with the Parisian censor; I had to reply [4:17] that he was unknown to me; the official *nihil obstat* had been delivered in accord with the favorable reviews made by my province and the *Imprimi potest* of the Provincial; in short, everything had gone as properly and normally as all the world. But in Rome, in the little circle that settled imminent decisions at that time, several were vexed: the book arrived too late to be inserted into the network of measures already prepared. In addition, it happened that a certain number of so-called conservative theologians, sometimes close to integrism, were interested (although in a rather different way) in the "spiritual meaning" of Scripture. This was fortunate. Despite a few things they tried to quibble about, the book came out unscathed by the adventure. It was moreover very sympathetically received, in long reviews, not only by a patristic scholar like Father T. Camelot (*Revue des sciences philosophiques et théologiques* [1951], 315–17) and by an exegete such as M.J. Coppens of Louvain but in the *Revue biblique* itself by Father Vincent, the faithful collaborator and disciple of Father Lagrange.[12] Among the letters it earned me was one, which I have kept, that is very curious; it was addressed to me by a lay sister of Belgian origin, the cook at the Regina laudis Benedictine monastery (Bethlehem, Connecticut, U.S.A.): "I cannot tell you, my Father, how much I thank you for speaking with so much love of Origen. I like your book enormously, which defends Origen against his enemies. Ah! How I would like to see him on the altars as a Doctor of the Church before I die! I love Origen, he does me much good, he is a saint." These naïve lines, similar to so many others from centuries past, would be worthy, it seems to me, to figure in a posthumous history of Origen. When I paid

---

[12] See the text of these three reviews in the Appendix [4:18].

a visit, seven years later, to Regina laudis, Sr. Geneviève had been dead for several months.

It was in June 1950 that lightning struck Fourvière. I will not give here the chronicle of events. It would be rich in dramatic and melodramatic incidents. Nor will I attempt any explanations of cause. As in what has gone before, I will bring up here only some of the details that concern me, in order to give a better understanding of the occasion and nature of my various writings. May I therefore be excused for the always resolutely egocentric character of these pages. The fact is that I then found myself at the center of the cyclone, or the anticyclone, as one prefers [4:19].

Since the Father General had written to me, in one of his letters during that period, that he had been obliged to remove me from the teaching assignment at Fourvière, I had to reply to him (it was necessary for me to seek ways of expressing myself so that a simple exposition of facts would not seem insolent) that he had long since been obeyed in advance, considering that I had not given a single hour of courses at Fourvière since the spring of 1940 and that I was in no way taking part in the faculty of the house. In fact, during the whole of my life, my teaching at Fourvière was limited to one special course in the history of religions between 1935 and 1940 (8 classes a year, from which students were easily dispensed), a mere "titulus coloratus" to justify my presence in the house; one year, however, I gave a few hours of course work on Tradition, to lighten the task of Father Fontoynont, whose strength was beginning to decline [4:20]. When, in September 1951, Fourvière had to send a twofold message of support to the Pope signed by all the professors, my case was embarrassing: not only had I already been living in Paris for a year but I had taught nothing to the scholasticate for more than ten years; but I was told that if the Pope did not see my name on the message, he would interpret that as a sign of my lack of submission (in Rome, I had been made out to be the "head of the School of Fourvière", and a whole legend had been created about it), and this might result in the closing of the school. In fact, the threat was serious, the situation tragic, especially since the notification coming from "Rome" arrived in Lyons (was this a calculated move?) only days before the beginning of the school term.[13] Summoned to Lyons by the new Provincial, Father André Ravier, I took part in the faculty meeting held in his office; the solution I proposed was in the end adopted: each

---

[13] Because he did not initiate in 1950 a message that would have publicly disavowed the five theologians who were sacrificed (a message for which no one had asked), Father Henri Rondet, prefect of studies, was himself dismissed, from that summer of 1951 on. He was always of an admirable uprightness, and he has remained a very dear friend to me.

indicated on the sheet of paper the title of the courses and the years taught, and I wrote: "History of religions, 1935–1940".[14]

The decisions made in Rome in June 1950 officially emanated solely from the General of the Society. The latter was motivated to make them, however, by the fact of "pernicious errors on essential points of dogma" maintained by the five professors in question, who had been removed from their duties and changed to a different residence: Fathers Emile Delaye, Henri Bouillard, Alexandre Durand, Pierre Ganne and I.[15] As soon as these decisions were known, I was called to the Archbishop, where the Professors of the Theology Faculty had gathered around Cardinal Gerlier, Lord Chancellor. All were very dissatisfied. They pressed me with questions to know what was behind the affair. They could not allow, they said, a dictatorial intervention by the Society of Jesus in the progress of our Faculty. I had great difficulty making them understand that any protest, any step on their part with reference to the Father General would be in vain, that all was certainly coming from farther up [4:22]. When, the following month, I took leave of the Cardinal, he told me again quite forcefully how much he himself, in solidarity with the Faculty, had been wounded by this affair; he added: "I do not want, of course, to urge you to disobey your superiors; but, you well know, your chair is yours; you could resume it each and every time you come back through Lyons." That was obviously just a manner of speaking. Cardinal Gerlier always afterward pleaded my cause, but without great success; it was too well known in Rome that he had a generous heart and that he was not what one might call a man of doctrine. Moreover, my case soon came by chance to be mixed with that of Father Montuclard, O.P., who was originally from Lyons, and his group "Jeunesse de l'Eglise" [Youth of the Church], which had emigrated from Lyons to Paris and which was to come to an end, as we know. Finally, Pius XII had been strongly circumvented; one day when the good Cardinal was interceding for me, the Pope interrupted him by saying: What is annoying about him is that one never knows if what he says or writes corresponds to what he thinks [4:23]. Traces of this mistrust are very clear in certain expressions in the encyclical *Humani generis*, where it is a question of certain professors, fortunately rare, who teach error "in a wary and covert manner"; the encyclical goes on: "If they speak prudently in printed books, they express themselves more freely in

[14] I have kept the text of one of the plans then hastily worked out for this message to the Pope. This was "Plan A", revised according the remarks of Rev. Father Provincial and Father Fontoynont, and reworked a bit more, I believe, before being sent off to Rome. This can be read in the Appendix [4:21].

[15] My personal reaction to these measures, or rather to their motivation, was expressed in a letter that I addressed to my Provincial on July 1, 1950 [4:24].

writings communicated privately, in classes and meetings."[16] This is what was said around the same time by a religious theologian, whose name I still prefer not to mention: "He is intelligent enough to make sure he always has an appearance of orthodoxy"; the expression is exquisite! It is also what an historian, Charles Ledré, would write in 1955 in his book *Un siècle sous la tiare*: In *Humani generis*, "Pius XII removed a whole group of methods, dear to the underground of all times, which the practices of Loisy and a few others had restored to honor. . . . It is only too easy to understand the kind of results such methods can produce. . . . So a well-advised master of higher learning did not hesitate to testify, soon after the encyclical, that there was nothing 'imaginary' or 'fictitious' in the uneasiness expressed by the Pope. . . ." (pp. 101–10) [4:25]. Father Congar's vision was more just, when he wrote at that time that the tarasque was in fact a very dangerous animal but that, happily, it did not exist. One fact that seems rather significant to me was that, with respect to the five professors affected, there was never the least defection on the part of their friends, their disciples, those who had any reason whatever to refer to one of them [4:26]—nor was there ever any need for any retraction.[17]

One of the men the most profoundly hit by the lightning of 1950 was our good adviser to all, a faithful man if there ever was one, attached by every fiber of his being to the tradition of the Church, of an unfailing loyalty, whose health had already been very shaken (he died, after a long illness, in December 1958). His feelings were expressed in a brief poem, dated November 1 [4:27]. Its title: "*Spes ultima*, Visitation 1950"; as a subtitle, the famous quatrain of Baudelaire: "O Mort, vieux capitaine, il est temps, levons l'ancre . . . ," [O Death, old captain, it is time, let us lift anchor], to which a note is added to the words: "This world bores us . . .": "It is 'disgusts us' that we must think"; then, in contrast, the

---

[16] I later found out, among other things, that one whole photocopied course, presumably of mine, had served as proof for this accusation of hypocrisy; I have never been able to find out where this course came from or what it contained; I have been told that it referred to a "De Ecclesia", but there was no indication of its origin. Other facts of the same kind, two of which were particularly serious but completely fanciful, have also been reported to me by men who had had inside knowledge in Rome and had even seen certain documents. —And here in May 1977, I learn in Paris through the Curé of Saint-Roch that the defection of Abbé Massin (with all his followers) was at that time attributed to me by members of the Holy Office and was added to my file.

[17] There must still be, at the old "Holy Office" (and perhaps at the S.J. General Curia) a file in my name. This file contains certain things (notably a theology course, judged at that time to be heterodox) that were freely attributed to me, of whose existence I was not aware and of which I still do not know the contents or the authors. I learned that by chance, from a good source, long after the events in question.

body of the poem, in the form of an address to the young Holy Virgin of the Visitation, full of subtle allusions to the liturgy of the feast:

> Mais il est un appel et plus humble et plus tendre:
> Courez à ma vieillesse, ô ma divine Soeur.
> Quelque chose en mon sein brûle de vous entendre.
> Une enfance endormie tressaille dans mon coeur.
> Vous viendrez cette fois par l'hiver et les ronces:
> La montagne a perdu sa parure de fleurs.
> —Mais vous m'apporterez votre divine annonce.[18]

I had thus now been replaced at *Recherches* by a committee of four members (Fathers Lecler, Rondet, Baumgartner and Lefèvre); the Father General was reserving the title of director for himself, I was later assured! The Lyons Faculty saved face and with the same stroke gave witness of its attachment to me by declaring me "on vacation" and by receiving as mere substitutes, supposedly chosen by me, those offered to it as my replacements. The houses of studies were forbidden to me. There was a question of sending me to Toulouse. In the end, I was sent off to Paris, rue de Sèvres. Father Henri Bouillard, also excluded from Lyons, became my neighbor, rue de Grenelle; this common exile was to bring us much closer together; although very different from each other, we still got along very well together; he became an adviser for me and a perfect friend. Results have shown the authoritative value and wisdom of his thinking. I will recall here only his great work on Karl Barth, which was a thesis for the Sorbonne. Barth came to be present at the defense of this thesis (June 16, 1956); full of good humor, he led us afterward to sample some shark-fin soup in a little Chinese restaurant; from all tables, people turned toward him to hear his animated discussion on justification; he also complained to us about the tragic turn of events in the Church in the time of Luther, which he did not like.[19] In 1957 and 1958, Father Bouillard helped the young Küng with his thesis in theology on Barth and rendered him some valuable service; in 1958, Küng nonetheless published a disdainful diatribe against Bouillard's work, which was not yet known in Germany; I took up the defense of the latter in an article published by Father du Rivau's journal, *Dokumente*, around the end of 1958.[20]

---

[18] "But it is both a more humble and a more tender call: / Run to my old age, oh my divine Sister. / Something in my breast burns to hear you. / A sleeping child leaps for joy in my heart. / You will come this time through winter and brambles: / The mountain has lost its adornment of flowers. / —But you will bring me your divine annunciation."

[19] These final words, to judge from other remarks heard from the lips of Barth, were a euphemism.

[20] "Zum Katholischen Dialog mit Karl Barth"; *Dokumente* 14:448–54 [4:30]. To judge from

The same day I arrived in Paris, around the end of August 1950, the encyclical *Humani generis* appeared in *La Croix*; I read it, toward the end of the afternoon, in a dark, still-empty room, in front of an open trunk. . . . I later wrote about it to someone asking me for information:

> It seems to me to be, like many other ecclesiastical documents, unilateral: that is almost the law of the genre; but I have read nothing in it, doctrinally, that affects me [4:28]. The only passage where I recognize an implicit reference to me is a phrase bearing on the question of the supernatural; now it is rather curious to note that this phrase, intending to recall the true doctrine on this subject, reproduces exactly what I said about it two years earlier in a article in *Recherches de science religieuse*. (So I could presume with some probability that the expression had been substituted, perhaps at the last moment, for another one by someone who was familiar with my article and favorably disposed toward me.) [4:29]

It is certain that those who had pushed the most for condemnations were not satisfied with the encyclical: they made this clear through many signs. But the quite objective and, so to speak, nontemporal sense of a document of this genre is one thing, the meaning given to it by circumstances and passions is another. It has been justly noted, for example, that this same encyclical *Humani generis*, by declaring clearly that one cannot avoid all evolutionism in the name of Christian dogma, supported Father Teilhard de Chardin against certain theologians in Rome who, on precisely this point, had just carried out their offensive against him: it is nonetheless true that, in the view of public opinion and in actual fact, Father Teilhard appeared vanquished [4:30]. As for me, to take another example, because the encyclical, in a first part, criticized existentialism, among other things, some have since then attributed to me a reputation as an "existentialist philosopher"; so too, Paul Tillich: an honor quite unmerited.[21]

On rue de Sèvres, at the back of the courtyard, in an old building that did not yet have a reception area or porter (one entered through the kitchen), parlor or library, nearly alone, I led the existence of a recluse for some time. Nevertheless, protests reached as far as Rome: I was going to corrupt the capital! I therefore had to seek lodgings elsewhere. Msgr. Gounot, Archbishop of Carthage, who had known me well through the priests' courses at Dax before the war, was sounded out by my Provincial [4:32]; he agreed

---

the reception that he continued to accord me after this, Barth was not displeased with this clarification. Father Bouillard died in Paris in 1981.

[21] When, soon after the war, the overwhelming reputation of Sartre and the existentialist fashion arose, I was so annoyed by it that I promised myself, even in discussions, never to use that word.

to take me for a few months.[22] New accusations: I was abandoning the houses of the Order, I was a "fugitive", my imminent, definitive defection was predicted. . . . A little later, around November 1951, I was therefore withdrawn to Gap, to a little residence built as an annex to the boarding school of the Sisters of Saint Joseph; I lived there alone with the old Father Roullet. At Gap I met once again one of my better former students, of whom I have already spoken, Abbé Paul Chevallier, later rector of the Catholic Faculties of Lyons; he was doing everything in his diocese and still took the time to accompany me on little walks. I finally returned to Paris, for an existence that was still secluded, without any decrease in the campaign that had been unleashed [4:33]. It was to last a long time yet.

Beginning with the summer of 1951, as I have said, the Provincial was Father André Ravier. He had immediately set about to inform himself about the "Fourvière affair" through an objective and patient process that soon left him without any doubts about the essentials. He made known to me his desire that I continue to work intellectually and to publish. Since theology was closed to me, we decided that I should write on Buddhism, which I did, under the conditions I have explained above. When the little volume *Aspects du bouddhisme* [Aspects of Buddhism] appeared, a reviewer, without malice but influenced by current opinion (a generalized phenomenon of which I have since seen many other examples, in very different senses), denounced it as contrary to the transcendence of the Christian faith. The Father General reminded sternly that everything written by me, on any subject, had to be submitted beforehand to a censor in Rome. Now I had taken as a spiritual adviser, in Paris, Father Jules Lebreton, who had a short time before defended me energetically in the *Surnaturel* battle. As I knew his work well and as I was much interested in the work he had done before 1914, together with Father de Grandmaison, I composed in 1951 a brief study on his antimodernist writings, for which Pius X had been anxious to express his personal gratitude. That, it seemed, was solid ground. I submitted my work to Father Lebreton, he approved it by a letter dated May 7, 1951, and, after approval by the censors of my Province, I sent the manuscript to Rome: the writing was not only rejected but reproved as modernist. Two other attempts, after modifications, explanations and competent recommendations, were to be likewise turned down. After Father Lebreton's death, which occurred unexpectedly in 1953, *Recherches* wanted to publish an homage to his memory: they ran into the same refusal.[23] The faction that was at that time triumphant, overstepping all lim-

---

[22] That was for me an experience of which I still have very good memories not only because of the extreme kindness of the Archbishop and his auxiliary, Msgr. Perrin, but because I was involved in the most varied ministries there.

[23] The article remained for several months in Rome. The review that finally arrived, at the

its both in the ideas as well as in the arbitrariness of its power, was hostile to the spirit of Fathers de Grandmaison and Lebreton, whom I had always been taught in the Society to consider as the best of masters. I have found among my papers the rough draft of a letter to the Father General, dating from December 1957, which I think might be instructive to quote:

> The last reviews that your Paternity communicated to me date from one year ago [this was in December 1956]. They have caused me particular pain. This time, in fact, it was not merely a question of me. I have become rather well used to having lies accumulate on my head, and, thanks be to God, that no longer troubles me—although I think with grief that if this were known one day, it would be a sad thing for the honor of the Society. But the censors of my work have also attacked the two theologians of whom I was the mere recorder, the surviving one of which had given me his approval in writing: Fathers Lebreton and de Grandmaison. Overstepping their rights in a shocking way, inspired by a completely false theology, they have condemned *ipsissimis verbis* a doctrine I have always been taught in the Society to regard as perfectly sound, a doctrine that had earned Father Lebreton the warmest congratulations from Saint Pius X. That is without ambiguity: the condemnation pronounced by the censors of your Paternity bear, I repeat, on the very texts in which this doctrine is expressed, and the paragraphs of my work that contain it are long, explicit quotations, with quotation marks. —Through a spirit of obedience, and because of the profound respect I feel toward your Paternity, I accepted in silence censorship that your Paternity seemed to want to make entirely your own—waiting to enlighten you later and to repeat filially, with new proof in support of it, what I had once said earlier: Your Paternity places his confidence, in this affair that has been unfolding for ten years, in men who, whatever might be their other merits, do not deserve it. If I decide in favor of this letter, it is for the two following reasons: (1) I believe I owe it to the memory of Fathers de Grandmaison and Lebreton, toward whom I have great gratitude; (2) I believe also that, if silent obedience is sometimes imperative, obedience is nevertheless not fully filial if it is not accompanied by an effort to enlighten the Superior, according to its means, when the truth is seriously at stake. . . .[24]

---

end of November, was so ridiculously severe that the peaceable Father Joseph Lecler, the principal person responsible for *Recherches*, wrote to me at the time: "I wonder if it would not be opportune to send to Rome a criticism of the Roman censors themselves. Were we to succeed merely in shaking the total confidence of the Father General in his ordinary reviewers, that would in itself be something." —According to two letters from Father J.-M. Le Blond, who had thought he could obtain the necessary authorizations later, while on a stay in Rome in 1959, the obstinate refusal came solely from within the Society [4:34].

[24] Either from a desire not to antagonize the Father General by writing to him too often (and without being able to tell if he would read it himself) or else out of distaste for an affair that had lasted more than ten years without anything ever having been clarified, I did not send this letter.

I should also have said above that, shortly after the publication of the encyclical *Humani generis*, a new measure had been taken. The order was given to withdraw from our libraries and from the trade, among other publications, three of my books: *Surnaturel, Corpus mysticum* and *Connaissance de Dieu*—as well as (from our libraries) the volume of *Recherches* containing my article on the "Mystère du surnaturel". It was Father Goussault, provincial of Paris, who communicated this order to me; he did it tactfully. The first of the three works had in fact been out of print for a long time; the second edition of the third was nearly so; but the second edition of *Corpus mysticum* had come out shortly before; almost the entire lot was still at the publisher's, and the Province of Lyons had to buy it. The copies got moldy from being piled up in two or three bad storehouses in succession before ending up in an attic at Fourvière; en route, some copies had been removed in order to satisfy individual curiosities or to feed the second-hand booksellers: a little black market of which I was not aware until a long time later. At the end of some fifteen years, what remained of them was bought back at a low price by the publisher, who would have liked to reissue the edition with a new cover, but the volumes were in such a bad condition that he had to give up the idea of putting them on public sale [4:35]. As for a new, corrected edition, it was not to be dreamed of during the fifties. Asked about the book's faults, the Father General had replied: Look at the reviews; since those had been favorable, a long criticism was sent to me from Rome, ending with the words: "The corrections necessary for the publication of *Corpus mysticum* cannot consist merely in the suppression or the modification of a few passages. Those passages that are the most open to criticism have extended ramifications in the author's development of the subject. The book would have to be profoundly changed in order for it to appear" [4:36].

Another attempt at publication was, on the other hand, strangely crowned with success. This concerned *Méditation sur l'Eglise* [The splendor of the Church] (1953). Many have believed that this book was composed following what have been called my "misfortunes". Some have praised me for it, others have blamed me. Actually this is not accurate.[25] During the years 1946 to 1949, at different times I had given several priestly recollection days, whose usual theme was some aspect or other of the Church. In 1949, in the diocese of Marseille (it seems to me it was on the premises of the major seminary, above the city), we had had a session of young priests that had lasted three days. The outline of my instructions, the title and the contents of each one were exactly those of the future

---

[25] The error, however, is quite natural. I find it again in the book: *Un théologien en liberté, Jacques Duquesne interroge le Père Chenu* (Centurion, 1975), 131.

book, whose publication was not brought about but rather delayed by the events of 1950 [4:37]. I later had only to supplement the quotations, to develop a few aspects that were treated too cursorily and to write, here and there, several new pages [4:38]. The reviewers chosen by the Provincial gave a favorable opinion very quickly; I think I remember there being three of them; one of them was Father Charles Baumgartner [4:39]. The manuscript was thus sent to Rome, in 1952. A formal order given to the Father in charge of the bureau of censure provided that any writing coming from me had to be transmitted to a certain censor designated by name. But Father Janssens was at his villa, and the censorship official was also absent. When the manuscript arrived, two Frenchmen were sought in Rome, in all innocence, to examine it. Only two of them remained, kept there by their infirmities: Fathers Paul Galtier, of the Gregorian, and Joseph Bonsirven, at the Biblical Institute. Both had been shocked by what had happened before and after *Humani generis*. Without acting in collusion, they each wrote an extremely laudatory review, anticipating possible objections, using official formulas from the Constitutions. (I learned all that from their own lips.) Faced with a fait accompli, the Father General (perhaps, deep down, happy at having his hand forced) did not dare to veto it; a scandal might have ensued. When I saw him in Rome, in the spring of 1953, and thanked him for granting his authorization (the book was then at the printer), he paled and, very frankly, told me that there was no reason to thank him, that it was quite by chance. Published shortly afterward, the book almost immediately went into a second, enlarged edition (1954). It was translated into Italian. Opponents then took a little revenge by having the *Imprimatur* refused by the Vicariate of Rome. But the following year the Italian edition appeared in Milan, under the patronage of the new archbishop, Msgr. Montini, who more than once cited the work and distributed it to his clergy.

I never saw Monsignor Montini or corresponded with him before he became Paul VI; once only, in 1962, I received from him a few words of thanks, for sending him my book on the *Pensée religieuse du Père Teilhard de Chardin* [The religious thought of Father Teilhard de Chardin] [4:40]. But twice already he had given me a sign of sympathy. In Paris, shortly after *Humani generis*, a religious, whom I did not know and whose name I have forgotten, came to bring me a word of encouragement from Msgr. Montini.[26] Another time, I received a letter from our ambassador to Rome, M. Wladimir d'Ormesson, announcing to me that Msgr. Montini had just

[26] Is my memory failing me, or does this refer to something else? I have found a note according to which Msgr. Pierre Veuillot, then attached to the Secretary of State, came to rue de Sèvres on November 9, 1950, to tell me on behalf of Msgr. Montini of his esteem "not only for you yourself but for your work".

given a conference there to which the leading members of the clergy, the ambassadors and other personages had been invited; he had treated the subject of the Church in the face of contemporary atheism and had then indicated that the essential points of his explanations had been drawn from *Drame de l'humanisme athée*, which he invited his listeners to read. The former under-secretary of State had just been named archbishop of Milan; he had thus acquired his freedom of speech, and through that conference he lost no time in officially taking a stand against the integrist faction, which at that time was all powerful. So I was not at all surprised later on when Paul VI, from the time of the Council and again in the period that followed, gave me various other signs of his confidence—although I had only seen him face-to-face once (in 1970?) in an audience that he had himself called for on the occasion of a meeting of the Theological Commission and which lasted scarcely ten minutes, for an exchange of cordial but rather banal words. On that day, taken unawares and on the point of leaving Rome, I did not think of following literally the advice given me by Etienne Gilson in a letter of September 3, 1968. "I have always been", he confided to me,

> extremely timid with my great men. I would never have dared to take a half-hour of Bergson's life for myself alone; the only time I had anything but a chance conversation with him, in Strasbourg, it was he who summoned me. I never went to see Claudel, that unique phenomenon in the history of our literature. I often ran into him, and for me our meetings were unforgettable, but I myself never presumed to occupy five minutes of his life. The idea of going to see Paul VI would never enter my mind, and that is perhaps a mistake, for this man of God, animated by a prophetic spirit, as you say with perfect justice, could well be in great need of both comfort and simple human affection, if only in compensation for the indignities heaped on him, which some of his sons heap on him. This is why I think that you, who are a priest, and a priest twice over since you belong to the Society of Jesus, should not hesitate to let him know how you feel. You have never had more than one adversary in the Vatican (to my knowledge), and that was a Jesuit. Msgr. Montini held you in the highest esteem, and I am certain that it has only increased with the passing years. A priest, a theologian as well known as you are and as universally esteemed(!)[27] has no reason at all to feel the timidity that restrains me, too often perhaps, from expressing my admiration to those I admire the most. —After all, our beloved Christ himself was not content to be loved, he wanted to be told of it: "Peter, do you love me?"

In truth, although I knew perfectly well that there was something more important to do, as Urs von Balthasar recalls,[28] with regard to an abused

---

[27] I would have had scruples about cutting this letter, but I must certainly recognize that in this passage its author is under a twofold illusion.

[28] In the fine chapter, "Etre pape aujourd'hui" from his *Points de repère* (Fayard, 1973).

Pope, than to offer him Veronica's veil, I regret having forgotten, at the desired moment, the advice of Etienne Gilson.

Méditation sur l'Eglise (which even those who seem to have read it closely persist in calling Méditation*s*) is an easy, not a technical, book, so that numerous readers could have access to it; the English translation dressed it up with the pompous title "The Splendour of the Church", which seems to rank it among the "triumphalist" writings and thereby to accelerate its obsolescence. It is no more a treatise on the Church than was *Catholicisme*. It has received various judgments.[29] Those who, through a curious conception of the Catholic Church, delude themselves in thinking that, as a Christian, one is less free to the degree that one is more respectful of the Magisterium and more inserted into the common faith of the People of God, have sometimes maintained the idea that through such a book I had in some way become estranged, that since then I was no longer myself, and so forth. . . . My own denials would certainly not be enough to reassure them; so I will quote here instead the letter received from a reader in September 1959, which said to me: "I had postponed reading your *Méditation sur l'Eglise* because X, often quick to protest against the Church of Rome, had said to me that, having been broken by your Superiors, you were no longer yourself in this book. It took your discreet allusion to this book, seven weeks ago, for me to assess for myself how much, on the contrary, you are fully yourself in it . . ." [4:41]. On the other hand, it would be a real misunderstanding of integrism—I understand this word in its proper sense, consecrated by history, and not in one of the abusive senses often given to it today—to believe that such a work had been in the least capable of satisfying it. Witness this long diatribe, from which I excerpt only one paragraph. After having enumerated the principal crimes with which I have strewn my career, the author continued:

. . . But, one will say, mercy should be shown for all sin. —Yes, undoubtedly, if the sinner is repentant. Now repentance is expressed by penitence and reparation. The repentant thief gives restitution, the repentant drunkard abstains, the repentant profligate controls himself. The writer, the author convicted of error and of a false spirit submits and is silent. At least, you will say, until he modifies and radically rectifies his thinking and his language. Now this is nearly impossible for a modernist. Pius X repeated this several times. No sign can be seen that would permit us to infer that Father de L., abandoning his evolutionist, existentialist and historicist errors, rejecting them, has undertaken to restore within himself the indispensable cult of principles, method and Thomistic doctrine rigorously required of all who teach in the Church. The chapter of his book "L'Eglise notre mère", filled with considerations

[29] It was the occasion for me of a friendly controversy with Father M.-D. Chenu, who thought he saw an "ecclesial monomorphism" in it. . . .

on obedience, will appear, in its historical context, to be impertinent and insupportable hypocrisy. . . .

Not all malcontents expressed themselves with such virulence, but this pamphlet, coming from South America, reconstructs well one whole aspect of the "spirit of the times" that reigned in France even during the fifties.[30]

After our General Congregation of 1946, which had given me the opportunity to make my first discovery of the City, I was not authorized to return there until the spring of 1953. During the whole affair set forth here in broad outline, an affair that would last so many years, I was never questioned, I never had a single conversation about the root of the matter with any authority of the Church in Rome or the Society. No one ever communicated to me any precise charge. Apart from the signature that I placed at the bottom of the address sent to the Pope by the faculty of Fourvière in 1951, under the conditions I have described, no one ever asked me for anything that would resemble a "retraction", explanation or particular submission. Even in that spring of 1953, when I finally saw the Father General two times, the latter was still evasive both about the basis as well as about the facts. I sensed that he did not want to depart from his role, even though undeclared, as a mere intermediary, a role that he exaggerated, moreover, and that left him all the more rigid and taciturn. He had already written to me, on June 29, 1952, and I had never been able to get any further specifics: "It is difficult for you to find in your works the errors that others claim to read in them, several of which have been attacked by the Encyclical *Humani generis*. If I had the competence, time would be materially lacking for me to study the question for myself, but numerous theologians, qualified by their knowledge and their good will, are and remain of a different opinion from yours. I do not really see what more I could do to form a conviction that I would be right in considering objective."[31] A pretext was found for me to come to Rome in 1953: a series of classes on the Church to young Ursuline religious of the "Roman union". It was their General Superior, the famous "Mother Saint John",[32] who invited me. She had been counselled to do so by two of my colleagues, and she wanted to be pardoned for having at first let herself be circumvented against me by a few integrist priests. Lodged in her gener-

[30] I have just learned that at the time this diatribe was written, it provoked a letter of protest signed by numerous young Jesuits, Canadians and others, addressed from Montreal to the Argentinian bishop to whom the author was subject.

[31] I knew later that he had let himself be tyrannized by one or two close advisers; he suffered greatly because of it.

[32] A quarter of a century earlier, a saying circulated in Rome: "There are only three men in the whole City: Pius XI, Mussolini and Mother Saint John."

alate house on Via Nomentano (the houses of the Society were not open to me), I was the object there of all her care, and I have kept a grateful memory of her solicitude toward me. During the free hours of that stay, I became more closely familiar with the work of Marie of the Incarnation, which led me to satisfy my old friend Father Hubert du Manoir by giving him a chapter on Marie of the Incarnation and the Blessed Virgin in one of the numerous volumes of his encyclopedia *Maria* (1954).[33] (He had me write the preface for another one.) Later, in collaboration with Father Claude Mondésert, we did a quick work on the history and spirituality of the Ursulines (1958) [4:42].

[33] This modest publication itself was at first rejected by a still distrustful censor. Various negotiations, concessions about words and disinterested explanations were necessary to get out of the impasse. The reviewer of the collective work, who was not aware of all this, asked me to suppress those lines, which he had marked as being irrelevant; I had to tell him that they had been imposed on me.

CHAPTER FIVE

From 1955–1956 on, a certain relaxation in official severity began to manifest itself. Two signs made me aware of this.

I was, first of all, allowed (thanks, at least in part, to a very kind review by Father Joseph de Finance, professor of philosophy at the Gregorian) to publish *Sur les chemins de Dieu*. This was in fact a new edition of *Connaissance de Dieu*, without corrections but enlarged (1956). It was furnished with a few new explanations, numerous documentary texts as well as with a postface that responded to the principal complaints recently formulated, passing at times into a discreet counterattack. I admit that this little victory gave me joy; it had been painful for me to see, in our libraries and bookshops, a writing that I knew from experience could encourage and accompany the reader on the road of faith replaced by another entitled "God, What For?",[1] from which undoubtedly judicious reflection was not entirely lacking but whose influence, I noted, was at times the opposite.

There was nothing basically very personal about *Sur les chemins de Dieu*, any more than there had been about the original little book. The passages that had been most criticized were scarcely more than translations or paraphrases of very traditional texts, as I have amply shown [5:1]. But some theological circles, even erudite ones, ordinarily had such a poor knowledge of Catholic tradition outside the traditions of their own schools! I understand nevertheless that even in its new form the work managed to displease a rather large number of readers. The reflections in the first chapter must have been more or less misunderstood by those who, not being sufficiently aware of the theories about the origin of the idea of God drawn from the history of religions, did not see to what I was responding: there was a true *ignoratio elenchi* on the part of some. But the opposition encountered by other chapters resulted from more general and fundamental reasons. On the one hand, even though it in no way favored an irrational tendency, the book did not insist inordinately on the exposition of proofs for the existence of God. It sought besides to remedy what seemed to me to be a deficiency of classical Thomism: for the latter, the necessary movement of negative theology creates a danger of agnosticism (for which Father Sertillanges had been reproached, rather justly, it seems to me, but illogically, in a famous controversy); so I wanted to base this same movement on a more fundamental positive exigency, there at the beginning and

---

[1] Montuclard.

constantly recurring, by which I sought to define the human spirit in its relation to God. This intuitive, or more precisely proleptic and dynamic (not thematized, as one would say today), element,[2] well founded in tradition, was diametrically opposed to the extrinsic and restrictive rationalism of one whole modern Thomistic school; it seems more important to me today than ever to stress this, at a time when an undue inflation of "negative theology" risks opening the way not only to agnosticism but to atheism.[3] On the other hand, still dependent upon awkward reflections dating from my beginnings as an apprentice philosopher, I was also moving in an atmosphere of "natural theology", outside of which, even today, I cannot breathe completely at ease—which does not mean that I admit a natural theology correctly constituted outside revelation, which would in that case come simply to be added onto it.[4] By the same token, I found myself unable to satisfy the new existentialist and biblicist trends, which, rejecting rationality along with rationalism, were then gathering strength and ended in conquering or at least intimidating a number of excellent minds in the Church.

Like *Catholicisme* and *Méditation sur l'Eglise*, *Chemins de Dieu* nonetheless pursued its course for some time. These three works were republished, slightly trimmed, during the sixties, in the pocketbook series "Foi vivante". The last of the three had brought me, from Etienne Gilson, a vivid letter that at the same time reconsidered the *Surnaturel* quarrel (July 8, 1956):[5]

I have just read the third edition of *Sur les chemins de Dieu* with so much pleasure that I could not keep from telling you. The theological anthropomorphism you are concerned about seems to me to be one of the main obstacles to belief in God, especially in the world of intellectuals. Father Sertillanges, whom you so appropriately cite, fought it with all his strength. Unfortunately, theological anthropomorphism has patronage in very high places, and

[2] Although less pronounced in Saint Thomas than in Saint Bonaventure.

[3] See on this subject the criticism addressed to a certain negative theology by Father von Balthasar and the more recent one by Claude Bruaire.

[4] I concur in this with the explanations given by Father Henri Bouillard in his *Karl Barth* and in *Logique de la Foi*. They seem to me to give, in addition, the best interpretation of Saint Paul's doctrine in the Epistle to the Romans. There is likewise a "natural religion" (not to be confused with the artificial and superficial religion that later philosophers have adorned with this term), which may have been mixed in practice with various sorts of paganism but which is nonetheless full of instruction. We know the importance that someone like Newman recognized in this.

[5] This entire letter was later published, along with others, in *Lettres de M. Etienne Gilson adressés au P. Henri de Lubac et commentées par celui-ci* (Paris: Cerf, 1986), letter 1, pp. 19–30 [English translation: *Letters of Etienne Gilson to Henri de Lubac Annotated by Father de Lubac* (San Francisco: Ignatius Press, 1988), letter 1, pp. 23–25].

this is precisely why such a large-scale enterprise is being pursued to bring Saint Thomas Aquinas to his senses. They manufacture a Thomism after the manner of the Schools, a sort of dull rationalism that satisfies the kind of deism that most of them, deep down, want to teach.

Our only salvation lies in a return to Saint Thomas himself, before the Thomism of John of Saint Thomas, before that of Cajetan himself—Cajetan, whose famous commentary is in every respect the consummate example of a *corruptorium Thomae*.

God is QUI EST; in God, that which in other beings is their essence is God's act of existing, the EST. Now, in the proposition *Deus est*, we know that what is said is true, but we do not know what the verb *est* means. I don't remember whether you cited the decisive text of the *Summa theologiae* I, 3, 4, ad 2m. Neither Father Sertillanges, nor you yourself, nor anybody will ever go farther in denouncing what Saint Thomas, over-boldly but correctly, called an "agnosticism of representation".

Yet, in order to have the right to go even this far, one must go as far as the Thomist metaphysic of the *esse*. The theologians fully understand this point because, even in the Order of Friars Preachers, from Hervé Nedellec right on up to Cajetan and beyond, so many of them have taken such great pains to camouflage the authentic doctrine of the master. Let us say, rather, to emasculate his doctrine and to make of his theology a kind of insipid *philosophia aristotelico-thomistica* suitable for spreading a vague deism for the use of right-thinking candidates for high-school diplomas and bachelor of arts degrees. Salvation lies in returning to the real Saint Thomas, rightly called the Universal Doctor of the Church; but one must accept no substitutes![6]

Please know, my reverend Father, how much I appreciate your sending your book. Why not consider so doing with other books, where you find your thinking correct but your language not impeccable, what you have just done with this one? Who has ever denied that, *de potentia Dei absoluta*, God could have created man without the possibility for beatitude? Nobody! But from the viewpoint of the final cause, which is the highest of causes, all evidence, both in the world *and in mankind as God created them*, points to the supernatural end for which God destined us. In short, according to the *Contra Gentiles*, the structure and nature of created man are those of a being called to beatitude. But who cares, these days, about the final cause? It is only the formal cause that counts.[7] Thank you again for so many fine, good books, which we (many of my friends and I) like too much not to wish them unassailable—if books do exist that certain people could not attack.

The second sign of a thaw given to me at that time was my participation in the Anselm Congress at the Abbey of Bec. That was in 1959. I was

---

[6] Although fully in agreement with everything M. Gilson says in this letter, and encouraged by the support of his high authority, I nevertheless thought that he had not fully noted the element in my book that sought to prevent the "agnosticism of representation" from sliding toward an agnosticism of thought.

[7] M. Gilson returned to the subject in later letters. See below, Chapter VII.

invited to it with very particular eagerness by the Abbot, Dom Gram-mont, who even wanted to have me preside over one meeting (which I resisted), and on the last day, the apostolic nuncio, Msgr. Marella, gave me emphatic praise in his address, presenting me as a master. . . . That little manifestation had obviously been arranged.[8] Sympathy, however, was not the only thing it would bring me.

I come now to another subject. In the second part of *Catholicisme*, there was already a question of the historical character of the Christian religion and the spiritual understanding of Scripture, in which many had long since seen nothing but pious and insignificant fantasy, expedients of a precritical age or allegorical rationalism imitating ancient mythologies. Familiarity with the Fathers of the Church and with the medieval greats had quickly persuaded me that that was a threefold misconception. My course in fun-damental theology always led me back, by a thousand avenues, to this cen-tral subject. I had alluded to it in *Proudhon*. I had also outlined the theme of the fourfold meaning of Scripture in a brief essay in *Mélanges offerts au Père Ferdinand Cavallera* (1948). I had drawn from Origen the subject of *Histoire et Esprit*. In order to write the conclusion of that book, I had amassed a number of texts from every era, many of which I had not used. The idea came to me, during these years when all properly doctrinal work seemed to me for the time, and perhaps forever, a dead end, to enlarge this conclusion, to correct hasty insights, to bring out the dogmatic back-bone of it. There was material in it for a new book that would retrace *per summa capita* the history of spiritual exegesis in the course of the Christian centuries. It was at Corenc, near Grenoble, with the Sisters of Providence that I set to work in the early days of April 1956. At first seen in modest dimensions, the book swelled beyond measure. I warmed up to the game and amused myself with classifying into little parcels the bits and pieces of texts (somewhat like I had done for *Corpus mysticum*); I made some curious discoveries, glimpsed unexpected ramifications, became attached to some little or poorly known figures. . . . Along the way, I became more and more strongly aware of the essential nature of the extraordinary connec-tion, always threatened but always maintained or reestablished within the great Church, between the two Testaments; I saw it more and more clearly dominating the whole history and the whole doctrine of the Church, from the first century to our own time; I verified through many examples the words of Newman, when he said that "There is something beautiful in this appointment."[9] I admired the marvelous synthesis of the whole Chris-tian faith, thought and spirituality contained in the so-called doctrine of

[8] Outside the Society.

[9] *Via media*, vol. 1, p. 308. Keble is known to have thought the same thing.

the "four senses" grasped as it welled forth. I was happy working to do justice in that way to one of the central elements of the Catholic tradition, so grossly unappreciated in modern times and nevertheless still the bearer of promises for renewal. I liked discerning the traces of it, sometimes incomplete or wrapped in strange forms, in a whole series of minor writers; following the systematizations, or even the deformations, of it in the course of the centuries. In a more general way, I liked thus discovering on all sides the historical symbolism, and the symbolic history, that already characterize our Gospels and about which one can say that they are one of the consubstantial characteristics of our faith. Of course, it would have been impossible for me to embrace a subject that was so vast both in itself and in its duration. Four volumes were nevertheless written, the last two of which are very long (1959, 1961, 1964). A fifth was to follow, which would have attempted to show the more or less caricatural surviving relics, the incomprehensions of the past, the transformations of perspectives engendered either by confessional controversies or by progress in criticism, more or less successful attempts at reappearance, and so forth. An already considerable file was prepared, but various unforeseen tasks, more urgent and more absorbing, diverted me from completing it and bringing it out.[10]

As an epilogue to the fourth volume, I transcribed in capital letters a text I consider to be one of the most beautiful of the New Testament. It is by a late, unknown author, at times considered insignificant. This anonymous person, clothed with the great name of Peter, was nonetheless a mind of astonishing perspicacity and depth. He has left us in a few lines one of the most decisive and I would dare to say one of the most intelligent professions of faith, still perfectly adapted to the situation of today. I take pleasure in reproducing it here, a little more at length than in my book, according to the Latin of the Vulgate: "Non enim doctas fabulas secuti notam fecimus vobis Domini nostri Jesu Christi virtutem et praesentiam, sed speculatores facti illius magnitudinis. . . . Et habemus firmiorem propheticum sermonem, cui bene facitis attendentes *quasi lucernae lucenti in caliginoso loco, donec dies elucescat, et lucifer oriatur in cordibus vestris*; hoc primum intellegentes quod omnis prophetia Scripturae propria interpretatione non fit. Non enim voluntate humana allata est aliquando prophetia, sed Spiritu sancto inspirati locuti sunt sancti Dei homines" (2 Pet 1:16–21).[11]

---

[10] Besides many other deficits, it seems to me that these four volumes of *Exégèse médiévale* lack two important chapters: one, on the relations between Jewish exegesis and Christian exegesis at that time, the other, on Exegesis and Liturgy.

[11] "For we did not follow cleverly devised myths when we made known to you the power and coming of our Lord Jesus Christ, but we were eyewitnesses of his majesty. . . . And we have the prophetic word made more sure. You will do well to pay attention to this *as to a lamp*

The Roman censor had given his agreement on the first part of *Exégèse médiévale* only on the express condition that a second part provide a critical restatement of what was as yet, he said, only the historical exposition of contestable views that both theology and science had since gone beyond. The historical exposition was in fact continued, the critical restatement did not come. Nor was my own wish, which was in part related to the demand of the first censors, ever realized. I had in fact vaguely nourished the hope that this long work—as formless as it was to remain and so unmethodical (its composition was ruled by whim and a kind of arbitrariness in its developments and omissions that is reminiscent of, though much more unwieldy than, certain defects in Henri Bremond's *Histoire littéraire du sentiment religieux*)—that this kind of Purana might provide a basis, or at least an occasion, for setting up a very desirable exchange between exegetes, (dogmatic) theologians and spiritual directors. My timid hope was disappointed. If there were any consolation in it, I would observe that the teachings of the conciliar constitution *Dei verbum* on this subject did not find an audience either: people take advantage of the freedom it recognizes for criticism, sometimes they even abuse it blindly; they hardly ever make an effort to accomplish the program it outlines. As for my work, it found acceptance with certain independent philosophers and theologians as well as in monastic circles—and even, almost to excess, with my colleagues of Louvain-Brussels, in their "Institute of Theological Studies". A very intelligent review, bringing out the profound interest of the subject for philosophical thought, appeared in the *Revue de métaphysique et de morale*. The work also had some success in certain Masonic circles much taken with symbolism: I was quite astonished the day a venerable French Mason came to ask me to inscribe a dedication on the copy he had obtained.[12] I also received a whole long memorandum, which seemed to me very penetrating, from a marine officer, an author of scholarly works on the problems of national defense, who thought he found in the "dialectic of the four senses", and also in the writings of Father Fessard, the ideal instrument for obtaining an in-depth understanding of the Christian mystery, accessible to minds of scientific formation. I admit to not having succeeded in following his demonstrations very closely—nor those of a young Belgian, Bolandist, colleague, Father Van Esbroeck, who later published an

---

shining in a dark place, until the day dawns and the morning star rises in your hearts. First of all you must understand this, that no prophecy of scripture is a matter of one's own interpretation, because no prophecy ever came by the impulse of man, but men moved by the Holy Spirit spoke from God."

[12] On the other hand, a very pious Catholic friend, authorized to remain in a mystical branch of the Masons, for a long time contrived, as a veritable apostle, to make my works known.

intelligent little book showing that the antithetical intellectual positions of Paul Ricoeur and Claude Lévi-Strauss could be reconciled in the higher Christian synthesis brought out by *Exégèse médiévale*.[13]

The very title of the work could in itself provoke opposition or at least reticence on the part of professional exegetes. It was also very difficult (and I hardly succeeded, despite clear proof and despite attestations as authoritative as those of Father Vincent, O.P.[14]) to straighten out the prejudices or to disentangle the complex of false ideas long entertained by most historians on the subject of the very word "allegory". Yet, as I have many times explained, it was not in any way a question in this study of discrediting, even so much as a little, modern disciplines in favor of those of the Middle Ages.[15] The word *exegesis*, placed in the title, is to be taken in its original meaning, a meaning much broader than that which prevails in our own time. It formerly included all the successive parts of Christian reflection being exercised on the basis of revelation handed on to us by the Holy Books accepted in the Church: that is, first of all, the "exegesis" of biblical texts, in the limited sense of our present usage, in its immediacy, as it were; then dogmatics, ecclesiology, moral theology and spirituality; a synthesis, a complete act, a theology that is both manifold and one in its various phases, the kind that even today, through renewed methods, all the better minds feel the need of, since "interdisciplinary" research and collaboration, incapable of furnishing a common soul, cannot truly supply it.

With respect to this work and to a few others, I have sometimes been reproached for abusing Latin quotations. Making allowance for negligence, or excessive haste, I will say in my defense that I often preserved the Latin of the texts because of their singular beauty, which all translation erases. Nonetheless, that is only a partial defense, for nothing stopped me from accompanying such texts, more strictly chosen, with a translation in a footnote. Yet I should also add that, at the time when I began to write, knowledge of Latin was much more widespread among those who might be my possible readers than it is now.

Since 1945, I had established friendly relations with Abbé Jean Steinmann, chaplain at the Bossuet School, then vicar at Notre Dame. Abbé Steinmann, a biblicist and Pascalian, had two mortal enemies: Origen and

---

[13] *Herméneutique, Structuralisme et Exégèse. Essai de logique kérygmatique* (Tournai: Desclée, 1968).

[14] See above, IV, his review of *Histoire et Esprit*, and below, VII, two of his letters (documents in the Appendix).

[15] I had already explained this, well before the publication of *Exégèse médiévale*, even before that of *Histoire et Esprit*, in a letter (which can be read in the Appendix) addressed to one of my colleagues at the Lyons Faculty [5:2].

the Jesuits [5:3]. In his eyes, therefore, I was affected by a twofold defect; he pardoned me, or at least tolerated them; our relations were never impeded by them, for we felt a lively sympathy for each other. I said to him: "If, instead of writing five volumes at full speed you would put all your care into only one, you would create only masterpieces"; he in fact had a taste for real work and remarkable gifts as a writer. He even accepted irony from me that was a little strong: as when I congratulated him on finally giving Origen his due, because he had quoted with admiration a page of Jerome in which I recognized the mark of the great Alexandrian.[16] In the years that followed 1950, however, I saw him only rarely. Besides, I was then living a rather solitary life; I had to avoid any meetings as well as teaching. Numerous ministries were refused me, either because in many cases I was no longer trusted or because my superiors, in their prudence or perhaps according to orders received, judged my activity inopportune. Or again—and such occasions were not rare—I had to defend myself against an indiscreet or even flashy, in any case hardly Catholic, exploitation of my situation. Any man, especially any priest, who finds himself with a reputation for having difficulties with the authority of the Church or who is considered to be its victim, is quickly surrounded by prowlers seeking to make some kind of spurious success of him. It is not always easy to escape this. Even if he manages to protect himself with respect to his own conduct, he nevertheless notices at times with grief that his name, mixed with equivocal praises, figures in recriminations or simply in expositions full of misunderstandings, precisely where he would not wish to see it. How many times—and even up to this present time itself —in journals, reviews, books, have I not also seen my name exploited against the Magisterium, against "Rome", often by the very ones who support positions they know I oppose and in quite different situations that would offer no plausible reason to their critics! I do not dare quote examples of this here. . . . As one can easily see, I am not speaking of faithful friends, who helped me in the bad days to "hold on", such as the one who, guessing my suffering, discreetly transcribed for me, without a word of commentary, these lines from Kierkegaard's *Journal*: "Each generation prepares someone who will announce Christianity in earnest. The more it persecutes and mistreats him, the more too it detaches his spirit from the world, so completely that God alone remains. And Christianity begins to be real for this man only when he is so unhappy and so tormented in this world that he seems a killjoy with all his suffering." —Nor am I speaking

[16] The tragic death of Abbé Steinman, in 1963, during a pilgrimage to the Holy Land, in the Petra gorge, is well known. I say nothing here of the priest, the educator and the zealous apostle, all of which he was, ever keeping to the point of view indicated in the foreword of this Memoir.

of certain tormented or anxious spirits, spontaneously drawn toward those they judge, because of their difficult situation, to be more accessible to their own search. Those who had recourse to me in that way during the course of those dark years were the source of one of my greatest joys.

Around the end of 1953, following an intervention by Cardinal Gerlier, I was for the first time authorized, not to resume regular teaching, but to give "a few conferences", outside the staff of the Theology Faculty and on a subject that would not be theological. Another condition had been specified: these conferences must not be announced publicly. The good Cardinal, who had since 1950 run into more radical refusals, tended to consider that to be a victory. This was hardly the opinion of the Faculty. The Father Provincial, however, thought that if I did not bring myself to do it, my silence would be interpreted as sulking and would make my case worse. So I brought myself to do it. In a little place with four or five charitable listeners, recruited by the dear and ever-faithful M. Ville-pelet, I made use of the authorization that had been granted by speaking about Amida, with which I had just become a little better acquainted at the Musée Guimet. It was a three or four-hour affair. And that was to permit me, in order to "save face" as much as possible, as my Superiors in France wished, to write in the Foreword of the book on *Amida* (1955) that it had its origin in conferences given at the Catholic Faculties of Lyons.

Three years later, at a new request by Cardinal Gerlier, Msgr. A. Dell'Acqua, assistant at the Secretariate of State, wrote to him from the Vatican:

> I am charged by the Holy Father to acknowledge Your Eminence's letter of last November 8, concerning the Rev. Father Henri de Lubac. —His Holiness has deigned to take your request into consideration as well as the religious and submissive attitude of the Reverend Father, after having confided the examination of this petition to the attentive care of the competent organisms. He charges me to inform Your Eminence that the Rev. Father de Lubac can henceforth *ad experimentum* give instruction at the Catholic Faculties of Lyons on Hinduism and Buddhism. —Deign to agree. . . .

Despite the sort of "good marks" that might be signified by the abandonment of any formula insinuating hypocrisy on my part, we had scarcely made any progress. My dean even feared, not without reason, that such a solution, with its threefold restrictive clause ("Catholic Faculties", "Hinduism and Buddhism", "ad experimentum"), might indicate a definitive exclusion from the corps of professors of the Theology Faculty.

Yet time did its work. In March 1958, a new step toward reconciliation was accomplished. Thanks to the persevering efforts of Father Ravier and the good will of Father Augustin Bea, the Pope's confessor, four of my books, bound in white, were presented to Pius XII. These were: two books on Buddhism, *Sur les chemins de Dieu* and *Méditation sur l'Eglise*. Father Bea had insisted that they be accompanied by an address on my part. I resisted at first, for two reasons, which I stated to Father Ravier (March 7, 1958): in the first place, "if my letter does not seem to be a kind of self-accusation, it risks being misinterpreted; people would not fail to say, and to have repeated in all the right places: it took him eight years to give in"; in the second place, "I have always thought that a religious should not take the initiative of personal steps of this kind outside his Superiors; in order to present my publications to the Pope, if it is I who am making the gesture, I must normally go through the Father General". Now the Roman authorities of the Society, sounded out by my Provincial, had declined to give an opinion—which could be interpreted as a repudiation and could encourage distrust toward me on the part of the Pope. In response to new requests, however, I ended up writing the following respectful and innocuous address:

> Very Holy Father, these books that are being presented to Your Holiness would wish to be a witness of the combat led for the faith of Holy Church by the most humble of her children. Their author is without merit; he hopes nonetheless to rejoice the heart of Your Holiness by opening to him his own heart and by giving him the assurance that during the course of an already long life he has always remained, through the grace of God, without the exception of a single day, in a disposition of faith, obedience and filial affection toward the Vicar of Our Lord Jesus Christ on earth. —The servant and very humbly devoted son of Your Holiness.[17]

Pius XII immediately had me thanked through a letter from Father Bea written in encouraging terms; he congratulated me on my activity at the service of the Church, without making the slightest allusion to a few false steps in the past. Here is this letter, dated March 29, 1958:

> I am happy to be able to communicate to you that the Holy Father has accepted with truly paternal kindness and with great joy the homage of your four volumes, which you presented to him through my hands, along with your beautiful declaration of dispositions of faith, obedience and affection toward the Vicar of Jesus Christ on earth. The Holy Father had a lively interest in the topics of your books and particularly of the fine work *Méditation sur l'Eglise*. He was delighted to see the scientific soundness attested to by the numerous notes and quotations. The Holy Father asked me to communicate

---

[17] I would write on April 6 (Easter) to my new Provincial, Father Blaise Arminjon: "I am happy to have finally been able to say to the Holy Father what I have been wanting to say to him for eight years, and I am still surprised that my words were so well received, although they might have appeared arrogant—for they constitute, unavoidably, a respectful protest against the essence of the accusations recorded in the encyclical *Humani generis*."

his great gratitude and to tell you that he expects much more from the talents
the Lord has given you for the good of the Church. He sends you wholeheartedly his blessing for your person, particularly for your health, and for all
your works, and he encourages you to continue with much confidence your
scientific activity from which much fruit is promised for the Church. You
can be sure, my Reverend Father, that you have given great consolation to
the Holy Father by your homage and your very devoted declaration. I myself
express to you my very keen joy at being able to bring you this good news,
to which I add, on my own part, the expression of my very sincere good
wishes on the occasion of the feast of Easter.

Father Bea followed this letter with two others, written in his own name,
one to my Provincial and the other to me again, specifying that the first
letter reproduced very exactly the thought of the Holy Father and that
the latter had not wanted to make a response through official channels for
fear that his thought might be more or less distorted.[18] He added that the
letter written in the name of the Pope had been written in such a way that
it could be shown to anyone. Since the Father General, to whom it was
communicated, declared that he did not wish to know about it since it
was not official, I did not spread it. There was no allusion to it in public
[5:4].

Was this finally the thaw? Not completely. From the end of 1957 until
the end of 1959, there was a labyrinth of complications. The attitude that
I just mentioned with respect to the Father General shows that there were
still some relentless strongholds of opposition. As far as I know, these
were, at that time, perhaps restricted to Father Janssens' advisers. Father
Janssens, very poorly informed about the very actions of his past government, seemed to believe that I had never done any teaching at the Theology Faculty other than a course in the history of religions; in a series of
letters from December 1957 and January 1958, he certified that it was not
he but my Faculty itself who had judged it good to dismiss me from it;
he declared that he was convinced that all had been henceforth settled by
the "permission obtained" of which I spoke above. For the honor of my
Faculty, as much as and more than for clearing up an impossible situation,
I had to reestablish the facts, cite the documents, prove to him that his
letters were full of untrue statements, specifying in addition what I knew
quite well: that, although signed by him, they had not been written by

[18] I suspect still another reason: without doubt (and I well understand why) the Holy See did
not wish to furnish an official document that would contradict another. The Father General,
for example, had written to me on February 23, 1951: "I would not dare to submit to the
Holy Father your protest of submission to the Magisterium if it did not also contain at the
same time a recognition of the objective errors for which the encyclical, in the unanimous
opinion of those who are conversant with the matter, reproaches you."

him. He ended by addressing me a letter that was embarrassed but loyal and which gave me further proof besides of his good heart; I will excerpt the essential lines: "It is clear that there have been misunderstandings on all sides. History teaches that men guided by the most honest intentions manage to have difficulties in being understood. What is important is to recognize at least the loyalty of those who make you suffer and whom one has made suffer. 'Diligentibus Deum, omnia cooperantur in bonum'."

We were not, however, at the end of the account. In June 1958, since the Society had not found anyone to look after the courses I had stopped teaching since 1950, I made a bold move. In order to get you out of the difficulty, I said to my dean, Msgr. Jouassard, I could perhaps quite simply begin again? Msgr. Jouassard wanted to get some assurances. Returning from a trip to Rome, he told me that the situation was "complex" and that intransigence in my regard was coming from within the Society— which I knew only too well.[19] In December, it was Cardinal Gerlier who reported from Rome a verbal approval for the resumption of my courses. Before or after that date, I do not remember exactly when, since the Father General had told my Dean that the question did not concern him seeing that he had never removed my chair,[20] our Faculty had the Congregation of Seminaries and Universities officially sounded out through the Procurator of Saint-Sulpice; they responded that since 1929, the year of my nomination, there had been nothing in my file and that they did not see why an authorization to teach was requested. In brief, no one wanted any more to have the least part in the interdictions that had weighed on me for nine years. After a few obscure negotiations, which still lasted nearly a year,[21] I resumed a little teaching, from November 1959 until March 1, 1960, and then handed in my resignation.[22] In the months that followed, the Faculty gave me the title of honorary professor.

[19] And in fact, an unbelievable thing, the Father General, visibly outflanked and a prisoner of those who informed him and wrote his official correspondence, had again, on November 26, 1958, harked back to the equivocations and errors that he had been able to acknowledge and apologize for in January: "Allow me to tell you how saddened I am to see the Lyons Faculty shift onto the Father General the responsibility of its own decisions"; he repeated to me the consent given by the Holy See to a course on "Buddhism" and upheld the demand of Roman censorship for any publication.

[20] Which was strictly true, since in 1929 I had been, not named, but presented to the Congregation of Seminaries and Universities, from which I held my chair and which alone could dismiss me from it.

[21] Letter from the Father General, June 19, 1959: "Agree, dear Father, to teach at the Faculty next year." See in the Appendix my letter of May 27, 1959, to the Father General [5:5]. New difficulties arose again at the end of June, caused by new Roman censors (of the Society).

[22] Father Blaise Arminjon, Provincial, had insisted, like his predecessor, Father Ravier, that I meet with students under regular conditions at least for a little while before resigning with honor.

Thus came to an end a long, complicated affair of which I have retraced here only the broad outlines.[23] As one prelate said in 1956, "Everything would have been much simpler if they had had the courage to send (me) to Nouméa".

Around 1956, I had been brought back again to the residence at Lyons, which Father Charles Nicolet, my old friend, now superior, had just established on rue Sala, but I would continue for several years to divide my time between Lyons and Paris. It was at Lyons that I saw the Visitator of the French Provinces, Father Clément Plaquet, a Belgian, who was very friendly toward me but at the same time very reserved; he refused to give the least glance to the file that I had sent him, the affair being, as far as he was concerned, already decided. (Without doubt he had received orders in that vein.) In the autumn of 1960, Father Arminjon had me go back up the hill of Fourvière, where Father Jacques Guillet, prefect of studies, and Father Jacques Misset, rector, received me with kindness. During the fifteen painful years that I had just gone through, nearly immediately following the trials of the nazi occupation, everything had been greatly eased by the affectionate confidence of my successive Superiors and by the very numerous testimonies of fraternity. At Fourvière, I found again some good advisers, kindly readers of many pages, in particular Fathers Henri Mogenet and Charles Baumgartner, as well as a younger active and courageous theologian, Gustave Martelet. I was going to live there, not without frequent absences, for fourteen more years, completely on the fringes of the internal life of the scholasticate (or of what was called so up until these recent times) before emigrating elsewhere.

Around the end of 1959, after various processes and consultations of Superiors, of which I was informed only at the end, I was elected a member of the *Académie des sciences morales et politiques*, which is one of the five branches of the "Institute of France". Some had proposed the name of Father Michel Riquet, who would have been very suitable and who later on, if only because of his habitual presence in Paris, would have been much better able than I to fulfill the (not very strict) obligations of such a post; but our Provincials, despite me, decided on my name. In the year that followed, I retraced the life of my predecessor, Msgr. Georges Chevrot, Curé of Saint-François-Xavier. At the Institute, a very "mixed" circle, I was well received by all, and I formed or drew closer the bonds of invaluable friendships. I met there once again Gabriel Marcel, Martial Gueroult, Pastor Marc Boegner, and so on; I made the acquaintance of

[23] On this whole affair, often called rather improperly the "Fourvière affair", I have kept numerous documents and several journals with day-to-day notes, which would permit as needed the completion or the correction of what is said in this Memoir. See several rediscovered dates in the Appendix [5:6].

Léon Noël, who soon became a true friend; among those who later joined us, I would mention Victor-L. Tapié, Robert Garric, now deceased, and Henri Gouhier, with whom I renewed old relations, and so forth.

There have been many pages here in which I have often strayed from my original goal, which was to give a few explanations about the nature and occasion for my writings. I now return to it by quoting the report that had been asked of me in 1959, as was customary, by the perpetual Secretary of the Academy of Moral Sciences in order to assist Pierre Renouvin, who had the responsibility of introducing my titles. This is how I expressed it:

> In the works classified under the rubric of "Theology", I have especially wanted to explore, on several fundamental points, the ancient Christian tradition, so as to show its richness, unity in diversity and creative vigor, which still today is not exhausted. Three examples, which were the subject of three works, seemed to me particularly important and significant. —In *Corpus mysticum*, through the history of these two words whose surprising vicissitudes I retraced, I tried to show the depths and the complexity of the bonds that unite these two realities of the Eucharist and the Church in Christian life and doctrine; that is, in the final analysis, to define the kind of relationship that ties, in the Catholic synthesis, the most "mystical" element to the most institutional. —In *Surnaturel*, it is a more fundamental problem from the point of view of the rational reflection that is approached: the problem of the relations between philosophy and theology, between reason and faith, between the development of the resources of human nature and the potential reception of a supernatural given, relations such as Christian thought conceives them in principle. What emerges from this essentially historical study, it seems, is the fact that a certain conception of two orders, the so-called natural and supernatural orders, which has been expressed in certain schools during these very recent centuries, resulting in the constitution of a "separated theology" that itself gives rise to a "separated philosophy", is not fully in conformity with either the whole of Christian tradition or the complete blossoming of the life of the spirit. —In *Histoire et Esprit*, it is the central idea of the ancient interpretation of Scripture that I tried to bring out by taking as the center of perspective its most brilliant representative, Origen. In so doing, I hoped to make a contribution, on the one hand, to the current research into the philosophy or the theology of history and, on the other, to the synthesis that is also being sought today within Christianity between exegesis, properly so-called, dogmatic theology and spirituality. It is a continuation of this study, this time adopting the early Latin Middle Ages as the center of perspective, that is occupying me at this time.
>
> These different themes are treated more broadly, from a less technical aspect, in two other works, which are in my thinking complementary: *Catholicisme* and *Méditation sur l'Eglise*. —At the foundation of the series *Sources chrétiennes*, which has been continuing its publications for fifteen years, is found the same

conviction that the renewal of Christian vitality is linked, at least in part, to a renewed exploration of the period and works in which the Christian tradition is expressed with particular intensity.

The works of a theological order could not keep me from reflecting with my times on an eternal problem, such as it is debated in our contemporary society and such as it controls its major orientations: the problem of God. That is the subject I have considered in a series of works grouped here under the title "religious philosophy": whether by setting forth and discussing in that regard the thought of Proudhon, Nietzsche, Feuerbach, Marx or August Comte, or by studying some of its more recent incidences, or again by reflecting on it freely for myself and by taking advantage for that purpose of the treasures of thought accumulated through philosophical efforts and through the mystical impulse of earlier generations. I have had the hope of assisting in that way some of my travelling companions "sur les chemins de Dieu" [along God's paths].

The writings that concern the "history of religions" deal almost exclusively with Buddhism. What is in question there is the most immense and complex spiritual fact in all human history outside the Judeo-Christian revelation. One work was devoted to the *Rencontre du Bouddhisme and de l'Occident* (chrétien) [Meeting of Buddhism and the (Christian) West] during the last twenty centuries. Two others attempted a more intrinsic confrontation. Through various means of approach, of the moral, cultural and symbolic order, they aim at penetrating to the essence of Buddhism, and, through a comparison with the most fundamental features of Christianity, at drawing attention to the two structures of thought, the two attitudes faced with the problem of man and the universe.

Through a copiously annotated edition of the correspondence between Maurice Blondel and Father Auguste Valensin, I hoped to be able to furnish, along with everything necessary for a full understanding of it, a first-hand document on the very active and very troubled period of our philosophical and religious history (between the years 1900 and 1913), a period about which we still have very few analogous documents at our disposal.

I have said nothing yet about *Sources chrétiennes*, to which, as we have just seen, this report alludes. Their foundation dates back to 1940. The initiator of the series, which at first was to include only the Greek Fathers, had been Father Victor Fontoynont. In an ecumenical spirit, he saw it as an instrument of rapprochement with the Orthodox Churches.[24] He thought for a long time about the accomplishment of it. On the eve of the Second World War, he discovered some support around him for his project. But

[24] The missions of our Lyons Province to the Near East placed a number of us in contact with the Orthodox: this is what suggested the idea to Father Fontoynont, who was in addition an excellent Hellenist. —As early as January 14, 1945, Abbé Charles Journet, greeting with joy, from Fribourg, the first progress of *Sources chrétiennes*, was actively interested in sending them to Russia.

as he was already advanced in age, the care of directing the enterprise was confided to Pierre Chaillet [5:7]. Scarcely had the latter begun the first steps when the mobilization of the summer of 1939 dispatched him to Budapest. When approached about replacing him, Father Henri Rondet, absorbed by his responsibilities as prefect of studies, declared himself incompetent. It was at that time that an appeal was made to me. The series got under way the following year, thanks to an understanding with Father Chifflot, O.P., editor of "Editions de l'Abeille",[25] who understood the interest of the undertaking immediately. We were encouraged by H. I. Marrou, then in Lyons, who was to give the series its fine edition of the "Letter to Diognetes"—and who would always remain very friendly toward me. When, demobilized, Father Daniélou had returned to Paris, he was our link with the "occupied zone"; he and I became co-editors; I have kept correspondence from him that gives witness to his great activity spent at the service of *Sources*.[26] Father Claude Mondésert served as editorial secretary. He later became the sole editor of the series, and it is to him, to his many areas of competence and to the team he was able to form that it owes its remarkable progress.[27] In the spring of 1973, it celebrated in Rome, Paris and Lyons its two-hundredth volume, and neither the spiritual crisis that raged in the Church of France nor the growing financial difficulties were yet able even to slow its pace of publication. I would have been incapable of pursuing such a work, which became more and more scholarly. If I have read and quoted much from the Fathers of the Church, I have never been able to study them as a specialist. I am nevertheless happy to have contributed in some little way to making others better aware of the current interest of the Fathers. "It is not a superficial current interest, and it is true that it will never blaze forth before all eyes. But it is a *fructifying* current interest [5:8]. Each time, in our West, that

[25] This was the successor of Editions du Cerf, "withdrawn" to Lyons. We also had several conversations with Father de Vaux, O.P. It was at that time that the idea for the "Jerusalem Bible" was born. In an overly ambitious dream, I would have liked the *Sources* (that was the simple title at first adopted) to include an initial series devoted to the books of the Bible in separate fascicles; then the Greek Fathers, the Latin Fathers, a medieval series; finally, each of the great modern languages would have had its series of Christian classics. . . . But I was not Abbé Migne!

[26] My more or less intense collaboration with Father Daniélou never ceased, so to speak: *Sources chrétiennes, Témoignage chrétien, Dieu vivant, Recherches de science religieuse*, the Council, Secretariate for Non-Christians, "Axes", and so forth. He rendered me many a service (correcting proofs, etc.) and gave many signs of his confidence.

[27] The very simple statutes drafted at the time of its foundation stipulated that the series was linked with the scholasticate at Fourvière and was not to be separated from it. Life almost immediately gave good reason for this clause. —In 1956, the "Association of Friends of Sources chrétiennes" was created; in 1969, the "Institute of Sources chrétiennes" was founded.

Christian renewal has flourished, in the order of thought as in that of life (and the two are always connected), it has flourished under the sign of the Fathers."

CHAPTER SIX

I would like to speak in this section of a few men whom I have known, whom I have loved, whose names have already appeared occasionally in the preceding pages, and several of whom left writings that I reviewed and published after their death.

We published seven volumes of Father Yves de Montcheuil (d. 1944). Two appeared in the "Theology" series: *Malebranche et le Quiétisme* (1947), which was his master's thesis in Rome, and *Mélanges théologiques* (1946), a collection of various articles and unpublished pieces to which I added a long introduction. *Malebranche*, undoubtedly the only one of the seven volumes that he would himself have published, after having completed it, still lacked a conclusion; this was to have been an overall view of the metaphysical problem of love; the controversy between Malebranche and Fénelon would have been clarified by the respective views on the subject by Saint Augustine and Saint Thomas Aquinas. That was an essential theme, which had occupied Father de Montcheuil for a long time and which, I believe, would have gone beyond the limits of a conclusion to become a large book. The *Leçons sur le Christ* and *Aspects de l'Eglise* (1949), works of more modest proportions, reproduce two catechetical courses given to students at the Sorbonne, in the "University Catholic Center" founded by him in 1941 with the assistance of some young friends, which was at the origin of our present "Catholic Center of French Intellectuals" [6:1]; a third course, on the sacraments, was not presented in a written form sufficient to enable us to publish it. The language of these two little books is always simple, avoiding any technicality; they are *elementary* works, which is to say, *essential*. There is nothing in these lines that seeks to shine or to please, rather, we find a fine, vigorous and ardent touch; nor was any effort made toward a surface adaptation that would already be out of date. The *Problèmes de vie spirituelle* [Problems of the spiritual life] (1945), composed of conferences given to young people and of a few personal notes that he does not seem to have used directly, is a master work, calling for reflection on subjects of profound timeliness, treated with robustness; the work, provided with an introduction by Father René d'Ouince, has been reprinted several times (not always as a whole); it would deserve to be so again.[1] *Eglise et le monde actual* [The Church and the modern world] (1945) gathers together various articles that appeared

[1] The fifth edition, complete, was in 1957.

97

in reviews or journals for youth as well as a course on the Church and
State and additional questions. In treating the ever-recurring problem of
the relations between "spiritual" and "temporal", between history and
eternity, between "liberation" and "salvation", and so forth, a problem
that still today catches so many minds off guard, there would be great
profit in referring to this course, in which the principles that determine
its solution, applicable in the most changeable situations, are set forth with
as much clarity as firmness.[2] Finally, *Royaume et ses exigences* (1957) gives
the text of a retreat destined for a group of J.E.C.F. (Students' Catholic Association), a text reproduced in part from the notes of his listeners.
These various books, of solid substance, firm writing, demanding thought,
have been much read and have done much good. They have increased the
number of those who, having known Father de Montcheuil, could not
help but dream wistfully of the commanding role he might have played,
within the Church and for her influence, in the troubled period after the
war (and again after the Council). A profound theologian, a remarkable
educator, Father de Montcheuil was an excellent chaplain for students.
It was for them that he gave his life. Those whom he formed first-hand
have remained under all circumstances intrepidly faithful. I will quote this
single maxim of his that happened to fall before my eyes this moment:
"Great causes are strengthened by the sacrifices they demand and not by
the concessions they make to the mediocre in order to hold them."[3]

In the following years, it was necessary to defend his memory, for he
was a posthumous victim of the senseless "Fourvière affair". A whole
novel was constructed about teaching supposedly given at the Faculty of
Paris that, it was claimed, introduced error on the subject of the Eucharist:
now what was in question was, in all and for all, only one phrase, understood the wrong way, exhumed I have no idea how from a paper on which
Father de Montcheuil had scribbled as a student during a class of Father
de Lanversin in 1930 or 1931 and passed to a neighbor sitting on the same
bench; a phrase that was, moreover, perfectly innocent.[4] But fifteen years
later, the suspicious group that mounted the "Fourvière affair" had lost
all reason. It was necessary to defend also the *Problèmes de vie spirituelle*,

---

[2] The work had three editions; the last was in 1959. Cf. *L'Ami du clergé*, May 15, 1947:
"Father de Montcheuil shows himself to be a master here not only by the robustness of his
thought but also, in a more eminent sense, by the courage with which he is able to enter into
this thought."

[3] I cannot note without sadness that, even among the best of the young intellectuals today,
his books are no longer read, even his name is unknown; they search in the dark without success for lights that would resolve their most current problems, lights that reading him would
furnish them in abundance.

[4] In 1947, Father de Montcheuil was admirably defended, on two occasions, by a "Menu
Propos" from Cardinal Saliège.

several chapters of which, they said, spread intolerable novelties. *Leçons sur le Christ* figured in the black list of books withdrawn from trade in 1950; several attempts at a new corrected edition miscarried; again in July 1959, I noted: "The new review finally made [in Rome] of *Leçons sur le Christ*, despite the appended explanations, is a worse condemnation than the preceding ones. Such tenacity, so stupid, so damaging to the good of souls, is confounding. They go so far as to reproach him for not having taught explicitly 'vindictive justice'. . . ." Father de Montcheuil was also much reproached for the fine introduction he had written for a selection of "religious pages" by Maurice Blondel [6:2], which was published by Aubier during the occupation;[5] from the point of view of doctrinal orthodoxy, these reproaches were very unjust; from the point of view of writing, we can regret that, because of the sometimes insurmountable obstacles encountered in communication between the two "zones" that divided France at that time, it was a rough draft and not the definitive draft of this introduction (which I still possess) that was published. Finally, a tinier detail but one that would lead to more widespread controversies, at the International Augustinian Congress held in Paris in 1954, I had Father Mondésert read an explanation of a controversial passage of *De libero arbitrio* (III, 20, 56) in view of defending the interpretation Father de Montcheuil had proposed for it (cf. *Augustinus magister* [1955], 1, 3).

~

Around the end of 1953, Father Auguste Valensin (born in 1879) had died in Nice, where he had resided nearly twenty years after leaving the Catholic Faculties of Lyons. He left a rather rich library, one large tier of which specialized in Dante, as well as numerous papers. As concerned to the extreme about perfection in writing as he was about perfection in thought, he had published little. Our Provincial charged me with making an inventory of everything, classifying it and drawing from it the best part of his manuscripts. For that purpose, I made two visits to Nice [6:3]. The books were divided into different lots, the Dante library was sold, various pieces of correspondence were sent back to their authors (among them, Teilhard's letters, forwarded to New York). With the help of Mlle. Marie Rougier, professor in the Lycée of Nice, whom I had known previously in Lyons, who had long devoted herself as a secretary to Father Valensin and who had a perfect knowledge of his work, I sought out everything in the papers that might be suitable for publication. We had to abandon

[5] In 1942.

the enormous file of courses from the Dante Institute, full of invaluable notes, but nothing of which was really written out. A collection of little meditations, written out extemporaneously by hand, was the first to be prepared; it was given the title (suggested by Father Mondésert) *La Joie dans la foi* [Joy in faith] (1954). The publisher Fernand Aubier accepted it, as an investment from which no return was expected, out of gratitude toward Father Valensin; it was the greatest success of his publishing house: it sold more than one hundred thousand copies and has been translated into numerous languages. We also published three collections of conferences under the single title *Regards* [Glances] (at philosophers, at writers, at Dante; 1955 and 1956). The "Theology" series received in 1954 a volume on *Christianisme de Dante* [The Christianity of Dante]; this was originally to have been an article destined for the *Dictionnaire de spiritualité*, which explains the rather schematic character of the whole and even the slightly bookish tone of some of the pages; it does not allow us to see the in-depth character of the knowledge Father Valensin had of the poet; putting all this in final form demanded rather a lot of work, coordinating the fragments, completing the citations, verifying certain details, and so forth, so that for a time I became a "Dantologist". Then came a kind of biography, not put together in a very strict arrangement, which nevertheless had a lively success among a select group; it was made up almost entirely of letters and fragments from personal journals; Mlle. Rougier and I had prepared it during a vacation in 1960; it was entitled simply *Auguste Valensin, textes et documents inédits* [Auguste Valensin, Unpublished texts and documents] (1961). I also republished the little volume *Autour de ma foi* [Around my faith], following it with a catechism for adults, *Initiation catholique* [Catholic initiation], which Father valued highly;[6] he said quite freely that it was his favorite work, because it had been written and perfected in the concrete exercise of his ministry and because it seemed to him to respond better than any other to the mind of Saint Ignatius of Loyola; a new edition of it appeared in 1974. In 1954, at a meeting in homage to the memory of Father Valensin, at the *Centre universitaire méditerranée*, of which he had been one of the founders along with Paul Valéry, I sketched some of the features of his personality. I took advantage of an inquiry made by the review *Christus* in 1955 to give them an article, "Présence actuelle du Christ" [The presence of Christ today], in which I invoked his testimony (several lines from this will be found in the Appendix [6:4] that serve to frame the presentation of a number of texts).

Father Valensin, like Surin and Fénelon, liked to set down his inner feelings and his prayer in little pieces of verse, which made no pretense at

---

[6] The first edition dated from 1941; it was a supplementary sheet in a journal from Nice.

literary effect and were not kept for publication. Here is one, which dates from 1928 and which I have here in a notebook:

> Me voici devant vous, mon Père,
> Avec mes péchés sur les bras,
> Aux lèvres le goût de la terre,
> Dans le coeur mille pensers bas.
> Je ne sens ni frayeur ni honte,
> Car c'est vers Vous que j'ai les yeux;
> C'est sur ma misère, ô mon Dieu,
> Et sur votre Amour—que je compte![7]

I consider the posthumous editions I have had occasion to provide of the works of Father Valensin and Father de Montcheuil, as well as of the correspondence of Maurice Blondel and later of the writings and letters of Father Teilhard de Chardin, to be one of the most useful tasks ever given to me to accomplish.

~

From the time he left the Faculty of Letters at Aix in order to enter, in the same city, the novitiate of the Jesuits of Lyons, Auguste Valensin never ceased to maintain relations of trusting friendship, mixed on his part with veneration, with his mentor Blondel. This was the source of a copious correspondence, covering a half-century. I published first, in two volumes, of which the greatest part was taken up with annotations, the entire series of letters exchanged between them up to the end of 1912. Visits to the Blondel archives in Aix, with Mlle. N. Panis, secretary to the philosopher, and numerous excursions into the books and journals of the period allowed me to carry out this work. I did not sign it, because it would have been necessary to submit the manuscript to the censor in Rome and thereby to expose ourselves to indiscretions, perhaps to ventures contrary to the respect owing to the memory of Blondel; but my Provincial—disregarding the surprisingly severe censures of two readers (some "young ones", he told me, undoubtedly newly arrived at Fourvière)—authorized the publication (September 1956); the work appeared in 1957.[8] A third volume appeared eight years later (1965), this one under my name; it contained

---

[7] Here I am before you, my Father, / With my sins on my hands, / On my lips, the taste of earth, / In my heart, a thousand base thoughts. / I feel neither fear nor shame, / For it is toward You that I gaze; / It is on my misery, O my God, / And on your Love that I count!

[8] Father Xavier Tilliette devoted an article to "Blondel and His Correspondents" in 1961, in the *Archives de philosophie*, that related to these two volumes and to the work I will soon discuss (*Au coeur de la crise moderniste*).

an annotated selection of the same correspondence, going from 1913 until the death of Blondel in 1949. This volume could only be comprised of excerpts because, on the one hand, with Blondel getting older, the letters were no longer of consistent interest and, on the other, there was often a question of persons still living. —I will observe on this subject that too many authors today take the liberty of publishing unverifiable gossip about their contemporaries, judgments they feel no need of justifying, and to the point of personal indiscretions; nothing is more harmful, either to accurate history or to the serious discussion of ideas. —Maurice Blondel's heirs also confided to me the publication (in two volumes) of a selection from the enormous correspondence exchanged between him and his friend Abbé J. Wehrlé; the selection was not entirely mine; I annotated it according to the same principles [6:5]. These are documents of primary value for the philosophico-religious history of the first part of our century; these are provisional materials for use in the great biography of Maurice Blondel, which would be a fundamental monument but which, I fear, will never be written. I had also begun to prepare a rather considerable collection of letters from Blondel to various correspondents, but the heirs could not reach an understanding among themselves on how to carry out the project, which came to nothing in the end; such was the origin of the little, quite invaluable volume of *Lettres philosophiques*, of which neither the selection nor the edition was mine. I have several times been asked to edit the voluminous correspondence between Blondel and Father Laberthonnière; it is of foremost interest, from many points of view; but it was a considerable undertaking and, on the other hand, the prohibitions set by the heirs of Laberthonnière made it impossible for me to do. Claude Tresmontant published a judicious but limited selection of it. One can hope that the project of publishing the whole of it will be taken up again soon; and similarly, the very interesting correspondence between Blondel and Msgr. Mulla. Other editions or republications are also envisaged.

In the 1950s, I had begun to prepare still another work of documents drawn for the most part from the Blondel archives. It finally resulted in a work that Father René Marlé published under the title of *Au coeur de la crise moderniste* [At the heart of the modernist crisis]. Because it was impossible for me at that time to publish anything without going through the censor in Rome (it was not a question of a mere edition of letters, even abundantly annotated, but of texts from different sources, encased in a narrative and containing many personal reflections), I was not long in perceiving that I would not succeed in accomplishing it. That is why, on the advice of my Provincial, Father Blaise Arminjon, who had just succeeded Father André Ravier, I forwarded files, rough drafts and chapter outlines to Father Marlé, who agreed to take them in order to make a selection of the better part, at his convenience. The authorship of the work has sometimes been attributed to me; this is an error. Such as it is, I disown it. The author has arranged the work in his own way, he has altered my prose, suppressed or abridged documents, left prepared files to one side, neglected developments and specifications that seemed necessary to me, and so forth; he brought forward various judgments that did not always coincide with mine. That being said (which is not a reproach, for he had well understood that he had full liberty), I think that we must be grateful to Father Marlé for having done very useful work outside the works of his own specialty and recognize that some of the criticisms addressed to him were excessive. Undoubtedly one of the most regrettable errors was his having neglected, despite my recommendations, to consult Msgr. Maurice Nédoncelle, an excellent expert on Hügel, who had studied and had made copies of the originals of the correspondence between the Baron and the philosopher of Aix; and also his having thought it good, in order to facilitate the reading, to abridge some letters and to replace in readable French a few picturesque but rather incorrect phrases of the Baron. As for the accusation brought by one scholar of having hidden a letter from Blondel to Loisy, that is pure calumny.

~

After Father de Montcheuil in 1944, Maurice Blondel in 1949, Father Valensin in 1953, Father Pierre Teilhard de Chardin died on April 10, 1955, on Easter Sunday, in New York. His overwhelming posthumous celebrity is well known as are the battles joined around his name and his work, still little and poorly known, most often by antagonists incapable of judging it soundly on one side or the other. As early as April 5, 1936, Msgr. Bruno de Solages had already written to me with respect to a series of long memoranda written by Father Teilhard over a period of fifteen years:

> My conviction only increases: we must manage to benefit our contemporaries with a publication of this kind, and it would have a much stronger effect if it were a concentrated whole than even if one were to succeed in getting pieces of it passed here and there. I had M. Devolvé, professor of philosophy at the University of Toulouse (who earlier agreed to collaborate on that detestable collection of Rougier: "Les Maîtres de la pensée antichrétienne") read what I had from Father Teilhard: it made a tremendous impression on him. He wrote me a long letter on the subject that gives first-rate testimony to the active force of Father Teilhard's thought in the modern world. He said to me, among other things, "If his word sounds in the secular world, I am convinced

it will find powerful echos there. . . ." We must work together, first to obtain from Father Teilhard the necessary work of reorganization, then to obtain an *imprimatur*. What do you think?

Father Teilhard had still written much after that, and, even if mentalities had evolved, if scientific interests had in part shifted, if the most vital problems after the Second World War were not those of the twenties or thirties, Teilhard's thought was too serious to have lost its timeliness. But in 1955, for the reasons we have seen, the hour was scarcely favorable. The Society of Jesus did not want to or could not take the responsibility of publishing anything of Teilhard's except for selected texts—which was impracticable. For several years we were even forbidden to write about him. Despite some rare good works, free reign was thus given to legends, to attacks of all kinds as well as to biased exploitations and aberrant interpretations [6:6]. Around 1957 or 1958, a friend had come to take me to Chantilly and had brought me for a few hours to the Teilhard days organized at the cultural center of Cérisy-la-Salle, in la Manche; I had to make an extemporaneous speech there, which led me in the days that followed to draft a rather brief text, which I entitled *Du bon usage du Milieu divin*. The revised text was mimeographed, without my knowledge, by a group of young officers in Algeria.[9] (This was due to the Teilhardian zeal of Claude Cuénot.) A little later, the journal of the J.E.C. in Paris gave a similar article, signed by Father Eugène d'Oncieu, the national chaplain, which I had written: a slight infraction, and the only one, against the law of silence under which I was living. It was not much. Abruptly, at the beginning of the summer of 1961, everything changed. On April 23, Father Arminjon was still reminding me of the formal interdiction against writing about Teilhard. Now, he called me in and gave me in substance the following talk: "People are writing everywhere, in every possible sense, for and against Teilhard; they are saying all sorts of nonsense about him. The Society cannot dissociate itself from one of its children; the four Provincials of France, with the approval of the Father General, want one of those who knew him well, who have followed his thought, to bring his testimony to bear about him; there are very few left in this world who can do so; we have decided on you. So set to work immediately; free yourself as much as possible from any other occupation and work quickly" [6:7].

The twofold order of silence that had weighed on me until then was thus subtly reversed. Actually, I did work quickly. I did not at that time have all the texts at my disposal, but I had many more of them than those

---

[9] In fact, as I was informed, by Colonel Michel Léon-Dufour; in an edition of 200 copies, on the equipment of the foreign legion in Sidi Bel Abbès, in 1960.

who had been fighting about Teilhard for six years; I had besides the advantage of having known him rather closely since 1921 or 1922, of having corresponded with him, of having been a witness to his private exchanges with Auguste Valensin; between 1946 and 1949, along with Msgr. Bruno de Solages, I had been able to help him review first-hand the text of *Phéomène humain* in order to satisfy with a few revisions some demands of the censor in Rome or to forestall others; I also had talked with him at length during his last visit in France, in July (or the beginning of August) 1954. The outline of *Bon usage du Milieu divin*, with hardly any changes, served as my starting point. The work was quickly drafted—too quickly; among other sacrifices made to the god of speed, I gave up two chapters, one of which would have been "La Matrice de l'Esprit" [The matrix of the Spirit], and the other, "Energétique de l'Amour" [The energetics of Love]. It was printed no less quickly, after revisions made in record time, in France (four), then, less quickly, in Rome. (Father Arminjon was afraid that "Rome" might change its mind, and that is why he urged me to hurry.) I should specify that no other order was given me except that of writing. The conception of the work was entirely my own. No one expressed to me any desire that I point out this or omit that. The few remarks made by the reviewers were purely a matter of form. (One of them was Father Paul Henry; he declared that he was enthusiastic; the most important remark came from him: he asked me to divide one chapter into two because he thought it too long.) On the delicate point of relations between "Rome" and Teilhard and their reciprocal judgments, I gave my opinion clearly, and I was not asked to suppress or change a single word. I had at first used the title: "La Doctrine spirituelle du Père Teilhard de Chardin" [The spiritual doctrine of Father Teilhard de Chardin]; while the book was being printed, Father Bottereau remarked that this title was too reminiscent (I had not thought of it) of "La Doctrine spirituelle du Père Lallemant", a classic work, and it might seem to be trying to compete with it.[10] At the very last moment, I therefore chose: "La Pensée religieuse . . ." [The religious thought . . .]; about which Msgr. André Combes was to construct a whole novel, attributing to me all sorts of intentions, as suspect as they were subtle. . . .

Published by Aubier in the spring of 1962, the work circulated very

[10] Cf. the letter from Father Jean L. Swain, assistant (and then substitute "vicar general") to the Father General: "January 26, 1962. My Rev. Father, P. Xti. I am happy to send on to you the equally favorable reviews given by the censors designated for the final revision of the manuscript by Father de Lubac: 'La Doctrine spirituelle du P. Teilhard de Chardin'. May the book thus be published and do all the good that so many competent judges expect from it." The same title is again mentioned in the permission to print given by Father Blaise Arminjon to the *Imprimatur* of Cardinal Gerlier, on January 31 and February 9, 1962.

quickly and drew me a considerable number of letters.[11] It was no less quick in creating a stir in the Holy Office. According to information furnished me by one visitor, Father Lamalle, the archivist of our General Curia, Msgr. Parente asked that it be placed on the Index. Several advisers of the Holy Office being of the contrary opinion, the affair was supposedly brought before John XXIII, who said: No. Hence the benign measures that were adopted. In public, there was a *Monitum*, with rather vague formulas, the importance of which was sometimes exaggerated; it was immediately commented on by Father Philippe de la Trinité (Joseph Rambaud, one of my former students from Mongré), a Discalced Carmelite, in *l'Osservatore romano*, in an article without signature or authority that criticized my book directly. On the other hand, on June 28, my Provincial informed me that any new edition of the book and any translation were forbidden [6:8]. In the letter that communicated these interdictions, the Father General specified in addition that he was only an intermediary, and shortly afterward he addressed an affectionate letter to me in which he expressed his complete solidarity with me:

> August 27, 1962. —I have examined your remarks on the anonymous article that appeared in *l'Osservatore romano* on July 1, 1962, with respect to Father Teilhard de Chardin [6:9]. It is not hard for me to understand that this article was painful for you; but *for the moment* an intervention on my part with the Holy Office seems inopportune. At this time, the cause of truth will be better served by our silent suffering than by untimely clarifications. In a little while —a few months?—we shall see. Many here and elsewhere are hoping for a change. —I am fully in agreement with you: your book constitutes a first, very important elucidation of the work of Father Teilhard, and, in the very spirit of the *Monitum*, a "warning" against possible extrapolations of Father's thought, not in conformity to the doctrine of the Church. It was my judgment that your book served the Church and the truth, and I wanted it to be published. I have not regretted that decision [6:10].

Nothing like that had come to me from Rome for a very long time. In his fundamental honesty, from the time he began to see that there was an acknowledged disagreement between the Holy Office and the Pope, Father Janssens had openly taken sides. From 1961 on, his attitude had changed. From then on, and up to his last days, during my stays at the Curia for the preparation for the Council and then during the Council, he gave many signs of his good will in my regard. He spoke to me one day with great liberty of the abuses of the Holy Office. I felt that he was freeing himself of a burden. He said to me more explicitly what he had tried to make me

[11] See in the Appendix the letter received from Msgr. Montini, a merely polite reply to my having sent him the book. See above, page 75.

understand earlier, on June 1, 1959, when he wrote to me: "There is no ostracism at work against you on the part of the Society.[12] The only thing I would recommend is that you avoid, in the light of the directives of the Holy See, the insufficiently clear statements that have in the past given the wrong impression of your true thinking. I know, my dear Father, that I can count on complete openness on your part; and the confidence is reciprocal." On December 9, 1963, he would write to me: "I understand that your community at Fourvière is preparing soon to celebrate your jubilee of religious life, which had been delayed by the second session of the Council. With all my heart, I am united in that prayer of thanksgiving, and I join in the sentiments of gratitude that your friends and students from the Theology Faculty at Fourvière are addressing to their professor and founder of the "Theology" and "Sources chrétiennes" series. The furrow you have thus opened, and sometimes watered with your tears, has yielded a fine harvest of which you can be proud, . . ." (The myth of my role at Fourvière was very strong!)

The good will of Father Janssens could do nothing about it: before leaving for the first session of the Council, I had to break several contracts signed with foreigners for my book on Teilhard. Two years in succession, the Italian publisher of "Morcelliana" (Brescia) besieged me with varied requests; he ended by obtaining the green light from Father Arrupe, several days after his election, and from then on other translations followed. The atmosphere had changed. The thin voice of Cardinal Frings, Archbishop of Cologne, had resounded in the conciliar aula. . . .[13] But the ban on a new edition had led me, in order to redress various widespread errors, to write (again too quickly) a new book, *La Prière du Père Teilhard de Chardin* [The prayer of Father Teilhard de Chardin], which was published in 1964, with a second, enlarged edition in 1967. After 1961, I became increasingly involved. First it was necessary for me to carry on some polemics with Msgr. André Combes, an erudite man who was nonetheless lacking in discernment, connected with Abbé Luc Lefèvre in the integrist undertaking "Pensée catholique" and fiercely anti-Teilhardian. It was in 1963, when I was in the hospital for two serious operations in succession, that his philippic appeared in *Ephemerides carmeliticae* in Rome; I responded to it during a convalescent stay in Saint-Gervais, around the end of the summer.[14] Our assistant from France to Rome, Father Pillain (who was soon to be dismissed from his position), showed me his warm approval in that situation.

[12] Which was not entirely accurate.

[13] An allusion to his intervention for a reform of the Holy Office—drafted, from all appearances, with the help of Dr. Joseph Ratzinger.

[14] My Provincial, Father Blaise Arminjon, accompanied my response with an energetic letter.

In 1961, I had published in the *Archives de philosophie*, at the request of Father Marcel Régnier, the memoranda exchanged in December 1919 between Maurice Blondel and Father Teilhard, through the mediation of Father Auguste Valensin. This correspondence was taken up again in 1963, copiously annotated and followed by two essays; it constitutes the first volume of the *Bibliothèque des Archives de philosophie*, in its new series. Another little book, *Teilhard missionnaire et apologiste* [Teilhard: Missionary and apologist], published in Toulouse in 1966, resulted from two conferences given in Rome; one, in connection with the Council, on Teilhard and Saint Paul, during which Henri Rambaud, cousin of Philippe de la Trinité and, like him, anti-Teilhardian, contradicted me; the other, about the proofs for the existence of God according to Teilhard, at a Thomist congress organized by Father Charles Boyer. It would take too long to recount how I came to give the latter, at the solemn closing session of the congress, in the great hall of the Cancellaria palace (September 10, 1965). The initiative goes back to Paul VI. What was most striking about the affair was that Father Boyer, who until then had had a reputation for being one of the most determined and influential adversaries of Father Teilhard and of my own doctrine, had himself invited me in a pressing way to come to Rome to speak there of Teilhard "with sympathy"; his letter let it be clearly understood that he had been ordered to do so by the Pope. As he had recently done in a more important cause (that of Catholic exegesis), Paul VI had wanted, by this gesture, to show that he did not approve of the frenetic anti-Teilhardian campaign that was then rampant.

Around the same time, I published two collections of letters by Teilhard of minor interest: *Lettres d'Egypte* (1963) and *Lettres d'Hastings et de Paris* (1965). A major work, *Ecrits du temps de la guerre*, also appeared in 1965, published by Grasset along with Msgr. Bruno de Solages (we had shared the task of annotation, which was intentionally sparing). Besides some articles here and there, I also contributed a chapter to the large volume *Teilhard de Chardin* in the "Realities" series,[15] and a commentary on the poem *L'Eternel Féminin*, which gave me an opportunity to bring out some fundamental aspects of Teilhardian thought that were generally misunderstood or distorted [6:11]. It was at the request of Father Bruno Ribes, editor of *Etudes*, that I had undertaken this latter work; he urged me to write something (his journal not wanting to be responsible for it) in order to reply to the insinuations that were being peddled about Father Teilhard's moral doctrine and conduct. Yet when the book was done, the two censors (Parisians, I do not know why, or perhaps I see it too well) were

---

[15] At the last moment, the publisher suppressed five pages of it that summarized Teilhardian Christology.

in agreement in their desire to block publication (something that might have seemed curious to anyone not knowing the situations and people concerned); one of the reasons acknowledged by both of them was that the book contained several quotations from Urs von Balthasar, and the editor of *Etudes* spread the rumor that I had "some serious trouble with censorship from the Society" and it was necessary to distrust me. My provincial, Father Eugène d'Oncieu, took the advice of a special censor (Father René d'Ouince), and the book finally appeared in 1968 [6:12].[16] The last of the Teilhardian series, a large volume of *Lettres intimes* (to Father Auguste Valensin, Msgr. Bruno de Solages and myself) came out in 1973. The publication of the letters to Father Valensin had been confided to me by Father Calvez, then Provincial of France, who several times urged me to complete it, but the annotation required long and detailed work. Thanks to Father Bouillard and to Mademoiselle Rougier, a new, carefully revised edition, augmented by letters to Father André Ravier, his last Provincial, appeared in the spring of 1974. Texts, notes and multiple references make this last work a favored tool for following the traces of Teilhard's peregrinating existence as well as the development of his thought and the vicissitudes of his interior life.

All these works on Teilhard, which were not of passionate interest to me, took much of my time over a period of twelve years or so and brought me many difficulties. In 1967, in an article for *Monde*, I acclaimed Msgr. de Solages' *Teilhard de Chardin* as "the first overall work based on integral information".[17] I directed, at the Theology Faculty of Lyons, two theses concerning Teilhard: one, by a Swiss priest, Peter Schellenbaum, on "The Role of Christ in Teilhardian Energetics", later published by Editions du Cerf, the other, by an American religious, Father Nemeck, O.M.I., on the "Passivities according to Teilhard", a judicious comparison of the mysticism of Teilhard with that of Saint John of the Cross, which is still unpublished.[18] I seem to have contributed to a twofold result: on the one hand, one had to recognize that Teilhard was a true religious and a faithful Catholic; but, on the other hand, and for that very reason, many then lost

---

[16] From Father d'Ouince, December 8, 1967: ". . . Very good conversation with Father d'Oncieu when he last came by. He admitted to me that in rereading the reviews, he had noted that they were not completely objective. Which delighted me. He is basically in agreement with you and . . . is doing what he can to redress the situation (of which he does not have a clear awareness, moreover) by striving not to be inhumane and by placing confidence in the good will of his subjects, even if they are irrational."

[17] The author made systematic use of the important journal kept by Teilhard from 1915 to 1925, the property of Mlle. Alice Teilhard-Chambon, which was then unknown.

[18] The work was published in 1975: Francis Nemeck, *Teilhard de Chardin et Jean de la Croix* (Paris-Tournai and Montreal: Edition Desclée et C. and Edition Bellarmin), 144 pages. A fair work, without great value.

interest in him. He could no longer be granted the same success as a scandal nor could he be denigrated as strongly. And then, fashions had changed. Certainly Teilhard's basic tendencies, however one judges them, are quite contrary to those reigning today in the so-called "advanced, postconciliar" circles, characterized by a critical, analytical, "pulverizing" mentality, by an empty formalism or by pronounced individualism and anti-intellectualism —and with even greater reason contrary to those tendencies reigning in all the "anti-establishment" stir. It is in no way paradoxical that he liked to call himself "hyper-Catholic". We must also recognize that his problems, thanks in part to him, are already no longer our own. In order to understand certain orientations and emphases of his thought, in order to do justice to what was both most daring and most timely in it, a work of historical reconstruction has become necessary. We must bring to mind again the situation of the religious and conservative world in France around 1900, the interior exile of Catholic society, the theology current at that time, as well as the positivist, determinist and antireligious mentality then dominant. Neither the denigrators nor the admirers of Teilhard ordinarily perceived the historical importance of his effort to establish, in the face of obstacles coming from two antagonist poles, a spiritual interpretation of universal evolution that included the transcendence of man, the value of the personal being, freedom, openness to God, consummation in Christ.

Nevertheless, Teilhard still today has an influence that is not negligible, more in various other countries than in France, and his work will last longer than others that are not judged to be more timely. I was reading recently in *Fragments d'un journal* these lines by Mircea Eliade, written on May 17, 1963: "What a joy to rediscover in a Western theologian, a 'man of science', the optimism of the Rumanian peasants, who were themselves Christians but who belonged to that 'cosmic Christianity' that has long since disappeared in the West. The peasant believes that 'the World is good', that it became so once again after the Incarnation, death and Resurrection of the Savior". That reminds me of the time a few years ago, when, invited to give several lectures in Greek before Orthodox audiences, I began to prepare one on Teilhard and Eastern Christianity, a subject richer than one might believe. More recently, in correcting the proofs of the new edition of *Lettres intimes*, I saw still more clearly, in addition to a rather simplistic hardening here and there in his later years, the greatness of this spiritual figure and the fruitfulness of his principal intuitions. His exchange of memoranda with Maurice Blondel, his long letters of conscience to Auguste Valensin, are of a beauty that will withstand the test of time.[19]

---

[19] On October 19, 1975, a lecture would be given on Teilhard at Notre-Dame de Paris by

Much has been said of Gabriel Marcel's opposition to Teilhard during the course of two meetings of intellectuals in Paris just after the war. Knowing that he had little appreciation for him, I had sent him my book on *La Pensée religieuse*. . . . Now, having bought it himself to read while traveling, he wrote to me from Brême, in April 1962: "I read it with an *emotion* difficult to describe, for at bottom, it was one of remorse. And I am making an act of contrition by writing to you. How upset I am with myself for having stayed on the surface and for having so poorly entered into its essence! When I have the joy of seeing you again, I will tell you something completely mysterious about that. . . ." Other resistance was more stubborn. "The apostolate", wrote Antoine Denat, "must have its true foundation in a certain solitude (that of Teilhard was long and crucifying) and not in the little successes of little journal articles or chatty lectures whose audiences are created and destroyed by fashion. One simply had to be in Maritain's circle in 1925. Then one had to gravitate between fashions that were changing. . . ." I do not quote this text to take a potshot at Maritain, whom I esteem for many reasons; I saw him once again a few years before his death at Toulouse, at the home of the Little Brothers of Jesus; he was already very weak, but his language remained lively, his thought clear, and I experienced the joy of a sincere understanding with him on many essential points; that only makes me all the more sorry that he as well as his friends Charles Journet [6:13] and Dietrich von Hildebrand, instead of discussing the real Teilhard, launched against him impassioned attacks stemming from misinterpretations or, more simply, from a lack of reading. They thereby helped to perpetuate harmful mistakes and lengthened a line of theologians that was not worthy of them. Father d'Ouince, in his excellent work on *Un Prophète en procès* [A prophet in process] (vol. 1, p. 30), believes that "the excessive resistance encountered by Father's vocation was less attributable to the narrowness of mind of a few theologians than to the intellectual and administrative climate then reigning in the Roman Curia". I am not of that opinion. Insofar as one can dissociate the two factors indicated by Father d'Ouince, I believe I can say, in full knowledge of the case, that their order must be reversed with respect to Teilhard and in other similar instances. Most of the superiors responsible, in the Society of Jesus as in the Church herself, without being competent specialists themselves, were prompted by liberal dispositions. Justified or not, according to the case, their restrictive measures were taken only under quasi-imperative and often prolonged pressure from certain theologians (not all of whom were in Rome). Teilhard was aware

---

Etienne Borne: "Teilhard de Chardin et la passion de l'unité" [Teilhard de Chardin and the passion for unity].

of this; he wrote, for example, on August 24, 1950, to his friend Marc Begouën, about "the integrist theologians who are persecuting us at the moment": "They keep us from adoring and loving *deeply*; they would like to keep God from growing in our eyes".[20] I will say even more: in the sense in which the two words "knowledge" and "authority" are used to distinguish (rather improperly) the authority of theologians from that of the Magisterium,[21] it is not rare, it seems to me, for "authority" to have exercised a liberating or "prophetic" role in opposition to "knowledge". From the day theologians, in the Church, became professors, it became difficult for them to be prophets at the same time; they were henceforth prophets only by exception, while their very organization into constituted bodies possessing "knowledge" brought them much rather to resist the great liberating initiatives of which the custodians of "authority" on more than one occasion proved capable.[22] It seems to me that views that are overly Manichean and oppositions that are too clear-cut should be avoided here.

~

When, in 1950, I had to interrupt my courses, I was anticipating a series of classes on Fénelon's writings in mystical theology (little studied up until then) and his doctrine of hope; nothing of any sustained nature was written about it; I sent the essence of it to Father François Varillon, who was able to use it in his very personal works on Fénelon. I would also have liked, in the following years, to conduct a course simultaneously, in fundamental theology and in the history of religions, on Christian mysticism, considered in its relation to natural mysticism, a question I had scarcely broached up until then. During my years in Paris, a sporadic attendance in the courses of Jean Baruzi (College of France)[23] and those of Henri-Charles Puech and Jean Orcibal (Higher Studies) was to keep me in

[20] Cf. our edition of *Lettres intimes*, note to the letter of September 2, 1947. I am not quoting Teilhard here as an indication of my full agreement with his judgment.

[21] Cf. *Un théologien en liberté, Jacques Duquesne interroge le Père Chenu* (Centurion, 1975), I: "What Is a Theologian?"

[22] And it is when "knowledge" demands or usurps "authority" that oppression becomes the heaviest, even if it claims to be exercised in the name of freedom. In addition, passing beyond this inadequate opposition and vocabulary, Father Chenu, p. 195, says very well: "The people of God organized into a hierarchical community is the subject of the Word of God. It is within this ecclesial community that theology is formulated."

[23] With Jean Baruzi, I took the place in some small way of Father de Montcheuil, who had often had discussions with him in an atmosphere of great sympathy and whom he still remembered with emotion.

this project. (Today, the subject would undoubtedly be transformed into a comparative study of faith and religion or would at least take that study as its primary basis.) I had already accumulated a number of notes for that and even written a first part. My years in Paris allowed me time to enlarge the file, thanks to numerous sessions at the national library. But the plan was too ambitious. None of it was carried through to completion. I consider the part I did write, which consisted only of prolegomena, far from satisfactory.[24] Besides, I never succeeded in determining a clear enough outline of the subject; in 1956, I wrote, in order to sum up my position, and it is still my position today:

> I truly believe that for a rather long time the idea for my book on Mysticism has been my inspiration in everything; I form my judgments on the basis of it, it provides me with the means to classify my ideas in proportion to it. But I will not write this book. It is in all ways beyond my physical, intellectual, spiritual strength. I have a clear vision of how it is linked together, I can distinguish and more or less situate the problems that should be treated in it, in their nature and in their order, I see the precise direction in which the solution of each of them should be sought—but I am incapable of formulating that solution. This all is enough to allow me to rule out one by one the views that are not conformed to it, in the works I read or the theories I hear expressed, but all this does not take its final form, the only one that would allow it to exist. The center always eludes me. What I achieve on paper is only preliminary, banalities, peripheral discussions or scholarly details.

Yet, when Father André Ravier asked me for a preface for the collected work he was preparing, which appeared in 1965 under the title *La Mystique et les mystiques*, I summed up in this preface some of the ideas that, according to my original outline, would have been developed in several volumes. In addition, I owe a twofold debt for this preface: one, to Father Louis Bouyer, who gave me a clearer vision of several of the specific traits of Christian mysticism; the other, older and completely fundamental, to Abbé Jules Monchanin. I said a word above about Abbé Monchanin; if I were writing memoirs here, I would have to speak at length about him, for my meeting with him and the friendship that followed were so decisive for me; I am aware of the fact that in our exchanges, it was I who received everything. He died in Paris, at the Saint-Antoine hospital, in October 1957.[25] He had been brought back, dying, from Pondichéry. Abbé Edouard Duperray obtained two precious little volumes of his for

---

[24] So I did not publish any of it. It would give a very false idea of what seemed to me essential in the matter.

[25] See in the Appendix a letter received after his death from Sr. Benedict Duss, O.S.B., prioress of the Regina Laudis monastery (Bethlehem, Connecticut), whom I was to see again twice during my trips to the United States.

us: *De l'esthétique à la mystique* and *Ecrits spirituels*; in 1974, a selection of
his writings relating to India, prepared with perfect competence and care
by Mlle. Suzanne Siauve, was published under the title: *Mystique de l'Inde
et Mystère chrétien* [6:14].[26] After too long a delay, I finally published a very
little volume of memories about him, *Images de l'abbé Monchanin* (1967),
which gave too faint an expression of my admiration and gratitude for this
extraordinary man, this genial priest, who was both a mystic and a saint.
All those who came near him knew concretely what spiritual fruitfulness
means. Dedicated to the priests of his diocese (Lyons), the little work
found scarcely any echo among them.

~

Shortly after his close friends Valensin and Teilhard, Father Victor Fontoynont died at Fourvière, in 1958. I have spoken about him, too, above. I
was asked to say a few words about him the day of his funeral. I reproduce
them here.

> Please allow the one who must speak to you to avoid too personal a remi-
> niscence at this moment. Allow him to be silent as well about the very rich
> and varied gifts that Father Fontoynont had received and which he cultivated
> so well. Of that life, which we saw little by little, so painfully, extinguished
> from his earthly form, we retain this morning only one thing: his essential
> example. Let us revive the memory of it so as to give praise to the Lord.
> —All those acquainted with him know it: that man of so delicate, timid and
> even fearful a nature was a strong man. For he was rooted in faith. That
> humanist, sensitive to all human beauty, was, in the strongest sense, a man
> of God. As wise and lucid as he was intrepid and faithful. . . . Free with that
> freedom that Jesus Christ bought with his blood. A true religious, truly dead
> to himself. All for his brothers because all for God. Let us not say that he was
> dedicated: he was dedication itself, and it was truly the depth of himself that
> was given. No one will ever be able to judge the extent of his action because
> he was too self-forgetful to imprint tangible forms on it. No one will ever
> measure the depth of it, because it was similar to those divine things that no
> one scrutinizes except the Spirit of God. Many could at least bear witness
> to it, I think: insofar as one was close to him and did not deliberately close
> oneself off from his influence, it was impossible to entertain other thoughts
> than thoughts of courage and fidelity. —My God, once again the enemy

[26] Other collections of various notes, which are always penetrating, and of letters should
appear if the present editorial difficulties can be ironed out. He himself published, in collaboration with Dom le Saulx, a Benedictine monk who had come to join him in his final years, a
brochure on their Ashram in both an English and a French edition: "Ermites du Saccidananda";
only the first chapter, the most important, is entirely by him.

Death has visited us. But you have already conquered him, and you already compel him to serve by stripping our earthly affections of anything that would still prevent them from leading us to you. Blessed are you, O God, creator of this universe in the midst of which we so often forget your presence, for having made such marvelous creatures! Blessed are you, Jesus, Son of Mary, for having raised up by your Spirit, from age to age, such pure witnesses of your charity, through which the light that you brought continues to shine! Blessed be the Holy Church of Christ, which never ceases to give birth to Christian generations, Christian families, in which such witnesses arise! —And we will also say, with modesty and without lacking a fair sense of the differences, yes, blessed be the Society of Jesus, which gives us such religious and allows us to call ourselves their brothers (December 8, 1958).

Father Fontoynont, whose *Vocabulaire grec* has a well-deserved reputation, was not able to complete a "Vocabulaire hébraïque", conceived along the same lines and long in preparation. In 1942, under the conditions I have described, he burned the notebooks of a Journal that was a veritable gold mine for religious history as well as a veritable "book of wisdom". He left among his personal papers a parcel of poems I would have liked to publish, but the project ran into several difficulties [6:15]. A little later, one of his disciples, Father Charles Nicolet, died. He had been my companion in the novitiate in 1914, then in philosophy, in "regency" and in theology (1920–1928), a faithful friend and demanding adviser.[27] Without saying too much to me about it, he found me a bit long-winded and would have liked me sometimes to be more biting intellectually. He never wanted to publish anything, although he had written, either for his philosophy courses or for his preaching or for his personal research, pages of great value in a condensed, solid style; but, he said, "one does not formulate the truth: one searches for it and one lives it", or again: "The definitive is foreign to me, one can write only when one has found". One could make a very fine collection of his scattered sentences. It would show in an eminent way what the interior freedom and spiritual demands were in a true Jesuit, in the generation that preceded the Council. I still cannot give up hope of accomplishing it.

---

[27] In 1950, after the encyclical *Humani generis*, he had addressed to our mutual Provincial, Father Décisier, a letter of which he gave me a copy. See the Appendix [6:16].

CHAPTER SEVEN

In these quick notes, I have constantly had to anticipate and mix dates, some of which are confused a little in my memory as well. We must now return to 1960. The death of Pius XII and the accession of John XXIII (which, as is well known, was not greeted with enthusiasm in France)[1] had not made any essential change in my situation, which was already much improved. But the new Pope, with whom I had never had the slightest personal contact, had been unhappy with what had happened at the time of *Humani generis*. He complained to my friend Paulus Lenz-Médoc, who saw him privately in Paris, that he had not been consulted in that affair and that he had not even known about the encyclical except through the newspapers. Anxious to make peace, he wanted to show me his good will. Very shortly after his election, he had a large donation made to the *Sources chrétiennes* series. It was not solely his interest in ecclesiastical history that had prompted him to make this gesture. Father Mondésert thanked him for his donation in a letter that I signed below his signature: then, fifteen days or so later, I received, addressed to me alone, a personal letter of thanks from him for this letter. I did not reply to it for fear of turning to artificialities.

Soon John XXIII made a second gesture, which was to change many things in the orientation of my life and work. In August 1960, passing through the town of Dauphiné where my companion had to stop in order to hear the confessions of some religious, in the parlor where I was waiting for him, I read in that day's issue of *La Croix* the list of theologians chosen by the Pope as consulters to the Preparatory Theological Commission for the Council. My name appeared there as well as that of Father Yves Congar. These were two symbolic names. John XXIII had undoubtedly wanted to make everyone understand that the difficulties that had occurred under the previous pontificate between Rome and the Jesuit and Dominican Orders in France were to be forgotten. (I have not said anything above about the difficulties of the Dominican Order, which are well known from other sources.) They were not, however, forgotten overnight by everyone, and in that commission, which was in operation until the summer of 1962 and which was practically an annex of the Holy

---

[1] When Paulus Lenz-Médoc said to an important ecclesiastical personage in Paris that Cardinal Roncalli had some chance of being elected Pope, the latter was heard to reply: "Don't be funny!"

Office, I in particular gave the impression of being a hostage, sometimes even of being a defendant. It was in the course of those two years that I began to get to know a new genre of literature, the product of a subtle mechanism whose process and vocabulary I had scarcely understood at first and to which I have had to devote myself on various occasions since: that of commission reports and counter-reports, *vota, animadversiones, modi,* and so forth. I was charged, among others, in 1961, with a doctrinal report on the various kinds of knowledge of God, a report that served no purpose, was never discussed and, I have sometimes thought, might well have been intended to serve as a test of my orthodoxy. The chronicle of those two years of the commission would not be lacking in picturesque scenes. There is reason to believe that it will never be written, since most of the participants would not have any desire to transmit the memory of it to posterity. As for me, out of perhaps excessive respect for the oath taken the first day, on our knees between two candles, before Cardinal Ottaviani, I abstained (at least the first year) from taking consistent notes on our meetings. Besides, this is not the place to speak of it[2]—or of the work of the Council during the four following years. For these six years, I wrote down facts and reflections in a series of notebooks that do not form any connected account and do not contain any sensational revelations. With respect to the Preparatory Commission, I will note only two things: the long defense, written and oral, that I made in opposition to the party that was demanding the explicit condemnation of Father Teilhard by the Council and that was making some outrageous misinterpretations of his thought;[3] and another defense, one of my own doctrine, which had also been falsified, the final episode of which was a written threat, addressed to the Secretary of the Commission, to hand in my resignation to the Holy Father, indicating to him the reason for this.[4]

My presence on the Preparatory Commission had brought me almost automatically to the Council in the position of an expert (*peritus*), which allowed me to attend regularly the meetings of the Theological Commission. Six consecutive years of constant stays in Rome brought me many

[2] I did however keep a summary with the title: "Notes sur la Commission théologique préparatoire au Concile Vatican II, 1960–1962" [Notes on the Preparatory Theological Commission for Vatican Council II, 1960–1962].

[3] There was a tragi-comic scene one day, when a Roman member of the Commission, after having paid me all sorts of kind attention while we were enjoying an *espresso* and after having invited me to visit his country, contradicted me fifteen minutes later with so much violence that he seemed ready to jump at my throat or collapse in a fit of apoplexy.

[4] On February 27, 1962, the wind having turned completely in the meantime, I received this little note from Father Sébastien Tromp: "The schema *De Deposito fidei* will not be presented to the Council. There is accordingly no reason to be disturbed about paragraph 22. Otherwise, Father X. would be prepared to change the text."

new acquaintances and several warm friendships. Among the latter, I will mention only those of Msgr. Jorge Medina, then dean of the Theology Faculty of Santiago (Chile), later pro-chancellor of the Catholic University and bishop, with whom I have often since had occasion to collaborate; Msgr. Cathal Daly, an Irishman, then professor of moral theology. Several of the bishops with whom I was able at that time to have personal discussions, whose pastoral experience, theological openness and evangelical spirit I can verify, have become cardinals in the curia, and I can testify that the way in which they are sometimes described in no way corresponds to reality.[5] I will say nearly as much of a totally different personage, whose actions were, I believe, at times harmful and who, even during the Council, pursued me with his hostility: Cardinal Ottaviani. Since I was able to observe him, I admired him in more than one respect. If I may be allowed this little detail, I imagine that the motto on his shield, *semper idem*, about which many ironical comments have been made and some have even been indignant, has nothing to do with doctrinal rigidity: it expresses rather, in my opinion, the disposition of a man of the Church who, reaching the highest responsibilities and the honors that they then include, intends always to remember that he is a humble child of the *Trastevere*.

As the Council continued and since it was possible to perceive as early as 1964 signs of a growing paraconciliar agitation, often far removed from the will of the Fathers, I remember having said to a certain number of them with whom I could speak frankly: "After the Council closes, as soon as you return to your diocese, do not fail to explain at length and at large the results obtained, to take the initiative in the orientations to be promoted; otherwise, you could have difficulties." One of them said to his secretary: "Father de L. is a wise man." This was, I do believe, the only fruit of my interventions [7:1]. The difficulties were not lacking [7:2]. The Yes said wholeheartedly to the Council and to all its legitimate consequences must, in order to remain consistent and sincere, be coupled with a No that is just as resolute to a certain type of exploitation that is in fact a perversion of it [7:3]. I will have occasion to return to this.

Beginning in 1965, meetings of theologians were organized. There was an international congress in Rome, in 1966, where Karl Barth appeared one day. There were others at Notre Dame (Indiana), Chicago, Toronto. I had to give some conferences in Montreal and in various cities in the United States, five times accompanied on these journeys by a very faithful

---

[5] Notably Msgr. John J. Wright, then Bishop of Pittsburgh (USA), a fervent Teilhardian, orthodox head of the American episcopate, with a generous heart and very well-informed about the situation in France. Or Msgr. Seper, then archbishop of Zagreb, a charitable and moderate man, full of good sense.

friend, Father William Russell (who had done his theology at Fourvière), who translated, explained and cared for me. I gave a few lectures at the Theology Faculties of Santiago, where Msgr. Medina had invited me, and in Buenos Aires, thanks to Father Mejía, professor of Holy Scripture and editor of the journal *Criterio*. A little later, there was an ecumenical visit in Greece; the two Theology Faculties of Athens and Thessalonica wanted to hear me speak on the Fathers of the Church and on the Catholic point of view on ecumenism; I remember even better the days spent on Crete with the Orthodox bishops of three dioceses whose guest I was: without any need for long discourses, they introduced me to an open, apostolic orthodoxy anxious for adaptation to all social demands and for a fully ecumenical spirit.[6]

In the two Secretariates created by Paul VI, one for "unbelievers" and the other for "non-Christians", of which I was a part until 1974, I never had much work to do: a few meetings, a few exchanges, some report or other,[7] some preliminary debates as well. I will not speak of my initial participation in the French section of the Secretariate for "unbelievers", which went its own independent way and from which I found myself quickly eliminated *de facto*. In an international meeting held in Vienna, whose theme was the examination of the great current fact of "secularization", I made a speech in which I distinguished a number of things that were often confused: the secular view of the Cosmos coming from positive science; the secularization of human societies beginning with periods in which the Church had had to take upon herself the great tasks of civilization, and so on; and finally the enterprises of secularization even from within the Church. This speech elicited no response and was not mentioned in the summary of the meeting; it became clear to me that the most influential organizers, under the pretext of a historico-sociological analysis, were pursuing a practical end; I myself saw in it the pursuit of an illusion and the seed of a denaturation of the Church. Another congress was held in Rome, for a meeting with important sociologists coming from nearly everywhere, particularly from the United States; there was a generous hospitality and a papal audience; the reports from the sociologists

---

[6] Another trip, occasioned by the commemorative celebrations at the University of Innsbruck, allowed me to meet the exegete H. Schlier, whom the study of the origins of Christianity had led from Lutheranism to the Catholic Church. A stay in Poland, organized by Cardinal Wojtyla, was at the last moment prevented by illness.

One memory of a conversation with an Orthodox archbishop; it can be summed up in three points: 1. It is absolutely necessary that union be achieved. 2. It is quite obvious that this can be achieved only around the Pope of Rome. 3. We are disconcerted at seeing that he is contested today from within Catholicism itself: that can only delay unity.

[7] I have discovered and give here in the Appendix [7:4] a copy of an opinion that was requested of me about a preparatory text for the 1967 Synod.

on the religious fact seemed to me in general rather flat, without much of any understanding of what Christianity represents either in history or in the present world; the rare Catholics who spoke seemed to concentrate their effort on showing that they too were capable of similar sociological work, not on explaining in the least the place that they recognized as belonging to sociology in religious studies nor, for even greater reason, how the understanding of the Christian faith differs from sociological analysis. In other words, there was a friendly reception but no real beginning of dialogue. Except for this rather unencouraging attempt, I had the impression that the concern for the world of unbelief, which had provoked the creation by Paul VI, had very quickly become, on the part of most, a concern for encounter, mixed with politics and diplomacy, with the Marxist world, favoring even on the part of a certain number an effort toward carrying Marxism into the Church. A plenary session of the Secretariate, held in Rome, confirmed this impression. —As for the Secretariate for Non-Christians, whose start was more modest and whose activity was a bit slow at first, it seems to me that it provided more serious work. It had a little difficulty in defining its role with relation to the Congregation for the evangelization of peoples: it had neither to encroach on it nor to risk disqualifying its work, although a false interpretation of the conciliar decree on religious freedom, stemming in certain circles from a weakening of the evangelical spirit, was already tending to discourage the missionary impulse. This danger seems to me to have been overcome, and several sections of the renewed Secretariate are in full swing.

One problem remains that has not yet been fully resolved, that of the necessary coherence of thought that should be assured between the two Secretariates. I posed this problem several times, in an intentionally paradoxical and provocative way, in order to draw more attention to it. With the non-Christians, I said, the Church says she wants a mutual understanding in a common exaltation of the eternal religious fact, in an active cooperation of all the religions in view of a better future; with the unbelievers, she seems to want a mutual understanding for a peaceful coexistence in a world finally become integrally secular, after having united with atheism in freeing man from a religious past that restrains his forward progress, in the name of a pure "faith" that is itself freed from its religious straitjacket. Of course, I was thereby pushing to the extreme the two opposite tendencies, I was expressing in the form of theoretical contradiction a confused situation whose twofold empiricism could, in practice, be accommodated at least for a time. But were the two extremities that I put forward not already in actual fact set in some minds? Many signs seemed to indicate this to me. —Here as everywhere, the Catholic spirit, which is a spirit of synthesis, must overcome the oppositions, but no more than in any other domain will this be achieved in an instant, without lucidity and without effort.[8]

~

Several little books came in large part out of the trips, congresses and discussions I have just mentioned. *Paradoxe et mystère de l'Eglise* [Paradox and mystery of the Church] (1967) contains two texts, whose subject had been dictated to me, coming from the International Theological Congress organized in March 1966 by the American University of Notre Dame, another text read at the Rome Congress of September 1966 (where I created a bit of a scandal, at least among the organizers, by expressing myself in French—but there was a Latin summary!) and various articles that had appeared in different places. *Athéisme et sens de l'homme* [Atheism and the meaning of man] (1968) develops a report given in Chicago: it was Fathers Bernard Bro and F. Refoulé, editors of Editions du Cerf, who requested it; I tried to include there in summary fashion a kind of follow-up to *Drame de l'humanisme athée* as well as an adaptation of my writings on the supernatural to the present problem of the relation between the earthly future and eternal salvation, in the perspective of *Gaudium et spes* and the Teilhardian vision; I gave it the subtitle: "Une double requête de *Gaudium et spes*" [A twofold appeal to *Gaudium et spes*]. The Council was wisely content to give this subject some general guidance; any attempt at overly specific theorization would have been premature, and it would have included too many elements drawn from human observation and judgment not to be debated *ad infinitum*. I nevertheless believe that if the authors had been better acquainted with the thought of Father Teilhard, they would have drawn from him some more solid distinctions, capable of averting with greater decisiveness certain aberrant musings, contrary to the Council as well as to all Christian tradition, which are making headway today. The theme that has come to the fore since then with respect to the "liberation of man" and "salvation in Jesus Christ" could also, it seems to me, find new clarity in the principles recalled by this little book, clarity that would displace or relativize somewhat the accepted facts such as many propose them. An address to the Congress in Toronto furnished the outline of *Teilhard et notre temps* [Teilhard and our time], published sep-

---

[8] For five years, I was also part of the International Theological Commission; at the end of three years, when it became too difficult for me to work in it actively, I offered my resignation in writing; on behalf of Paul VI, I was asked to be patient until the five-year renewal in 1974. —The French episcopate has always shown reticence in regard to this Commission, which it qualifies (= disqualifies) as "Roman".

arately in a little volume (1970) after having been placed in an appendix to *l'Eternel féminin* (1968); as I warned the reader, it is not a study of what is most original or singular in Teilhard's thought; in it, I drew attention to his most basic convictions and his most fundamental behavior, which he consistently maintained, preferring them for sound reasons to his own particular research and individual temperament; it had seemed useful to me to collect his major teachings, expressed in some very beautiful texts, concerning faith in God, love of Christ, obedience to the Church, esteem for the tradition of the Church. America was also responsible for *l'Ecriture dans la tradition* [Scripture in tradition] (1966), a book that provided nothing new, composed solely of excerpts from *Histoire et Esprit* and *Exégèse médiévale*. It was requested by a New Yorker, who was editing a series more or less patronized at the beginning by Maritain (she went into raptures, eyes raised to the heavens, at the very name of "Jack"). When the project was sent to her, a little behind schedule, she no longer wanted it: the wind seemed to her to have changed, and she preferred to devote herself to religious syncretism. Madame Gabail, who since 1960 had succeeded her father, the publisher Fernand Aubier, then wanted to publish the volume in French; two letters from Father Vincent, from Jerusalem, were added to it in an appendix. I do not think it had much success. Nevertheless, another American publisher did a translation of it. How astonished I was to read as its title on the cover: "The Sources of Revelation" (1968)! I, who had fought against the famous theory of the "two sources"! Was it the blunder of an ignorant publisher? or perhaps (though I scarcely believe so) the deed of some malicious intention?

Editions du Cerf had undertaken the publication of a copious commentary, of rather loose proportions, of all the texts of Vatican II. Father Dupuy, O.P., charged with the two volumes concerning *Dei verbum*, asked me to comment on the introduction and the first chapter. I felt rather well equipped for this task, I liked the text, I was personally interested in the vicissitudes of its elaboration. When I had finished my work, I had it reviewed by Father Pieter Frans Smulders, S.J., from Holland, who along with Dr. Joseph Ratzinger had been one of the principal authors of this chapter. The work appeared in 1968. In 1973, Father Refoulé wanted to use the main part of my contribution in a little volume of "Foi vivante"; to make it more accessible, he proposed that I leave out all the annotation (which was very abundant and intended principally to show the traditional character of *Dei verbum*), all the historical developments about the working out of the text (necessary for a complete understanding of it), and finally all the passages deemed too technical. I ended by agreeing to his plan, leaving the task of carrying out this threefold surgical intervention up to him. I only had to make a few sutures and to inform the eventual reader that he should refer to the complete edition if he wanted to obtain a slightly deeper knowledge of the text concerned. The little volume appeared in 1974, under a title chosen by the publisher: *Dieu se dit dans l'histoire* [God expresses himself in history]. (By a mistake, provoked perhaps unconsciously by the widespread theories of "permanent revelation" invoking "the signs of the times", the title was sometimes quoted as: "Dieu se *lit* dans l'histoire" [God is read in history].)

In 1965 two volumes appeared, though they were ready long before that, both of the same height and nearly the same width, which I call my two twins. (I should have put them together under one title, as Balthasar did in his translation.) One, *Le Mystère du surnaturel*, develops point by point, in the same order and without changing the least point of doctrine [7:5], the article published under that title in *Recherches* in 1949; in 1960, as all hope of publishing in France still seemed fanciful, my old friend and colleague Gerard Smith, of Marquette University (Milwaukee), and Dr. Pegis, director of the Institut d'études médiévales in Toronto, had offered to publish it in America: they took charge of everything: translation, printing, publishing; that is why the book is dedicated to Father Smith. The second, *Augustinisme et théologie moderne*, reproduced with similar fidelity the first part of the old *Surnaturel*, enlarging it with new texts. Sending these two books at the same time to Etienne Gilson earned me three successive letters from him, which seem worth reproducing because of their vividness as well as for their doctrine; they might also constitute a useful contribution to the history of Thomism in the twentieth century:[9]

June 19, 1965. . . . You are right to insist on the natural vocation of the intellect to a vision of God of which it is naturally incapable. Your Thomistic texts are conclusive, but I don't even know whether people are conscious of the centrality of the problem. I recently heard an eminent Dominican theologian publicly state his admiration for the notion of obediential potency, so appropriate for settling the argument. But I do not believe Saint Thomas ever spoke of obediential potency in this context. The beatific vision is *supernatural*, but it is not a *miracle*! But then, I am carrying coals to Newcastle. . . . [From Paris.]

June 20, 1965. [From Vermenton, Yonne.] A belated, but providential, inspiration made me add the first volume to my baggage at the last minute. I have done nothing but read it—all the way from Paris to Vermenton and, once I got here, all the rest of the day and a good part of the night. How could I have remained insensitive to this whole first part of the old edition of

Surnaturel? In the first place, I have never had a copy of my own, and it has become impossible to find; then, too, the unbearable Baius, so prominent at the beginning, put me off (he'll put others off too and I am not sure that he is in the right place). Finally and above all, my abysmal ignorance of post-medieval theology, which causes me untold misery (I've never even *seen* a volume of Soto), makes it hard for me to follow a guide, even one as wise and careful as you, through such extremely subtle arguments. It is like trying to picture, with the help of a guidebook, a country one has never seen.

This time, I think I am almost there, and I owe you my deepest gratitude for that. I think volume 2 will be easy for me, since I am already familiar with it. I agree completely with you on the root of the problem. Besides, you call my attention to some texts I didn't know about, or whose importance perhaps escaped me when I first read *Surnaturel* (in the well-thumbed copy belonging to the Montreal Dominicans). I would have taken them into consideration if I had known about them when I wrote the little essay you were kind enough to quote. The short quotation from Saint Thomas, III, 9, 2, which I considered conclusive, was already in your book, p. 243, note 4. I do not think either of us has ever found a set of terms adequate to define the Thomist position, and that is quite to be expected, since he himself could not find one either. In fact, his terminology is extremely free, for he never misses an expression if it is possible to justify it *in some sense*. Obediential potency is an instructive example. He came upon the term ready-made; strictly speaking, it is applicable only to miracles, where nothing in matter either prepares for, expects, or makes the phenomenon possible; in general (your excellent quotes on page 244), all nature is in a state of obediential potency to whatever it may please God to do with it, provided that this is not, in itself, contradictory or impossible. You are right to say that in the case of the beatific vision, one could not say that the human soul might be, in that respect, in a state of *potentia obedientiaetantum*, but I do not know of a text where it would be expressed that way, nor even whether he spoke in this regard of *potentia obedientiae* in any sense at all. Why? Because his whole purpose was to make it clear that the word *obedience* is a poor way of expressing the relationship of nature to grace. A creature made in the image of God does not have to "obey" in order to want to grow in likeness to its model; no doubt it is obedient, but it obeys the same way we obey an order that coincides exactly with our own dearest wish. Nobody will ever be able to capture in one sentence the synchronous, but not in the same respect, natural and supernatural character of this natural desire to see God. . . .

June 21, 1965. [From Vermenton, Yonne.] *Le Mystère du surnaturel*, which I have just devoured, is absolutely perfect. I really have the impression, not that the question is closed, because people always have to muddle everything up, but that it ought to be. You have said all that can be said, particularly the very important counsel that one must be silent in the end. It truly is a mystery that is at issue here. Your pages 179–183, not to mention others, are cast in the mold of the most reliable Thomistic thought including, which is so important, Saint Thomas' manner of speaking. Others (those who are not of the breed of masters like Augustine and Bonaventure, for example) take theology as their object, while Thomas, Augustine and all the great ones take for their subject the One theology is all about, created reality seen in the light of divine revelation and God himself before everything else. This is why every theology worthy of the name ends by stopping, not short, but stumbling and groping before the essential ineffability of God. Saint Thomas possessed this sense of mystery in the highest degree, but since he was, at the same time, imbued with boundless admiration for the intellect—the two great wonders are the existence of being and knowledge—he often sets us to grappling with positions that consist in defining exactly the intelligible shape of a mystery whose complete philosophical elucidation is impossible.

It seems to me that Cajetan is done for. Very soon we will be called upon to defend him, and you have already started. I am fully aware that sometimes I go too far in my remarks, but after due reflection and in all objectivity, I think I would still label it a *corruptorium*. For two reasons. His commentary on the first article of the *Summa Theologiae* gets the whole book on the wrong track from the very outset; then, professing to interpret the meaning of the work, he misleads Saint Thomas' readers. It took me years to figure that out. When I finally did and said something about it, fearfully, as if it were something new, I was astonished that I got no reaction at all. I did not know that everybody already knew this but wanted to keep the *skeleton in the closet*! Thanks to you, I get the picture. But Bañez (whom you do not like very much) is practically unobtainable; Soto, and that Tolet whom I knew about only through his commentary on Aristotle, are entirely so; and the sand is running low in the hourglass.

You made me very happy by remembering me to C. A. Pegis and Father G. Smith, from Marquette. Pegis, a one-hundred-percent Greek, born Orthodox, converted by his Jesuit teachers, especially the Rev. J. F. McCormick, is a close friend of Father Smith, who was one of my first students at the Toronto Institute. I assigned him a paper on some point or other from Saint Bonaventure; I was getting ready to give a mark to a student; but as soon as he began, I put aside my pen and paper to listen, spellbound. When he was ready to write a thesis, I asked him to do one on Molina, so I could be clear in my own mind on that subject. He did an excellent job, which, despite our entreaties, his Superiors never permitted him to publish.

You have revealed to me a side of the Rev. Father Carlo Boyer I was not acquainted with, and right at the moment when I had been making an effort, if not superhuman, at least super-Gilsonian, to like him. At the last Thomist Congress but one (in any case the last one I attended, under the authority of Father Garrigou and the permanent censorship of Father Boyer), our Carlo took Pegis aside to explain to him *all* the passages in *Humani generis* that he assured him were directed against you. "How do you know that?" asked Pegis. C. B. replied that everyone in Rome knew that. "But," Pegis persisted, "someone in authority must have told you this: who was it?" The Reverend

Father remained silent. I am telling you these things because it seems to me that with books like yours we are beginning to come out into the open, where *unimaginable* propositions, like Father Boyer's, p. 62, note 1, can no longer be formulated.

I certainly would not dare write what I nevertheless think: that all this, Boyer included, is a sequel, or simply a manifestation, of the philosophism endemic to the Church from the beginning but which has taken up permanent residence in Scholasticism since the thirteenth century. For every Saint Thomas and a few others like him, who magnificently destroyed the obstacle, or even hoisted and boosted themselves over it, there have been hundreds of low-flying "rationalists" who foundered on it. Father Boyer asked me one day for an article for an issue of *Doctor communis* (no relation to the *Universal Doctor!!*), and proposed, among other possible subjects, the following two: (1) *Philosophia fundamentalis necessaria ad salutem*; (2) *Doctrina S. Thomae Aquinatis in omnibus sequenda*. My answer to him, more or less, was that the two propositions were contradictory. I tried to say it tactfully in an article, but I am not sure he understood.

This is what is frightening: orthodoxy in the hands of her destroyers. The tragedy of modernism was that the rotten theology promulgated by its opponents was in large part responsible for its errors. Modernism was wrong, but its repression was undertaken by men who were also wrong, whose pseudo-theology made a modernist reaction inevitable.

I see redemption only in a Thomist theology as you perceive it, in the company of Saint Augustine, Saint Bonaventure and the great theologians of the East: they are all welcome because, despite unavoidable *philosophical* differences, they all try to draw an *intellectus* from the same Faith. I wish I could unreservedly include Duns Scotus (to please my friend Father Balic), and I do include him, certainly! but with one reservation: he taught that the object of *our* theology, for us men, is not God, but the *ens infinitum*. . . . And he seems to me to make the vision of God into the object of a *potentia naturalis* with no mystery to it, instead of the way it is with Saint Thomas, for whom the whole of the divine mystery is already present in the very nature of the intellect. There are but three "intellectual" beings: God, Angel and Man. This is why the creation of *Man-intellect-image* makes sense only within the framework of the master-plan of creation. Of course God could have created man without raising him to the beatific vision! The real mystery, for me, is not that there are the Elect; but that there are not only the Elect. . . .

The preceding year, I no longer recall the occasion,[10] Gilson had written the following letter to me from Toronto (April 1, 1964), which I quote also because of its vividness:

[10] Yes. Etienne Gilson had just published a very warm article about me in *La Croix*. Reproduced in *Lettres*. This note corrects p. 55, note 1, of the *Lettres* [p. 70, note 1, of the English edition].

I was blessed, literally, to be able to express my friendship with you publicly. I have never read anything of yours without feeling I am in a friendly atmosphere. I think minds behave like cats: they sniff noses for a second and know immediately if God has disposed them to friendship or to enmity. I recently experienced this again in Montreal. I spent a week with the Dominican Fathers, giving four lectures on *The Spirit of Thomism*. The second one had to do with "The Master-Plan of Creation" (a rather showy title for publicity's sake), and for that occasion I planned to reread *Surnaturel*. I could only say you were right, because what you say is true. *No doubt is possible on this subject.* I am going to say the same thing again in two weeks' time at the 175th centenary [*sic*] of Georgetown University, S.J., in Washington. I don't think it will provoke a scandal. Your credentials as a theologian are the highest, but you are also a humanist in the great tradition of humanist theologians. The latter do not care much for the Scholastics and the Scholastics generally detest them. Why? It is partly, I suppose, because Scholastics understand only propositions that are simple and unequivocal, or that seem to be so. You are more interested in the truth that the proposition is intended to express and that always eludes it to some extent. When the Scholastics do not understand it well, they get nervous, and since they cannot be sure that what is eluding them is not false, they condemn it on principle because it is *safer*. Your priceless pearl brings me to my point.[11] In my third lecture for Georgetown, I wrote the following: "Thomas Aquinas was not a particularly safe Thomist; rather than safe, he preferred to be right, which is not the same thing. The safe Thomist prefers not to say the whole truth if to assert it unqualifiedly risks misleading his readers. Thomas proceeds differently. Having first made sure of the truth, he states it as forcibly as possible; after all, if his meaning is clear, those who misinterpret it are responsible for their own errors." Your theologian's ghastly comment is a perfect witness to the indifference of so many pious souls to the meaning of the word truth. There is some Father Boyer in that (I don't like everybody). . . . When I quote them Saint Thomas on the Faith, they accuse me of fideism. No! Not of fideism, but of "leaning dangerously toward fideism". I never respond to them. My great strength, alas! is that I am not a priest. Had Maritain and I been monks or priests, neither of us would have been able to write the hundredth part of what we have written. We would have been, as they say, *crucified*. But I have nothing to teach you on that score, have I? Nonetheless, there will have to be a new edition of *Surnaturel*.

It is snowing here today and I am thinking of you in that marvelous town of Aix, near Pernes-les-Fontaines, where people really understand the art of living. I am happy you are there. Please don't worry any more than you have to about the opinions of those who have so much trouble thinking. I know they do some harm, but as I once said to a monk-friend of mine: it would be

---

[11] I do not see what he is alluding to here. —Yes, it referred to some words plucked from the lips of a theologian in Rome: "*Ea quae dicit Excellentia vestra sunt quidem verissima, sed prorsus periculosa*" [What you said, your Reverence, is all too true but certainly dangerous].

only too lovely to be a monk, if only the Church didn't take it upon herself to make you do a little penance for the privilege. . . .

I had at first had the intention (twelve or fifteen years earlier) of preparing a new edition of *Surnaturel*, as Gilson was still proposing in 1964, and for that new edition I had written the following foreword:

> The appeal contained in the last lines of this foreword[12] has been widely understood. Among the numerous studies occasioned by our work or treating related subjects since its appearance, a notable proportion furnish truly positive elements. Several are important. This second edition attempts to take them into consideration. Some unpublished texts have appeared, notably by Fathers Gauthier and Gillon, O.P.; by Father Renwart, S.J.; by Abbé Philippe Delhaye. Memoires such as those of Father Henri Rondet, S.J., Father Antoninus Finili, O.P., and Father Smulders, S.J., have clarified some points that were still obscure. The recent work by Etienne Gilson on *l'Etre et l'essence*, by explaining the evolution of traditional philosophy in the West, cannot fail to make the parallel evolution in theology better understood. The discussion instituted by Father Gerard Smith, S.J., and Anton C. Pegis, President of the Institut pontifical d'études médiévales in Toronto, at the Congress of American Catholic philosophers held in Boston in April 1949, also seemed very instructive. The serious but polite objections addressed to us by Father L. Malevez, S.J., Father Philippe de la Trinité, O.C.D., and several others gave us profitable food for reflection. Other studies, perhaps of too polemical a purpose to help much in probing deeper into the subject, are nonetheless invaluable because of the numerous texts they cite and comment upon: such as the articles by Father Gagnebet, O.P., on the natural love of God in Saint Thomas. . . . Many criticisms formulated at the beginning from the point of view of history seem already to have disappeared on their own, as the judgment of specialists as qualified as Dom M. Cappuyns, O.S.B., Canon G. Philips and Anton C. Pegis advise us to believe. Some sprang from obvious confusion. We nonetheless did not want to overlook all of them, as the reader will see. As for criticisms on the doctrinal level, they would have affected us more if it had not been clear in more than one instance that they were addressed to ideas that are in no way ours. We are grateful to theologians such as Msgr. Bruno de Solages and Father Victor White, O.P., for having ascertained and declared this without ambiguity. On other points, the favorable judgment of eminent reviewers as well as that of numerous other theologians, approving even when they do not themselves hold all the positions that were not taken without due consideration, is enough to reassure us. We must add, finally, that the "traditional interpretation" of Saint Thomas, in the name of which some have reproached us for introducing a "new theology", is today held by no serious historian of Thomistic thought, while what was

---

[12] The end of that foreword: ". . .We cite here only a few studies, monographs on a very limited subject, which might help to prepare [the theology of the supernatural], if they are succeeded, completed, corrected perhaps by many others."

declared new is recognized by a certain number of these historians as the authentic thought of Saint Thomas. Surprise has been expressed in various quarters that we did not reply to such accusations. To explain our silence, allow us to borrow these few lines from Dominic de Soto: ". . . Enimvero vix iniri potest concertatio ulla, ubi stylus ipse contradicendi non aliquid pariat vel amaritudinis, vel saltem asperitatis; quae, ut ab ingenio christiano procul esse debet, ita meo certe est ingratissima." [One can hardly engage in any controversy where the language used does not itself breed contradiction or bitterness or at least some lack of courtesy. These are far from Christian attitudes, and I certainly find them unpleasant.]

Yet, if there were misunderstandings, it is possible that this was not unrelated to the style of publication we chose. It was not without some awkwardness. "Historical studies" were followed by a "conclusion" of a different character. It had in fact seemed to us—and good judges had thought the same—that the clear orientation of these studies and the consequences that had to follow, in the eyes of any reader sensitive to the argument of tradition as well as to the rational problems, were evoked in at least several pages where it would be shown how, if one rejected the modern idea of "pure nature", one could do so without falling into the idea of an exigency of the supernatural. Precisely at this point, as experience has shown, there was undoubtedly too much, or too little. For some thought it possible to believe that we had wanted to present in brief a whole system, a "new system", and, as they did not find it in our text, they sometimes imagined they could. This is what led us to give, in *Recherches de science religieuse*, several complementary explanations, which have been received on the whole favorably enough to encourage us to reproduce their main points at the end of this second edition.

Despite the care we have exercised in preparing it, we know that this second edition is still far from perfect. Various monographs would be necessary to complete it. On the other hand, even when there is agreement about history, or about a part of history, everyone will not agree with all our value judgments. But we are not that ambitious! Besides, as much as we believe in doctrine, we attach only a relative importance to many of the theories. This work, once again, does not propose anything new. Through a still-incomplete examination of tradition, considered from various, overlapping slants, it attempts merely to show what little value and in-depth interest there is in one modern theory, which has besides the disgrace of being, as it were, the symbol of a separated theology—of a separated Christianity—and the error of constituting an obstacle to any slightly sustained effort of Christian thought. If, subsequently, many of the problems are still posed, we do not claim to resolve them. We do not have an answer for everything. It is enough for us to be placed, as we believe we are, at the authentic axis of Tradition. Others, if need be, will enlarge or straighten out the bed of the great river of tradition: we have wished only to clear the way.[13]

---

[13] I undoubtedly should have made the observation, either in this new preface or after 1950, in a more explicit way that Orthodox theology never made use of the modern Western

It did not take me long to see that such a plan for a new edition of *Surnaturel* was fanciful. Nevertheless, following a practice I had long before adopted and which I always maintained for each of my books, I continued, according to circumstances, to enlarge the file of what had already been published. This is what had allowed me to publish my supernatural "twins", in that year of 1965, since the times had become more lenient toward me. I had even intended doing two other books, prepared by the same method, with the two following parts of *Surnaturel*: "Esprit et liberté dans la tradition théologie" and "Histoire du mot surnaturel". There was no lack of documents: I was beginning to have almost an overabundance of them. But I had to recognize rather quickly that the latter one of these studies would not be definitive and would provide nothing substantially new. As for the former, I was at first more inclined toward it, because it seemed to me to be, along with *Corpus mysticum*, one of the rare things of rather formal construction that might come from my pen, and because what was at stake is (or was) important, as I have said above (II). But I lacked the time for finishing this reworking—and then, I had the feeling that it was superfluous to insist on a point that was already settled.[14] Two signs, among others, were given to me of this. The *Archives de philosophie* of 1964 (January–March) contained a long paper by Father S. Dockx, O.P., "Du désir naturel de voir l'essence divine d'après saint Thomas" [On the natural desire to see the divine essence according to Saint Thomas], a very scholarly paper that justified entirely the positions of *Surnaturel* and which did not, to my knowledge, arouse the least objection. On the other hand, the *Bulletin de théologie ancienne et médiévale*, reviewing the two new published volumes in an almost annoyed tone, was surprised to find me returning again to a question that had already been sufficiently clarified and that, besides, did not offer in itself any further interest. The notice thereby given was all the more significant as this review came, if I am not mistaken, from the same author who, in the same Bulletin, had in 1947 upheld integrally and with some warmth the cause of *Surnaturel*.[15] I therefore judged it more worthwhile to occupy myself with something else [7:7].

A part of my time, after *Catholicisme*, was thus spent gathering material for new corrected and enlarged editions, but most of these projects were not carried out—ordinarily for the simple reason that the first edition sold

---

theory of "pure nature", that it always ignored or rejected it—and that this never constituted the least obstacle in the search for Unity. See in the Appendix [7:6] the review given of my "twins" of 1965 by Father Xavier Tilliette.

[14] *Mystère du surnaturel*, however, includes a preface destined to show the still current and even urgent interest of the question treated, in an endlessly renewed problematic [7:8].

[15] Dom M. Cappuyns, O.S.B., *Bulletin*, 5:724 (October 1947), 251–54 [7:9].

too slowly. On the other hand, time rushes by at an accelerated speed, carrying along the life of the Church; in the desire to perfect a work too hastily done at first, one lingers uselessly on the bank. . . .

Another work from the sixties grew out of a fraternal discussion with a group of youth chaplains initiated in Chantilly by Father Blaise Arminjon in 1959 or 1960: this was *La Foi chrétienne, essai sur la structure du symbole des apôtres* [English translation: *The Christian Faith: An essay on the structure of the Apostles' Creed* (San Francisco: Ignatius Press, 1986)], which had two editions (1969 and 1970). The numerous observations that I had occasion to make, during the years 1945–1960, of the "spiritual depression" (Karl Barth) that followed the Second World War made me diagnose a crisis of faith, less by the clash of adverse thoughts or the aberration of a few superior minds than by a slow loss of consciousness, by a shift of interest, indeed, by the deep-seated disgust with the supernatural reality, which can transform the entire being, brought to the world by Christ and spread by the Church. The distribution of a certain anti-intellectual program in Catholic Action, which was already debilitated, was to make young people even more vulnerable. But when I explained these things, each of my listeners seemed to have but one idea: to defend the purity of his flock; each replied to my diagnosis, without looking any farther: "My little ones are very good". None perceived within his radius of action the least cause for uneasiness with respect to the quality of the evangelical spirit, the soundness of the Christian faith, the perfect loyalty toward the institution of the Church in the soul of French Catholics. —How, in retrospect, can we be surprised to see a dozen years later, in the midst of the storm, a highly placed archbishop, without any doubt full of good sense as well as good will, declare publicly with assurance: one is not right to speak today in the Church of our country about a crisis of faith? —As far as my interlocutors were concerned, everything was going along famously. . . . This lack of awareness was painful for me. The Council made me hope at first for a reawakening. Within certain limits, even though it was often misunderstood, it was efficacious, and the generations to come will perhaps see the ripening of many fruits that are as yet unsuspected. But on the whole, it did not at all succeed in stopping that spiritual depression of which Barth spoke and whose destructive consequences are unfolding before our eyes.

La Foi chrétienne makes few if any allusions to this. The young Father Michel Sales, then a theologian at Fourvière, helped me by his remarks to clarify the text and suggested that I place at the beginning an "outline" that would facilitate reading. Drafting the book was a slow process, which allowed me to introduce, in the first edition and even more in the second, several developments adapted to the theological situation in the postconciliar period, for example on faith and religion, on the idea of "functional" revelation and again on the process of elaboration of dogmatic formulas. One of the reviewers observed that the "point" of the book was difficult to see. This was because there was in fact no point; as mediocre as the result of my efforts may have been, I had sought, in each subject approached, to respect the two aspects of reality, which are too often opposed, by uniting them, persuaded as always that such an effort toward synthesis is the proper one for the Catholic mind. A free summary of *La Foi chrétienne* appeared in January 1975 in the German edition of the journal *Communio*.

Again in 1969, Editions du Cerf published a little booklet on *l'Eglise dans la crise actuelle* [The Church in the present crisis] (and not on "the crisis of the Church"). The *Nouvelle revue théologique* had at first published it as an article, thanks to its editor, Father Matagne. It was the amplified text of a conference given at the University of Saint Louis (Missouri) [7:10]. Given the advanced state of the crisis, perhaps I made an error in publishing so brief and summary a text, which rather assumed the tone of a manifesto instead of patiently examining a single, well-chosen point in order to throw light on it. Yet how can one react effectively to a state of mind that penetrates all sectors of thought, that brings everything into question at once, on principle and on every level, without anything being really studied and discussed?[16]

Next, in 1972, came another little volume in Aubier's white series, which for some time took the title "Intelligence de la foi" [Understanding of the faith]. This was *Les Eglises particulières dans l'Eglise universelle* [English translation: "Particular Churches in the Universal Church", in: *The Motherhood of the Church* (San Francisco, Ignatius Press, 1982)]. Again, a work rising out of the Council and the postconciliar period. The precise occasion was quite fortuitous. Msgr. Pignedoli, then secretary of the "Propaganda" (a Cardinal today), had addressed a circular to various theologians, asking them how they understood the relations between Rome and the local churches in mission lands. They had to draw up a "synthesis report" from the collection of responses. As for what concerned the application to missionary territories, I declined to give an opinion; but they wanted to print in the files of the Propaganda ("Euntes docete") the statement of doctrinal principles that I had thought it impossible to deny. I then had the idea of developing this text. I also used a conference given a little earlier on the San Giorgio Island in Venice, under the auspices of the

---

[16] In this same booklet, I was imprudent through omission, by recalling the necessary love of Jesus Christ without specifying that Jesus was the Way to the Father: I was still so little aware of the "Christian atheists" and "Jesusism" that were beginning to flourish. It has since then been necessary to specify that "christological concentration" was in no way "christological reduction" leading to "anthropological reduction"! Later I would have to specify still further, in the opposite sense, that "christocentricity" is not necessarily an exclusion of the Holy Spirit.

Benedictine Monastery on the island and of the Fondation Chigi, on "La Maternité de l'Eglise" [The Motherhood of the Church] [7:11]. It seemed to me that these two texts complemented each other well enough to be printed together. Msgr. Poupard, from the Secretariate of State, wanted to review my manuscript. Before the book was published, a summary of its first part was given at a conference in Rome, in October 1971, to the Saint-Louis-des-Français circle. The date by chance corresponded with the last, very unsettled days of an episcopal synod, and the subject was, as they say, "in the air", so much so that this conference created quite a stir. Vigorously attacked by some (as early as the next day, in *La Croix*), warmly approved by others, it appeared in a little booklet from Editions de la "Civiltà cattolica", after having been reproduced nearly *in extenso* by *l'Osservatore romano* (only one paragraph, of minor importance, on the method of electing popes, was left out). Various journals, in various languages, then took it up; there was even an edition of it in Zaire.

In writing *Les Eglises particulières*, I approached directly for the first time the subject of institutions. In addition to the circumstances of which I have just spoken, the present situation impelled me to do so. I explained this in the introduction by saying:

> I do not believe that problems of structure are in themselves the most important. *I do not believe that structural reforms, about which there has been much debate for some years, are ever the main part of a program that must aim at the only true renewal, spiritual renewal.* I even fear that the present-day inflation of such projects and discussions furnishes an all-too-convenient alibi to avoid it. The conciliar formula "*Ecclesia semper purificanda*" seems to me as to others "much superior to the '*Ecclesia semper reformanda*' which is used so extensively nearly everywhere" (J.J. von Allmen). But *I do believe, on the other hand, that any disturbance, any change, or any relaxation of the essential structure of the Church would suffice to endanger all spiritual renewal.*

There had long since been no need of such texts to make me lose my reputation in anti-establishment or simply so-called "progressivist" (a very equivocal term) circles; but the work surely withdrew from me what remained of the confidence of a certain number of theologians I esteem as well as the hearing I might still have been able to obtain with a certain number of bishops. I was trying to restore there the true idea of episcopal collegiality, traditional and conciliar, which is very different from that which tends more and more to prevail in a certain ecclesiastical ideology and in the very practice of our episcopate.[17] What I said was rejected, with-

---

[17] See in the Appendix [7:12] the conclusion drawn by Cardinal Gouyon from his study of the French episcopal conference, in *L'Année canonique* of 1978.

out having aroused, as far as I know, the least discussion.[18] One theologian friend, more sensitive than I to currents of opinion, was kind enough to observe that the documentation of the book was borrowed from *Méditation sur l'Eglise*; yet I doubt, at the very least in the first, principal, part of the book, if more than one or two citations in common could be found, since the subjects on both sides are so different and since the latter of these two books depends so much on the Council and the problems suggested by some of its teachings, problems that I had never before treated.

For the German-language edition, I wrote a new preface, in which I summed up the broad outlines of two or three essential ideas that I thought it particularly timely to bring out.[19] I reproduce that here:

A friend suggested to me that having shown the *Particular Churches in the Universal Church* in a recent little book, I might do well to show the *Universal Church in the Particular Churches* in a parallel or rather symmetrical book. I could only reply that this had already been done. If he would read the first work well, he would find the second there at the same time. Our era no longer tolerates long, drawn-out titles, otherwise the two formulas could have appeared on the cover. A correlation, a reciprocal inclusion, exists between each particular Church (or also each group of Churches) and the unique universal Church, at their very base. Many historians and theologians, in the course of these recent years, have recalled this, and the matter is so important that it is good to recall it again, without claiming the least originality.

Yet, in order for the inclusion to remain effective and for the same life to circulate everywhere, it is equally necessary that there be a unique center. Now, if it is true that today (Orthodox and even Protestants have, with sadness, recently made this observation to me) the essential role of this center is the object of theoretical and practical contestations within Catholicism itself, it was equally necessary, in order to help maintain or reestablish the equilibrium, to recall what the essential role of that center consists of, independent of all accidents of history.

On the other hand, it was necessary to clarify certain questions of terminology; not that we cling to the words themselves, but so as to keep from being mistaken about things. In fact, since reflections on the local Church are multiplying, it often happens, that this expression is employed in completely different ways. Without being aware of it, we easily pass from one to the other, and this has given rise to much confusion. At the present time, the confusion is only growing.[20] Hence the distinction we proposed between

[18] Many have preferred to take their inspiration from a certain ideology of collective government rather than from the teaching of the Council concerning the episcopal college. Yet in the Council itself, more than one speaker among the warmest partisans of the text had warned against such a confusion.

[19] *Quellen Kirchlicher Einheit* (Einsiedeln, 1974), trans. by Hans Urs von Balthasar.

[20] "Local church" is used in all kinds of senses: from the village parish up to the Church of France, for example, or the United States! It is not merely a question of differences in size.

"particular church" and "local church". But, once again, the words are of little importance to us if only we succeed in calling attention to a problem that is itself important.

No less important in our opinion is another proposed distinction, between "collegial" and "collective". The very word "collegial" (or the noun "collegiality") seems to us to need protection against quite abusive usage, as was emphasized at the Second Vatican Council, according to a traditional doctrine whose practical effect had become blurred. It cannot be stressed enough: a very strong tendency exists today to divert this teaching from its meaning— against the letter of the texts and also manifestly against their spirit. That is in no way progress, or, as some say, a way of "going farther": it is a serious attack made against the constitution of the Church as well as an obstacle to the smooth running of her everyday life.

We must not be overly surprised at this or, whatever judgment we might have, believe it to be some very new phenomenon. The temptation has always existed to change in one sense or another (in many senses!) the original structure and original idea of the Church to accord with the secular doctrines or societies in the milieu in which she lives. But in all times as well, with more or less success, through battles that were sometimes harsh and long and despite situations that were often very involved, the Church has passed through these reefs, pursuing her divine mission. Besides, in large measure, for everything that has to do with contingent, endlessly variable organization, it is not a question of temptation but, on the contrary, of an appeal to a completely desirable effort toward adaptation; hence, for our generation, there is a large field of possible research and progress. This was not, however, the most central and limited, the most radical, if one might say so, subject that we wanted to treat by recalling the precise doctrinal meaning of the word "collegial".

The second part of the book to which we are referring, closely united to the first, wishes in the end to recall only one thing—but a thing that is so essential that when it is misunderstood, all Christianity falls. It seems to us that year by year the question takes on a livelier keenness, and that is why we stress it again. Christianity is a life. We are given birth in it, and the mother who gives birth to us in it is the Church, the spouse of Christ. Such is the meaning of the apostolic ministry, perpetuated down through the centuries—which one calls the "ordained", "pastoral", "presbyteral", "sacerdotal" ministry or some other name. The wish to make this be an emanation from the community, which would delegate some one or other of its members as "responsible" or as "president", is to reverse the order of things; it is to put man in the place of God and to deny the saving work of Christ. It is all the more important to explain this clearly today, for all kinds of new ministerial formulas are being proposed to us that, even though they wrongly invoke the authority of New Testament exegesis, are in reality little concerned about all the fundamental ideas given in Scripture and have little in common with the faith or with the two-millenia-old practice of the Church. Yet, let me say explicitly that it does not follow from this that the Christian people must be a passive flock, that a thousand initiatives cannot freely arise among her members or, to put it another way, that each assembly, each Christian community does not constitute around its pastor and with him a unique whole, for the exercise of a common essential work, in a common overall responsibility. And even less does it signify, if I might say so, that the so-called "hierarchical" order surpasses the order of sanctity. But what would Christian activity or sanctity be if its principle were not received? What kind of salvation can man give to himself, either by recourse to some wholly individual inner experience that he would then set up as the norm, or by any search whatever for social unanimity, in a celebration where the community would constitute itself by "finding itself"? It would in any case no longer be Christian holiness, it would no longer be Christian salvation. Coming from man, our rites would be empty and our union artificial. We would be left to our solitude and our misery. Issuing from Christ and animated by his Spirit, the Church, through her ministry, pulls us out of this. Through her, it is God who saves us, it is God who gathers us together. We are introduced into a new universe, the universe of grace. As Paul says, it is a "new creation" (*kainè ktisis*). We, obviously, must consent to it. We must "become what we are".

The reader will perhaps allow us a final consideration. For the past dozen years or so, much has been written on the new situation created for the papacy by the evolution of contemporary society and by the orientations of the Council, notably by its teaching on the episcopacy. Without having constantly to speak ill of a past that, as always, included many an abuse but that was especially at fault in corresponding to historical circumstances that are entirely transformed today, two things are, in my opinion, imperative. It was first a matter of freeing the Apostolic See of the last inoffensive but cumbersome vestiges of its juridico-spiritual suzerainty and its temporal power. One could say that this has been accomplished. In the second place, it was necessary to proceed to a decentralization that gave back to the episcopacy, with the full awareness of its responsibilities, the full exercise of its charge: a profound reform that required, that still requires, a certain number of years for its accomplishment. On the part of the center, the conditions for this have already been largely set in place; with respect to the periphery, as is normal, the effects are perhaps slower to manifest themselves, and they do not always succeed in being produced without a certain chaos. For a better realization—which neither could nor should take the same form everywhere—we must trust in time, which the Spirit of God himself does not usually dispense with. It would be regrettable if, as one whole, rather unsound trend in ecclesiology seems to be inclined to do today, we were to infer, on the basis of a good and necessary decentralization, a straining of the bonds between the episcopal college and its head—a straining that would inevitably soon spread between the various members of that college, to the great detriment of each particular Church and of the whole Christian people. Nothing would be more contrary to the perspectives opened by the Council or to the necessities of this time.

Returned, on the one hand, to the purity of its spiritual function, relieved, on the other hand, of its excessive administrative apparatus, which may have had its advantages but which nevertheless risked paralyzing itself as well as hindering the vitality of the Churches, the papacy in our opinion has never since the beginnings of the Christian era more closely approached what it was supposed to be according to the words Christ addressed to Peter. This is without doubt the deepest reason why it is contested so warmly today, to the surprise, indeed the scandal, of many non-Catholic Christians. And in a world that, for the first time, finds itself unified, not certainly in unanimity of minds and hearts, but in the ever-growing means of communication, is it not natural, and at the same time in some way indispensable, that the voice of the one who has received the responsibility of "confirming his brothers" might resound with greater clarity through all the Churches? To confirm is not to weaken or supplant or always to precede. It is to strengthen, by unifying.

Quite recently, in his acceptance speech to the Académie française, Maurice Schumann gave a summary of the resolutions made by his predecessor, Wladimir d'Ormesson, the fundamental truth of which is not at all lessened by their political overtones. They agree so well with what I was trying to say that I would like to quote them:

The Church has been universal since her origins; but this universality is only beginning to exist; technical revolutions (the only ones that are irreversible) are abolishing distances; the end of the European hegemony, the inevitable growth of young nations, the displacement of the axis of the world toward Asia . . ., there is nothing that does not tend to charge the word ecumenical with its true weight, applicable to the "whole inhabited earth". If this evolution were to fragment the universal Church into national chapels, we would have a humanity more cruelly divided against itself. But if, on the contrary, it gives new birth to the international authority of the Holy See, relieved from its temporal forms, we will have a new dawn breaking (January 30, 1975).

It remains for me to say a word about two more recent books. One is *Claudel et Péguy.* Only the first part is by me; the second is the work of my friend Jean Bastaire, secretary of the Amitié Charles Péguy. They were looking for someone rather neutral, who had friends in both camps, Peguyst and Claudelian, who do not always get on exceptionally well together, to edit and give a commentary for the rare exchanges of letters, direct and indirect, that these two great men had between 1910 and 1914. The confidence of Pierre Claudel had made me accept this task. But I had conceived too vast a plan to accomplish it. In 1971, having fallen ill without any hope of a real recovery and in the face of having to reserve what remained of my strength for more everyday tasks, I had to excuse myself. Bastaire agreed to carry on the work, reducing the proportions I had had in mind. Finally we agreed to a joint publication together. Thus, late in life, I was able to salute two geniuses with whom I associated (nearly in secret, for neither one of them was at that time of much recognized value among those around me) from before my entrance into the novitiate in 1913, in a notebook that has long accompanied me. Comparing one to the other, loving them in their contrasts, I have so to speak never ceased to drink in their substance. Reading Claudel exalted and fatigued me; reading Péguy, even in his haziest polemics, always refreshed me. Although this was a writing of only minor interest, I am happy to have been offered this occasion to acquit symbolically my debt toward the two of them. In the preface given recently to a collection of Claudel texts on the Credo, I had tried to give a glimpse, based on some rare examples drawn from this collection, of what riches Claudel's work offers for doctrinal reflection, what at times unexpected perspectives, having nothing to do with the clichés of Baroque thinking or "triumphalism", easy pretexts to be avoided.[21] As for Péguy, about whom scholarly ground work is increasing at the moment, I admire more and more the acuity of his prophetic views. I am equally persuaded that in the end we will come to understand both the essential justice of his social project and the marvelous depth of his Catholicism without having to sacrifice one for the other; Father Daniélou, with whom I discussed this more than once, had the correct intuition about this. —Claudel and Péguy: two poet-theologians of exceptional stature, not monopolized or exploited, as some have said, but on the contrary too neglected in the Church. Two universes, both still insufficiently explored. At the present time, when a contorted rejection of the most recent past is spreading like an epidemic in many Christian consciences, their work is suffering an eclipse. But tomorrow's generation, if it were trained in their school, would surprise its elders by the boldness and the lively strength for renewal that would come from their inspiration.

And finally, coming last, a young and old friend, Giovanni Pico della Mirandola, was published as a book around the end of 1974. I had been reading him in my spare time for some forty years. By chance, my frequent stays in Rome over some dozen years permitted me, with the help of an excellent friend, Canon Hilaire Torney, to deepen my acquaintance with him a bit. The book that I devoted to him slowly took shape. It was

[21] I would like also to express my deep gratitude to a man who is often referred to harshly and yet was capable of delicate goodness. When, in 1950, he knew my situation as a proscribed person, he, who knew me on the whole rather little, addressed a rare edition of one of his books to me in homage, he said, with warm gratitude. Our relations, moreover, always remained episodic. Among his not very numerous letters, I have one in which he has fun feigning stupidity with respect to the Solomonic origins of the Song of Songs. —In December 1968, at the Catholic Institute of Paris, at a meeting organized to celebrate the centenary of his birth, I gave a brief speech, serving in some way to "raise the curtain" on an enjoyable conference given by Etienne Gilson on "Claudel—Catholic poet".

not a complete account of his life nor an integral analysis of his work: too many elements were lacking for that; it was a mere series of "studies and discussions", as the subtitle indicates. I tried to show through a number of topical examples, as I had already done in lesser proportions for Erasmus (*Exégèse médiévale*, vol. 4) and for Charles de Bovelles (*Mélanges M.-D. Chenu*), that even the most serious historians of humanism and the Renaissance, for the reasons I stated, were not able really to understand the great Christian humanists.[22] But there are certain currents of opinion in the intellectual world that it would be illusory to hope to turn around. As Giovanni Pico is not a current hero, on the other hand, I had thought at first that, in the publisher's boxes, he would peacefully continue a sleep that had scarcely been disturbed by him in France for nearly five centuries; but a happy circumstance suddenly hastened his awakening [7:13].[23]

[22] Yet, through his long thesis on the *Ratio verae theologiae* of Erasmus, Father Georges Chantraine seems to have won the game, at least with respect to some. Cf. the article by J.-P. Massaut, "Histoire, humanisme et théologie", in the *Revue d'histoire ecclésiastique* (Louvain, 1974).

[23] See in the Appendix my letter of July 8, 1976. Since then, the work has been well received by more than one specialist, and Italy has done me the honor of publishing a translation (in Editions Jaca Book of Milan). I returned to Giovanni Pico in a preface for a work by Father Henri Crouzel, *Une controverse sur Origène à la Renaissance: Jean Pic de la Mirandole et Pierre Garcia* (Vrin, 1977).

CHAPTER EIGHT

There you have, as requested, a review of the character and occasion of various writings; I have mixed in a few memories connected with them, but always attempting to avoid generalizations. I have been a more or less direct witness of many things that were more important than the ones I have reported, about which I say nothing and, with all the more reason, about which I do not wish to make any judgment. In order to be complete, I am going to say yet a word about what was written and not published, and even about what was at first considered but will perhaps or certainly never be written.

One manuscript sleeps in a box. It is a series of six monographs, some unpublished, other recast, on various subjects having to do with the history of theology. The first, a sketch of which appeared in 1950 in the *Mémorial Joseph Chaîne*, constitutes, on the subject of several texts of Origen's homilies on Jeremiah, a kind of analysis of the Christian demythization of the last ends and more generally of biblical revelation, which could be contrasted to those worked out by Spinoza or Bultmann. Another, whose origin was a brief contribution to the Anselm congress of 1959, follows step by step the progress, in its broken line, of Anselm's *Proslogion*,[1] from which a certain type of understanding of faith arises that is not completely that of Augustine nor that of Thomas Aquinas and that culminates in a hymn to hope. A chapter on Charles de Bovelles enlarges the subject I had treated in the *Mélanges Chenu*; but recent works from Maurice de Gandillac and carried on by a young team from the Renaissance Center of Tours, much better equipped than I, will doubtlessly render it superfluous. Next came a study on the legend of the "fall of Origen" from the end of the Middle Ages to our time: it completes the section I had devoted to this legend, for the earlier period, in *Exégèse médiévale*.[2] I would have liked to end with a final chapter, which would contribute nothing really new and whose perspectives are today largely transcended, but which would constitute a homage finally made publicly to two venerated masters of whom I spoke above: this is the article, once rejected, on revelation and dogma according to the antimodernist writings of Father Lebreton.

A seventh chapter had been foreseen for this collection. Having taken

---

[1] See below, p. 154.

[2] Father Henri Crouzel wanted to take this study to publish it in the *Bulletin de littérature ecclésiastique de Toulouse*.

on larger proportions, it was detached from the rest. It is the general historical view of what I call the "Joachimite succession", that is, sacred or secularized dreams of a "third age" taking over from the Christian age. If I had the strength to carry it out, it would immerse us fully in our present time.[3]

Parallel to the essays attempted around the problem of mysticism, I sketched out a supplementary work of spiritual anthropology, according to the tradition springing from Saint Paul, 1 Thessalonians 5:23; it has remained in a shapeless state; I regret this, for it was one means, at least for me, of bringing some clarity into all kinds of fundamental problems relative to reason and revelation, moral and spiritual life, freedom and grace, the spirit of man and the Spirit of God, and so forth.[4] Other files for other projects were gathered, but they never took shape and were long ago aborted: such was a study I considered doing about René Guénon, as representing the "eternal gnosis" in the twentieth century; another was on Erasmus, of which I had given an advance summary in the fourth volume of *Exégèse médiévale*. One of these still-born projects was more ambitious and was to be a collective work. It was a treatise on theology, conceived according to a new plan and in another spirit than the manuals still in use; I wanted it to be at once less systematic and more deeply traditional, integrating the best works of the century in matters of exegesis, patristics, liturgy, history, philosophical reflection. . . . The initial idea for it came from Msgr. de Solages, who had talked about it freely with me; we had had the approval of Fathers Congar and Chenu, after a meeting of which I was reminded by Father Chenu in a recent work;[5] we had obtained the collaboration of Jean Mouroux, Canon Dondeyne, Fathers Malevez, Holstein, Baumgartner, of M. Chavasse and several others as well. It was to be a Catholic undertaking, in all the vigor and range of that term. The general outline had been simple; about six volumes were foreseen, in an order that presently escapes me: "Anthropology", "Christology", "Ecclesiology", "Eschatology", "Theology" (= on God), perhaps "Ecumenism". The need was great but the combination of circumstances not very favorable; I had to warn my colleagues that my collaboration would compromise them. Then the lightning bolt of *Humani generis* entered the scene.

Now, I should write at least some small work on the life of Father Pierre Chaillet (d. 1972), particularly on his charitable work and his defense of

---

[3] See below, pp. 155-57.

[4] One part of this manuscript has nevertheless been published in the Italian edition of my *Opera*, vol. 6, *Mistica e mistero cristiano*, 39-163.

[5] *Jacques Duquesne interroge le Père Chenu—Un théologien en liberté* (Paris: Centurion, 1975), 130.

the Gospel during the somber years of nazism. It would not merely be a question of fulfilling a duty of friendship. It would be an important document for the history of French Catholicism. The scarcity of written and accurate testimonies, my lapses of memory, the impossibility of stating the whole truth on certain essential points without rousing the passions and inciting polemics,[6] made me fear that the project, which was nevertheless close to my heart, could not be accomplished. Father Chaillet had deepened his love of the Church and of her divine charity by placing himself in the school of the Fathers of the first centuries and by frequent reading of the great Catholic theologians of Tubingen. He had undertaken a thesis on Drey, the principal initiator of that celebrated School, as well as a translation of his works. He had, in the intrepidity of his faith, achieved this tour de force: the publication of an important collective work, in both Germany and France, as an attestation in the face of nazi paganism and the rifts threatening Catholic unity: *L'Eglise est une, hommage à Moehler* [The Church is one, homage to Moehler]. It seems to have been forgotten today.[7] I will cite these words by him here, words that apply so well to his own life: "We have an irresistible mistrust of those constructions where logic alone and an insistence on established systems place little value on reasons of the heart and on personal commitments that give a work, just as they give life, its profound unity and interior rhythm, its lived logic." The memory of Father Chaillet and that of Father de Montcheuil should be sustained among us as high and pure examples and as pledges of hope [8:1].

Several young thesis-writers have written about me. A more important study was on its way to completion when its author had to interrupt it when he was called to the episcopacy. One chapter was devoted to me in a large work published in Germany and translated into French, on the "theologians of the twentieth century". While I am grateful for the extreme kindness of this biographer, I must nevertheless say that a certain number of factual errors have slipped into his text and that some of his interpretations are rather far from mine. I am indebted for a brief correction, whose final lines I give here, to the recent republication (1975) of a bibliography provided (in German) by Fathers Karl Neufeld and Michel Sales:[8]

---

[6] Some of the correspondence I still have seems to me to be unpublishable to the very degree in which it is illuminating.

[7] Even Fathers Congar and Chenu, who speak of a Moehlerian revival in their recent works, are silent with respect to Father Chaillet, who was the principal architect of it. —With respect to this work, I had published in the *Bulletin de l'Union apostolique* (September-October 1939) an article on "Moehler et sa doctrine sur l'Eglise" [Moehler and his doctrine on the Church], taking my inspiration from Father Chaillet.

[8] The complete text is provided in the Appendix [8:2].

Without contesting in any way the author's freedom in his judgments, I have the strict duty to declare that I do not always share them. I have never confused what I thought to be unjustified criticism coming from men I respect and revere with "stupid", "malicious" or "cruel" attacks; I owe it to the memory of my Superior General to say that he was, insofar as he could be, of great kindness to me; finally, the idea, stated without restrictions and in language lacking any moderation, that it would be appropriate to resist any "repression" in the Church and that the latter "should never inflict suffering or punishment" is so far from my unchanging opinion that it seems to me contrary to the nature of the Church and to her whole tradition, made manifest from the earliest times and testified to in the writings of the New Testament.

To those who ask me, with a gentle irony, "what are you writing", I usually reply that I am not a machine for making books. As one can see, nearly everything I have written has been as a result of circumstances that were often unforeseen, in scattered order and without technical preparation. In consequence, the professionals as a rule rarely took seriously what I proposed to them. I did not in fact receive any specialized formation at the outset, I am very ignorant of languages, I did not go through the salutary testing of a doctoral thesis. One fine day, Father General Wladimir Ledochowski granted me (that is the right word) a doctoral diploma from the Gregorian University, in which I had never set foot and where no one knew me, because they needed me to fill in a gap at the Theology Faculty of Lyons; I have never since obtained the time requested to make up for this, and the large amounts of free time granted me by Providence since 1950 worked only to put me at a greater distance from all "scientific" theology. Besides, I sincerely believe that if, at that date, some of my writings had not been—or had not seemed to be—publicly repudiated by the authorities, the importance that was sometimes attributed to them afterward would not have been recognized. It would be fruitless to seek in such a diverse collection of writings the elements of any truly personal philosophical or theological—or, as some have said, "gnoseological"— synthesis, whether to criticize or to adopt it. In this multi-colored fabric gradually formed according to teaching assignments, ministries, situations and appeals of all kinds, it nevertheless seems possible to me to discern a certain texture that, come what may, creates a unity. Without claiming to open up new avenues to thought, I have sought rather, without any anti- quarianism, to make known some of the great common areas of Catholic tradition. I wanted to make it loved, to show its ever-present fruitfulness. Such a task called more for a reading across the centuries than for a critical application to specific points; it excluded any overly preferential attach- ment to one school, system, or definite age; it demanded more attention to the deep and permanent unity of the Faith, to the mysterious relationship (which escapes so many specialized scholars) of all those who invoke the name of Christ, than to the multiple diversities of eras, milieux, personalities and cultures. So I have never been tempted by any kind of "return to the sources" that would scorn later developments and represent the history of Christian thought as a stream of decadences; the Latins have not pushed aside the Greeks for me; nor has Saint Augustine diverted me from Saint Anselm or Saint Thomas Aquinas; nor has the latter ever seemed to me either to make the twelve centuries that preceded him useless or to condemn his disciples to a failure to see and understand fully what has followed him.[9]

When I left Jersey (I was then 27 years old), where a Suarezian spirit still reigned, I had been put down severely as a Thomist (of a Thomism, it is true, revitalized by Maréchal and Rousselot). At that time, this was called "not holding the doctrines of the Society." I have never renounced that fundamental orientation. I even believe that I have worked (with varying degrees of success) to lead minds back to the authentic Saint Thomas, as to a master considered ever-current. As for the "Thomism" of our century, I have too often found in it a system that is too rigid and yet at the same time not faithful enough to the Doctor it claims as its authority. I have also seen it raised too often (in complete good faith) like a pavilion to cover the most diverse merchandise to be able to take it seriously. I have known a traditionalist Thomism à la Bonald, a Thomism as patron of "*l'Action française*", a Thomism as the inspiration of Christian Democracy, a progressivist and even a neo-Marxist Thomism, and so forth (to say nothing of innocent fantasies such as the Thomism of the scout rule, among others). And no salvation outside of each in its turn. I have read, from the pen of a theoretician rejecting any fidelity to Catholicism, that he would never forget his debt of loyalty to the doctrine of Saint Thomas Aquinas. I have more than once observed a "Thomism" that was scarcely more than a tool in the hands of the government, the rallying point of a party, the password of a troop of ambitious careerists, or even the empty shell of a thoughtless conformity, the padlock closing the door to all understanding of the thought of others. Even today, despite all the supervening changes, this still makes it difficult for me to be very loud in proclaiming that I am a Thomist [8:4]. Besides, to each his task! I have never claimed to be doing the work of philosophical systematization or of theological synthesis. That is not out of contempt on my part, quite the contrary. But, leaving this twofold kind of task to others with the necessary gifts, it is in a more

[9] See in the Appendix [8:3] my response to a theology student who had questioned me about these things.

general way to the great tradition of the Church, understood as the experience of all Christian centuries, coming to enlighten, orient, expand our poor little individual experience, to protect it from aberrations, to open it to the paths of the future, that I once again recently made appeal in the introduction to *La Foi chrétienne* [The Christian Faith], just as I had done long before in *Catholicisme* [Catholicism].

What I have more than once regretted in highly regarded theologians, experienced guardians, was less, as others made it out, their lack of openness to the problems and currents of contemporary thought than their lack of a truly traditional mind (the two things are, moreover, connected). I inwardly reproached them for not having an acute enough awareness of what they were representing or should have been representing: like those Romans who seem to be ignorant of their claims to Christian nobility, taking no interest deep in their heart either in the catacombs or in the mosaics of the churches of their city, and who, going up to the Cadius [Monte Celio], crowd along the same pavement that Saint Gregory once trod without being in any way affected by it. They were, for me, in Péguy's sense, the "moderns". Such a state of mind, which was too generally widespread in dominant spheres during the preparation for the Council, was in my opinion at the root of a contempt that was not without grave consequences. It was the state of mind that characterized the party (I believe that word is appropriate here) that had hoped to control, not to say confiscate, the Council and that was, from the very first session, spectacularly overcome. But in the consequence of the confusion that I have just pointed out, it seemed in its defeat to entail the defeat of Tradition as well, although the latter, on the contrary, was in fact liberated. A necessary reaction, a condition of the desired "opening", was taken to be revolutionary, and, in public opinion, which was very poorly informed, it was the tradition of the Church herself, with all her fertile but misunderstood richness, that seemed to be crushed. Many were no longer attentive to the very work of the Council, to the substance of its teachings, to the spirit that emanated from it: for them, through them, it was a new "modernity", in restless excitement but without a compass, that triumphed over a petrified modernity.[10]

What can be said, since then, of the new powers of the day, who, in the reverse situation, suffer from a blindness that is more dense and all the more confident! What I had wanted to offer as savory nourishment and, as it were, a propelling force, I see them push aside as a dry fruit or reject as a cumbersome burden. Despite the efforts of the better interpreters of

---

[10] I could cite here a number of precise and characteristic facts. —See, in the Appendix, the judgment of one of the principal actors in what I have called above the "para-Council" [8:5].

the Council and above all the efforts of him who through his supreme office never ceases to guide us in its wake, I see with sadness the spread of an indifference, when it is not a flaunted scorn or a resentment full of bitter hatred, with respect to this tradition, which alone has the promise of life and of renewal because it is the bearer of eternity.[11] At the same time, I see a harsh demand for "pluralism" [8:6], which, in its worship of differences, shatters the harmony of the great Catholic concert and tends, not to enrichment, but to the dislocation of Unity.[12] How I would like to be able to cry out with the same persuasive tone to those of my brothers who are letting themselves be seduced by this music of perdition what in the last century Newman declared to his contemporaries!

> There is [he said] a depth and a power in the Catholic Religion, a fulness of satisfaction in its creed, its theology, its rites, its sacraments, its discipline, a freedom yet a support also, before which the neglect or the misapprehension about oneself on the part of individual living persons, however exalted, is as so much dust when weighed in the balance. This is the true secret of the Church's strength, the principle of its indefectibility, and the bond of its indissoluble unity. It is the earnest and the beginning of the repose of heaven.

Even though, in hindsight and undoubtedly with too much complacency, I find in my scattered works a certain direction or at least a certain common intention, I am plagued by a doubt about the good use of my time. This doubt is prompted by a reflection, to which I have already alluded, on the present situation of the Church and the crisis she must face.[13] Those who have been most affected by this crisis seem, in their blindness, to feel it rather to be progress. Few in the Church know how to interpret its signs because they do not discern its roots. For several years, I have seen it spread and bear its fruits of death by means of these two kinds of unawareness. I am not giving in to pessimism. I see many efforts of authentic renewal at work; even in certain mixed achievements, I have confidence in the Spirit of God who is shaping them. Signs of hope are not lacking to sustain the essential hope given by God alone: every

---

[11] "Tradition", wrote Maurice Blondel in *Histoire et dogme*, "anticipates the future and prepares to throw light on it through the very effort it makes to remain faithful to the past." See also the little book pointed out by Msgr. Guimet, *Existence et Eternité* (1973), for which I wrote a brief introduction.

[12] There, it is a question of something quite different from a legitimate, inevitable and desirable "pluriformity", all the elements of which constitute, as it were, so many converging lines. With respect to the two ways of understanding the "freedom of the theologian", see the Appendix [8:7].

[13] The latter has an incomparably more painful effect on me than the trials on a more personal level that have not been spared me—and I do not have to defend myself from this pain as from that of times past.

day brings me one. I also know that sometimes, in unforeseen and at first hidden forms, evil does not generate more evil but gives rise to a greater good. But neither do I want to give in to a conformity that would reject a priori any realistic view or effort of discernment as contrary to "openness", "renewal", to "forward progress" [8:8]. Nothing is more fatal to true renewal than the conviction of inevitable progress. Our "postconciliar" era has certainly been visited by the Spirit of God, even if it be by rather severe jolts; I even believe that more signs of this are beginning to appear, and I want to make my own the expression of a correspondent who wrote to me recently: "Hope no longer seems to me to be a duty but a springtime." But we do not have the right to forget—and it seems to me that the reality still reminds us of this with sufficient force—that this period is not for all that any less subject than other periods to aberrations, mistakes, illusions—to attacks by the spirit of evil.

What I perceive of these attacks today does not make me curse my era, it rather forces me to question myself. Would I not have done better, taking from the beginning my character as a believer and my role as a priest and as a member of an apostolic order, in brief, my vocation, more seriously, to concentrate my intellectual work with greater resolution more on the very center of the Christian faith and life instead of letting it be dispersed on more or less peripheral fields at the mercy of my taste or timeliness? Should I not have followed more strictly the program that Saint Augustine once outlined in these terms: ". . . cum, neglectis atque rejectis voluptatibus nostris, pro fructu Matris Ecclesiae laboramus" [When we neglect and put aside our own pleasures to work for the benefit of Mother Church]?[14] Should I not, even in less favorable circumstances, have made more of an effort toward humble patience? Would I not have been prepared in that way to intervene with a little more competence and especially moral authority in the great spiritual debate of our generation? Would I not be at the present time a little less at a loss to enlighten some and encourage others [8:9]? I cannot help thinking that it is a certain spiritual superficiality rather than the feeling of my intellectual deficiencies or even than the conviction that I am far too unequal to such a subject to dare ever to approach it head-on, that has always made me postpone undertaking that work on Jesus Christ that would have been dearer to me than all the others, and in view of which I did much reading and recorded many reflections but which I never really attacked.[15] I was invited to do so one

---

[14] *De diversis quaestionibus* 83, p. 67, n.2.

[15] Although I have always tried to keep abreast of serious works, I have always lacked the technical knowledge indispensable for a work in which exegesis, even if not put on display, must have a large part. I have often had to deal with these things, but only in correspondence or private conversations.

day by an unknown correspondent, who, after having spoken of my little
work on "the knowledge of God", read in his youth, said to me:

> Today, I experience another need: to know the person of Jesus. So, having
> read several of your books, I am writing to ask you for this life of Jesus, as
> you alone[!] can write it today. In the impersonal form that is characteristic
> of you, tell us what you know of Jesus. . . . In the course of your life bent
> over so many questions of our faith in God, you have had this person present
> in your heart at every moment. It has drawn us, annoyed us, filled us with
> enthusiasm, crushed us, in this dialogue of silence in which we live our faith.
> If you could describe for us, through your remarks, your dialogue, I am sure
> it would reach the hearts of many. . . .

Such letters enlightened me about the illusions one can engender by
writing books. The latter made me feel my powerlessness to the point
of being crushed by it. There are, thanks be to God, even in the form
of books, other witnesses more solid than my own. Without claiming to
refer to anything other than the Gospel such as the Church transmits it
to me, I can nevertheless make my own the words of Moehler on Jesus,
with little concern for the whiff of pietism that some of our adult minds
would criticize in them: "I think I would no longer want to live if I were
no longer to hear Him speak."[16]

A few months ago, the editor of an Italian journal observed, seeming
to reproach me, that my reservations concerning a certain "postconciliar
theology" had become more pronounced. The observation was accurate,
but the cause escaped him: it is because this "theology" is moving farther and farther away from the norms of the Catholic faith and from the
very teachings of Vatican II [8:10]. It is not, thank God, the whole of
postconciliar theology, but if it is not the most living part of it, it is the
noisiest. Powerfully orchestrated by most of the masters of "opinion", its
destructive action is considerable. It is not an exaggeration to say that the
Council has been betrayed by it: it neither "extends" nor "transcends"
the Council, in the name of what it sometimes calls its "dynamic" or its
"spirit": on all the essential points, whether it is a question of the mysteries of the faith, of the constitution of the Church and in particular of the
episcopate, of tradition, of religious freedom, and so forth, it is moving in
the wrong direction. It supports and accelerates that vast phenomenon of
the Church's "self-destruction" and "inner apostasy", indicated so many
times these past ten years or so. Good minds seem to lose interest in it.
Good theologians, even, seem to minimize the effects of it and sometimes
give proof of it. I have no doubts about their good faith, or even their
courage, but I deplore their apparent euphoria [8:11]. Some have been

---

[16] *L'Unité dans l'Eglise*, 16.

led to believe that I am exaggerating and that I am "closing my mind" in getting old. I reply to them in substance that formerly, in quite different circumstances, I refused to bend the knee before those successive Baals that had the name of Maurrasism, Hitlerism, integrism: I now see other Baals, having invaded the sanctuary, demand the same adoration, and their servants use the same kind of procedures that characterized the old integrism with the opposite sign, from as early as 1914.[17] I like neither hypocrisy nor the intimidations of social pressures nor intellectual terrorism. I do not accept the practice of covering the worst enterprises with the magic words of progress, forward movement, opening or renewal. It seems to me that this is on my part no more a matter of simple individual disposition than it is an effect of age, but rather a feeling of a responsibility that is, of course, limited but grave.[18]

That is why, as much as I disapprove of any sort of obstinate opposition, sterile dogmatism, poorly enlightened traditionalism, politico-religious blocking, any rejection of evolutions controlled and guided by a living Magisterium—all that Blondel once designated as "traditionalism" [vétérisme]—I do delight in the healthy reactions, even if they are a bit simplistic, coming from the Christian people, without however seeing the essential ground for my hope in this. And although I could no longer bring any effective support to them, I am in sympathy with the various efforts made toward clarification, for example, by H. I. Marrou, with his "Quatre Fleuves" Notebooks, by Father P. M. Laurent, with his "Groupe sacerdotal 'Lumen gentium'", and by Gérard Soulages, who is gathering Catholic intellectuals together under the sign of "Fidélité et ouverture". On All Saints' Day, 1971, in Strasbourg, Soulages had organized a meeting, presided over by Msgr. Elchinger, for which the opening conference was given by Gabriel Marcel; as I was ill, I was not able to take part in it nor to write a whole report, as he had wished; I had to content myself with a simple address, from which I excerpt one sentence: "Perhaps it is harder to give witness to one's faith before the eyes of brothers who have a mocking smile or naïve incomprehension than before a hostile tribunal." These words reflect a daily experience. Yet they do not say everything.

[17] Nearly every day the press brings examples of it (and it is the same with many others). For my part, I have received insulting letters, I have been treated as a "court theologian", it has been written that I spent my time "infatuating Paul VI", I have been excommunicated for not having supported the crude maneuver of a manifesto and for not having taken part as a hostage in a sham congress; my name has been fraudulently abused on various occasions, and so on. The more moderate among them say with a sad tone of voice that I have become "traditional", because I remain faithful to the teaching of Vatican II, which is not for me an "opening" allowing me to make any "breakthrough" whatever outside the faith of the Church.

[18] From time to time some echo also reaches me of attacks coming from little relentless integrist circles. I sometimes amuse myself by replying (by private letter) to some of them.

There is a twofold complicity that favors the ravages made by the destructive maneuvers. On the one hand, there is a false idea of "opening to the world", shamelessly preached as being the thought of the Council, that takes away from the mass of the faithful what was always the strength of the Christians most involved in the world—the consciousness of their obligation to be an enlivening soul in it—in order to make them poor beings without an identity tagging along behind it. There is, on the other hand, and most particularly with numerous clerics, a frightening dearth of intelligence and education, which hands them over without any defense to all the most contradictory speculations, to the most pretentious fantasies, sometimes as brilliant as fake glass jewelry; visits to Catholic bookdealers and the innumerable copies of papers I receive, coming from private or even official agencies, bear an overabundant witness to this. Two philosophers, both of whom are personal friends of mine, are among those trying to remedy this latter aspect of the crisis: Etienne Borne and Claude Bruaire (d. 1985). It is also well known, without any insistence from me, what an important role Father, then Cardinal, Daniélou played, one of whose last books was entitled precisely: *La Culture trahie par les siens* [Culture betrayed by its own]. It was likewise a wish to get on one's feet again that was at the origin of the "Revue théologique internationale" *Communio*, launched by a group of German theologians, in the foremost ranks of whom were Joseph Ratzinger and Hans Urs von Balthasar.[19]

One chapter was devoted to von Balthasar in *Paradoxe et mystère de l'Eglise*, of which I have spoken above. It is of interest only as a testimony, for I was then and am still very far from knowing the whole of von Balthasar's work, which was already immense and which never ceased to increase. It was an article that had been asked of me by H. Gut, the editor of the journal *Civitas* (Lucerne), in order to celebrate in 1965 his sixtieth birthday. (He had refused to allow a volume in honor of him to be prepared for this occasion.) Von Balthasar has nourished me through those of his writings that are accessible to me. His theological work, so diverse and yet so one, dominate our century. It is regrettable that it has still only partially been translated into French, and in a scattered order: *Herrlichkeit*, the five large volumes of which constitute the first section of an anticipated triptych (the first of the second section, *Theo-Dramatik*, was published last year), appeared in French, under the title *La Gloire et la Croix*, only at a very slow pace; in reserving the work for the "Theology" series, the Fourvière scholasticate had contracted a moral commitment to the author that has

---

[19] After many difficulties, the French edition of *Communio* has just begun its career in October 1975, thanks in particular to a group of young academics. In this first issue, I wrote three pages on von Balthasar, which supplemented briefly, but on two essential points, what I had written about him previously.

not been kept; there would still be time, in a certain measure, to repair the fault, by deciding finally to translate the central volume, which was senselessly left aside.[20] A year ago, I wrote a memorandum with this in mind, which our Superiors seem to wish to consider. Von Balthasar's work silently makes a path into minds and spirits. Despite the efforts used to stifle it, its greatness has in the end compelled recognition. In the measure that the present crisis has grown worse, von Balthasar has appeared more and more what he has always been: a man of the Church, more devoted to the often unrewarding tasks that fall to him because of this than to personal creation [8:12]. —I owe much to my association with such a friend. And this worker, as friendly and serene as he is relentless in his work, has still wished to spend a considerable amount of time translating some eleven of my books into German (a twelfth will soon appear),[21] as well as numerous articles. Since he has an admirable skill as a writer, I am well on my way to having a reputation in German-speaking countries as a writer, which verges on fraud.[22]

~

I am still haunted by the questions I have asked myself, and which I just admitted above, concerning the choice of subjects approached in the course of my life, to the degree that these choices depended on me. Thinking of the pressing necessities of the present time, I feel some shame in having been able to offer to so many disoriented minds, as the final fruit of my work, only a study of Pico della Mirandola, whose usefulness no one would assert to be imperative. —But we cannot start our lives over again, and regrets are pointless. Moreover, the pages I have just written for the sake of a little group of friends were not intended to be an examination of conscience. —Neither have I wanted to write memoirs. That is

[20] It is humiliating for us to have the author find himself forced to warn the reader, although in the most delicate terms, that between the second volume and the fourth, "a volume of some thousand pages is missing, entitled *Dans le domaine de la métaphysique*", which is necessary to the understanding of the integral work. [Since then, this volume appeared in three parts, as volume 4 of *La Gloire et la Croix*, Theology 84, 85, 86 (Paris: Aubier, 1981, 1982, 1983). The entire seven-volume English translation of the complete work has been published under the title *The Glory of the Lord: A theological aesthetics* by Ignatius Press (San Francisco, 1982–1990).]

[21] *La Foi chrétienne: Essai sur la structure du symbole des Apôtres* (Paris: Aubier, 1969); German trans., *Credo. Gestalt und Lebendigkeit unseres Glaubensbakenntnisses* (Einsiedeln: Johannes Verlag, 1975); English trans., *The Christian Faith: An Essay on the Structure of the Apostles' Creed* (San Francisco: Ignatius Press, 1986).

[22] Never have I so regretted my ignorance of German as when faced with my inability to translate von Balthasar's works into French.

why I have kept from recalling here the many friends God has given me throughout my existence, a gift for which I thank him every day. Only a few of them have been cited in these pages. By way of an epilogue, I would nevertheless like to say in closing a few words about my mother.

My parents were hardly well-to-do. We were six children. They raised us according to the principles of a strict economy, but we were bathed in their tenderness. My mother was a simple woman. Her entire education was received in the country and in the cloister of a Visitation monastery, according to the custom of the times. Her entire upbringing rested on the foundation of Christian tradition and piety. I never saw anything in her but self-forgetfulness and goodness. After the death of my father, who had worn himself out in daily labor, she said to me one day: "We never had the least disagreement." She remained a widow for a quarter of a century, and the intimacy between us grew. When, somewhere around 1950, an indiscreet religious thought to do good by coming to disturb her on the subject of my orthodoxy and my conduct, she replied to him sweetly: "I know my son; I know that he will always be a submissive child of Holy Church." When she learned that I had been elected to the Institute, and, a little later, that I had been called to Rome for the Council, disturbed by what seemed to her to be honors, the two letters she addressed to me said, each in nearly the same terms: "I pray Our Lord to keep you in humility." She died at 95 years of age.

EEGENHOVEN, DECEMBER 30, 1973
CHANTILLY, FEBRUARY 23, 1975

CHAPTER NINE

Since, despite a few jolts, my earthly life has been prolonged, I am completing this memoir with an additional chapter.

In 1977, I again published a little book on Father Teilhard de Chardin. In this *Teilhard posthume*, which contains a few reminiscences, my essential goal was to show how far a "certain Teilhardism", which has spread everywhere, is from Teilhardian thought. I left aside the grossly polemical or naïvely laudatory authors to cite, on the other hand, only serious authors and to oppose them in each instance with precise texts. I also tried to explain why, at least with us, Teilhard found scarcely any hearing any more. One of the reasons seemed to me to be his synthetic character, whereas for some time now a pan-critical, "pulverizing" mentality has reigned, "crushing everything that comes under its millstone" (von Balthasar)— a phenomenon already observed by Jean Ladrière in 1969 [9:1]. A few of this book's pages upset some friends of Jacques Maritain; but I believe that it was read by very few.

In 1978, *Sources chrétiennes* was preparing to publish the celebrated *Dialogue on the Priesthood* by Saint John Chrysostom. Father Claude Mondésert, editor of the series, had asked me to give a theological introduction for it, which *Nouvelle revue théologique* agreed in advance to publish (November–December 1978). When the volume was published, the promised introduction did not appear in it. A circle of people, small but powerful, had been opposed to it. The editor had not given in to their blackmail; but I had withdrawn my text so as not to deprive *Sources chrétiennes* of an excellent volume. In the months that followed, Father Mondésert insisted on publishing the article in a pamphlet in order to give it wide distribution. If I call attention to this slight intrigue, it is as an example of the "terrorism" exercised in the course of the seventies against anything that could oppose, through the simple exposition of unquestionable facts, an enterprise destructive to Catholic tradition. I had made the mistake of recalling that the ministerial priesthood, in the Church, is not the result of a belated "blockage" between the noble "ministry of the word" and the humble "worship functions", conceded to the popular need for the "sacred" [9:2].

My friend Father Marcel Régnier, indefatigable editor of *Archives de philosophie*, which he had made a center for manifold human as well as intellectual relations, had opened in 1965 the new series *Bibliothèque des*

Archives with the annotated correspondence of *Blondel et Teilhard de Chardin*. Later, he again wanted to publish something of mine. This was the origin of *Recherche dans la foi* [Research in the faith] (1979). The work brings together three studies: on Origen, on Saint Anselm, on Christian philosophy. This latter reproduces, nearly unchanged, an article from 1936 [9:3]. The first two are reworkings, considerably augmented, of more recent texts. One gives a commentary on an exclamation by Origen (borrowed from Jeremiah): "You have duped me, Lord!"; the other, on an exclamation by Anselm: "Lord, I seek your face!", which seemed to me worth being examined as introductions to the thought process characterizing each of these two great minds and even more to the fundamental movement of their soul. A few lines of the foreword will suffice to show the intention that guided me in this publication: the two cases of Origen and Anselm are "appropriate for making us see, across the differences of two eras as well as of two individualities, a more essential relationship. And we too 'are of their race'. All those nourished on the indefinitely fruitful substance of one and the same great tradition are brothers." Thus I tried, once more, to communicate the feeling of unity in a ceaseless plurality, at a time when one sees and wants it above all the ruptures and when the risk of a dissolution of the Catholic conscience is increasing. With Origen, I seek the principle of his exegesis, which is also the heart of his thought. With Anselm, I observe the conflict between the satisfaction obtained from the understanding and the always unsatisfied impulse of the soul, a conflict whose solution is expressed in the final formula of the *Proslogion*, which is commented upon far too rarely: "majus quam cogitari possit" [more than can be thought].

Beginning in 1977, the journal *Communio* had been joined by a series of works in which I published, in 1980, a *Petite catéchèse sur Nature et Grâce* [English translation: *A Brief Catechesis on Nature and Grace* (San Francisco: Ignatius Press, 1984)]. My goal was twofold: on the one hand, to summarize the doctrine of the supernatural, such as it emerged from my previous historical studies on the subject, in a simple and up-to-date way, in order to draw the conclusions from it; on the other hand, to complete it with an exposition on grace, the liberator from sin. Both parts, closely connected, seemed to me in fact to be of a similarly obvious timeliness. But I had no illusion about believing that my voice might awaken a very powerful echo! My aim was modest; but each is accountable for the effort he can supply [9:4].

Various particular points of more immediate importance are treated in the appendices. One of these analyzes an expression dear to Father Schillebeeckx, on "the Church as sacrament of the world", an expression he attributes incorrectly to the last council and one that he invokes in favor of a process of secularization. Father Michel Sales was kind enough to entrust me with a brief study on the bases of the truly sacred in every man and to bring the volume to an end with a bibliography.

Around the end of this same year, 1980, another little volume appeared through Lethielleux that I had been in a hurry to publish before dying, considering it to be a kind of testament. It was thanks to a grant made available by Rev. Father Madelin, Provincial, that its publication was possible. Its title was *Trois jésuites nous parlent: Yves de Montcheuil, Charles Nicolet, Jean Zupan* [English translation: *Three Jesuits Speak* (San Francisco: Ignatius Press, 1988)]. It contains only a few pages by me, necessary for the introduction of these three Jesuits [9:5]. All three were intimate friends of mine. If I chose them, it was because they offered me texts I could use, thereby permitting me to let them speak for themselves. But I do not separate them from a number of others. For me, they are the voice of them all. It was this voice that I wanted to have heard, as a witness of my gratitude to the Society of Jesus, which formed them to meet the test, and which, through them, was a source of help to me. Neither did I want, even in appearance, to oppose their generation to any other. It was simply that, belatedly, after many years had passed, I would have reproached myself, an unfaithful steward, for having buried the treasure I had inherited instead of handing on at least something of it to the next generation.

Jean Zupan, Yves de Montcheuil, Charles Nicolet, very beloved brothers among so many others, lights for my life, whose memory I call forth in my heart! You are not for me models that I would invite others to reproduce. You are much more: a threefold source of inspiration that, in new fields, can nourish new growth.

A final work has dragged on. It is the *Postérité spirituelle de Joachim de Flore* [The spiritual posterity of Joachim of Flora]. The first volume appeared in 1979, the second in 1981, in the Sycomore series, which carries on or revives at Namur the *Museum Lessianum* of Louvain; it has offered me an asylum I could no longer find in the defunct "Theology" series.

In volume 3 of *Exégèse médiévale* (1961), I had devoted a long chapter of 122 pages to Joachim of Flora [9:6]. I had not been seduced by this strange Calabrian abbé but had been vividly struck by the powerful originality of his exegesis and methods as well as by the fullness of his dream. He had seemed to me like such an enormous boulder in the course of Christian thought. Little by little, however, I would discover the extent of his influence, and I was all the more surprised that our historians of theology accorded him such paltry attention. At the same time, I let myself be tempted by the idea of carrying on my work. Even before the fourth volume was completed, notes were accumulating in view of a fifth, which would cover the various phases of the old exegesis as it continued and caricatured itself through the modern period. One of its chapters was to describe the twofold posterity of Joachim: on the one hand, a properly exegetic line, that is, the immense forest of commentaries interpreting the Apocalypse "literally" as a prophecy of the history of the Church, and, on the other, a spiritual line with numerous ramifications, that of the thinkers or men of action who (whether or not quoting him as their authority but all more or less betraying his dream) tend, like him, to conceive of a third age, an age of the Spirit, succeeding that of Christ of which the Church was the guardian.

Too ambitious a program! I soon perceived that it was not one new volume that was needed but four and that I would lack both the competence as well as the time. And then, from day to day, other concerns were waiting for me. But since the Joachim file had grown, I undertook to use it for one little volume. Even that was a wish to include too much. I reduced my project to the second half of the chapter I had first envisaged. Nevertheless, the more I explored the field, according to the books encountered and the hours available, the more the objective I had narrowed down was still shown to be immense. Two volumes resulted from it, published in 1979 and 1981 [9:7]. As such, it is still a very incomplete work. Three notes stress this, on pages 336, 434 and 450 of volume 2. But, as Ecclesiastes would say, there is a time for going on and a time for stopping. In the spring of 1980, I felt that the time for stopping had come. Through a literary artifice, I have thus entitled "Conclusion" a final chapter, itself too brief, on "Contemporary Neo-Joachimisms". It cannot take the place of the doctrinal conclusion I had envisaged and in view of which I attached to this work an interest that was more than mere inquisitiveness.[1]

The work is presented as a series of monographs that are rather loosely connected, for the authors successively considered differ greatly from each other, and, if Joachim of Flora can be thought the ancestor of most, the lineage is far from always being legitimate, as I recalled on many occasions. For some whose case merited a close examination, the established facts even proved negative, and this is to their credit: such was the case with Philippe Buchez, Adam Mickiewicz and Vladimir Soloviev.

Under the various forms it has assumed, I consider Joachimism to be a still-present and even pressing danger. I recognize it in the process of secularization, which, betraying the Gospel, transforms the search for the kingdom of God into social utopias. I see it at work in what was so justly called the "self-destruction of the Church". I believe that it can only in-

---

[1] After the event, I noticed that the outline for this missing conclusion was traced in 1952 in my *Méditation sur l'Eglise*, 175–80.

crease the suffering and bring about the degradation of our humanity. Still, I would not be far from admitting that a kind of semi-Joachimism (perhaps less unfaithful to the aim of Joachim himself), of which I spoke with regard to Buchez, was, on the contrary, the tentative search for what was to be the normal development of Catholic tradition. A development that has no connection with that cancerous proliferation of abstract deductions within an ever more rarefied atmosphere, as the unconscious excesses of a certain modern Scholasticism have succeeded in making us fear; which is no longer that "opening", or rather that servile adaptation to the world and its changing idols, sometimes presented as the necessary route of progress—but the discovery by the Church herself, all along her pilgrimage, of the perpetual fruitfulness of the Gospel, from which she draws, with each new situation, in a global view at times difficult to grasp at first in its authentic tenor, *nova et vetera*. This is what seems to me to be the kind of development at work in the Church's consciousness today, as in many periods of the past. In 1977, I had received a visit from Sante Bagnoli, a very active member of the young movement "Communione e Liberazione" and the very enterprising editor of the Milan "Jaca Book" publications. He was accompanied by his assistant Elio Guerriero. The two had conceived an immense project: a translation of all my writings into Italian. I had objected to them that it was an insane undertaking. But they were set on it. Soon they drew up a plan for *Opera omnia*, in nine sections and thirty-two volumes! The guiding principle of the edition was to join to each work the articles or other minor writings whose subject was related to it. In 1978, the series began with *Catolicismo*. At the present time (autumn 1981), eight volumes have been published, and another has been announced as imminent. More than one-third of the volume entitled *Mistica e mistero cristiano* (pp. 39 to 163) has not been published in French; it is the summary, rather halting in composition, of two courses given, one at the Faculty of Lyons and the other at the Institut de sciences des religion founded after the Council at the Institut Catholique de Paris. *Spirito e Libertà*, which translates the second part of *Surnaturel*, also includes a few unpublished developments. But I suspect that all will stop well before the thirty-second volume. The problematics, in the kinds of subjects I approached in turn, has changed too profoundly in recent times for any of my books to maintain any lasting timeliness.

∼

In February 1976, on the occasion of my eightieth birthday, I received a long, "handwritten" letter from Paul VI. As I recalled above (Chapter IV,

p. 75), I had long known the kindness of the Pope in my regard; yet I was very far from expecting such a gesture. I offered the letter to my rector, who did not want to read it. Shortly after, at the time of my manifestation of conscience, I did the same with my Provincial: the same lack of success. That put me in a rather difficult situation, for the terms used by the Pope clearly showed that the letter was not meant to be strictly private, but, on the other hand, the meaningful reserve of my Superiors dissuaded me from seeming to oppose them by making it public. So I kept it secret, except for two or three close friends [9:8]. Well, in March 1977, the editor of *France catholique*, who had obtained (I don't know how) a copy of the papal letter in French translation, wrote to me to receive authorization to publish it. I immediately advised my rector, who had no objection; the letter appeared in the March 25 issue. In May, our monthly bulletin *Compagnie* drew attention to the thing with a few lines; anyone could have thought as a result that I was the author of this indiscreet publication. At the end of the year, the mail brought me from Argentina an issue of *Stromata*, the journal of the Universidad del Salvador (the Society of Jesus scholasticate of San Miguel), January-June 1977, which reproduced the whole of the papal document in Castilian translation, even adding the cover letter from Cardinal Villot, Secretary of State. Shortly after, a friend sent me an issue of *Vida cristiana* (April 3, 1977), a humble leaflet of two pages on poor paper, the only authorized Catholic publication in Cuba, which gave a summary of the document. So in a way it may have been Fidel Castro who first granted the wish of the Pope—unless there had first been a publication in *l'Osservatore romano*, which one of my correspondents has supposed but which has never been confirmed for me [9:9].

If I recount this minor fact, it is because it is symbolic of the awkward situation that had existed for a long time but was made still worse following our last General Congregation (1974). The period following the Council was (and still is) a time of systematic and multiform opposition to the papacy. Paul VI was its first victim. I greatly admired that Pope. The most contradictory judgments have been made about him; he has often been criticized unjustly and at times with shameful calumny. Recently I wanted to defend his memory, in one of the appendices of my *Petite catéchèse* (A Brief Catechism on Nature and Grace), by reestablishing the true meaning of the discourse he had given in 1965 at the closing session of the Council; a passage from this discourse, although very clear, continued to be the subject of absurd interpretations and impassioned attacks [9:10]. I gave as a subtitle to this defense: "In Reparation to Paul VI", because one of my confreres had played a very vocal part in this campaign of abuse.

Throughout his pontificate, Paul VI suffered due to a "self-destructive attitude" he encountered within the Church. "We did not expect", he said one day in 1974 (July 10), "this phenomenon of intolerant agitation and even subversion desired by the people of our own house."[2] Now the truth obliges me to say that in so grave a circumstance, despite several reminders from our Father General, the Society of Jesus in France has not played the role incumbent upon it. Through many of its members, sometimes placed in the highest positions of influence, it has played precisely the opposite role. By their constant hostility to the papacy, in forms that were sometimes violent and sometimes scornful, they accelerated that process of "subversion" deplored by Paul VI. I have seen, read, heard too many things (which I prefer not to say here) for the most skillful argument possible ever to change my judgment in this regard.[3]

The second successor to Paul VI was very right in saying that

> his greatness finds its basis in the mystery of the Cross of Christ. He not only carried the cross in his hands, as he did each year on Good Friday to the Coliseum, but also in his heart, in his whole mission. He was the apostle of the Crucified, as was Saint Paul. He knew the insults, the spitting, the sadness and the agony evoked by the first reading [of Sunday, September 14, 1979] and the Psalm that followed it. He overcame the trial through prayer, through unshakeable trust; he responded to the trials both inside and outside the Church with that unshakeable faith, hope and charity that made him the Peter of our times. The great wisdom and humility that accompanied this faith and this hope made them firm and unbending.[4]

During a stay in Rome just after the Council, I went to see once again the tomb of Adrian VI in the choir of the church of Santa Maria dell'anima. Engraved there is this melancholy inscription, whose literal translation is difficult but whose meaning is only too obvious: *Proh dolor! Quantum refert in quae tempora vel optimi cujusque virtus incidat!* [Alas! What a huge difference it makes when a man of consummate virtue happens to live at the wrong time!] [9:11].

~

Many friends have vanished during these recent years. I would like to recall a few of them because of the part they had in my own work.

---

[2] *Documentation catholique*, no. 1659 (August 4–18, 1974), 701.

[3] It is very clear, however, that these "many" were, in relation to the whole, only a small number—and that many of the tirades have died down. My filial and entire confidence in the Society of Jesus has not been affected by it. Cf. above.

[4] John Paul II, homily at Saint Peter's, anniversary Mass for the repose of the soul of Paul VI (*La Croix*, Tuesday, September 16, 1979). Anyone would be blind to see these words as merely a conventional eulogy.

The death of Father Pierre Chaillet in Lyons, in April 1972, was passed over with indifference by that Fourvière house where he had taught and from which he had launched the *Cahiers du Témoignage chrétien* enterprise,[5] the honor of the Society of Jesus—but which, since then in full spiritual decomposition, had rejected any memory of a past that it had decided to abolish. In 1973, it was the death of Father René d'Ouince in Paris, a discreet confidant, a sound adviser, a faithful support in all circumstances, to whom I was bound as well by a twofold, joint friendship with Father Fessard and Father Teilhard de Chardin. On January 31, 1974, Father Robert Hamel died in Nantes, having spent his final days praying "for the unity of those who believe in Jesus Christ" and "for the Peace of the Catholic Church in the solidity of the Faith". How many times he had encouraged, counselled, enlightened—and picked me up again—since the distant time of our philosophy on Jersey! He would have liked me to be bolder in spiritual combat. His was a soul on fire—a very pure fire, that which Christ came to bring to the earth. The papers he left behind were too scattered to allow me to publish a collection of them as requested. I will quote one page from them in the Appendix [9:12].

This same year, in May, came the death of Cardinal Jean Daniélou. Never so much as on this occasion have I felt to what decadence a decline in the religious spirit can lead: it was a group of his confreres, such a ferocious pack, who immediately set out to hound his memory, launching a slanderous campaign against him that was to be sustained for years. In truth, I then saw the face of fratricidal hatred. On his return from Rome, where Paul VI had just made him a cardinal, he had written to a confidant: "I already know what it is to sacrifice one's reputation for the honor of God and the Church and to see oneself removed from one's brothers and friends". And several years before, taking Saint Paul as a model for the apostle: "Saint Paul is a lost man, a hunted man . . . his reputation ruined, rejected, scorned. . . . That is true of all those who take Christ seriously". One journalist, a specialist in the commonplaces of dispute, wrote that "in contrast to Newman, he was a dilettante", and that he had been "embittered by secularization and demythologization". Nothing could be less true. On essential points, Father Daniélou was always committed to the depths of his soul, with a strength of total conviction. The journalist in question, who was not without some complicity among us, could only denigrate the one who had fought with courage against the disintegration of the faith. Daniélou's intelligence, his education, as well as his kindness,

---

[5] The journal that continues to bear that name today has just celebrated (November 1981) with solemnity what it called its fortieth anniversary by having a long series of official tributes addressed to itself. None of those who had formed the original team around Father Chaillet had even been approached. The spirit of the *Cahiers* was thus totally falsified.

preserved him from all fanaticism, but his zeal was nonetheless ardent, "without respect of persons". He knew how to observe both those outside the Church and the men of the Church, as one aspect of the vast human comedy, and how to cling to the Church and to his faith with a profound sincerity and a rock-like firmness.

He was at ease everywhere. Those who thought him worldly because they had heard of him only in respect to some ceremony, knew nothing of all his hard labor, of his spiritual apostolate and of his hidden devotion. For a long time, in the interest of a better ministry, he had, despite his gifts, renounced any pursuit of writing. In his final years, without losing any of his liveliness, continuing to be interested in everything, he had achieved a rare degree of self-renunciation. More and more, his freedom as an apostle made him everything to everyone. He was also without rancor. Even among those who did battle with him, those who knew him well knew that if they were in trouble, they could have recourse to his charity. I could cite many pertinent examples of it.

He rendered me very numerous services, and we often collaborated. He engaged in intense activity, from 1942 on, in the service of *Sources chrétiennes*.[6] More than once, right or wrong, I had occasion to make use of my seniority to give him some advice (frequently requested by him) or even some slight warning; he never took offense at it, and his trust was not altered by it—no more than it was by some little difference in our evaluation of the Fathers of the Church. During the Council, we constantly met together, had discussions, exchanged many a note, worked out more than one text together. Cardinal Garrone has recalled what effective help he had found from him, particularly for the preparation of *Gaudium et spes*. But whatever some ill-informed person might say about it, his conciliar activity was much more extensive; in that area, the most effective interventions are not always those that leave recorded traces. In the years that followed, the friendship between us remained without a break. It increased with time and, for my part, the better I knew him from within, the more it was joined by an ever more lively admiration.

Soon after his death, at the invitation of Father Roger Heckel, I published, in the *Cahiers d'action religieuse et sociale*, the following lines about him:

> It is impossible to describe in a few lines, even in outline, the many-sided, truly extraordinary activity of Father Jean Daniélou. Others have already done so, others will do so more fully. The readers of the *Cahiers* will permit someone

---

[6] It was to him, moreover, that we owe the good start of this series in the difficult conditions of an "occupied" France. —The *Bulletin des Amis du Cardinal Daniélou* has begun (no. 2, June 1976) to publish the letters he wrote to me from 1941 on.

who knew him for nearly half a century, who often worked with him in the most varied tasks, who received from him many confidences and was able to observe him up close on many occasions to bear this brief testimony in his regard.

Father Daniélou was *a free man*. At ease in all milieux, with men of the most varied opinions. Creating faithful friendships everywhere. Taking or encouraging all kinds of initiatives. Open to all kinds of pursuits. Without prejudices. Nothing was farther from him than the tendency, frequent among clerics of all kinds, to see salvation only within the confines of their own system. He was not a man of slow reflection or literary subtleties or of minute analyses—even his most technical works feel the effects at times of a certain haste—but the acuity of his observation made him discern, in a nearly infallible way, the central point of a tangled question, the major interest of a new subject, the real stakes of a confused discussion, the essential need of some given situation. His already long experience of the life of the Church made him a resolute and very well-informed worker for conciliar renewal. He was from the first day—and at times with what passion!—among the "active element" of the Council, and his momentum did not slacken in the days that followed. With the same spontaneity, the same youthfulness of heart, he maintained his direction, without letting himself be led into errors or giving way to the falsifications we can observe every day.

He had read much of Péguy—the real Péguy, which a series of good workers is striving to make better known to us today. Like him, very open to social problems, he had also, like him, soon recognized their essential connection to the total human problem. So one of his principal efforts was turned toward the question of education. He thought with good reason that it was especially necessary since the frequent lack of education, linked to a kind of morbid anti-intellectualism, was one of the great misfortunes of the Church in our country: the source of so much confusion, naïve ignorance, inferiority complexes; so many aberrations, too, the abortion of so many generous undertakings. . . .

How could some have believed that he had ended by giving way to conservatism, indeed to "integrism"? It was precisely the contrary. Few men have given proof of such freedom of spirit. He was always opposed to all integrisms. He never let himself be seduced or intimidated by any clique. He did not flatter the powers of the day, those who manipulated opinion—and we know what strength of soul is required today to resist it, so long as one does not resign oneself to silent withdrawal. Thanks to that freedom of spirit, he could truly be, like the Apostle, "everything to everyone". There could have been no better choice made for the second reading at his funeral Mass than the passage from the Epistle to the Corinthians (9:19–23), in which Paul talks of this. The vast crowd, as varied as possible, moved and praying, who filled Notre Dame, gave witness to it.

This free man was a true Christian. *A man of faith*—not of a blind or "habitual" (Péguy) and hardened faith, but a faith that was living, springing from the depths of his soul, permeating every sphere of his action. That is why he fought so courageously for it, could not endure to see it degraded, "secularized", shaking the cowardly indifference of many, waking sleepy consciences, taking up the defense of believers without defense, all the while pursuing his effort to enlighten, educate, enliven. That is why he dared (it is not without shame that one finds oneself forced to say so) to support the See of Peter, although so many men of the Church around him were silent, bowing or trembling beneath the effect of the propaganda. That is why his cardinalate took away nothing of his straightforwardness or spontaneity.

For fear of lapsing into panegyrics, it often happens that one lingers over describing little shortcomings, noting each of the slight faults of men about whom one could just as well gather a rich harvest of admirable traits. I prefer to say what is essential. It is the most true. Father Daniélou was an *evangelical man*. There was no pharisaism in him. Behavior that was modeled on that of Jesus—which exposed him to the same kind of criticism. Like his master, he welcomed sinners. A priest, he judged that the best part of his time was owed to souls. Not on the periphery but at the heart of his activity, it was a discreet work of spiritual education that one discovers. And more than ever after he became a cardinal, a poor life: without a car, without a secretary,[7] hardly dressed decently, housed like the poor. All without affectation. An example more fruitful than so many declamations on poverty, which are truly naïve even when they are sincere.

What is most essential I have yet to say. I will make only a brief allusion to it. Cardinal Daniélou (who could fail to mention it?) was the object of a persistent campaign of disparagement that was so successful that many who had never come near him and had scarcely read a thing by him knew him only in a false light. He was insulted, mocked, slandered. He was at times treated shamefully by his brothers. Others systematically avoided him. They plotted against him. He knew all that—and he did not want to know it. "If I stopped to think about it," he confessed one day to a friend, "I would let myself become irritated or discouraged." He remained smiling, obliging, brotherly. If he fought, it was without mixing personal polemics with his battle. There was no bitterness, no rancor in him. In that way, above all, he was evangelical. It was for that that I loved him most [9:13].

Cardinal Garrone could write that, from the human viewpoint, the abrupt departure of Cardinal Daniélou was "a catastrophe" for the Church. He is right. As for me, I associate his memory with that of Father Yves de Montcheuil, whom we missed so much in the years after the war, at the time when that "spiritual collapse" began to be produced of which Karl Barth spoke and whose consequences are accelerating, despite the effort of renewal by a betrayed Council. A martyr of charity, Father de Montcheuil fell in bearing witness to Christ before nazi paganism. Father Daniélou used his strength to bear witness to him within a Church where the temptation to corrupt the Gospel was rampant. The one was condemned by the enemies of

---

[7] On account, it must be said, of the ill will of our order.

his faith. The other succumbed in an effort opposed by the very ones who
should have supported it. Yes, from the human point of view, those were
both catastrophes. But we would be unfaithful to their spirit if, in our grief,
we allowed ourselves to give in to the sadness of these human views.

HENRI DE LUBAC, S.J.

P.S. This article was written before the end of May. Today, I would make
it more precise and still more laudatory. When certain truths are better
known, the figure of Cardinal Jean Daniélou will emerge from the campaign of which we are well aware not only intact but greater in the eyes
of any man with a sense of the Gospel.

~

Father Gaston Fessard died on June 18, 1978 [9:14]. It was with him that
I enjoyed the longest and closest relationship of friendly collaboration.
We had known each other in the "juniorate" of Canterbury, in December
1919, on our return from the great war. Three years of joint reflection on
Jersey (1920–1923), under the rather suspicious gaze of Fathers Picard and
Descoqs (who could not stand our Thomistic tendencies), had bound us
together forever.[8] We had met again during two years at Fourvière (1926–
1928). As early as 1922, he had laid the foundations of a work on "the
method of reflection of Maine de Biran", which would appear only in 1938
(he presented it to me at that time "in memory of the already distant years
that saw its birth and burial"). His first public work was to be "*Pax nostra*: An international examination of conscience" (1936), which carried as
an introductory quotation these words of Saint Paul: "IPSE enim est Pax
nostra"; it contained the seeds of the principles, spirit and method that
would subsequently unfold. What memories are evoked by the dedication
"of this occasional writing", he said to me, "in which, from the main outlines—so far back does the friendship go that saw the first sketch hatched
—to the well-placed commas—so diligent to the very end was the care
taken by the corrector—I can no longer distinguish what is yours from
what is mine". From then until the end, there was scarcely a writing for
which Father Fessard did not communicate to me the outline, successive
drafts and final edition in order to submit them to my criticism, which was
always frank and often finicky. This is what resulted in our voluminous
correspondence [9:15].

[8] See above, IV, p. 64.

Already, at the request of Father Auguste Valensin, he contributed much to a reworking of Blondel's secondary thesis on the *vinculum substantiale* for publication in the French language (1930). He had published (1935) a critical study on the thought of Le Senne, and he had entered into correspondence with Brunschvicg—his two masters at the Sorbonne. He had established a close friendship with Gabriel Marcel,[9] who never ceased to entrust him with his confidence. It was in 1926, in Munich, that he had discovered Hegel; from 1934 to 1939, he was a part of a little group that was studying the "Phenomenology of the Spirit" with Alexandre Kojévnikoff ("Kojève"). In 1937, he published "La Main tendue: Le Dialogue catholique-communiste est-il possible? [The extended hand: Is Catholic-communist dialogue possible?]", and in 1939, "Epreuve de force [Test of strength]". If I mention these two works, it is as signs, first, of a thought that was always engaged in the tragic actuality of our century and, then, of the continuity of that thought, contrary to the idea that some have sought to spread, according to which he later changed his orientation through his fight against community ideology.

The war came, and then the collapse, as we know. Demobilized, Father Fessard spent several months in Lyons before rejoining our two friends René d'Ouince and Yves de Montcheuil in Paris, at the Etudes house. It was in Lyons, with Pierre Chaillet, that the plans for the *Cahiers du Témoignage catholique* were worked out in secret. At least six months of preparations were needed for the appearance of the first *Cahier* (whose title was changed at the last moment). It was *France, prends garde de perdre ton âme* [France, take care not to lose your soul!], of which Father Fessard was the author. It excited considerable interest. It was the first side of a triptych, whose second was to be, in 1945 and 1946, *France, prends garde de perdre ta liberté!* [France, take care not to lose your freedom!] and the third, posthumously, in 1979: *Eglise de France, prends garde de perdre la foi!* [Church of France, take care not to lose the faith!]. The last two required no less courage and faith than the first. In order to appear, as Father Chaillet wished, in the Jeunes Editions of the *Témoignage chrétien*, the second had to overcome a tenacious obstruction (the author reminds me, in his dedication, of the "great concern" that his publication caused me), and in the months that followed, he was violently attacked [9:16].

When, soon after, discussions were raised in the Church that were going to become a tempest, he wrote to me one day, although we knew ourselves to be in union of thought: "You are suspected of heresy, and I, of being the

---

[9] Their correspondence has been published: Gabriel Marcel-Gaston Fessard, *Correspondance (1934–1971)*, introduced and annotated by Henri de Lubac, Marie Rougier and Michel Sales. Introduction by Xavier Tilliette (Archives de Philosophie library. New series, 45) (Paris: Beauchesne, 1985).

herald of the Inquisition!" He himself, however, was no less "suspected of heresy" by those who saw a sacrilege in any critical examination of "progressivism". On more than one occasion he was reproached as if for some defect because of what they called his "Hegelianism". The attacks were revived in 1960, when his masterly work "De l'actualité historique" appeared. Confronted with the clearsightedness and rigor of his analyses, it is staggering to note the blindness of those who fought against him: "Thomism" covered everything, and the bugbear of "Hegelianism" was enough to dissuade them from studying a work that constitutes perhaps the most competent and most radical criticism of Hegel [9:17] as well as the soundest synthesis of Catholic understanding produced in France during the course of this century [9:18].

Shortly after the death of Father Fessard, his long study on *Chrétiens marxistes et théologie de la libération* (1978) appeared, whose final proofs he had managed to correct. Since then, two posthumous writings have been published: one, *Eglise de France. . .* (1979), which I mentioned above; the other, *La Philosophie historique de Raymond Aron* (1980), which contains an appendix on "the mystery of Israel". At this time, another posthumous writing should be ready for printing: a third volume of the work that is undoubtedly Father Fessard's most important and one about which I have said nothing yet: *La Dialectique des Exercices spirituels de saint Ignace de Loyola* [The dialectic of the Spiritual Exercises of Saint Ignatius of Loyola] (volumes 1 and 2 were published in 1956 and 1966). Studies on language and symbol,[10] undertaken beginning around 1960, are still in large part unpublished.

I never stopped urging him to put an end to his minute analyses and publish at last. But he made up his mind only with difficulty to cut the thread of his research, and, in his scrupulous integrity, he pushed the concern for objectivity to the extreme. (Often incisive, or at times a bit finicky, his criticism was never polemical.[11] In 1945, I literally tore the manuscript of *Autorité et bien common* from him, a study that was an honor for the newly founded "Theology" series; it was the same in 1948 with *Le Mystère de la société*, published in the *Recherches de science religieuse*. His unbending love of Truth—which is the incarnate Word of God—made him disagreeable to many: they wanted to see in it the mark of an extremist character, or an abstract logicism—when it was not of a natural "conservative". In recent

---

[10] Some appeared in the third volume of *La Dialectique des Exercices spirituels de S. Ignace de Loyola*, vol. 3: *Symbolisme et historicité*, Le Sycomore series (Paris-Namur: Lethielleux-Culture et Vérité, 1984). Father Fessard's studies on Hegel will also appear in a volume prepared by Father Michel Sales.

[11] In *De l'actualité historique*, he explained the meaning he gave to "criticism" as opposed to "polemics" (vol. 2, pp. 395–98).

times, some have reproached him for his lack of "pastoral sense". That was to misunderstand him completely. His conscience was unashamed and calm [9:19].

In living a life full of difficulties, he gave proof of a perfect uprightness and exemplary obedience. Long delayed in his studies, then expelled for no valid reason from Paris, where he was exercising a fruitful ministry, he never let one complaint be heard outside. But increasingly, in those years when a certain distancing from the Church passed for the criterion of adult Christianity, he made people uncomfortable. Even those who had to recognize his worth deplored a fidelity they no longer understood. (I am speaking here only of a small number, but it was they who laid down the law.) His death was not even announced in *Etudes*, for which he had been a writer for thirty years, or in *Recherches de science religieuse*, for whom he had been the secretary. Any review of his later works was forbidden. One weekly had two articles published that crushed his entire work beneath a funeral oration in cleverly calculated expressions and omissions. A secret intrigue brought about the rejection of the clarification that had obtained the *nihil obstat* from the Provincial of France [9:20]. A fine example of the police methods practiced by a certain intelligentsia then reigning in France in the Society of Jesus! He who had written a commentary upon and lived this thought of Saint Ignatius: "We believe that between Christ our Lord, who is the Bridegroom, and the Church, His Bride, one and the same Spirit governs and directs us" was rejected even in his death by the new "Ignatians".

Fortunately he had a fervent disciple, Father Michel Sales. It is to him that we owe the publication of his last three works, the preservation of his archives and the hope of later publications [9:21].

The death of Father Henri Bouillard, 73 years old, occurred unexpectedly in July of this year, 1981. He had come from the Sulpician seminaries to the Society of Jesus. A distinguished philosopher, a believer always in search of understanding, as steady as he was moderate, of calm courage, who made no accommodation for flashy novelties, he was capable of admiring the most varied ways of thinking when he recognized the mark of a committed conscience in it. He was an eminent master, whom the "seminaries" had followed through a fervent elite group. I can no more enter here into an examination of his works than I can give a summary of his life; the logic in it was rigorous, the form, classic, sober, without display, but not devoid of elegance. He gave penetrating interpretations of the authors he studied—Saint Thomas, Barth, Blondel, Bultmann, Eric Weill. . . . In 1941, he had defended at Fourvière (because of the war) a thesis prepared at the Gregorian under the direction of Father Charles Boyer, who presided over his jury: *Conversion et grâce chez saint Thomas d'Aquin* [Conversion and grace in Saint Thomas Aquinas]. In 1944, this opened the "Theology" series, of which he was the founder.

I did not know him very well at that time. The "Fourvière affair" brought us together. From 1946 on, we were companions in misfortune, first exposed to the lions without defense, then, in 1950, exiled. For more than thirty years, our friendship did not weaken. Although we were very different, our trust was mutual. He took a close interest in my work, and I in his. When, after the Council, he became a professor at the Theology Faculty of Paris, he nevertheless remained until the end excluded from any influence in the Society and subject to many a harassment: this was because, in a study on Saint John of the Cross that appeared in 1962–1963,[12] he had dared to discuss competently (in the most measured terms) an interpretation given by Father Georges Morel: hence this new ostracism, more persistent than the first.

I still have our correspondence. I have had some excerpts from it typed, parts that seemed to me to be instructive. I will quote a few of them in the Appendix [9:22]. He wrote to me again, in September 1975: "If I grant critical exegesis the place that it deserves, I hardly appreciate a theology that neglects philosophical reflection as well as the tradition and concrete life of the Church." He had written to me in 1968: "I think as you do that we must not let ourselves be discouraged by what disconcerts us in the present situation of the Society and the Church. The excesses will end by arousing reactions, and the Spirit of God will not abandon us."[13]

~

Again integrism. The "opening" of the Council had not extinguished all its fires. Recently again some journalists have written (they must really have been inspired) that after the lamentable weaknesses of Paul VI, John Paul II was going to take my fate in hand; I was even assured that an article to this effect had appeared in *l'Osservatore romano*. . . . One little thing after another, forgotten one by one. I remember one of them, nevertheless, because it was symptomatic. In 1975, an Italian publisher addressed some photocopies to me of a work that Cardinal Siri, Archbishop of Genoa, had just published in Rome. I was named in it as the first of three authors responsible for the doctrinal crisis raging within the Church

---

[12] "Sagesse mystique, selon saint Jean de la Croix", in *Recherches de Science religieuse*, 50 (1962), 481–529.

[13] An important work of philosophy and fundamental theology, which he had given up supplementing further, should have been able to be published without delay.

(my two companions were Karl Rahner and Jacques Maritain). This crisis resulted from an "historicist mentality", whose "three principal expressions" were "the historical conscience", "hermeneutics" and "the existential reference". At the origin of such an evil, there was *Surnaturel*. No middle term was indicated to show the possible connection between this book (even understood the wrong way) with the three above-mentioned errors. On November 15, I wrote to Genoa:

Monsieur le Cardinal, I have received a photocopy of the pages in which you speak of me in a recent work. —If it had been a question of a polemicist, I would not have paid any notice to it. But the respect I have always professed for the shepherds of the Church makes it a duty for me to write to you. —First of all, it is impossible for me to accept the praise contained on page 73: "In questi ultimi anni. . . ." The opposition that such an expression suggests with respect to my attitude in the past is an insult to me. My concern for the Christian faith and the life of the Church has not waited until these recent years to exist and manifest itself. —As for the heart of the matter, I have no intention of debating it with Your Eminence. I will merely allow myself to say that you have ventured into territory that you seem not to know well, that you imagine some monstrous filiation without giving a single piece of evidence for it—and to contrast this to the testimony of a man whose eminent competence everyone, in the Church and in this century, must recognize: Etienne Gilson (precisely the man to whom the Holy Father has just given a glowing homage). —You will find attached a copy of an entire article by Mr. Gilson [9:23],[14] which appeared in *La Croix* in 1965, and excerpts from two letters that he has addressed to me. —Please accept, Monsieur le Cardinal, along with the expression of my grieved amazement and my hope that you will be able to make the public gesture of reparation that is imperative, that of my profound and religious respect. —P.S. Only a discretion that I have never wished to relinquish dissuades me from sending you as well a copy of the letter that His Holiness, Pius XII, had addressed to me during his life. In congratulating me for my works, and without the least allusion to the fact that any of them might have strayed from the right path even so much as a little, the Holy Father encouraged me to "continue with much confidence a scientific activity from which much fruit is promised for the Church".

I received no reply. But in 1981, Cardinal Siri (who in the meantime, it is said, had failed to become pope) had had published in French translation his large volume: *Gethsémani. Réflexions sur le Mouvement théologique contemporain* [Gethsemani. Reflections on the contemporary theological move-

---

[14] *Lettres de M. Etienne Gilson au R. P. H. de Lubac* (Paris: Cerf, 1986), 145–49; English trans.: *Letters of Etienne Gilson to Henri de Lubac* (San Francisco: Ignatius Press, 1988), 177–82.

ment].[15] And to speed up the distribution of it, one troop of diligent disciples was going to offer it at the homes of some outstanding personages.

Again Teilhard. 1981 was the year of his centenary. Conferences, colloquia, exhibitions, various publications came one after the other. The Church and the State, Notre Dame and Unesco, the Hotel de Ville and the Jesuits rivalled each other in zeal. In the bookstores, topical emptiness. Praises sprinkled with reservations. Incompetence in every form. Fireworks that were in fact artificial, without substance. Teilhard will not be better understood because of it. And the union of the celebrants will reinforce the equivocation. As a result, despite a few honest statements, "Teilhardism" will come out reinforced against Teilhard; this same Teilhardism of which some have made themselves a school and others a bugbear—and which is not worth considering.

"All spiritual ventures are a Calvary." Teilhard had noted this sentence from Bernanos in his notebook. And the great Newman, whom he so admired, had written humbly to Father Perrone: "Cum bene mihi sim semper conscius me non esse theologum. . . . [Since I am always well aware that I am not a theologian]." Teilhard spoke in this same vein— but no more than Newman could he ignore that it is through this kind of non-theologian that theology receives the most life-giving transplants.

In *Teilhard posthume*, I alluded to the conference that I had had to give about him in Rome in 1963. The invitation had been addressed to me by Father Charles Boyer, prefect of the Gregorian. I have just rediscovered his letter. When one knows that Father Boyer was Teilhard's great adversary in Rome (and no less mine), this letter takes on its full flavor:

> Pontificia Accademia romana de S. Tommaso d'Aquino e di Religione cattolica. Rome, June 10, 1963. My Reverend Father, P.C. You must have received at the proper time the announcement of the Sixth International Thomist Congress. I understand that other occupations have not permitted you to take an interest in it. This is why I dare to speak to you again about it. Having recently been received by the Holy Father, I had occasion to note the great esteem he has for you and your writings. At the same time, he expressed, although not without reservations, a judgment on Father Teilhard

---

[15] The series of the Fraternity of the Most Blessed Virgin Mary. Téqui. The translation was apparently made from an enlarged edition, but the part that concerns me is unchanged. In his conclusion, the author invites us to enter "into the mystery of Gethsemani" in order to "find there the meaning of man". It is with the most profound sympathy that we wish to follow him there; but that in no way changes the fact of our regret over his errors. A very benevolent reviewer observes, with respect to several theologians criticized by him: "We have the impression that, perhaps because of some question of language or through ignorance of the whole of their thought, he has not understood them well" (J. Daujat).

that would not have displeased you. —My reflections then led me to think that we must hear at the Congress a presentation that is sympathetic to the thought of Father Teilhard de Chardin on our theme ("De Deo"). No one could do this better than you. —So I am coming simply to ask you to take part in our Congress, whose date is just before the opening of the fourth session of the Council: from September 6 to 11. You could come only for the final days and, if you can do no more, merely give a brief paper. . . .

At the height of the Teilhardian celebrations (September 1981), *La Croix* published two unfortunate articles, one a criticism, the other praise, both incompetent and erroneous. Thanks to the energetic support of Rev. Father Madelin, Provincial, I was able to have a correction of the former published (in the "Mailbox" of the journal) [9:24]. Nothing could be done about the second, which vaunted an "extraordinary superecumenism" in Teilhard that had nothing Christian about it. A little later, the Father Provincial asked me to make up for it through a chapter that would be added to a collective volume prepared in the Society. Undoubtedly he also wanted to correct in that way the exclusion to which I was subjected when appeal had been made to "all" those (rare from then on) who had known Teilhard well. But again, circumstances did not allow for it.

~

I will end this rather disorderly memoir with a few words on my relations with His Holiness John Paul II. I had known Bishop Wojtyla in Rome, at the time of the Council. We worked side by side at the time of the arduous birth of the famous Schema 13, which, after a number of hasty modifications, became the Constitution *Gaudium et spes*. It did not take long observation to discover in him a person of the very highest qualities. He knew my works, and we were soon on good terms. He had asked me to write a preface for the French translation of his book *Love and Responsibility* (in a later letter, he complained of the poor quality of this translation). On March 17, 1966, he wrote to me that my preface "had a great deal to do with the decision of His Holiness to call [him] to the Commission on questions relating to marriage." In the course of the following years, we saw each other occasionally in Rome, particularly at the Gregorian, and we became friends.

He wrote to me in February 1968, shortly after he became a cardinal, following a few personal words,

I devote my very rare free moments to a work that is close to my heart and devoted to the metaphysical sense and mystery of the PERSON. It seems to me that the debate today is being played on that level. The evil of our times consists in the first place in a kind of degradation, indeed in a pulverization, of the fundamental uniqueness of each human person. This evil is even much more of the metaphysical order than of the moral order. To this disintegration, planned at times by atheistic ideologies, we must oppose, rather than sterile polemics, a kind of 'recapitulation' of the inviolable mystery of the person. I firmly believe that the truths attacked compel with more urgency the recognition of those who are often the involuntary victims of it. . . .

Several times I had the occasion to send him books or articles that I or others had written. He once replied to me, in 1969: ". . . I, too, do not lose hope that the great crisis that now shakes us so painfully will lead humanity to the royal way. Perhaps it will no longer be open to us, but we have firmly hoped, we will always hope, and we are and will be happy." Two years later, in 1970 and 1971, he invited me to Poland; in conjunction with the Superior of the Society, he had himself arranged for a three-city visit to Warsaw, Lublin and Cracow; but other obligations and then illness stood in the way. He never failed to send me a little note for Christmas and Easter. In 1972, he worked to translate into Polish my article on "Particular Churches and the Universal Church"—in which too great a fidelity to the Council had caused a few ripples in France. In letters from 1975, with respect to the next symposium of European bishops, he had shared with me, among other things, a concern about which we have since had other signs: that of assuring union with "bishops who live in another part of Europe and who are up against diametrically opposed problems."

For a long time I had happened to say in friendly conversations: "After Paul VI, my candidate is Wojtyla." A half-serious, half-joking remark. Besides, I added: "But he doesn't stand a chance." Learning of his election, I was as surprised as I was happy. Yet my joy was not unmixed. I thought, and I afterward said to others: "The night of that election I lost a friend." At the urging of others, I sent him a few lines; he replied immediately, with a very personal letter, sent through the mail without going through any office. After the assassination attempt in May 1981, when he had returned to Castelgandolfo, I again addressed him a few words of affection, under similar urging [from friends]. He replied to me on October 20, telling me of "the joy and consolation of feeling that you remain a faithful and discreet friend" and wishing that my "evening oblation might still be fruitful for the Church and for the Society of Jesus, to which you have given your life." I had had the happiness of seeing him again for a moment the preceding year in Paris. I suffered to see that many continued to have the same belligerent attitude toward him that they had had toward Paul VI, an attitude that springs above all from a hostility to the papacy, to the guardian of our Faith. I suffer doubly today because of the attitude of some of my brothers in his regard and because of all of which this is a sign. But, as he wrote to me, "we have firmly hoped, we will always hope, and we are and will be happy" [9:25].

DECEMBER 1981

PART TWO

APPENDICES

APPENDIX I

[*1:1*]

Shortly after, following a diatribe from Father Laberthonnière, aimed both at Saint Thomas and Blondel, published in the *Archivio di Filosofia* of 1933, Abbé J. Wehrlé wrote to Mlle. T. Perrin (February 14, 1935): "It is not a description of doctrines. It is a complete distortion, in my opinion, not only of the intentions but of the thoughts themselves. There is not only no equanimity, no impartiality in it, there is not even any fairness, any true objectivity. It is mad, really pathological writing. . . . Surely, one can ask for a strict revision of the Aristotelean-Thomist doctrine of the material principle of individuation of form. One can also have reservations about the way in which the thesis of predestination is proposed by Thomism. But this is not a pamphlet that will enable a clarification of things, nor is it a flood of vitriol that will help to rectify certain chemical compounds. . . . I am not unaware that Thomism is plagued by an inner dualism born of the intrinsic opposition between an originally and entirely pagan philosophy and a spiritual doctrine of evangelical and Christian origin. I admit that this dualism has not been completely reduced and brought around to an infrangible unity. But I do not admit any of the consequences that Father Laberthonnière draws from this with a virulence nearly unrivalled to this day." Let us add merely that Father Laberthonnière had many excuses: the unjust war of extermination that his implacable enemies had waged against him in the name of a Maurrasian "Thomism", the isolation to which he found himself condemned, painful attacks of illness that inspired his most regrettable excesses in writing. . . .

[*1:2*]

The article is reproduced in *Recherches dans la foi* (Paris: Beauchesne, 1979), 127–52. Letter from Msgr. Bruno de Solages, April 5, 1936: ". . . M. Blondel has written to me about your article on Christian philosophy, expressing his joy about your agreement with his position. He adds: 'As for the last pages, I admit that I have some doubts about the considered opinion I would have to give of them if I were to take up the problem again.' I will admit that, after having read your article with much attention this morning, these last pages also leave me with an impression of hesitation.

Why? Because it all still seems to me to lack sufficient clarification and because this final direction does not seem to me to be connected well enough to the others. Imperfect clarification not only in your article but in my own mind. . . ."

In *Nova et vetera* (1936), 108, Abbé Charles Journet gave the following review of the article:

"There are some Catholic philosophers who find philosophy as conceived by J. Maritain to be too Christian. For Father de Lubac, however, it is not Christian enough.

"Father de Lubac (who wrote before reading *Science et Sagesse*), moreover, gives a very inaccurate representation of J. Maritain's position. So inaccurate that he identifies it with that of Father Mandonnet.

"For Father de Lubac, it is M. Blondel who has found the true solution. By undertaking a similar path, Father de Lubac no longer manages to distinguish philosophy from theology. He realizes this himself. From which come his singular lines, which will astonish many other readers besides us: 'Will it be said that this is not philosophy but theology? The words scarcely matter. But in the present meaning of the word, *theology* calls to mind today, and has long done so, especially since the sixteenth century, a more specialized knowledge. It is not entirely the understanding of faith, it is much less understanding through faith. It is the science of revealed truths, it is not the science of all things in the light of faith. If we do not have any special word to designate this science, *would this not be because this science itself no longer corresponds with anything important in our thought?* By drawing our attention to it, the debate over Christian philosophy renders us an eminent service.' (The italics are ours.) These are singular reflections.

"If an intermediary position exists between that of Father Mandonnet and that of Father de Lubac, it would have much chance of being the true one."

There was a series of misunderstandings. Such was the purpose of our first exchange of letters, with a completely peaceful tone.

MAY 9, 1936

MONSIEUR L'ABBÉ,

The *Nouvelle revue théologique* forwarded to me the March issue of the *Nova et Vetera* journal, which contains your review of my little study concerning Christian philosophy. I want to thank you for it. To tell the truth, I am a little surprised at the summary you gave of it. I admit to having been completely unaware that I no longer managed to distinguish philosophy from theology. . . . The passage you quote in no way contains such an admission, even when taken out of context; and in any case, in its proper context, it seems as clearly as possible not to have the least bit of the meaning you apparently suppose of it: merely look, for example, at the last lines of the immediately preceding page, p. 246. Permit me to add that, in the pages in question, I am in no way referring to Christian philosophy in the sense of M. Blondel, but to *something quite different*: so I consequently no longer understand at all the meaning of your remarks, which I would otherwise have found it very pleasant to consider.

Nonetheless, I still have the satisfaction of being able to congratulate you on the fine standards of this journal, for which you, I believe, are the moving force, and particularly for that study on "L'Esprit divinateur de l'Eglise" [The prophetic spirit of the Church], which I am very happy to have, thanks to you, in this form, while waiting for the day (not-too-distant, I hope) when we will read your great treatise on the Church.

Please know, Monsieur l'Abbé, that I still remember with great gratitude and pleasure the welcome I received several years ago at the Major Seminary in Fribourg, and that I am sincerely and respectfully yours in Christ.

Nova et vetera
Catholic review for French Switzerland.

                                    FRIBOURG. MONDAY. SEMINARY.
MY VERY REVEREND FATHER,

Deep thanks for the cordiality and charity with which you replied to my review in *Nova et vetera*. My intention was far more to draw attention to your study than to summarize it. I felt incapable of doing that. Although I read several times passages like the one on p. 249 where you seem to sum up your thought, I did not succeed in satisfying myself that I understood it well. I see by your letter that I have attributed a thought to you that is not yours. I regret that very much. If I return one day to this subject, I will be happy to take your remarks into account. I must say that that famous p. 247 had caused me an uneasiness that your letter has just completely dissipated. I had indeed read p. 246: philosophy appears there to be, as it were, a very vast discipline in which, besides a purely rational *phase* (is it a question of a *science* having a specific, proper, objective and valid object?), one must include other things that are not so purely rational, things that are the product of a heteronomy, and I believed that on this point you agreed with the opinion of Blondel, whom you quote here with praise. In a general way, I thought I could say you classified the three principal responses made to the problem of Christian philosophy around three names and that it was the third, that of Blondel, that seemed to you to represent the true solution. I was aware that you mention a fourth position, that of G. Marcel. But, either this fourth position is reducible to the solution of a specifically rational philosophy, having a distinctive object of specifying, but receiving objective and subjective conformations from the supernatural order: this is the solution with which I myself am in agreement. Or else it is reducible to a discipline objectively specified by the supernatural, and then I do not see how to distinguish it from theology. Forgive me, my Father, for allowing myself these remarks, which have no other purpose but to excuse myself in part for having misunderstood you. Thank you for the great indulgence with which you speak of the study in *Nota* on the Holy Spirit in the Church and for the invaluable encouragement you give me; and also for the very gracious memory you keep of the Seminary of Fribourg: when will we have the great pleasure of seeing you there again? I am, my very reverend Father, sincerely and respectfully yours in Christ.

ABBÉ JOURNET

I will have occasion to speak of Msgr. Journet again. For a long time he had difficulty understanding anything that was not strictly in conformity with the "Thomist" model he had received. At a time when our relations were more trusting, I allowed myself the pleasure of teasing him on the subject. He had sent me his little book on Savonarola, which was an unqualified defense. I said to him in my reply: "Perhaps it is fortunate that the great goodness of your heart is not always free to go its full limits when the subject is someone not of your dear School: otherwise you would end by falling into laxity! . . ."

[1:3]

C. F. Laberthonnière, *Annales de philosophie chrétienne*, 159:292: ". . . God does not want us, know us, love us as *things*; he wants us, knows us, loves us—which for him is to make us exist—as *beings*, so that we, in our turn, might want him, know him, love him as Being. This implies a relation between him and us of known being to knowing being and, in consequence, a knowledge by us about him just as by him about us. But this knowledge does not at all resemble the knowledge of things. And this is what the mystics have well seen."

406–7: "Considered in its movement, in its development, [the life of faith] is a transformation at work in one's manner of seeing at the same time as in one's manner of being. And, like all transformation, it is a death as well as a birth. It is a matter of winning a new mind, a new heart, a new will, and of winning them from an already existing will, heart and mind. It is a battle to be instituted by oneself against oneself, by what one should be against what one is, by what one should think against what one thinks, by the new man against the old man. And it is not some make-believe battle, a simulated battle; it is combat without a truce, without mercy. To win ourselves, as has been said, we must lose ourselves. It is over ourselves that we gain our victories. And while these are a rending by which we cast aside illusions that bind us as if by magic to perishable things, they always bring us at present only a foretaste, a light more or less mixed with shadow, which, instead of satisfying our appetite for 'true intuition', for full participation, make it feel ever more deeply the emptiness that remains to be filled. This thus produces two kinds of suffering, the suffering of the old man who is dying and the suffering of the new man who has not reached the goal of being what he would like to be. And in fact it happens that the best among us, each in turn, falls from weariness on the road, complaining of his distress. But this is only in order to gather more vigorous speed, because at bottom there is a strength that overcomes all weariness and a joy that overcomes all suffering. —And it is faith itself that gives this strength and this joy, 'scio cui credidi' [I know in whom I have believed], because, instead of being, as one might on the contrary imagine, a chain that stops the mind's momentum, faith is the divine impetus that leads the mind to light, to freedom, to indefectible love. And if the life of faith understood in this way is burdensome and painful, this is only through the obstacles that it must overcome and through the incompletion that leaves it unsatisfied. But in itself, it is a blossoming and not a compression, victory and not passivity."

413: "Faith is the initial Yes we say to God in the depths of ourselves with all ourself. This Yes, so long as we are in this world, always remains, in some respects, precarious; even when we say it the most heartily, it is still only a stammering, only a rough draft of the ineffable Yes that will fill eternity. . . ."

165 (February 1913), 548: "If there are thus grounds to distinguish the two theories of faith indicated by M. Rousselot, . . . it seems to us that from another point of view there are grounds to distinguish a third, which is proper to Augustinianism in opposition to Thomism, and according to which the light of faith acts not only *per viam voluntatis* [by way of the will] but *per viam intellectus* [by way of the intellect], by raising the mind, by conferring on it through grace a connaturality with supernatural truth, in such a way that it is enlightened by it and lives by it."

As much and perhaps even more than Rousselot, Laberthonnière was aware very early of the imperative necessity to clarify the idea of the supernatural and to transform the representation of it that had prevailed in modern Scholasticism. He wrote in April 1901 to Marcel Hébert, in response to certain criticisms formulated by the latter: "The manner in which the supernatural is represented seems to me to have considerable importance. It is this, in my opinion, that gives rise to all the ambiguities and misunderstandings. That is above all what I would have liked to make understood." (*Laberthonnière et ses amis*, files of correspondence introduced by Marie-Thérèse Perrin [Beauchesne, 1975], 31.)

[*1:4*]

From Father Joseph Huby, September 15, 1945:

"You had spoken to me . . . about a project of gathering into one volume scattered articles by Father Rousselot, including 'les Yeux de la Foi' [The eyes of faith]. [I posed] the question to Rome (Father de Boynes). I have received the reply, deplorable. Here are the conditions for it: 'You can publish all the articles that do not relate to the question of the Eyes of Faith, but I cannot authorize the publication of those that treat this question. You know that I am only a mere Vicar General. It is true that I have all the authority of the General, but I must govern "ad mentem Patris Generalis defuncti". It is the only restriction made on my authority. You understand that the thought of the Father General was too clear on this painful question for me to go against it. The future General—let us hope that we will have him without too much delay—will have full freedom to act as he judges best'. . . ."

Since then, several important studies have been devoted to Rousselot: E. Kunz, S.J., *Glaube, Gnade, Geschichte: Die Glaubenstheologie des Pierre Rousselot* (Frankfurt, 1969); J. de Wulf, S.J., *La Justification de la foi chez s. Thomas d'Aquin et le P. Rousselot* (Paris, 1946); John M. McDermotte, S.J., "Love and Understanding, the Relation of Will and Intellect", in *Pierre Rousselot's Christological Vision* (Rome, 1983); cf. M. Nédoncelle, "L'Influence de Newman sur 'les Yeux de la Foi' de Rousselot", *Rev. des sc. religieuses* (1953). Some of his writings have been published. But his work has not been collected.

[*1:5*]

In the third volume of the *Correspondance Blondel-Valensin* (1936) and in the edition of Father Teilhard de Chardin's *Lettres intimes*, I have given a number of details about this affair. See the analytical tables.

Blondel also did this in several studies in his later period. Etienne Borne remarked on this to the Société française de philosophie, on January 25, 1975 (*Bulletin*, 9–10):

"Considered in its relation with Christianity, philosophy [cannot be reduced] to a preliminary or intermediate function. . . . The Christian Blondel will also use philosophy like a descending dialectic, and, departing from revelation and faith in the Word, he will try to smooth out a certain number of antinomical difficulties in which, in its supreme effort, philosophical thought ends. There is most certainly no way to pass from the philosophical idea of the absolute to the Trinity-God, who is of another order. But a certain dilemma that Plato had already encountered in 'The Sophist' on the apparently contradictory necessity of attributing to the absolute both identity and life could be removed in the perspective of the Christian God. This was the way in which Blondel renewed and practiced the 'Fides quaerens intellectum' [Faith seeking understanding]."
On April 8, 1936, I wrote to Blondel, who had just sent me *l'Etre et les êtres*, "It seems to me that I should have added a paragraph [to my article], or rather perhaps completed it, gone into more detail in the last few pages. For . . . we have never been more in Christian philosophy than with your last work."

On April 3, 1932, I had addressed to Blondel this sort of sketch of what would later become my book *Surnaturel* (1946):

"A few free moments now, at the end of vacation, allow me to thank you once again for the 'Problème de la philosophie catholique'.

"You had asked me, very kindly, to tell you if any of the theses you present in it seemed to me to 'overstep the mark'. . . . To tell you the truth, it is rather the opposite reproach that I would be tempted to make, and I cannot help being a bit annoyed with those theologians who, through their lack of comprehension, obliged you to give so many explanations and insistences. Not that in themselves these explanations are not invaluable. But (allow me this excess of frankness, as you would a child) hasn't the perpetual retrospection to which they have obliged you already somewhat obstructed for a long time the free development of your thought? The latter was spontaneously Catholic enough not to have been hindered by excessive timidities. Yes, if I admire the minute care you take in criticizing yourself, I am a bit saddened at the thought that this labor perhaps slows down the more important works we await from you with so much impatience. . . .

"None of that gets to the root of things. But it is a point about which I would like to offer a few reflections, if you would allow me to. Three times (pp. 25, 37 n. 2, 159–60), you make allusion in your book to the hypothesis of a state of nature in which man might have been created and left. I am well aware that several of your strongest supporters have proved the orthodoxy of your doctrine by appealing to this distinction between 'essential' nature and 'historical' nature. But I believe that the question needs to be taken up again in its entirety.

"First of all, I note that no ecclesiastical document imposes belief in a realizable state of 'pure nature', in which man would have had only a natural destiny. Such a belief would be indissolubly linked, one would think, to the belief in the gratuity of the supernatural.

"Now, it does not seem to me that this link is so indissoluble. In fact, if the possibility of pure nature were denied, one would not for all that be obliged to say: 'God, having created human nature, owes it to that nature (or owes it to himself) to grant it a supernatural end', if it is true that we can say: 'It is because he wants to grant it a supernatural end that God creates human nature.' How can one say that the means being willed in view of the end, once willed, demands the volition of the end?

"Moreover, this concept of a pure nature runs into great difficulties, the principal one of which seems to me to be the following: How can a conscious spirit be anything other than an absolute desire of God? The reasons ordinarily alleged to explain that this desire must be 'ordered', 'conditioned', 'impulsive', are rather weak. In particular, they pass from the notion of inefficacious appetite to that of simple impulse: Is the assimilation not gratuitous? They argue from the divine independence: Is that an intrinsic reason? They try to show that the desire of God must be neither efficacious nor absolute; but they are less concerned to show how it cannot be so. . . .

"If we now question Tradition, we will see what can be called the 'system of Pure Nature' born from the womb of decadent Scholasticism. It seems that one might say, on the whole, that there we have one of those 'pieces of Scotism' that the great stream of the Thomist tradition itself began to carry along unconsciously; theology adopted it only because it was extremely convenient for the refutation of Baianism. But it was unknown to Saint Thomas. As for Saint Augustine, he would have been absolutely unable to accommodate it.

"Finally, would this system not be in large part responsible for the evil of 'separated theology', an evil from which we still suffer greatly today?

Is it not this that still sets up a barrier in opposition to every effort of Christian thought?

"These reflections will undoubtedly appear very rash to you. Their aim, however, is only to recapture the most traditional teaching: So long as this teaching is not freed from the artificial theories that still encumber it (although great progress has been made in the last forty years), I do not believe it will be possible to form a fully coherent theology of the supernatural.

"You see, Monsieur, how I let myself speak to you with all the freedom of a disciple. It is in fact the study of your work that made me begin, some eleven years ago, to reflect on these problems, and I believe that I have remained faithful to its inspiration. If it were necessary to try to define it, I would willingly take as a formula this text from your 'Itinéraire': 'There is a fear of mixing, confusing; there must be a fear of not uniting enough. . . . It is in fact when one does not know how to unite things well that one particularly fears confusing them. If the general life of humanity today too often withdraws from Christianity, it is perhaps because Christianity has too often been uprooted from the inner viscera of man.'

"Please be kind enough, Monsieur, to pardon me this letter, which I feel, despite everything, is a bit pretentious, and please believe in my very respectful wishes as well as in my faith remembrance *in Christo Jesu*."

Blondel replied to me on April 5th:

"Your very kind and very provocative letter merits all my gratitude; it increases my debt to you, which I like to feel grows greater each day, as I constantly count on the support of your prayers and of your manifold assistance. I would like to prove my gratitude to you by responding without delay and without evasion to your very useful admonitions.

"Your theological reflections are a singular encouragement for the philosophical initiatives I am reserving for *l'Esprit chrétien*, which is in large part already dictated. I will profit from your desiderata, which it seems to me I am in large measure satisfying spontaneously. Allow me today to say to you only and simply in what respect you seem to me to be a bit hard on the past and in what respect I deviate from some of what you express.

"First of all, when, over 40 years ago, I dealt with problems for which I was not sufficiently equipped, an intransigent extrinsicism reigned, and if I had said, therefore, what you wish, I would have been thought rash and I would have compromised all effort I might have made, all causes I might have defended, by braving the censure that would have been nearly inevitable and certainly retardative. It was necessary to take time for my thought to mature and for rebel spirits to be tamed. The slownesses you regret are, from this twofold point of view, excusable. And, before going on to debatable theses, I was anxious to make the unperceived essence discerned, the incontestable that is nevertheless contested; it was for this reason that it was necessary to accept traditional modes (recent tradition, moreover, but now become pedestrian) and to adapt myself to the customary perspective, at least as a point of departure for a renewal, for a further deepening. You know the difficulties, the risks—not yet disappeared—through which I pursued a plan made still more burdensome by the trials of health and the professional tasks and even the counsels of prudence and waiting that were poured out upon me. So I am not completely responsible for the delays and timidities that you deplore as a 'child' of a new generation and as a master of a theological knowledge that I have always been far from possessing.

"I now add that it is not my part to 'play the theologian', as your desiderata seem to imply. Even if in fact one were to imagine that the supernatural were unconscious, I could in no way observe it and speculate as a philosopher on the finalist antecedence of the supernaturalizing design and on the content of the supernatural plan of God or the transnatural state of man. My role, my goal does not involve an observation from above of what is below, I could only observe the above from below without piercing the cloud where the God to be revealed is enveloped. And if there is in fact a place to deepen and renew the very theological analysis of the supernatural, one of the questions to be elucidated is that of knowing why, in fact and undoubtedly through intrinsic reasons, the supernatural as such remains unconscious even when it is present and acting in us.

"I would like to touch here on that central problem of which you have such a lively sense: an integral revival of the concept of the supernatural should be attempted. But it is necessary that it be integral, that all the facts of the statements, all the conditions of the solution be brought together, considered normally and organized harmoniously. It is not as a function of discussions or artificial and fragmentary distinctions that it is possible to explain and resolve such a difficulty. One of the errors in perspective that must be avoided, it seems to me, has to do with the bad habit of considering that the state in which the supernatural vocation places us eliminates the 'state of nature'. No, the latter remains immanent to the divine adoption itself. And it is in this sense that one can, as a philosopher and as a theologian, speak of the essential and indestructible incommensurability of created beings and God, in order better to understand the creations of the divine Charity, the paradoxical ways of transforming union, the metaphysical and properly hyperphysical wonder of our *consortium divinae naturae* [sharing in the divine nature]. Like you, I believe that God created only with a view to a deifying elevation; but that does not prevent the radical heterogeneity of the first gift of rational life and the second (and *antecedent* in the order of finality) gift of supernatural life, which, in order to be both received and acquired demands of us a *denuo nasci* [new birth], so that, as participants in the *Ens a se* and becoming *Entes a nobis divinitus*, we restore, so to speak, God to God in us who could exclude him and (?), if we did not return to him our original being and our native gifts.

"Please excuse my scribbling and this disorderly rough draft. I wanted only to give you a sign of my gratitude and to reveal in some way what great hopes I place in you. Sincerely yours."

I thanked him on April 8th:

"Even at the risk of giving you the impression that I am overstepping, it is impossible for me not to reply to the letter I have just read, at first with confusion, then with a satisfaction that increased with every sentence. The severity of which my preceding letter gave witness was aimed *entirely* at those extrinsicist theologians with whom you have clashed and for whom you have had to make allowances. I nonetheless understood your will to remain on the philosophical level, proceeding always from below to above, and if I let myself dream before you about the elaboration of a theology of the Supernatural, it was with the idea, not at all that you should do it, but that it could now be done because your philosophical work had paved the way. And it is precisely because you have been able to show the radical heterogeneity of the 'first gift' and the 'second gift', the indestructible incommensurability of created beings and God, the state of nature immanent to the divine adoption itself, that this imagination of a 'pure nature', which, with the whole series of its corollaries, still encumbers our classical theology, becomes unnecessary.

"Moreover, you did not have to combat this imagination directly. I only regret that the very ones who have defended you have sometimes in a way shielded you behind it, as if it had been the only means of saving your orthodoxy, and that no theologian well enough aware of the total tradition could be found to make everyone see that you are much more in the right than some of your most faithful disciples believe. Although incompetent in pure philosophy, my ambition would be to demonstrate that one day, on the level of the most positive theology. The completion and implementation of the already-voluminous file I have gradually put together awaits only a renewal of strength that Providence will perhaps not grant me. But it is nevertheless invaluable for me to see, by the explanations that you have been good enough to send me, that you do not discourage my efforts, and this gives me the courage to hope that I might have occasion to submit the rough draft to you.

"In the meantime, Monsieur, please accept once again the expression of my very deep gratitude. Do not think that I am merely being polite in saying this: modesty actually makes me fall short of the truth. My debt in your regard is known only by God, before whom I have for a very long time remembered you daily."

When my book appeared in 1946, I sent it to Blondel, who wrote to me on December 19: ". . . I had not until now been able to complete my reading of your fundamental, truly monumental work, *Surnaturel*, and I find in it a light, a power, a joy for which I cannot thank you enough, without forgetting the gratitude I owe you for the care with which you raise me above disparaging remarks and objections. —I find myself strengthened by it to pick up once again my efforts to finish the multiple drafts of Volume III on 'La Philosophie et l'Esprit chrétien'. . . ."

[*1:8*]

Here are the beginning and the end of this letter.

POITIERS. MAY 8, 1934
MY REVEREND FATHER,

My very deep thanks for having sent me your study of the history of the word supernatural. I have read it with great interest. These are questions I often had occasion to discuss with your colleague Father Fessard when he was here, and I am particularly happy to have all the historical and dogmatic details from your study. There are very many points in it about which I had only a vague knowledge, and I did not see the exact, often accidental, reasons behind the evolution of this term. [The body of the letter is found on p. 25].

But I won't go on forever trying to express the reflections your study suggests. I am convinced it is a collection of invaluable remarks to which I will often have to return. Please accept, my reverend Father, my warm thanks and the assurance of my deep respect.

A. FOREST

[*1:9*]

I had prepared a twofold follow-up to this study on the authority of the Church in temporal matters; one was a critical examination of the concept of "political Augustinianism" adopted in our century by a certain number of historians; the other concerned the evolution of ideas and facts during the contemporary period with regard to the relations between the Church and civil authorities. These two studies have remained uncompleted. Several fragments from the first have been collected in a volume of the Italian edition of my works undertaken by Jaca Book (Milan).

APPENDIX II

The misunderstanding, however, was persistent. In August 1952, I was at Gemen, near Münster, for an international meeting of Catholic youth, organized by Paulus Lenz-Médoc. Father Wetter, who had come from Rome, was present. According to what he recounted to our host, I was being reproached in Rome for having long before rejected the primacy of the Pope. One proof for that could be found in certain silences in my *Catholicisme*. Father Wetter immediately added that the thing seemed so ridiculous to him that he hardly dared report it. Through delicacy, he did not speak to me directly about it but managed to tell me that he had read this work, that he had found it very helpful and that he greatly valued it. In the following years, I heard the same reproach made again several times.

In his review, published in the *Nouvelle revue théologique* (1939), 1254–55, Father L. Malevez noted that "Father de L. did not have to make a theology of the Church" (1255). To quote this text in its entirety:

We are seeing these days an increasing number of studies on the Mystical Body of Christ; few of them succeed as well as this one, we believe, in giving or returning to the Christian the authentic and, so to speak, native sense of the Church. If we were to try to summarize it, we would undoubtedly distinguish, as it were, two "moments" in the thought of the author. The first: the Catholic concept of destiny is essentially social; as the dogmatics of the sacraments and the principles of the ancient interpretation of Scripture show, the hope of the Christian is fixed above all on the common salvation of humanity and, through this salvation of the human race, on his own personal salvation. The second moment: "The whole history of the world is the preparation for this common destiny" (98). Precisely because the mystery that is accomplished is that of the whole race, for that reason, this mystery can only be carried out within the duration of time; the progress of history possesses a meaning [*sens*], which is to say, a direction and a significance; and the succession of centuries develops a design, a divine idea, whose content is the fullness of the Body of Christ. Father de L. does not express these two interdependent theses at the conclusion of speculation about the Church; they emerge, according to him, from the works of the patristic period, they form two constants in the thinking of the Fathers, and it is to show that very thing that the author applies himself in most of the chapters. We believe that he succeeds: the abundance of testimony gathered by him makes these conclusions very convincing.

Nevertheless, insofar as the second thesis is concerned, one could suspect that the author was led to formulate it under the influence of a certain philosophy of history. All that is real is rational; all historical reality displays the moments of a thought. Such is undoubtedly the secret doctrine to which Father de L. is indebted for having been attentive to the historical character of the patristic conception of destiny. That is not a reproach, if it is true that this character is well attested by documentary evidence; in this case, the author's philosophy would not have invented it, it would only have made the perception of it possible. If we have any reservation, it would bear on this: the reader is requested to think that the Fathers had to have a progressive concept of Christianity; precisely because Christianity unfolds the phases of a divine idea immanent in history, it must anticipate what those who present it to us as such affirm with respect to new phases: that they constitute, from some points of view, progress over the preceding phases. Is this affirmation not quite the opposite from what one encounters in quite a lot of ecclesiastical writers! The apostolic period was the golden age of Christianity, and the truth, as Bossuet said, echoing the ancients, initially had its full perfection; history had reached its summit with Christ; the humanity coming after him could add nothing to his splendor (except, it is true, for its final transformation; but that, being eschatological, was thereby conceived as being metahistorical). Father de L. is undoubtedly aware of this patristic perspective; he even points to it explicitly (p. 197), but he has perhaps obscured it slightly in obedience to entirely modern modes of thought that are theoretically legitimate but historically distorting.

In the last two chapters, "Person and Society" and "Transcendence" (both remarkably nuanced), the investigation into the facts has ended; here we try to "think" the Church. In particular, in the first of the two, the difficult problem is broached of reconciling the unity of all in Christ, in which the Mystical Body consists, with the distinction and ultimate value of our individual persons for eternity. The author is content to point out the direction in which it seems to him we must look: abstract logic knows as categories of unity only identity (numerical unity) and participation (the imitation by several of an example that this imitation does not multiply); with these intellectual resources alone, we will not overcome the antinomy; rather, we will sacrifice one of the terms, we will absorb the person into the One or at the very least we will subordinate it into the whole as to an end that transcends it. But an apperception exists, not logical but real, in which we grasp in a single glance the place of the personal and the universal: in a single exercise of concrete thought, we can comprehend that, far from endangering the definitive otherness of persons, it is their spiritual unity and their circuminsession that establishes or frees it; the "I" exists in all its dimensions only in the act by which it consents to create society, to unite itself to the university of minds. This, we believe, is the thought of the author; and it is, it seems to us, full of promise. We regret, however, that it was not able to profit from the fine analyses of the recent book by G. Madinier, *Conscience et amour* (Paris: Alcan, 1938; Father de L. quotes it p. 259); it was more clearly evident in what act the desired unity could be revealed to our eyes. It is in the practice of love-devotion, of charity, of the gift of self, that the I sees all at once its proper perfection accomplished and the union of all achieved. In addition, it would remain to be seen if, on the path thus traced, all the fundamental givens of Christian thought on our union "in Christo" would be satisfied. The author speaks somewhere of the "mediation of Christ, in whom all [persons] are enveloped, within the Trinity itself" (p. 260). And farther on: "Bringing humanity to completion in himself, Christ at the same time brings us all to completion—but in God. . . . We are fully personal only within the Person of the Son, by whom and in whom we have a share in the exchanges of the trinitarian life" (p. 267). These final words would give us to think that, according to the author, it is in the divine Person of the Son that the universe of spirits is achieved. That is fair enough; but it is self-evident that, according to Christian dogma, the Incarnation and the humanity of Christ also exercise a function in this formation of the Mystical Body. What exactly is this function! The direction of thought indicated by the author suggests nothing regarding it, or, at least, the author himself voices no very definite suggestion.

But that itself does not constitute a lacuna. Concerned to understand the Fathers, Father de L. did not have to make a theology of the Church. Let us say in conclusion: his book is of such density and the quality of thought, soul and expression in it are so rare, that a review must despair of doing justice to all its merits.

L. MALEVEZ, S.J.

[2:2]

Letter from Father J. Lebreton, publisher of *Recherches*, September 7, 1939:
"I have received the page proofs of your article. . . . Once Father Fessard has done the make-up on chaps. V, VI and VII, this whole section will

appear in the October issue. The rest will appear in December. We have chaps. VIII and IX in galleys. I would be happy to have the rest as soon as possible. . . . The study you are allowing us to publish in *Recherches* will have a lasting importance; it is an honor for us, and it will long be of service to the Church. The treatise on the Church and that on the Eucharist, which are so closely linked, shed light on each other in the course of this long history, and many of the texts, in which only objections are usually seen, recapture their meaning and make the faith of past centuries more intelligible and alive for us. . . ."

Similarly, on October 27, 1939:
"I received your new parcel [chap. X] the day before yesterday; it is worthy of the others and I will very gladly publish it . . . in the following issue. Chapters VIII and IX, which arrived too late for the December issue, will appear, I hope, in February; this chapter X, probably in April. . . ."

That, merely to fix a minuscule point of history and to show by this example how myths are born. At the same time, it can be seen that an experienced theologian, one of the best of his generation, who was rather severe in his judgment and had given many a proof of his clear-sightedness, did not perceive in this poor *Corpus mysticum* any of the numerous and grave errors that others were to denounce in it during the late 1940s. But during those latter times, there were official representatives of "Thomism" for whom nothing good could have existed in Christian thought, for twelve centuries, except to the degree in which it prepared the way for *their* doctrine.

The perspective of my book was different from that of the excellent work by Father Emile Mersch on *Le Corps mystique du Christ*, which I had reviewed in 1934; I quote this review here (I no longer remember where it appeared) because of the place held later in the "Fourvière affair" by secret criticism directed against my own work:

Emile Mersch, S.J., professor at the Faculties of N.D. de la Paix, Namur: *Le Corps mystique du Christ*: Etudes de théologie historique. 2 vols. (XXXVIII, 478 and 446 pages), (Louvain: Museum Lessianum, 1933).
"At a time when we are seeking to rediscover the full meaning of the Church's catholicity, nothing could be more opportune than this important publication. The author does not claim to trace a complete history of the doctrine of the Mystical Body in precisely measured proportions. For example, the Eastern tradition according to John Damascene remains unexplored; and, likewise, our own spiritual tradition, except for one chapter on the French School. The lengthy expositions devoted to the Scholastics

would risk creating a false illusion if the author himself had not taken care
to warn us that the quotations he lavishes upon us, 'put back into their
context, scattered as they are in immense works, lost in expositions from
which the idea of incorporation in Christ is absent', lose much of their
relief. What one might call the 'dynamic' of the Mystical Body, the explanation of that providential plan according to which the Mystical Body
is prepared, takes shape and grows throughout history—an explanation
that looms large in the patristic tradition, notably in Saint Irenaeus—is not
dealt with. But these 'studies', such as they are, the fruit of vast reading
and expert reflection, offer us a truly invaluable collection of texts with
commentary that is nearly always of very lucid soundness. Some chapters,
particularly those on Saint Augustine, are admirable, in our opinion. For a
Christian life that is both more interior and more consciously Catholic, for
a less individualist and less extrinsicist theology, for a better understanding
of the mystery of the Church, for the mystical foundation of our social
action, this work brings us a mine of treasures. H. L."

[2:3]

A long, anonymous review appeared in the *Revue de métaphysique et de
morale*, 51 (1946), 376–77, giving a very intelligent summary of the work,
ending with these words: "After this, there is no need to insist on the
necessity, felt by the believer, of a return to the ancient doctrine, which,
without overlooking contemporary statements, offers an unequalled fullness and richness."

[2:4]

The off-print of this article reached me in Rome (sent on from Lyons) on
September 29, 1946. The same day, I learned that a formal denunciation
had been made against Fathers de Montcheuil, Fessard and Daniélou; a visitor, Father Lang, S.J., came to complain to me about the doctrinal errors
of Father von Balthasar. In the days that immediately followed, students
reported to me the thundering declarations made at the Angelicum against
the modernism of Father Bouillard; Léon Bérard repeated the accusations
formulated against Father Daniélou and me; Father Boyer supported the
campaign directed against Father de Montcheuil, etc. (see above, Chapter
IV). All these conjunctions explain why we were affected by the article
by Fathers Labourdette and Nicolas. Soon (around April 1947?) the little
booklet of controversies entitled *Dialogue théologique*, prefaced by Father

Bruckberger, O.P., was to appear, about which we had not even been informed. On the initiative of Father Decisier, we had sought to organize a meeting for a peaceful examination of the disagreement; Father Labourdette's timidity would not consent to it. But Bishop de Solages offered his good offices; there was an exchange of letters between Father Nicolas and him in the *Bulletin de littérature ecclésiastique*. On September 16, 1947, Father Nicolas (then provincial of the Dominicans in Toulouse) came to Fourvière to confirm the peace. All went very well. I was to make the acquaintance of Father Labourdette in the autumn of 1960, in the antechamber of Cardinal Ottaviani, where we were the first two to arrive for the opening of the theological commission in preparation for the Council called by John XXIII.

[2:5]

The thesis was undertaken in 1941. The *nihil obstat* was given by Fathers C. Boyer and H. Rondet on March 12. Delayed by wartime difficulties, the work appeared in 1944.

From 1945 on, an offensive was launched against him: on November 5, 1945, Father Huby wrote to me from Paris:

"On October 17th, there was a meeting of the Security Council at the archbishop's; I represented the Society with Father Villain from *l'Action Populaire*. In opening the session, the agenda of which had not been communicated to us in advance, Cardinal Suhard announced that he had received a mandate from the *Holy Office* to have an examination made of Father Bouillard's book, about which, moreover, he knew absolutely nothing. The examination had been entrusted to two reviewers, Levassor-Berrus, superior of the Sulpician seminary on rue du Regard, and Father Cayré, an Assumptionist, a regular member of the Vigilance Council. The latter had shifted the responsibility for the task to Father Farne (or Farme), the professor of dogma in their scholasticate at Lormoy, near Montlhéry, who had therefore come to the Council to read his statement. The report by Levassor-Berrus was favorable; he praised the care with which Father Bouillard had conducted his historical investigation; he had a few reservations, which were themselves benign, about the conclusion, which he found rather onesided; he would suggest a few corrections or additions to indicate, alongside the relative aspect, the progress and enrichment of which theology is capable. In sum, no complaint serious enough to motivate a condemnation. The report by the Assumptionist Father was noticeably less benevolent because less intelligent; the author is a young professor, who seems not to have much philosophical breadth or historical knowledge, nor to be able to depart from a textbook theology. I had the impression that he believed himself obliged to formulate accusations from the moment the Holy Office requested an examination of the book. . . . His complaint against Father Bouillard was not regarding his historical investigation, the accuracy of which he would in any case have been incapable of judging, but against personal preferences that he manifested in two or three passages (pp. 137, 166, 171, insofar as I remember): Father Bouillard seems, as far as he is concerned, to be disposed to abandon a 'classical' explanation in theology, that of the grace-habitus or grace-quality. Father Farne seems to attach great importance to this point: he narrowly misses making the grace-quality a teaching of the Council of Trent. The other complaint concerned the conclusion, which he attacked, without nuance or intelligence, because of what it says about the relativism of theology. He even saw in that a threat to the progress of dogma!

"After these reports, Pressoir and Boisard intervened to express their great esteem for Father Bouillard, whom they knew at Saint-Sulpice, and to say that a condemnation seemed deplorable to them. I myself supported the point of view that Saint Thomas had not achieved a satisfactory synthesis of the Pauline conception of grace with the conception of the grace-form according to Aristotle's categories and that the second conception is no longer 'preachable' to modern minds: it is as foreign to them as Aristotle's Physics. I joined Pressoir and Boisard in affirming that a condemnation would be unjustified: all that could be asked would be a few editorial changes.

"The Cardinal gave no reaction: he simply asked the two reviewers to agree on a note that would be sent to Rome. I am a little afraid that the Assumptionist theologian does not show much spirit of conciliation.

"Father Villain had kept Father Bith up to date. Before his departure for Rome, Father Bith had had Father d'Ouince ask me for a statement in favor of Father Bouillard; unfortunately I was mistaken about the date of his departure, which, instead of being on Friday, as I had been told, took place on Wednesday. When I carried in my statement on Thursday, the Father Provincial had already left; I immediately sent the paper to Rome in the hope of reaching Father Bith before his return. In any case, the statement will reach Father de Boynes."

Around the same date, Father Guérard des Lauriers, O.P., gave a sharp criticism of Father Bouillard's work in an issue of *L'Année théologique*. I wrote, on January 13, 1946, to one of his colleagues about it:

". . . Saint Thomas is not always an easy author, and differences in interpretation in his regard do not in the least scandalize me, even if they lead to rather sharp criticism here and there. But here, one senses something else. The large number of mistakes Father Guérard des Lauriers makes in reading Father Bouillard's text itself denotes a degree of passion that no longer permits either the equity or the intelligence of the author he is criticizing. Moreover, I would attach less importance to it and would not speak to you about it if I had not heard from several quarters in the course of the past months that Father G. des L. is saying some really strange things both about Father Bouillard and about another colleague of mine at Fourvière. I would like to think that his remarks were exaggerated when they were reported. It is difficult for me to believe that they were completely distorted. I confess to you my surprise and my sorrow."

[2:6]

"In our world of semi-culture, someone like Jules Monchanin is a second-class citizen, without a passport. Pressed by time, elliptical like the flashes of his lightning, he was so precisely because supremely and universally cultured. . . ." Pierre Emmanuel, in *France catholique*, May 9, 1975.

[2:7]

My first two books on Buddhism earned me the following letter from a young man whom I did not know at the time but who was soon to become an excellent friend:

"My Father, I would like to thank you for your last two books published on Buddhism. . . . They bring me the nourishment I need. I too, in 1949, had noted the two invaluable allusions that Romano Guardini made to Buddhism in *The Lord*. Despite their brevity, they nonetheless, to my mind, pointed to what might be written with greater relevance on the question from the Catholic point of view. More precisely, I felt the problem finally posed there in its true light, and I waited for some response. You have appeared. —I should tell you that I came to Catholicism only three years ago from a fundamentally dechristianized milieu through the instrumentality of that 'Eastern spirituality' whose great diffusion you rightly emphasize. So I am a recent Christian, still very poorly seated on the doctrinal foundations of his faith. My attitude toward Hinduism, Buddhism and occultism feels the effect of it, as you might imagine. I believe absolutely, to be sure, that the truth can be found in Christ alone (position of principle), but I am led to wonder nevertheless, in practice, if there are not other ways by which to arrive at the same Lord (tactical position). For I am troubled—it is undoubtedly a question in me of character—

more by living examples than by theories and mysteries. Now I have in mind the example of my best friend. Let us call him an occultist, with a strong Buddhist and more specifically Lamaist hue. I have never received from him anything but an extraordinary incitement to exercise self-control and to strive for love. It is to him that I owe first of all my having left a dense materialism, then (my conversion to Catholicism having occurred afterward, apart from him), each time I met him, my sense of greater calm and strength for following my own Christian path, even though it is so different from his own. In our thinking, we part ways entirely. But we are in communion in the heart of the same realities that I dare to call 'supernatural'. —My friend certainly owes the dignity of his life to the one he recognizes as his master: Jean Varagerat, whose disciple he was for several years and who has been dead now for some two years I believe. I have read the works of this man. Their doctrinal tenor differs little from the concepts of the Theosophical Society. But, through this emotionalism, there is witness to a profound spiritual experience. How can I respond to his disciple, who is in the process of reviving it in a more clearly Buddhist sense? Forced to keep silent, I wait—and I have longed—for the Church to instruct me. That is why I am grateful for your work. —Continue to pursue it, and please inform me of others moved by the same concerns. I am already familiar, for example, with several of the all-too-rare writings of Abbé Monchanin. I would like to read other pages of that quality. . ." (July 1, 1952).

[2:8]

In fact, the work had taken sufficient shape in 1941 to be submitted for review. My Provincial, Father Joseph du Bouchet, chose Fathers Lebreton and Huby as reviewers, and they asked for a few modifications. Once these were supplied, a new review was made at my request; the Provincial entrusted it to Fathers Baumgartner and Fontoynont and signed his *nihil obstat* on February 2, 1942. Yet there could be no question of having it printed at that time. The book appeared, slightly enlarged after some other revisions, only in 1946. The *Imprimatur* is dated October 20, 1945.

[2:9]

In my opinion, two things at least were lacking in this book:

1. I should have stated clearly, from the beginning, that it presupposed a basic abstraction in taking the question as all Scholastic tradition had done

so and as it continued to do so: which was the reason for a nearly total absence of any consideration of historic revelation or of creation in Christ and for Christ, etc. Father Henri Bouillard supplied this in his study on "L'Idée de surnaturel et le mystère chrétien" [The idea of the supernatural and the Christian mystery] in *L'Homme devant Dieu* (Aubier, 1964), vol. 3 (Theology series, vol. 58), 153–66. This was because, shortly after I wrote my book, the so-called "existentialist" perspective began to invade theological speculation, which had remained until then more formal and more respectful of methodological distinctions. Consequently, as Father Bouillard observed, "statements that would otherwise have been entitled 'the supernatural order' are called today 'the Christian Mystery'" (154). A more concrete and more synthetic mode of proceeding, which has its advantages and its disadvantages.

2. I should also have been more specific, with respect to "independent" thinkers and historians of philosophy even more than with respect to Scholastics, about the sense in which the word "nature" was taken: it referred to a concept of the "supernatural" and not to an idea that would be opposed, for example, within philosophic thought, to ideas such as that of person or history or culture, etc. (I gave some elementary details on this subject in my *Petite catéchèse sur Nature et grâce*, chap. 1 [Fayard, 1980] [English trans.: *A Brief Catechesis on Nature and Grace* (San Francisco: Ignatius Press, 1984)]).

Finally, the transformation, or rather the turning around, of the desire for God under the action of grace, its (partial) metamorphosis into charity, was only just pointed out with a few words in the conclusion, but that would have been the subject of another work.

Nevertheless, influenced by controversies current at that time and then because of the confused situation that resulted from them, an interpretation of the book appeared that was quite contrary to reality. One expression of this is to be found in the work of an Italian Protestant, Vittorio Subilia: "During the ten years preceding the second half of our century, works by Catholic theologians, Jesuits in particular, have appeared, volumes and articles symptomatic of a vast spiritual malaise. . . . Thomism, the central theology of Catholicism, . . . is judged to be a medieval doctrine no longer adequate for expressing correctly the gospel truth in a language responding to the needs of present-day problematics." And, in a note, he cites *Corpus mysticum* and *Surnaturel* in support of this (Vittorio Subilia, *Le Problème du catholicisme*, translated from the Italian by Emile Ribaute [Paris: Librairie protestante, 1964], 129–30. I have abbreviated slightly). The author obviously had not read these two works. In neither of them is anything said in favor of such "new language" nor against the "medieval doctrine" that is in fact its subject. Quite the contrary, *Surnaturel* is an argument in favor of a return to the authentic doctrine of Saint Thomas.

Writing to Msgr. Charles Journet, on March 17, 1952, I had occasion to say, with respect to one page of his second volume on *l'Eglise du Verbe incarné*: "I also would have preferred that you not attribute to me the idea of a 'postulation' of the beatific vision. I did not use that word, and I rejected the thing itself. I can be reproached for a lack of internal coherence, but an assertion that I reject cannot be attributed to me. I do not want in any case to be obstinate in defending any personal opinion, but I persist in thinking that one of the weak points of the modern Thomistic school is its objection to a methodical and unprejudiced historical study of the thought of Saint Thomas in this matter. I am very far from claiming to have done this whole study myself, which would be a complex and difficult task. Yet, nearly all that has been said in opposition to me has seemed more to have nonacceptance as its purpose (to say the least) than any serious search for historical truth."

[2:10]

Yet, as early as the end of August 1946, Father Creusen, professor of theology at the Gregorian and consultant to the Holy Office, had seen Father Lebreton in Paris, at *Etudes*, and had told him that *Surnaturel* was being threatened and that he, Lebreton, was being criticized by some for having given it the *nihil obstat*. The latter had then given me a lively defense. But by that date, the campaign, some of whose features I am recalling here, had already long since begun for other reasons.

The following are extracts from the reviews of the book made in 1942 by Father Lebreton and from two letters that he wrote to me in 1942 and in 1946 on this subject:

Surnaturel. From the review by Father Lebreton. About the conclusion: "Divine exigency and natural desire. Very fine pages where the author, comparing this desire to merit, makes it well understood that the independence of God is not compromised by these two concepts, quite the contrary: by crowning our merits, God crowns his works; by fulfilling our desire, he answers his own call."

Overall judgment: "Above all, I am anxious to repeat that I endorse the judgment of the author about the system of pure nature. It is a thesis of great importance; it is established particularly in the first part, the historical notes and the conclusion."

From Father Lebreton, February 2, 1942. "I am in complete agreement with the thesis you are defending, and the only goal of my demands is to insure the complete efficacy of your demonstration. I am delighted to see its appearance."

(This refers to his previous review; in this "interzonal" card, he thanks me for the letter I had addressed to him about this review—with which I complied completely.)

March 31, 1946. *Etudes*: "I have just glanced rapidly through this book, which is of such rich scholarship and above all of such sound theological sense. This new study has confirmed my judgment of the first reading; I wish and hope that this work will not be without effect and will make us understand better the work of wisdom and infinite goodness that God is pursuing in us."

Father Henry, O.P. wrote to me on June 17, 1946:

"I have just read with unfeigned joy your fine book on the supernatural. So much so that others have been saying to me here: 'But write that to Father de Lubac.' It is simply for this reason, my Father, that I am writing to you.

"This book is a veritable deliverance. I have been waiting for it for a long time without suspecting it, and it is closely related to much of the work and research I have done in this direction following a more attentive study of the precise meaning of Saint Thomas. I would be happy to do a long review of it in *La Vie spirituelle*, but I wonder if our censors would let it through. . . .

"One Father to whom I presented it said to me: 'But my Father, you do not realize that you are in the process of demolishing my whole theology.' In particular I put before him that view of a unique world, physical and spiritual, which is brought out so strongly by the exposition you made of the ancient tradition and of the theology of Saint Thomas. Besides, I had the impression he was not without a certain delight in seeing 'his' theology collapse like that. One must also admit that several masters at Saulchoir over the past fifteen years have prepared the way for us to receive this teaching.

"You are much to be thanked, my Father, for this excellent new book you have given us. It will make as much, if not more, of a mark, I hope, than your *Catholicisme*."

On December 16, he wrote me again: ". . . I had told you how happy I was for this book, which had been a long-awaited liberation for me, and I wrote a review of it with joy. Unhappily, as I rather expected, the good traditionalist elements in our censorship committee found that it could not be accepted as such, that it revolutionalized one whole part of theology and that it could not be introduced by so brief a review. Several Fathers wanted this review to go through, but, in the end, it was not adopted."

From the major seminary at Saint-Dié, Abbé Mathéry, the director, wrote me on February 5, 1947:

". . . Here, we are following with great sympathy the theological effort of the School of Fourvière, which seems to us to be completely providential and so urgent! We understand, nonetheless, the reaction of some theologians, representatives of a 'certain' Scholasticism, for it is very true that you overturn—without violence, but the result is the same!—positions in which they have been comfortably settled for several centuries.

"Personally, I have just reread your *Surnaturel*. It seems to me that one would have to have understood nothing in it in order to see in it an attack on the gratuity of the supernatural. Quite the contrary, you reinforce that gratuity by showing that, contrary to what is ordinarily taught, it is not only in its existing state but *in any hypothesis* that *human nature can realize its destiny only by the reception of a gratuitous gift.*"

On July 21, 1957, from Father Gerard Smith, S.J., of Marquette University (Milwaukee): "I have just read some of the works coming from the Fourvière Faculty (not all, as I have not even been able to get them all, due to some difficulty in reprinting), and in particular your *Proudhon, Athéisme humaniste, Surnaturel*. I cannot tell you how much I like them all, especially your *Surnaturel*. The restoration to human nature of its true end has been too long awaited. And then, to do that in so decisive, so fine a manner, with a style that bears such a weight of doctrine so lightly—truly it makes one think of the Fathers of the Church. —That sounds terribly like mere flattery, I know, but my excuse is my inability to say things elegantly in French. But they must be said nevertheless, and to the devil with style. Finally, I like your *Surnaturel* very much. . . ."

In January 1949, a letter from Dietrich von Hildebrand, coming from New York: "My dear Father, I have been wanting to write you for a long time now. I have read and studied in depth your great work, *Surnaturel*, and I cannot tell you what light and what intellectual profit I have drawn from that reading." And, after some praises I could never transcribe, this judgment about the conclusion, which was so criticized by others: "The conclusion is of a beauty, depth and truth that have quite carried me away. I cannot express what importance I attribute to this reintegration of a fundamental truth. . . ."

On April 23, Father R. A. Gauthier, O.P., wrote to me: "I admit that at my first reading I felt only sympathy for most of the positions you defended in

Surnaturel, and particularly for your interpretation of Saint Thomas, which is very captivating. If, on reflection, a few reservations seem called for, I nonetheless deplore, here as on other points, the tone of certain polemics and the narrowness of mind of which they are the proof. . . . I remain convinced that you have contributed progress in the interpretation of Saint Thomas that will have to be taken into account and for which in the end you will be thanked."

I will also quote here a letter sent from Saulchoir, Etiolles, on January 13, 1966, by Father Jean-Pierre Jossua, O.P., even though it is of later date, because it seems very characteristic to me in some of its rather abrupt expressions:

". . . In reading 'Augustinisme et théologie modern' and 'Le Mystère du surnaturel', I renew the total agreement I gave in former times to the theses in *Surnaturel*. My entire personal vision of faith is centered on it, just as at another time I was converted to Christianity by reading the *Confessions*, and my whole teaching of 'Christian anthropology' rests on it. The obstinacy of some in not seeing is astonishing. But let us not accuse them of lacking lucidity; on the contrary, they sense quite rightly that such a return to the sources sweeps away their mediocre scaffoldings, their simultaneously rationalist and nonhumanist universe—whence their foul temper. Thank you for contributing so much to this liquidation. This reading has renewed my conviction—which I expressed to you two years ago in Strasbourg at Father Congar's celebration, with an enthusiasm that perhaps seemed a bit naïve to you . . .—that I owe you, that the Dominicans of my generation owe you, as much and more than we owe our own masters. . . ."

[2:11]

As documentation, we reproduce here some of the reviews of *Surnaturel*, by:

1. Joseph Huby (*Etudes*)
2. Gérard Philips (*Erasmus*)
3. Albert Chavasse (*Revue de moyen âge latin*)
4. Vincent Turner (*Letters and Notices*)
5. M. C. (= Dom Cappuyns, *Bulletin de théologie ancienne et médiévale*)
6. Paul Vignaux (*Revue de l'histoire des religions*)
7. x. (*Revue de métaphysique et de morale*)
8. A. Van Hove (*Revue d'histoire ecclésiastique*)

It goes without saying that I do not agree (far from it) with all the expressions, all the analyses and, a fortiori, all the judgments contained in these reviews. The one written by Msgr. Philips, professor at the Theology Faculty of Louvain, will provide an opportunity to admire the irenicism and concern for balance that were to gain him, even in the field of politics, a well-deserved reputation for calming diplomacy and that attained their perfection in his role as secretary to the Doctrinal Commission of the Second Vatican Council.

Etudes, 251 (1946), 265–68:
Joseph Huby: Henri de Lubac, *Surnaturel, Etudes historiques*. Theology series (Paris: Aubier, 1946). 8vo, 498 pages.

Some readers will perhaps be surprised to see this new book by Father de Lubac coming so soon after works as important as *Corpus mysticum, Le Drame de l'humanisme athée, Proudhon et le Christianisme*. Let them not presume on that account, however, that they have some makeshift work before them. Quite the contrary, it is the fruit of several years of research and reflection, as witnessed solely by the list of Fathers and theologians consulted by Father de Lubac. If it had not been for the difficulties arising from the war, the book would have appeared three or four years earlier: the *nihil obstat* is from 1942.

The subtitle specifies the character of the work. The latter is not presented directly as a systematic construction but as a series of historical studies, several pieces of which had already appeared in the form of journal articles. There are three of these studies: "Augustinianism and Baianism", "Spirit and Freedom in the Theological Tradition", "At the Origins of the Word 'Supernatural' ". A half-dozen historical notes and a few pages of conclusion complete the work.

These studies relate to one and the same fundamental subject, the "supernatural", considered from different angles. One of these angles will particularly hold the readers' attention: it is the doctrine of the final end of man or the immediate vision of God and, in relation to this doctrine, a critical review of the theological system of "pure nature". Father de Lubac retraces the history of this opinion: he shows its relatively recent introduction into theology, since, unknown to the Fathers and Saint Thomas, it makes its appearance only in the sixteenth century; he follows its development and shows the role it played against Baianism in defense of the gratuity of the supernatural end.

In order to understand how this system of "pure nature" was born, it is necessary to go back to the questions posed by the ancient Scholastics about the state of the first man when he left the hands of the Creator.

Had sanctifying grace and original justice along with the gifts of integrity and immortality been conferred on Adam from the instant of creation or had he received them only afterward? Could one not conceive as possible a creation of man with only the constitutive elements of his nature and without possessing, even before any sin, original justice and the gifts of integrity and immortality that accompanied it? The answers had varied.

The Baianist controversy had brought these questions to the fore once again. Against Baius, who denied the gratuity of the gifts made by God to Adam, the theologians are not content to defend the possibility of a *state* of pure nature, that is, of a state in which man, *while being created for a supernatural end*, would have been able to know, "not by virtue of the pain of sin, but by the very reason of his nature, the mortality, concupiscence and the whole procession of evils of which the heirs of Adam bear the heavy experience"; through an almost imperceptible deviation, they transform the possibility of a *state* of pure nature into the possibility of a purely natural *order*, suitable for reaching a purely natural *end*; in that way, they introduce a relationship of finality unknown to the ancients. While Saint Augustine and, after him, the great Scholastic doctors, Saint Thomas as well as Saint Bonaventure and Duns Scotus, basing themselves on the very dignity of the created spirit, conceived only one single ultimate end for it, union with God in intuitive vision, the theologians of the sixteenth century and the following centuries envisaged the possibility of another final end, some natural beatitude of an order inferior to intuitive vision. We can see in Father de Lubac (pp. 133–35) the different ways, each as unsatisfactory as the rest, in which they tried to represent this natural end.

This possibility of two last ends, one accessible to the sole forces of nature, the other transcending them, was for these theologians the way to defend the gratuitous character of the supernatural end. This system of "pure nature", notes Father de Lubac, certainly did not fail to render eminent service. "It permitted them to use more than a mere denial in opposing error: it was a positive explanation whose clarity and apparent logic satisfied the rational needs of the period. Thus, for a time, orthodoxy was saved." But the system was to have other effects that were less fortuitous. "Did it not effect a separation between nature and the supernatural that would prove fatal?" By supporting the possibility of a substantial natural order, giving satisfaction to the needs and desires of nature, by presenting the latter as a well-closed whole, having the power to achieve its own balance, it made the supernatural order something superfluous, which man was tempted to do without, since this supernatural found no anticipation, no desire, no aspiration in him. This conception of the supernatural as a superstructure coming to rest from outside on an edifice that stands on its own opened the way to a philosophy and a morality that were separate, being constituted in complete independence not only of any positive revelation but of any fundamental orientation of the soul to the beatific vision. The desire for intuitive vision, which Saint Thomas, as inclined as he was toward Aristotelianism, had maintained in his doctrine as essential to the spirit although not achievable by natural powers alone, was reduced to a vague and inconsistent stray impulse. "In order better to assure the dominion of grace over a region of human activity", the system of pure nature "risked allowing another whole region be secularized".

After having criticized this theological thesis, Father de Lubac had to show how it is not necessary to have recourse to it in order to maintain the gratuity of the intuitive vision and how the desire for this vision, while being "the most absolute of all desires", is nevertheless not a requirement of nature. This is what he has done in his conclusion, in pages that must be pondered carefully. In this question as in many others, the essential thing is to pose the problems well, to determine precisely the given facts concerning them, to avoid equivocations and all those false suppositions in which decadent Scholasticism too often takes delight. Here, what is above all important is to penetrate, to "realize" to the depths our condition as creature, who can demand nothing from God because it has no rights over him. "I am the One who is, and you, you are the one who is not", said Our Lord to Saint Catherine of Siena: mystical intuition concurs with the most profound theology. To forget even partially this condition of creature, which affects not only our origin, our position in existence, but our essence, to withdraw in theory any part whatever of the being or of his action from the sovereign domain of God, is to envisage man in his relations with God as an absolute in the face of another Absolute, as a being in the face of another Being toward whom we have duties but over whom we also have rights, in the image of a human servant in his relations with a human master. This is the spontaneous tendency of our spirit and it is also the inheritance from ancient philosophy, which was unaware of the dogma of creation: which, despite the corrections imposed on Aristotle by the Scholastics, has not been without some influence on their concept of a plan of human sufficiency.

In order to form a true idea of our relations with God, it is necessary to go beyond these representations, to cease looking at man and God like two beings, who, while certainly unequal, are nonetheless treated practically as one-to-one, to dismiss radically any right or demand on the part of the creature. Father de Lubac uses multiple expressions to make us grasp this unique case of the condition of creature, this paradox of a created spirit who desires God essentially without demanding anything. The spirit desires God, but it desires him as a gift. "The spirit desires not only God himself but God such as he cannot be, God giving himself freely in the initiative of his pure love." Let us not speak of an exigency of nature but rather of an exigency *in* nature. "If there is in our nature a desire to see God, this can only be because God wants for us this supernatural end that consists in seeing him. It is because, willing it and never ceasing to will it, he places and never ceases to place the desire for it in our nature. This desire is consequently nothing other than his call."

If one considers the question from not only an anthropocentric but a theocentric point of view, the conclusion is the same. In creating the world through generosity, God necessarily created it for himself and for his glory, so that this world might be related to him entirely through the medium of intelligent and free beings. "The spirit gives God the world by giving itself in an act of total surrender. Now this act attains its perfection, that is, it is achieved in all its purity, only in the supernatural order, which is the order of pure charity." In order that this external glory, "which adds nothing to his Being but which even the superabundance of his love cannot make him renounce", might be rendered to the Creator in fullness, God can create spirits only in order to make them participate in his life of blessedness. He thereby obtains the sacrifice of perfect praise, which is the necessary end of creation.

By deepening our understanding of the relations of God and man, Father de Lubac draws us outside the categories of law, interest, commutative justice, all those juridical concepts that in this domain would easily lead to doctrinal deviations. He renders theology the invaluable service of disencumbering it from a certain number of pseudo-problems and of placing it in the light of true perspectives. The religious sense can only profit by assuming a more lively awareness of the transcendence of God and of the total independence of his love. A theology that radically dismisses any right and all demand of the creature in his relations with God does not diminish the value of the created being but situates it in its true place, not in a certain natural sufficiency and independence with regard to God, but in that indestructible call to charity and to the intuitive vision, that "fiery seed" (Claudel) that God deposited in the depths of our nature.

JOSEPH HUBY

Erasmus (1946), 202–5.
G. Philips (Louvain): Henri de Lubac, *Le* (sic) *surnaturel, Etudes historiques* (Paris: Aubier, 1946), 496 pp., 8vo. Studies published under the direction of the S.J. Theology Faculty of Lyons-Fourvière, no. 8.

Father de Lubac's "historical studies" prove to be of very great importance for the theology of grace. They constitute a vigorous attempt to reunite, on the other side of certain impoverishing deviations, the theological riches of the Greeks and Saint Augustine. While doctrine, since Baianism, has ordinarily stressed above all the difference and almost the rupture between grace and the natural "order", Father de Lubac emphasizes the continuity that binds the human spirit, the image of God, to the blessing of divinization. The book obviously does not form a homogeneous whole. Yet these historical monographs converge on rather unexpected speculative conclusions that one regrets not finding presented in a more systematic way.

The first part is devoted to a comparative study of Baianism and Augustinianism. It is the most original and the strongest part of the book. It would be difficult to find a more penetrating analysis of the Baianist spirit. Under the pretext of positive theology, restricted moreover to the Augustinian heritage, in contempt of Greek thought, Baius and Jansenius present us with a rationalizing system of an extreme religious poverty, in which a fierce literalism has completely falsified the doctrine of the Doctor of grace. A most well-informed historical sense has allowed Father de Lubac to detect in the arid Jansenist literature the lines of force that in a strange way link up with the errors of Pelagianism. A fine Jesuit revenge in a secular dispute. The author does not shrink from a minute examination of the most subtle questions of interpretation, particularly with respect to certain chapters in *De Correptione et Gratia*. Yet the style always remains lively and the reading enjoyable; a rather rare gift in theological publications. The pages, for example, on the prayer of Adam are beautiful. The author then sketches the progressive formation of the system of "pure nature", which is at the origin of the nature-grace dualism, a dualism to which the author attributes, perhaps with a bit of exaggeration, the most dismal consequences. The apparent clarity of this system allowed an easy victory over Baianism, but it was obtained by sacrificing a traditional, fundamental element, notably that of the innate appetite for the supernatural beatitude. The war-cry of Ripalda is understandable: "Exterminandus est appetitus innatus!" [Inborn appetite must be uprooted]. The verdict that Father de Lubac heaps upon the Jesuit theologian is also understandable: "Verbalism, absurd hypotheses, pretensions of high metaphysics, dangerous subtleties, cunning arguments *ad hominem*, an entirely superficial understanding of the great traditional ideas, Ripalda's work presents all the symptoms of a decadent theology. One wonders what religious idea presides over this glib, lucid jumble. One searches in vain for the glimmer of intuition that would give meaning to this reeling-off of concepts . . ." (p. 299).

The second part is devoted to an inquiry of rather secondary importance: Is a spiritual creature who is naturally incapable of sin conceivable? The question raised, however, does have importance in relation to the problem of evil and of destiny, and in general in its relation to the philosophy of the spirit and of freedom. Tradition replies without hesitation that any creature is naturally defectible, and Saint Thomas Aquinas did not abandon this position in his analysis of the fall of the angels. Father de Lubac's demonstration is solid and enlightening: the Angelic Doctor did not profess the sinlessness of the celestial spirits in an order of pure nature. It can be seen how this discussion is linked to the conclusion of the first part. In the course of his exposition, the author is not sparing in his criticisms of the famous "obediential power" of nature with respect to grace. But it seems to us that he understands it in a way that is too restrictive, as a pure noncontradiction.

In his third part, he describes for us, without sacrificing the least detail, the prehistory of the word "supernatural". The term ended up designating not only a good added onto a natural good but a finality added onto a natural finality. It is this splitting of finalities into two that has broken, in nearly every School, the fundamental unity of the relations of the created spirit with God. Saint Thomas himself knew only one final end for man, and that consists in the beatific vision. Father de Lubac gives proof everywhere of an immense erudition that is perfectly assimilated as well. Insights such as those about Ruysbroeck and Cardinal Deschamps are particularly evocative. The supernatural is not abnormal; it does not point to something adventitious, but it remains gratuitous, even if it is deeply rooted in our nature.

There we have the critical point. If Father de Lubac resolutely rejects the possibility of pure nature, he is not more condemnable than the Augustinian authors whom the Holy See has more than once taken under its protection, as it recently did on behalf of Maurice Blondel. If he admits a natural, innate desire for the beatific vision, he in no way compromises the gratuity of grace; he teaches with M. Vialatoux that "the appetite for the supernatural, far from making demands on its object, demands on the contrary that its object be not at all subject to demand". In this way, he retains the richest and strongest meaning in the affirmations of Saint Thomas.

We can only applaud his intention to dismiss for good "a timid, doubly extrinsicist theology, which would cast dogma outside of thought and the supernatural outside of nature, in the illusory intention of better maintaining them above nature and above reason" (p. 437). And yet one could nevertheless wonder if the study of pure nature, considered as an hypothesis, merits the massive condemnation that he inflicts on it. It is licit to wonder what might be a natural end and a natural beatitude of the rational creature, even if the response will always be hesitant. The ancients did not consider this problem. It is Baius who introduced it. Once again, heresy proved useful. The sense of God is a call and a preparation for the total possession of the divinity, but human nature would not be completely absurd if the beatific vision were not achieved. The opening to the supernatural is the very constitution of the spiritual creature. This paradox marks his congenital nobility. If it *does not demand* its solution, as the author stresses, the question of pure nature retains a certain meaning. The natural finality will never be the *last* end, since it is included in the vision that transcends it. But we are not forbidden to see if it could have some consistency in an unverified hypothesis. Father de Lubac has chosen a radical position. He will be attacked, but he is a man who can defend himself. It is not every day that we can welcome, in theology, so personal and so intrepid a contribution.

G. PHILIPS

Revue du moyen âge latin, 2, no. 3-4 (1946), 352-54.
A. Chavasse: Bulletin critique. Henri de Lubac, *Surnaturel, Etudes historiques* (Paris: Aubier, 1946). One vol., 8vo, 498 p. ("Theology", studies published under the direction of the S.J. Theology Faculty of Lyons-Fourvière, no. 8).

The major influence that this new book by Father de Lubac will have on theological thought will one day be measured. It comes at the right time. The uneasiness that many theologians and philosophers were already feeling about admitting the possibility of man having a twofold end, natural and supernatural, the impression they thereby experienced of tearing man between two "human orders" that were nearly foreign to each other, will henceforth be understood in the fullest sense. They will give thanks to Father de Lubac for having made them definitively aware that they do not have to twist their minds in order to accommodate a theological explanation that might have had its temporary usefulness but that, far from having been a part of the mainstream of tradition, was introduced only recently and not without opposition in theological thought, at times causing catastrophic results besides.

By making us go back to the historical sources of the hypothesis of "pure nature" and by revealing the evils that it has produced in theology —without concealing, however, the services it has rendered in the face of the naturalism of Baius and Jansenius, of the philosophers of the Enlightenment and their modern disciples—Father de Lubac has effected on this point a "psychoanalysis" of the theological conscience, like Bachelard tried to do for the scientific conscience. And our conscience comes away truly "liberated" by this analysis.

Freed from this unfortunate hypothesis, theological thought is ready to open itself anew to the breath of tradition and to work out a Christian anthropology in which the man of today can recognize himself and in which above all he can acquire the conviction that union with God is the profound meaning of the life of the spirit and that Christianity is not some artificial accretion to the world and man. That was the deep conviction of all the Christian thinkers before the sixteenth century. Now the hypothesis of "pure nature", in the face of a more or less virulent naturalism, had the effect of relegating the supernatural among things of indifference to man: if someone speaks of the "pure nonrepugnance" of nature in the face of the supernatural, does that not, translated into intelligible language, leave me perfectly indifferent? And when I hear theologians teach that the angel has the effective power to sin only once engaged in the supernatural order, am I not going to experience, rather than indifference, some indignation and even some repulsion with respect to this "gift, which, instead of purely and simply perfecting the spiritual creature, introduces such a disorder to it"?

If, on the other hand, we put aside the hypothesis of pure nature, the supernatural immediately becomes once again the gratuitous consummation of an anticipation that defines the spirit as such. In creating the spirit, God wants a being capable of receiving him. The ancient theologians, to say nothing of the Fathers, had an acute sense of this essential destination of the spirit, and it is wonderful to reread these old texts from, for example, Hugh of Saint Victor or from the unknown theologian who wrote the *Summa Sententiarum*, in which, developing the Christian vision of the world, their authors formulate from the outset the free plan of God to give himself, which sets in motion the work of creation and assures total and fundamental gratuity to its unfolding.

We are not surprised, moreover, at having to set aside this hypothesis of pure nature. The history of sciences has accustomed us to these changes of hypotheses. It has even taught us that no hypothesis is ever abandoned completely; that the truths it had momentarily taken up and preserved survive it; and that any subsequent hypothesis must satisfy this while, at the same time, it proves capable of explaining facts that the preceding hypothesis did not know, neglected or even deformed. Father de Lubac is very sensitive to this dialectic of "hypotheses", and we should take care not to forget the grave warning he gives to present and future theologians about the necessity of safeguarding more explicitly than the ancients did the truths to which the hypothesis of pure nature has strongly drawn attention: in particular the gratuity and the inaccessibility of the supernatural.

Rather than giving a dry, and consequently deceptive, summary of a book of extraordinary richness, in which the ideas are never simplified, in which the historical facts are grasped with all their countless contingent nuances, I have preferred to relay some of the impressions this book has occasioned in me. I wish it would become bedside reading for every young theologian and that theologians grown old in the trade would read it with the greatest care, and even with the will to "refine" their hypothesis of pure nature, if they cling to it despite everything. It is never forbidden to correct an hypothesis, if one does not want to abandon it, when facts are brought forward that discredit it at least in part!

Father de Lubac's inquiry relates to almost all the theologians since the sixteenth century, but, in order to show the distortions that have been produced since that date, he has had to go back at times much farther into the past: multiple probings that are more or less extensive according to the needs of the inquiry and that at times, especially with reference to the Middle Ages, reach back to Christian antiquity. Father de Lubac's documentation and the erudite critical apparatus upon which his very diverse research is based has at times been criticized with varying degrees of justice—and pertinence (cf. G. Le Bras, in the *Revue de l'histoire des religions*, vol. 129, review of H. de L., *Corpus mysticum*, or R. Maublanc [hostile] in *Pensée*, new series, no. 5 [October-December, 1945], 63–64). To tell the truth, they have turned up only trifles. And what author is there who, in inquiries so vast that one wonders how one single man could have conducted them, has never stumbled? Only specialists, limited to their little, very little domain can pride themselves with having always cited the right edition, the exact page, the precise paragraph!

As for us, we will willingly forego condemnation of these trifles in the face of the prodigious richness of such works, and we will express our deeply felt gratitude to the thinker and historian who has never left our mind where he took it up and who has so enriched it once more in writing *Surnaturel*.

A. Chavasse

Vincent Turner. (*Letters and Notices*, vol. 55, no. 294 [January 1947], Library notes, Theology, 47–48):

Another author whose work is already known and appreciated in England is Father de Lubac. The extent (and originality) of his patristic knowledge have long since been an object of admiration; but his recent works have attracted considerable attention for the vigorous and sustained effort he has devoted to them. His last book, *Surnaturel* (Paris: Aubier, 1946— which is a part of the Theology series, published by Lyons-Fourvière) is of magnificent quality and deserves to be called authoritative. In truth, it may very well be that after having passed through the preliminary barrage that it is very likely to arouse, it will take its place as one of the rare classic works of theology of this half-century. It does not make its appearance without others having introduced and prepared the way; much rather, it sums up, and, with great historical erudition and an abundance of very discriminating theological views, it carries to perfection a work that has been pursued by such men as Father de Broglie, one of Rousselot's disciples, Father de Montcheuil (who wrote the best essay we have yet had on Blondel), Abbé Tiberghien, and others. The mere mention of these names, however, is enough to indicate the nature of the criticism that will of necessity be faced by *Surnaturel*. But Father de Lubac is in a stronger position to withstand it than many of those who wrote on this subject previously.

His book is an imposing work. It is comprised of nearly 500 pages. It bears the subtitle: *Historical studies*; that is the method followed. The first part is a long study on Augustinianism and Baianism and Jansenism, concluding with chapters on the concept of "pure nature" and on the theology of grace from Jansenius up to our own time. Then comes a very interesting history of Scholastic theology through the centuries (again a part that will cause many frowns of indignation; and yet similar things have already been said—for example by Father Lennerz—in the pages of *Gregorianum*). The third part is a history of the *word* (but also of the *concept* and of closely related ideas and views) "supernatural", and the book ends with various Notes on "natural beatitude" and the "natural" desire for the supernatural, and so forth. From this results a richer and more positive concept of the supernatural, and much of the dust falls away when we see that it was raised by pseudo-problems.

This gives only a brief indication of its contents. After all, these pages give only notes and not critical reviews. Perhaps, however, we should still add that, if Father de Lubac is mature and balanced, cultivated and full of a refined courtesy, and that, if he is the last man in the world to take pleasure in misrepresenting opinions that have become conventional, he has a gift for incisive clarity that can be devastating. Nowhere else has the concept of nature, as it is used in the theological context, been handled with a dexterity comparable to that of this book, and nowhere else has the nature of this concept been shown as well. *Surnaturel* is a work of great importance whose influence will be truly profound not only in theology but also (especially in France) in spirituality. For there is a great difference between considering supernatural glory as only the final stage of a pilgrimage and, on the contrary, as a gift that nevertheless carries with it a responsibility with regard to a finality in nature, in the strongest sense of that ambiguous term.

M. C(appuyns). *Bulletin de théologie ancienne et médiévale*, vol. V, no. 720–24, pp. 251–54.

H. de Lubac. *Surnaturel. Etudes historiques* (Theology, 8) (Paris: Aubier, 1946); 8vo, 498 p., Fr. 300.

Father de Lubac likes fundamental and complex ideas. Not in order to simplify them but in order to bring out their essential richness, their historical adhesions, the relativity of their expression. After *Catholicisme*, after *Corpus mysticum* (see *Bull.* V, no. 277), after *Humanisme*, and so forth, here is *Surnaturel*. We are still far from the complete historical syntheses and treatises on religious semantics for which Father de L. makes such strong appeals. But the "monographs of very limited object" (p. 6) that he brings together in his volumes will make the achievement of that more accessible.

In *Surnaturel*, we find first (9–183) a long essay entitled "Augustinianism and Baianism", in which the interpretation of Saint Augustine by Baius and Jansenius and then the supposed historical antecedents of the hypothesis of "pure nature", the principal weapon of anti-Jansenist theology in the defense of the supernatural, are submitted to an ever-benevolent and comprehensive but close criticism. Then, pp. 187–321, under the title "Spirit and Freedom in the Theological Tradition", the examination turns to one of the essential aspects of the spiritual "nature"—its freedom of choice with respect to its end—from the Fathers up to the seventeenth century. The third part of the book, about the origins of the word "supernatural" (pp. 325–428), is a sort of essay on semantics. The fourth part finally groups together six historical Notes (pp. 431–80), devoted to Saint Thomas and his interpreters: Natural and supernatural desire; Immediate natural vision; Supernatural beatitude according to Saint Thomas; What does Saint Thomas wish to demonstrate by the natural desire to see God?; Has Saint Thomas chosen Aristotle?; Three exegeses of the *desiderium naturale*.

We do not have to give the case against modern theology here. Besides, the above outline gives a hint of Father de Lubac's principal conclusions: the hypothesis of "pure nature" as well as, correlatively, the rejection of man's "natural desire" and the acceptance of the impeccability of the angel in naturalibus, such as modern theology professes them, were asserted only belatedly. Such a perspective was still unknown in the Catechism of the Council of Trent, and, if the anti-Thomistic problematic from which they are derived was itself born of the medieval speculations on the *potentia Dei absoluta* [absolute power of God], their effective introduction dates— O irony—from Sylvester of Ferrara, Cajetan and Bañez. Even then they became established only gradually, with the help of Suarez, Ripalda, John of Saint Thomas, the Salamancans, by means of the fight against Baius and Jansenism. The new theology of nature brings about as a consequence a new conception of the supernatural unknown to the ancients and in which predominates the hybrid notion of an "end superadded" onto a "natural order" complete in itself.

Let us turn for the moment to antiquity and the Middle Ages. Father de Lubac's notes and commentaries are not easily summarized. Proceeding by integration rather than by analysis, by successive expositions rather than by systematization, approaching the doctrines as a psychologist rather than as a philologist, he illuminates his conclusions and their numerous aspects rather than draws them. But the light he throws most often makes the facts emerge. Here are those that seem the most important to us.

The thought of Saint Augustine, as systematized by Baius and Jansenius, most often by means of his own formulas, could not be farther from his historical thought. Father de L. has no trouble showing throughout his exposition the incompatibility between atmosphere and principles, which is even much more profound than is generally said. But it is especially in the exegesis of particular texts that he gives proof of shrewdness and perspicacity. Witness, pp. 46–63, the famous chapters XI–XII of the *De correptione et gratia* on the subject of the distinction between *adiutorium sine quo non* and *adiutorium quo* [indispensable aid and sufficient aid]. The opposition that exists between Augustine, on the one hand, and Baius and Jansenius, on the other, however, is not always that which the theologians endeavor to establish. This is the case for the celebrated hypothesis of "pure nature". It is as foreign to Augustinian thought as it is opposed to the systems of Baius and Jansenius. Much more, it will remain practically unknown by the theologians of the Middle Ages up to Sylvester of Ferrara, who lays the basis for it while interpreting in his own way—which is equivalent to a rejection—the *desiderium naturale* of Saint Thomas. The problem of *pura naturalia* and that of *desiderium naturale* are, in fact, intimately linked: to accept one is to condemn the other, and vice versa. Now, if it is true that the Middle Ages did not accept the former—in the modern sense—it is also clear in other respects that it unanimously admitted the second. The exegesis that Father de L. gives in this regard for texts of Saint Thomas (pp. 118–20, 129–38, and especially 431–80) is as luminous as it is conclusive: human nature tends, of itself, necessarily toward God, that is, toward the supernatural end. This is the nearly general interpretation today of historians of Thomistic thought, but freed from the useless subtleties with which they often encumber it.

Another related problem—and one which we think deserves to be treated concurrently with "pure nature" and "natural desire"—is that of the impeccability of the angels *in puris naturalibus*. Here again, the exegesis of the texts of Saint Thomas is perfect, notably that of *Summa theol.* Ia, q. 63, a. 1. It is clear that Thomas always taught, along with the whole of earlier tradition, that the angel, impeccable in relation to the intrinsically

natural goods that are presented to it, is necessarily peccable—insofar as finite spirit—in relation to its end, which in any hypothesis is God himself,
that is, the supernatural. As for earlier tradition, Father de L. pays particular attention to illustrating the patristic parrallelism between *natura* and
imago et similitudo Dei. He dwells for a moment on Saint Anselm and Saint
Bernard, some of whose expressions are eloquent, then at greater length
on the influence of the introduction of Aristotle and of the doctrine of
"separated intelligences" on our problem.

The traditional and Thomist doctrine relating to spiritual natures necessarily oriented to a supernatural end obviously implies a conception of the
supernatural about which it is necessary to be specific. This is what Father
de L. undertakes to do on pages 325–428 of his book. The method used
there is more philological and the inquiry into theologians less extensive,
but the results are significant. Let us pass over the cosmological antecedents
of the term, which to our eyes seem somewhat irrelevant, theology having
taken possession only of the spiritual sense of it. The word *supernaturalis*
appears for the first time, it seems, in the sixth century, in the Latin translation of the letters of Isidore of Pelusia. In the ninth century, Johannes
Scotus Erigena introduces it in theological terminology, but it is only with
Saint Thomas that its usage greatly expands. The meanings of the word
would still be variable, but they "are, in the final analysis, reduced to two
fundamental significations . . . : an essential, ontological meaning; on the
other hand, a modal, active meaning. They run the gamut from one to the
other of the two poles, which we can designate by the two words miraculous and transcendent" (p. 401). It is a subtle mixture of these two parallel
significations that produces the modern definition of the strict supernatural, into which the notions of end, transcendence and superaddition enter
simultaneously. There were mystics, Eckhart, Tauler, Ruysbroeck, who
—curiously enough—put a curb on this process of confusion for a time
by opposing "supernatural" to "superessential". But the distinction gained
scarcely any ground, and the movement of fusion continued to develop.
The factor that perhaps contributed the most to distorting the meaning of
supernatural was its encounter with the word *superadditum*, which ended
in invading the very definition of supernatural. The pages Father de L.
devotes to it (pp. 385–94) reproduce an article that we review elsewhere
(*Bull.* V, no. 810). Let us merely recall that for ancient tradition, and for
Saint Thomas in particular, it would be meaningless to call the supernatural end *superaddita*, that word being reserved for "the whole aggregate of
means destined to procure that end" (p. 393).

This review, which is too long already, is far from giving even a glimpse
of all the wealth of material in Father de L.'s book. Neither does it stress
the inevitable lacunae or the several points that to us seem weaker. In

conclusion, however, we must take Father de L. to task a little for one tendency. His benevolent love for tradition prompts him, it seems to us, to harmonize excessively. He measures perfectly the distance that separates Saint Augustine from Saint Thomas and Aristotelianism from Augustinianism. But his sense of the relativity of formulas and concepts makes him round off the angles of thought at times. It is in this way that he seems to us to exaggerate the doctrinal agreement between Saint Augustine and Saint Thomas (see, for example, p. 182), notably with regard to the ideas of nature and grace. In addition, even within Augustinian doctrine and while telling about its evolution, Father de L. sees scarcely any opposition between the early teachings and those of the anti-Pelagian period. If it is true that these latter are not exclusively infralapsarian, they nevertheless on many points escape a Jansenist interpretation, we believe, only thanks to the inconsistencies that are part of Augustine's genius. Baius' and Jansenius' lack of understanding was assuredly profound and determined by their lack of historical sense as well as by all the other reasons described by Father de L. Perhaps it should be added that, drawing their inspiration from this ensemble of reasons, they combat the hypothesis of pure nature by using a terminology that was unaware of that hypothesis. Seen from this angle, their transposition of theological Augustinianism does less to diminish their intellectual renown and can offer some analogy to the transposition that the great Scholastics imposed on Aristotle.

With regard to what this latter transposition precisely is, Father de L. is justified in his judgment that Saint Thomas "did not always succeed in fusing the elements received from two different traditions into a perfect unity" (p. 435). He does not hide the interference between the two Augustinian and Aristotelian currents in the doctrine of nature and of natural desire (for example, pp. 434–45). But it seems to us that he should have taken greater note, in the exegesis of the text, of the antinomies that result from this duality of inspiration. Thus, in particular, the *desiderium naturale cognoscendi causam* [natural desire to know the cause] of Aristotle and the celebrated Aristotelian principle *desiderium naturae non potest esse inane* (especially if one translates, with good reason, moreover, the last four words as: "destined actually to be fulfilled one day" (p. 469), both suffer an Augustinizing transposition that it would be much to the advantage of the exegetes of Saint Thomas to discern more carefully. Perhaps Father de L. will help them by developing his *Historical Notes* a bit more?

M. C.

Paul Vignaux. *Revue de l'histoire des religions*, (1947), 225–26. Henri de Lubac, *Surnaturel. Etudes historiques* (Paris, Aubier), 498 p.

This volume constitutes no. 8 in the Theology series published under the direction of the Theology Faculty of the Scholasticate of the Society of Jesus at Lyons-Fourvière. Father de Lubac is himself the most representative figure of this group of theologians and historians. Leaving aside the brief but very brilliant Conclusion on the relationship of desire between the created spirit and God, *Surnaturel* is presented as a series of "historical studies". The work is in fact comprised of three long essays, the first on "Augustinianism and Baianism", the second on "Spirit and Freedom in the Theological Tradition", the third entitled "At the Origins of the Word 'Supernatural' ".

The interpretation provided by Father de Lubac on the nature-grace relation in Baius and Jansenius (chaps. I, II and III) is so powerfully constructed that in the future no interpreter of these two famous "disciples of Saint Augustine" will be able to disregard it. Disciples, moreover, who were unfaithful, according to Father de Lubac, to the very intention of their master (cf. particularly chap. IV on the "Prayer of Adam"). The last three chapters of this first part set forth—in a truly new synthesis—*the system of "pure nature"* that was asserted in reaction against Baianism and Jansenism; then follows the *stages of its transformation* and its development *from Jansenius to our day*. Father de Lubac brings out from the mass of texts a movement of thought shown by his analyses to be essential: the passage from the distinction between the *naturalia* and the *gratuita* to the hypothesis of a state of *pura natura*; more: to the conception of a purely natural *order*, in which the destiny of man reaches completion in an end *proportionate* to his nature, on this side of the Beatitude of believers and theologians.

In that, we touch on one of the leading ideas, perhaps the central idea, of the book: through "a kind of peripatetic orthodoxy" (p. 119), "the spirit, which is open to the infinite", has been assimilated to "beings of nature, whose end is proportionate to their limits". The same reasoning by analogy has supported "the assertion that the natural perfection of the angels must render them impeccable, since the most perfect of bodies, that is, celestial bodies, are indeclinable in their course as well as incorruptible in their essence" (p. 117). This representation, according to the Aristotelian "physics", of the perfection of a spirit has not only been *the temptation of the thirteenth century*, but again "that of the sixteenth" (p. 286); if Saint Thomas resisted it, that was not true of Bañez. . . . Such is the line of thought followed across a multitude of very complex texts by the second part of the book, which brings out of the speculations about angels the *spirit and freedom* problem and begins by invoking the *ancient tradition*, prior to the thirteenth century, in order to lead us up to the *modern period*.

It is to the Greek Fathers and to those who introduced their doctrines into the West that the first two chapters of the third part refer: *At the*

Origins of the Word "Supernatural". Chapter III provides a very fine analysis of the metaphor contained in *superadditum*. In chapter IV, "supernatural" is compared to "miraculous" and "transcendent". This is obviously only a first study, from an overall view, whose fullness embraces very complex fundamental principles. In it will be found suggestions and analyses, some more limited, some more extensive.

A fourth part, smaller than the preceding three, brings together some simple *historical notes*, most of which relate to the now theologically current problem of the "natural" desire for the "supernatural" beatitude, especially in the doctrines that profess to be "Thomistic".

As a whole, the parts of which are not equally developed, Father de Lubac's book includes, skillfully and without weighing it down, a considerable mass of invaluable references and proposes to those at work in this field the central ideas that will help them find once again the philosophical and religious meaning of often abstruse texts. It will be useful even in what it suggests without perhaps sufficient specific detail: for example, with respect to the influence of "nominalist" theology on the evolution of the notion of "nature", or with respect to the place of Duns Scotus in the history of the same idea, which is central in Christian anthropology.

Revue de métaphysique et de morale, vol. 53 (January 1948): *Surnaturel, Etudes historiques*, par Henri de Lubac. One vol., 8vo, 498 p. (Paris: Aubier, 1946).

In 1944, Father de Lubac published a volume of historical studies, *Corpus mysticum*, in which the minute analysis of certain theological expressions brought to light, thanks to prodigious erudition, the relations between the Eucharist and the Church in Christian tradition. The present volume, entitled *Surnaturel*, is in the same vein: the same richness and the same sureness of erudition; but also, as before, a very lively sense of what comprises the depth of the traditional teaching in the Church. It is a major book.

The main part of the work is made up of three studies, which in appearance seem independent—"monographs of very limited object" (p. 6), the author declares too modestly: first, "Augustinianism and Baianism", which retraces the formation of the idea of "pure nature", such as modern theology understands it; second, "Spirit and Freedom in the Theological Tradition", which touches on the discussions relating to the impossibility of an impeccable spiritual creature; third, "At the Origins of the Word 'Supernatural'", which explains the circumstances under which the term "supernatural" first appeared and how the corresponding notion was progressively defined.

But, at bottom, all these studies are connected. What Father de Lubac has constantly in view is the—relatively recent—dualist system, according to which a human essence, having by itself a certain sufficiency, would at first be constituted and capable of being the subject of philosophical analysis; then a supernatural order, wholly contingent and wholly extrinsic, would come to superimpose itself on the first nature, in virtue of a pure grace. Now, history shows that such a system was not imposed by tradition: the problem of beatitude and the question of freedom in its relation to the idea of the spiritual creature give occasion to verify this. It was quite late, in the sixteenth century, and even in the second half of that century, with respect to discussions brought about by the doctrines of Baius, that the dualist theory was formed: Father de Lubac works out in detail the evolution of thought that led to this result. The earlier tradition, when better examined, lets us see a very different and more profound conception, of Augustinian inspiration, which claims that there is no opposition between nature and grace but rather inclusion, the human soul being illuminated and fortified by the unceasing action of God. "This is, in fact, because whether it is a question of innocent man or sinful man, the salutary act that brings about in him the divine image is always a true creation. . . . Man, undoubtedly, cooperates in it—and the conditions under which he cooperates can vary—but God is always, of necessity, the true author of it. Through the first creation, he set nature into being; he produces, maintains, and makes his activity effective, he presides over its development. But for this attainment of another genre of being that the free effort of the moral will must achieve, for this passage to another order, a second cycle of creation must be opened: a higher gift, of a supereminent gratuity, through the effect of which the created spirit, transcending its nature, enters into the supernatural order" (p. 81).

This gives a better understanding of the relation of the creature to God. One in fact cannot "envisage man in his relation to God as one would envisage a being of nature with the exterior and finite agent, another being of nature, who must by hypothesis procure his end"; one cannot imagine "two beings *confronting* each other" (p. 485): in such a case, the desire that carries man toward God would seem inevitably to be either like an *exigency*, that is, like a demand that would place God in a position of dependence on the creature, or like a mere *inclination*, that is, like a desire that, far from being absolute, would remain limited. "In reality, if there is in our nature a desire to see God, this can only be because God wants for us this supernatural end that consists in seeing him. It is because, willing it and never ceasing to will it, he places and never ceases to place the desire for it in our nature. This desire is consequently nothing other than his call. . . . Natural desire for the supernatural: it is the permanent action in us of the God who creates our nature, just as grace is in us the permanent action of the God who creates the moral order" (pp. 486–87).

By showing the profoundly traditional character of these views in Christian theology, Father de Lubac intends to do the work of a pure historian. But is it necessary to observe that the conclusions to which he is thus led have at the same time a properly philosophical value? From all points of view, this work is of the first order.

Revue d'histoire ecclésiastique (1947), 176–78.
A. Van Hove: Henri de Lubac, *Surnaturel* (etc.)

The history of theological doctrines is always instructive, but it is not always equally edifying. In the present case, it invites at least theologians to a serious examination of conscience, and in an area that is assuredly not peripheral, since what is at issue is the very notion of the supernatural and of the relations of the latter with nature.

The work is comprised of three parts, consisting of historical studies that are clearly distinct and separable as well as very closely connected by the general inspiration that animates them and by their fundamental object.

Under the title "Augustinianism and Baianism", the first part in reality studies nearly the whole history of the theological doctrines established on the hypothesis of "pure nature". It is first of all the case against Baianism and Jansenism. The author stresses the opposition of these doctrines to true Augustinianism and shows that, while Baius and Jansenius may use more than one Augustinian expression, the spirit of their doctrine differs totally from Saint Augustine and in essence comes very close to Pelagianism. Their fundamental error is therefore not, as is sometimes said, having denied "pure nature". Here, on the contrary, we are witnessing the criticism, through history, of this relatively recent concept, to which modern theology accords so much importance. That is because this concept is closely linked to the idea of a natural beatitude that would supposedly be the normal and essential end of man and would not consist in the vision of God; now this idea is completely foreign to true Augustinian tradition. But in it were sought the means for refuting Baius. If this concept thus proved useful, it also led, on the other hand, to a "deadly" separation between nature and the supernatural. We are in reality encouraged here to return to authentic Augustinianism.

The second part also invites us to a similar return to tradition. We know that several modern theologians admit—or are disposed to admit—the impeccability of the angel in a purely natural order, and they like to pride themselves on the authority of Saint Thomas. An attentive and extensive study establishes, on the contrary, that tradition is unanimous in rejecting this conception, that there can be no doubt that Saint Thomas shared the same negative attitude on the subject, and that it was only quite late—notably from the time of Bañez and his followers—that the equally new distinction between the natural and supernatural orders, or the theory of the two ends, made the elevation to the supernatural order the essential condition of the peccability of spiritual substances.

The third part is no less provocative. This time the question refers to the origin and history of the meanings of the word "supernatural". A rather complex history. It seems that the word *supernaturalis* made its first appearance in the sixth century (in a Latin translation of the letters of Saint Isidore of Pelusia); it does not enter into theology until the ninth century and comes into current usage only beginning with Saint Thomas Aquinas. But a related terminology, which itself has a whole history, prepared the way for this first appearance, and the term itself, once admitted, does not always have the same meaning and takes on, according to the circumstances, very different nuances. Another term, *superadditus*, used in the theology of grace, will in the end influence the doctrine of the supernatural and fix a definite meaning for the word; at the same time, it will help to make the supernatural be conceived as an order of things clearly distinct from "nature". This evolution is in reality a revolution, which raises once again the question of two ends, the question that is the central point of the work. This inquiry is pursued up to the nineteenth century.

The three historical studies to which we have just briefly referred are followed by a series of six notes, of less breadth and importance, relating in different ways to the question of the natural desire to see God. Let us point out in particular the judicious criticism of the *expression* "natural desire for the supernatural" and the study of natural beatitude according to Saint Thomas, in which the effort is made to establish on the basis of the texts that, with the holy Doctor, it is not a question of a twofold end and a twofold beatitude of man.

Obviously the author is not writing history for its own sake, rather he wishes, through the lesson given by that history, to justify a theological conception of the relations between nature and the supernatural. It is a matter in reality of establishing that the supernatural is less "supernatural" than some imagine, that there is no radical separation between the order called natural and the one of the beatific vision, that man does not have two distinct ends, the one natural and the other supernatural. It is therefore, essentially, the thesis of the "natural desire for the supernatural". The author, in response to the "war-cry" launched by Ripalda: *Exterminandus est appetitus innatus* (p. 173), is concerned to show that the "desire to see God" has traditionally been considered the first explanatory principle of man and the pivotal point of Christian philosophy, and he understands that it is to this conception that we must absolutely return. We will leave to the specialists the task of judging if all the elements of the history have been interpreted correctly, but we nevertheless insist on paying homage as much to the remarkable erudition that is at the foundation of this study as to the concern for objectivity that served as its connecting thread. Let us also point out the fact that the author does not only juxtapose the historical stages of the doctrinal development but excels in showing how the variations in theological climate have brought about those in the doctrines themselves. The line of history appears only more clearly because of it.

Must we say, in conclusion, that, despite everything, the question of the relations between nature and the supernatural will still long remain a subject of controversy?

A. VAN HOVE.

In 1983, Raymond Winling presented *Surnaturel* in the following way (*La Théologie contemporaine, 1945–1980* [Centurion, 1983], 99–100):

Some theologians are taking up again, at new expense, the problematic of the relationship between nature and the supernatural. In *Le Surnaturel* (sic), Father de Lubac delivers the results of an historical enquiry. According to him, it was not Saint Thomas Aquinas who was at the origin of the distinction between nature and supernature but Cajetan and Suarez. The author is led to criticize the conception of "pure nature". He recognizes that this conception was capable of rendering service during the course of the discussions on Baianism but judges it to be dangerous from several points of view. To begin with, this conception, because of the extrinsicism it introduces, furthers the claims in favor of a natural order considered as properly human and in favor of a secular culture and a secular morality. On the other hand, this conception is insufficient for giving an account of the destiny of man: it represents an hypothesis that has never been achieved historically, and it lacks the personal and dialogical dimension. Logically, one must use the concrete and historical nature of man as one's starting point and not a hypothetical construction.

[2:12]

Haubtmann quotes an unpublished fragment (the "Boutteville leaf") from Proudhon, dating from 1862, that we think confirms our own conclusion and whose importance and beauty are manifest: ". . . There is one thing about God at least we can affirm from experience, it is that the idea of him possesses us and preys on our mind tremendously. . . . God is hidden, but once again there is no doubt that he torments us, that at every moment we think we will see him appear, that we seem to hear him knocking at the door; and that we cannot keep from crying out: *Wer da?* Who is there? . . . We do not know who God is, what the constitution of his being and of his attributes is, and so forth; but we say, whether we like it or not: *There is someone!*". . .

[*2:13*]

A correspondent whose name I have lost sent on to me a long, unpublished letter by Proudhon. I had planned to publish it as a supplement to my book or in a second edition, but the occasion was wanting. It is addressed to one of his former fellow workers, when he was a printer in Besançon. I have excerpted a few lines from it here:

"If the February Revolution had not moved so quickly and had left me the time to get together 3 or 4000 F by working a little, it would be in Besançon that I would live—among the memories of my youth, in close contact with five or six old friends, among whom you are surely in the first ranks. How that would refresh my imagination! How you would revive my spirit! And what sparkling pages would be written under the influence of that pure country spirit and of the fellowship we enjoyed in other times. What skeptics we were already in 1834, and how bold in style were our resolutions! Ever since that time, my dear Plumey, I have been out of my element. I have seen much, observed much; it seems to me that I have achieved nothing. I live on my wealth from 1827–1836. I have tried to get some Franche-Comté, and particularly Arboisian, irony, which is so invaluable for complete freedom of understanding, into our romantic, drawling, dense, cynical, prudish literature. Can you believe that in Paris those in literary circles have seen that as blasphemy. . . . What imbeciles I have seen in Paris, my dear Plumey, among politicians, literary figures, men of law, and above all in the Assembly! . . ."

APPENDIX III

[3:1]

He died accidentally in 1974 in Rome, where he was ecclesiastical advisor to our ambassador to the Vatican. "A mind infinitely open to all creative forms of culture in attachment to essential values, nourished by the most authentic and the most spiritual traditions of Christianity, all too aware as well of what was at stake in the philosophical debate, Fernand Guimet could only suffer profoundly from the lack of consideration with which, at a certain period, hasty theologians played with the weapon of dispute and claimed at times to teach him a lesson. This man, for whom listening and dialogue in absolute respect for the other had been the golden rule, could only have been deeply wounded by certain manipulations of theological opinion by what must truly be called pressure groups within the Church. —Only his closest friends knew that. . . ." Fernand Chapey, in *L'Echo des Carmes*, p. 10.

[3:2]

MONTAUBAN, MAY 31, 1936. MY REVEREND FATHER,

As you wished, I am giving you written confirmation—your kindness will pardon me for doing it so belatedly—of the reply I made to you on the subject of Father de Lubac's courses at the "Priests' Month" at Dax in 1934 and 1935.

I heard each of the conferences in its entirety. M. Pardes, presently superior of the house of studies of the Congregation of the Mission at Dax (he was professor of dogma there in 1934), and my colleague M. Jordy, professor of dogma at the Major Seminary of Montauban—both doctors in theology from the Angelicum—also followed them very attentively. Msgr. Mathieu, Bishop of Dax, was present at three of them and has had the text for all of them in hand. None of us has found anything reprehensible in the teaching of Father de Lubac. We all admired the profound, exact and nuanced doctrine of the learned theologian, the aptitude of the professor and the charming simplicity of the humble religious.

No astonishment was evident among the audience in 1935. In 1934, to my knowledge, the first conference (in which the problem of human origins was discussed?), which presented at length the latest discoveries from China and Palestine, aroused some surprise with two or three of the priests in the group. The reverend Father had simply and very conscientiously furnished the given facts of the problem, which posed in all its acuteness the question of the origin of the first human body. In the exchanges of views that followed the class, principles for solution that were fully conformed to the demands of the decree of the biblical commission of June 30, 1909, were considered, to the final satisfaction of all. In the face of difficulties of a scientific order, the fact of the special creation of man by God being obviously placed beyond doubt, this decree in fact leaves in its fifth, sixth and seventh responses a rather broad latitude for interpretation with respect to the mode of this creation. At the end of this conference, I quickly noted a few conclusions, the very precisely recorded text of which you will find attached: these are positions similar to those of the Rev. Father Pinard (conf. of March 8, 1936), of *L'Ami du clergé* (March 5, 1936), of M. Périer (Rev. Apol., May 1936), of M. Paquier (in a volume that carries the *Imprimatur* of Msgr. Baudrillard), of the Rev. Father Sertillanges and of a host of others (among whom, it appears, is the Rev. Father Höpfl in Rome itself). I do not believe that the Rev. Father de Lubac is blameworthy on this question.

Four of the other conferences, which is to say nearly the whole, have been published, word for word, as far as I can judge. One in the *N. rev. théol.* of March 1936; another in the *Union missionnaire du clergé*; a third in the *Chronique soc. de Fr.*, March and April 1936, and a fourth in the "Somme contre les Sans-Dieu". I do not believe they have aroused any criticism that would place the perfect orthodoxy of the Rev. Father de Lubac in doubt.

I wonder if a few teasing remarks made to M. Lahitton by one or another of his former students might not be at the origin of this tendentious case against one of the most justly esteemed professors of the Priests' Month at Dax. M. Lahitton is said to be easily irritated; perhaps he is also dangerously unconcerned about the scientific, philosophical, historical and scriptural problems of our times.

Deign to accept, my Rev. Father, with the assurance of my prayers, the very cordial homage of my deep and religious respect.

(M. Gounot, Lazarist, Superior of the Seminary of Montauban and of the Priests' Month of Dax, to the Rev. Father Demaux-Lagrange.)

Letter from M. C. Gounot, priest of the Mission, Superior of the Major Seminary of Montauban, Superior of the Priests' Month of Dax in 1934 and in 1935 (future Archbishop of Carthage).

MONTAUBAN, NOVEMBER 13, 1935, MY VERY DEAR FATHER,

Do not abandon the Priests' Month. You have done only good, and much good. You have said what it was necessary to say in order to enlighten our young priests on the problems that are arising at this time in Apologetics, and you have done so with delicacy and perfect accuracy. None of your students whom I know has been troubled or surprised by your teaching. Monsieur Pardes, superior of our house of studies and an excellent professor of dogma, has admired, as I myself have, the soundness of your doctrine on the most difficult points.

As for Msgr. Mathieu, I have been informed, through his Secretary General, how much he appreciated your course. He expressed to me yesterday, in Toulouse, his deep regret at having given you any occasion to fear the least disapproval on his part. His delay in writing to you is due to excessive work, and if he wanted to see your lectures again, it was because they interested him to the utmost degree. He absolutely insists on your participation in the Priests' Month.

So you see, there is no reason for uneasiness. May Our Lord grant you perfect health and continue to bless your fine apostolate. . . .

Letter of His Excellency, Monsignor Mathieu, Bishop of Aire and of Dax.

DAX, NOVEMBER 17, 1935, MY REVEREND FATHER,

How ashamed I am to be so late in thanking you. I wanted to reply as soon as I read your work. Unfortunately, I am very pressed: I leave tomorrow for a lecture tour in Belgium, on a subject that has required long preparation. That explains and perhaps excuses my delay a bit.

Let me say once again how happy I was to be among your audience at the Priests' Month. I am sure that in reading your typed pages, my enthusiasm will remain the same. I hope that you can continue for a long time to lend your assistance to the intellectual apostolate exercised by the Priests' Month. We would lose a great deal if, for any reason whatever, you stopped coming to Dax.

I send you, along with the expression of my religious gratitude, my cordial blessing.

+ CLÉMENT, BISHOP OF AIRE.

From Father Ferdinand Cavallera. Toulouse, February 4, 1936.

. . . I will take advantage of this occasion to bring you up to date—M. Gounot would rather have dissuaded me for doing so—about an incident others must have spoken to you about, since our Superiors have been informed of the way in which they might defend you. Well, several days ago, in January, when I was in Montauban to give a conference to a *Semaine sociale* for priests, M. Gounot had me read a letter that had been sent to him by M. Pardes, Superior of the Lazarists in Dax, in which M. Pardes confided to him—under the greatest secrecy with regard to what concerns the intervention of M. (?)—that the latter, Superior of the Major Seminary of Dax, had written to him that *M. Lahitton had boasted publicly about having been commissioned by Msgr. Ruffini*, the secretary of the Congregation of Seminaries and Universities, *to investigate your course at the Semaine in Dax*. Since the Archbishop of Toulouse and Rector, Msgr. de Solages, was at that same *Semaine* in Dax, they were informed by Msgr. Gounot and declared that they would act energetically in your favor. The Bishop of Dax was also informed and could only do the same with even greater forcefulness, since he had both read and heard you. *I was asked to inform our provincial*, so that he might inform yours in turn. I was then told to say nothing to you so as not to cause you any needless concern. *I know that the Father General is informed and that he wants to be given all the facts.* Under these conditions, I do not see why, as a colleague, I should continue to keep silent instead of doing for you what I would want for myself under the same circumstances, that is, to inform you of what has been said to me by *M. Gounot*, who, having come to Toulouse a few days ago, *told me again of his complete indignation* and repeated to me that M. Pardes had found you to be almost too moderate. Whatever happens, you can count on the support of my prayers and also my entirely favorable testimony. I hope that the matter will go no farther and that we will have the pleasure of meeting together again next session. . . .

[3:3]

I am getting a little ahead of myself. It was in January 1943 that Claudel came to Fourvière, where I saw him for the first time at length. He wrote to me from Brangues on the 21st:

"My dear Father, I was very happy to meet you, and it is a great comfort for me to know that my manner of understanding Scripture is approved by a man like you and like Father Fontoynont. I was very happy too to have your book *Catholicisme*, which has interested me profoundly and which treats a question of vital interest in a masterful way. The little collection of *morceaux choisis* at the end is a treasure from which I will allow myself to draw, for example this fragment from Pseudo-Chrysostom. . . ."

Claudel continued by discussing a text from Saint Gregory of Nyssa and speaking to me of his friend Romain Rolland.

P.S. I have, however, found a note according to which it was in July 1942 that I had the meeting with Claudel.

February 1943: "This little book merits attention because of the importance of its subject, the personality of its author and the evident nobility of its inspiration. All those who, during this troubled era through which we are passing, have not abandoned their special task as men, which is first of all to reflect and to judge, would profit from reading it. We must congratulate the author, convinced as was Péguy that 'the frightful lack of the sacred' in the modern world was the profound cause of our misfortunes, for having tried 'to collect the most humble vestiges' of this sacred, 'as one collects in the course of an excavation the least fragments of marble in which the letters of an ancient inscription can still be discerned', so as to guide us from there, as if by a mysterious Jacob's ladder, to the Being whose 'Splendor surpasses all images and who at last makes sacred, by his presence, all that we have loved and venerated here below'. His goal and his method thus defined seem excellent in all respects. We only regret, for our part, that instead of having brought back from his exploration in search of 'the smoldering wick' a certain mystique of the leader (elements of which would be difficult to find in our national tradition or in Christian tradition), he did not make a greater effort, after having spoken so well of the family and work, to discern in the people of France the many 'vestiges' of the sacred that it still preserves from its Christian past. That effort might have saved him from a tendency, which for us was excessive, to hypnotize himself about our present degradation. It would also have allowed him to direct his analysis of the sacred along a slightly different route and to show us more clearly, among the various analogous notions that history offers and theology brings out, that the difference is not only in its object but also, principally and by that very fact, in its nature. From this point of view, has what we could call the Christian revolution not consisted precisely in transforming (or rather in completing the transformation of) a pagan idea, a pagan sense of the sacred, which we might sum up in the word 'taboo', into a totally different sense and idea? It has not only shifted or completed their objects, it has interiorized and moralized them. Without doubt, religion remains something else and more than the moral, and the sense of the sacred cannot be reduced to a simple sense of duty; but it is now impossible for us to recognize the least trace of anything authentically, respectably sacred in a sense that does not take such a transformation into account. Undoubtedly there were still in paganism many human (let us even say: divine) elements of permanent value, which would be saved by Christianity and which we must retain or rediscover. Péguy said, and Father Doncoeur is right in repeating: 'A certain innocent and unfortunate paganism did not have the gods it merited.' But, as Father Festugière explains very well in the work he recently devoted to Holiness, and as Péguy himself also understood, that part of the ancient heritage is the fruit of a reason that, piercing the mist and shaking off the chains of superstition, sensed the God of justice and goodness, the God who was 'before us': the only true God who, after having made himself known to Abraham, then to Moses and the Prophets, was to reveal himself fully to us in his Son. We are sure as well that there is no fundamental disagreement between the author and us. But if these and other analogous distinctions had been clarified, it seems to us this would have dispelled completely the ambiguity in the atmosphere into which the reading of this little book plunges us, and we would have been able to enjoy with unalloyed appreciation the admirable pages for which any Christian reader would be grateful to Father Doncoeur for having provided the benefit."

[3:5]

Here is this note: "Monday 29. Dear and Reverend Father. You and two or three around you are my secret link with my Church. From my little hospital bed in Aubenas, I want to send you a sign, to restore this link. Two priests, duly reprimanded by my police chief, have refused me the sacraments. I forgive them, for, in view of the relations with Cerbère and the impossibility of my being open under the seal of the confession they refuse me, I cannot tell them all the shades of meaning in what I did. But their arguments! —I wanted you to know and to pray for me. —Do not be too alarmed about the news that is or will be rumored about me. I am holding up well, and we are waiting for a solution in the very near future.

My affection and my faithful remembrance. E. M."

[3:6]

The *Menus propos* [Small talk] of Cardinal Saliège, the complete collection in seven parts. Editions *L'Equipe*, 18, rue de Metz, Toulouse.

Seven beautiful little volumes: the format and presentation were so appropriate for these *Menus propos*. The editors also did well to classify by subject and not chronologically. What did the occasion of each one matter? (although it might be good to recall that at times these occasions were actions, at times even great actions). So grouped, the reading of it is more profitable. The reading? Let us say rather the meditation. For these short texts do not surrender their meaning to the hurried reader. Before us, in each of the volumes, file successively: the Christian, the Frenchman, the educator, the social man, the interior man, and finally the parish team and the team of action. In an alert, pungent and paradoxical form, in that spare, abrupt style without any fat, which several ringing texts have made famous, the principal problems of the Christian today, in the Church and in the city, are taken up one by one. And right away, with a firm stroke, the heart of the problem is reached.

"Small talk", little nothings, on the whole, these fantasies that one would not put one's name to, that one would hardly admit. . . . But let no one be mistaken: they are not at all mere amusement. Surely, nothing could be less solemn, nothing less "doctoral"—and often nothing more serious. Nothing less conformist—and nothing more likely to arouse profound fidelity. Some sharp remarks and, overall, some deep feelings. Some boldness, and always such good, solid sense. No eloquence, and so much persuasive force! One can only admire the union that has been accomplished between the freest of personalities and the most concerned of Church leaders about his pastoral responsibilities. This little encyclopedia, so easy to handle and so varied, is a perpetual school of realism and optimism at one and the same time; for whoever is fully open to its message, it is a school of sanctity.

And, for future historians, a magnificent document, the most sincere and the most expressive, on the Christian life of our time.

[3:7]

This is why I could not accept what my friend Father Congar recently wrote, in the written interview he gave to Jean Puyo (Centurion, 1975), 92: "My anti-nazi reflex was in essence patriotic; it was also supported by my Christian convictions; but it did not issue forth, I admit, in a political commitment like that made, in France, by friends like Fathers Chaillet, de Lubac, Chenu, Maydieu." It is quite natural, however, that Father Congar, then a prisoner of war in Germany, could not grasp exactly the nature of our commitment.

[3:8]

On the first beginnings of the *Cahiers du T.C.*, see my letter to my Superiors, Lyons-Fourvière, April 25, 1941, published in 1983 in Jean Chelini,

L'Eglise sous Pie XII, la tourments (1939–1945) (Fayard), 293–310. It reflects the common preoccupations of Father Fessard and Father Cahillet, with whom I was in constant communication at that time in Lyons. Our Provincial, Father Joseph du Bouchet, and the rector of Fourvière, Father Auguste Décisier, proved very encouraging, particularly for our fight against anti-Semitism. (Someone else saw tendentious political undertones in it.)

[*3:9*]

Interned at the Gonne barracks, which served the Gestapo as a prison, he was submitted to two interrogations. In the course of the second, which was long, the police captain asked him: "Were you the chaplain?" Not being that, he could not reply: Yes. But he did not want to seem, through a denial, more or less to disavow those to whom he had completely devoted himself. He replied: "I have come from Paris for the express purpose of being with them." He had written a little earlier: "There is a greater intensity and quality of existence in the act of dying in order to be faithful to one's duty than in a long, full life." I have devoted some pages to him in my preface to his *Mélanges théologiques*, to which I will refer later on. See also *Trois jésuites nous parlent* (Lethielleux, 1980), chap. 2 [*Three Jesuits Speak* (San Francisco: Ignatius Press, 1988), chap. 1].

When the fortieth anniversary of the first *Cahier du Témoignage chrétien* was commemorated, I agreed to Renée Bédarida's request to give an interview on "the birth of 'Témoignage chrétien'", in order to cut short various tendentious interpretations. This interview appeared in *Le Monde dimanche* on December 27, 1981.

[*3:10*]

I record here four texts, which appeared after the liberation in 1944 and 1945, in *Témoignage chrétien*. The first was written in union with Father Décisier, then rector of Fourvière, and Cardinal Gerlier, in order to plead for an increase of peace and unity among the French people (if my memory is correct; I have not been able to obtain the entire publication). The second is a reminder of what the Christian resistance to nazism was in Germany. The third was written to celebrate the return of M. Richard to Lyons. The fourth wished to draw attention to Msgr. de Solages' attitude in Toulouse before his deportation.

I.

". . . Liberation seems very close. (Since these lines were written, it has been nearly accomplished.) Victory is on the horizon. The promise of it is magnificent. But no exterior event, no matter how marvelous it might be, can suppress, as if by a magic wand, an evil whose causes are, as we see it, far-reaching and profound. Unless the heroism that compels the victory at this moment is accompanied and followed by another heroism, sustained at great length; unless the military epic that France is in the process of living can appear to us as the pledge of another effort subsequently made to accomplish self-mastery, the enthusiasm of which we already have a presentiment will soon give place to a new despair.

"Without doubt, the belief that any restoration whatever would be possible under a national-socialist domination was pure utopia. Nothing was more injurious to us during these four terrible years than the blindness of these good French people who could not see—we are not speaking of those who did not want to see—the true face of nazism. They will never know what they escaped, what corruption and what horror. Whatever the future holds for us, anything would be better than that implacable suffocation of the spirit. No Antichrist could invent a more cunning and sinister instrument than the swastika. . . .

"But, this being said, now that we are soon going to find ourselves once again in an atmosphere of openness and freedom, now that it will once again be possible for us to speak and fight honestly, in the open, it is important that we place before us two of the principal conditions upon which we will leave the trial regenerated:

"In the first place, let those who, in fact, were more perspicacious not show themselves unjust or hard toward the others. Let them not interpret evil in their attitude. Let them be able to recognize not only the purity of their intentions but also the profound truth and excellence that may have been in their plan. Let them not claim to have the monopoly on patriotism or Christian fidelity, and let them be able to admire the devotion to the public good of which others give proof even in some of their errors. The traitors to be punished will be only too numerous: it is not necessary that, tomorrow and perhaps for a long time in the future, the relations between the French and particularly between Christians also be poisoned by exclusions, resentments, recriminations or infinite retrospective quarrels.

"Then, let all together turn toward the future and give themselves to the work of regeneration that remains to be done and that nothing can replace. An immense task, capable of employing all good, and a task suited to divert us from vain disputes. Let those engaged in working toward it renounce even the dream of privileges! Let it avoid all clericalism! Let it break with that morbid atmosphere of pseudo-penitence that, in truth, was only resignation! Let it be done, not in a spirit of harsh moralism and suspicious paternalism, but, on the contrary, in a spirit of confidence in man and of social boldness, in such a way that it might infuse, for example, all Catholics with the admirable pontifical Christmas message for 1942. Then, despite all the obstacles, whose weight we are not tempted to underestimate, France will find new ways of greatness." (1944)

II.

". . . In these days of anger, when the terrible fate Hitler's Germany has called down upon itself is crashing over it, it will not be said that the *Témoignage chrétien* did not have a word of sympathy for those Christians in Germany who paved for other people the way of resistance in the face of nazi barbarianism. —We are all seized with horror before the spectacle of the deportation camps. Are we always sufficiently aware that their system was at first conceived against Germans and that, up to the end, deported Germans and foreigners were suffering in them side by side? From the beginnings of the regime, the Dachau camp enjoyed a sad reputation. We cannot count the number of priests who found death there. —Nor do we know enough about all that was done by a number of German Catholics, on many occasions, for our prisoners and deportees. Everywhere a faithful Catholic population was located, a kind of honorable complicity was established rather quickly on the level of charity. More and more numerous testimonies have come to us about it. Many of them are touching. The facts recounted to us presuppose not only a movement of the heart but often of heroism, a love stronger than the fear of death. How many priests, in particular, provided some of us with sustenance, for body and for soul, at the peril of their freedom and their life, despite all the prohibitions and the police controls! How many then paid for it in the clutches of the Gestapo! —Many Germans have shown it: brotherhood in Christ, in the twentieth century no less than in the first, is not an empty word or a concept to be used in easy times or a comfortable refuge in the depths of the spirit without external commitment. We will not forget that. —Today, we think with grief of those men who, after having been the first victims of nazism, after having often seen their superiors and their companions in the Resistance fall, one after the other, are now led into the ruin of their homeland! Yes, we pray for them, and we hope. The world will again be more than once surprised by the unifying power represented, for the earth itself, by the divine principle of Catholicity." (X)

"Lyons has just celebrated the return of Abbé Louis Richard, Sulpician priest, professor at the Theology Faculty and director of the university seminary, finally freed after twenty months of captivity and deportation. Richard was a friend to the *Cahiers du Témoignage chrétien* from the very first days, and he himself had wanted to become its distributor. When he was arrested by the Gestapo in September 1943, this was not only because of his high spiritual and doctrinal authority: it was, very precisely, because of the *Cahiers*. Embracing him soon after his return, before all his students and joyful friends, Cardinal Gerlier was eager to confer on him immediately the high position of canon of the Lyons cathedral. Questions of ecclesiastical dress lend themselves naturally to some joking, and the rite was well observed. This time, however, the Cardinal's gesture took on an unaccustomed importance. It appeared to all as the official approbation and consecration of M. Richard's attitude and of his activity in relation to the *Cahiers*. A witness had to be given, M. Richard said simply, and the *Cahiers* did so. Without doubt, he added, the *Cahiers du témoignage chrétien* did not claim to be identical with the "Christian witness" as such; yet it was nonetheless true that, at that tragic hour, while the Hierarchy found itself in a delicate situation, the *Cahiers*, at their risk and peril, assured the freedom of Christian witness, that freedom which is essential to the Church and which is no less essential to the soul of France." (1945)

The *Bulletin de littérature ecclésiastique*, which is the organ of the Institut catholique of Toulouse, has just published in its *Chronique* two admirable discourses. These are the two speeches given by the Rector of the Institut, Msgr. Bruno de Solages, in 1942 and 1943 at the opening of the school year.

The one for 1942 was devoted to "Truth". "Must we not, now more than ever," said the orator, "hold on to the truth with all our soul, in these grievous times when a tide of lies seeks to submerge us, to the point that we often have the impression that we are going to be engulfed despite ourselves if the Gospel of Jesus Christ does not remain, like a lifesaving buoy?" —The Vichy censor naturally wanted to cut this passage as well as one other. When notified of this measure, Msgr. de Solages replied, in a letter dated December 17: "I was obliged, in consequence, to order the printer to suppress the whole of the text of this discourse (in the *Bulletin*). The truncated publication of a document—unless one can indicate that the text has been subjected to such cuts—constitutes a falsehood. It is not at the moment when I am rising, in the name of the rights of truth, against falsifications of all kinds that I am going to agree to make myself an accomplice to them."

The following year, the atmosphere having become still heavier, he expressed himself more emphatically. —The Church, he proclaimed, judges "the whole of human life, public as well as private"; she judges "its conformity or its nonconformity with moral law, which is that of the conscience. . . . From this doctrinal and moral angle, her Magisterium touches everything, and it is that Magisterium which has the final word. Any intervention to prevent it from making itself heard—from whatever side it may come—constitutes a disorder. That is the doctrine of Saint Ambrose, who received it from the Apostles: It is better to obey God than men; we cannot fail to speak out." And he added, with a sober and firm dignity: "Anxious, for my part, to remain faithful to the mission that has been confided to me, being conscientiously vigilant never to depart in my teaching from the doctrinal and moral point of view and, when it is a matter of burning questions, from weighing the terms I employ, if I might use the expression from the oath of the Conclaves, before Christ, who is my judge, I admit no other censor that that of the Magisterium of the Church."

In this discourse of 1943, whose theme was "Moral Theology", the Rector of the Institut spoke out indeed. And these words, published today, help to wash us from some sense of shame. He said there, for example: "In no way and at no time does anyone have the right to commit injustice, not alone, not in one's family, not in one's profession, not in one's city, not even against one's enemies. . . ." He said there, recalling the Christian teaching on the State: "The fundamental starting point of the Catholic doctrine of the State is not the established authority but the common good." What a timely elementary catechism lesson! "Whence", he added in more detail, "the protest of the human conscience against what is arbitrary, which rages in our day as always." And, to be still more precise: "The sovereignty of the State is not absolute. It has limits, the very limits of the common good it must protect. What does not contribute to the common good is not its concern. All the more reason why the State does not have the right to go against the common good. Now, the common good is essentially a human good, and thus a moral good. The sovereignty of the State is, consequently, limited by the moral law. Any decision contrary to the conscience is, by nature, null and void. . . ."

Finally, let us quote the conclusion of this discourse. No one who, reading it and thinking of the situation of 1943 and of all that followed, can fail to feel the weight of it: The juridical organization of the social life "needs a soul, and this soul is the passion for justice. I observe with indignation the inhuman arbitrariness that rages through the world in our time; but that does not keep me, on the other hand, from feeling too with an immense sadness the rising tidal waves of vengeance and hatred in the period after the war. Will we never see in the world 'justice and peace embrace'? For there will be true peace only in justice, and to have that, totally pure, evangelical, there must be pardon and love. It is our role as Christians to use all our power over the progress of the world in favor of justice; to adhere to it ourselves, fiercely, and, if need be, to suffer for it. Blessed, said Christ, are those who suffer persecution for the sake of justice!"

Words that were weighed, measured; proud and courageous words; words of *commitment* that were already bearing witness. What followed was inevitable. Arrest, deportation. Since last September we have been prevented from even pronouncing the name of Msgr. de Solages. Still today, we are without news of him—as of so many others. . . . But from now on, we are permitted to say: the Rector of Toulouse was in those four atrocious years a witness to Christ such as one wished them to be. By his noble fidelity to the Gospel, he was yesterday and will be tomorrow one of the great supports of the Church of France.

[*3:11*]

Msgr. Saliège had been one of our great moral supports. I have saved these two notes from him, written after his elevation to the cardinalate:

TOULOUSE, DECEMBER 28, 1945

My Reverend Father, The Seminary of the Missions of Syria has been a light, a strength for me. I am only a rather awkward reflection of what came to me from it. It is with joy that I see in my elevation to the Cardinalate the consecration of the activity of the Seminary of the Missions of Syria.

TOULOUSE, JUNE 1, 1946

Do you know that the nuncio is not pleased that in Rome I quoted the "scholasticate of Fourvière", whose doctrine he claims is suspect. It was to Msgr. Théas that he said this. You are not unaware that in Paris there is a center of virulent integrism.

Such as that by Father Camelot:

Corpus mysticum. The work by Father H. de L., C.M., is now appearing in its second edition. We have already said here all that must be thought of this fine book, of its immense erudition, of the wealth and fecundity of its suggestions regarding the relations between the Eucharist and the Church as well as regarding the history of theology. This new edition differs from the first by a few, but very few, changes, by several additions and above all by a *Foreword* in which the author undertakes to respond to the uneasiness aroused in some of his readers by tendencies that appeared to be manifested in this book. "A few inadvertencies" had made it possible for them to suppose that Father de L. had the purpose of bringing an action against rational thought and classical theology. Filled with wonder at the riches he discovered in the ancient Christian heritage, he did not for all that nourish some archaist's dream, nor did he plan to disparage a more dialectical form of understanding. On the contrary, he had recognized that the dialectical excess of someone like Béranger itself marked the direction of progress, and he had expressly noted that the Thomistic synthesis, in which the contributions of the past culminate, so nourished by tradition and so strongly balanced, was the bearer of the future (pp. 7–8, and cf. pp. 225–56, 297). Although they use another dialectical apparatus than Saint Augustine or Hugh of Saint Victor did, the great Scholastic doctors do not separate rational effort from religious respect before the *mysterium fidei*. Augustine's or Anselm's understanding of the faith "must retain for us the fullness of its dynamism and its power", and we must "return constantly to the roots, to the original implications, in order to be nourished"; otherwise, we are in danger of "withering" or "being led astray" (C. Journet, quoted p. 265, note 71). But that would be rather vain if we were not concerned at the same time to retain the benefit of other acquisitions from Christian thought and other traditions. We willingly grant these frank explanations to Father de L.

T. CAMELOT, O.P., Revue sc. philos. et théol. (195), 380.

I had drafted the following reply, which remained among my papers:

Professor Hommes is the author of a large work, *Der technische Eros*, which I assume to be very wise, even profound. Neither is he averse to pleasant fantasies, if I can judge by several passages that have been quoted to me from his book. I learn in fact that, according to Professor Hommes (op. cit., p. 40), I have undertaken to "baptize the communist social philosophy" and that I perceive "the salvation of the human community in the union of Kierkegaard and Marx". It is always instructive to see oneself through the eyes of others: one thereby discovers in oneself unsuspected regions. It is not the first time I have had this experience. Yet, I do ask Professor Hommes' pardon: if he had discovered a propagandist for Pelagius in Saint Augustine or a partisan of Averroès in Saint Thomas, it would not have been a more revolutionary find. The subject would simply have been more notable. I will not undertake at all a personal defense that would be only an excess of zeal. My writings are at the disposal of anyone at all. That Professor Hommes did not waste his time in reading a very secondary author, writing in a foreign language, is a very natural thing. All the same, the little that has been translated into German would have been enough to clarify his religion.[1] But above all, I think, he could have chosen better informers.

HENRI DE LUBAC, S.J.

Similarly, a page published in 1947, in the issue of *Esprit* on "Monde chrétien, monde moderne" [Christian world, modern world], reproduced several years later without my knowledge in *France catholique*, reportedly told readers, whose feelings tended toward the left and who had not noticed the source of this page, that I "was veering to the right". The same experience again with some chapters from my *Paradoxes*, praised, undoubtedly with confidence, by "progressive" minds and then subsequently criticized by the same ones, while Gustave Thibon was at the same time addressing me an enthusiastic letter in their regard. Whatever one says or does, one does not escape these kinds of successive and contradictory judgments.

Still in 1962, I read, in a Polish book translated by Paul Cazin, "The Vatican . . . had secretly withdrawn from circulation the works by Father de Lubac, *Le Surnaturel*, *De la connaissance de Dieu*, permeated with an intolerable flirtation with regard to communism." (Tadeuz Breza, *La Porte de Bronze, chronique de la vie vaticane*, 83–84. The author had obviously not seen these works.)

My real attitude, which the second *France prends garde . . .* by Father Fessard had made me support in 1945–1946, was expressed more than once again in the following years. Witness, among others, this letter, which I

---

[1] A critic above suspicion, Jean de Fabrègues, the editor of *France catholique*, wrote in his journal, in reference to precisely the same writing to which the Professor is referring, that it was to his knowledge one of the best refutations of Marxism. "Each phrase is right on target", he wrote. Whom shall we believe? Which way shall we turn?

addressed to a young friend on February 3, 1949, and which today, thirty years later, does not seem to me to have lost any of its timeliness:

"My dear friend, you wanted to question me last month about 'Progressive Christians'. As I predicted, the discussion did not begin well, I am distressed at the turn it risks taking. That does not prevent me from thinking, although I state it very reluctantly, that this movement is going astray; it is, unfortunately, often easier to see evil and condemn it than to give positive advice and to create good. Duty must always be more or less discovered: how can we be surprised then that all discoveries are not happy? It is not a question of throwing stones at anyone. Yet, I would like to tell you my point of view in a few very simple reflections.

"1) These 'progressive Christians', in fact, play into the hands of the worst of totalitarianisms. The leading ones among them, who have fought against totalitarians of the nazi party and the nazi state, fail to perceive that they are fighting today for the totalitarians of the communist party and the communist state. They want social liberation, and they are lending their assistance to a suffocation of man, to a tyrannical police organization, to an external control of thoughts and consciences, to an enormous attempt to tear away the principle of spiritual freedom that Christianity inserted into the world. They do not perceive this because they are caught up in its magic appeal and their sensibility avoids all evidence that would risk doing harm to their new faith. And they do not understand that they are not giving totalitarianism its due.

"2) Consequently, in opposition to their desire, they work to ruin any hope for an authentic and effective social impetus in contemporary Catholicism. Without wanting to, they play a kind of role as *agents provocateurs*, which, in a reaction devoid of Christian spirit, contributes to a rejection of many of the elements that might have been won over to a better ideal. The more their social program claims to be free and bold, the more it finds itself coinciding in certain points with claims preached by the communists, and the more they should, if they do not wish to compromise everything, insist on separating themselves clearly from the communist party instead of giving their adherence to it, as they do in practice, whatever might be the more or less labored distinctions they maintain. Their desire for realism and efficacy plays against them in any case: for if communism triumphs, the result will be what I said in no. 1; and if it is eliminated, at least for a time, the social cause itself to which they have devoted themselves, compromised along with it, will also suffer the consequences. Besides, on the more personal level, this premature desire for efficacy in many cases risks dropping the substance for the shadow: no longer placing confidence in anything but the communist revolution, which must be brought about by a wholly political action, to achieve what they dream of, they soon risk becoming mere sterile political agitators, who are more or less deformed, withered, humanly speaking, at the same time as they are passionate, while those who pursued more humbly a task of social builders would have been more effective in their action and would have much more effectively saved both the man and the Christian in themselves. This is not an attempt to depreciate political action but to put it back in its proper place.

"3) Finally, what I fear, and events show only too well that my fear is not groundless, is that those responsible for the formation and for the so closely communizing orientation of 'progressive Christians' are working, again without wishing to and even against their deepest wish, to prepare the way for apostasies. This is being done in two ways: first because of the positive attraction of the communist party, which fascinates them and which constitutes one of the most formidable anti-Christian machines there is. It is easy to say: we are guarding our Christian faith in the spiritual realm, and we are giving our faith, with respect to temporal things, to Marxism. But, apart from the fact that it is already an abdication to place one's faith in an order of things that is not answerable to faith, it is not true that Marxism is careful to govern only temporal things while setting aside another domain: what is true is that, admitting only the solely temporal order, it claims to enclose all of man within it. And the one who delivers himself over to its influence is in serious danger with respect to his faith as well as to his Christian behavior. Here again, they are not giving totalitarianism its due.

"In the second place, danger comes from that atmosphere of criticism with respect to the Church, which is so debilitating, particularly for young minds. I do not want to preach complacent conformity nor to reject the existence of a healthy self-criticism nor to be scandalized by certain cries that are at times a little harsh. I do not even wish to insist too strongly on the distinction to be made between the mass of Catholics and the Church as such, and so forth. . . . One cannot require young laypeople to make a whole series of learnedly balanced theological considerations. But what is serious is that kind of disposition that tends toward disparagement, as if one were oneself outside, as if one had lost the consciousness of being one of the faithful, as if one were judging from outside and almost as if one no longer loved; —a disposition that is in sharp contrast with the kind of magic appeal I noted a little while ago, which systematically avoids any quasi-shadow of criticism. A little Marxist ideology having come to be mixed with it, this so-called social detachment with respect to the Church risks causing a loss of faith more quickly than steps taken on a more purely intellectual level.

"You see, I am speaking above all about lack of awareness, about blindness, about dangerous orientation. I am not speaking about heresy. The way in which some of them try to justify their position through the distinction of the realm of God and the realm of Caesar is simplistic and illusory; hardened, it would become formally erroneous. It has not yet assumed enough ideological consistency for that. But in practice, it comes to the same thing.

"On the other hand, I understand, and I dare say I share, the whole initial impulse, the whole initial uneasiness, indeed the whole initial scandal that today impels a certain number of young people in this group of 'progressive Christians'. I know some who are very likable, very admirable in certain respects, who do not see the political situation of the group well or who do not discern the danger because this aspect of the question scarcely matters to them, concerned as they are to work then and there, in more or less close union with a few communists, at a task of the social order; to whom connection on the human level hides the fact of political adherence (and, more or less, dependency). I know all too well, in addition, that they have great excuses and that the first responsibilities are not theirs. But I would not like an insufficiently enlightened and overly lax sympathy to prevent us from using the utmost of our power in the years and perhaps the months ahead to save them from a terrible tragedy. And that is why, being capable of nothing else, I am sending you these few reflections from my bed, where a state of intermittent illness has kept me lately. It only remains for me to assure you once again of my friendship and my prayers."

[*3:14*]

In what follows, I will confine myself to what concerns me most closely. I will not undertake to give a chronological account of the debate that was to shake the Church during the years that followed the war, a debate scarcely allayed by the encyclical *Humani generis* (1950). With even greater reason, I will not to try to analyze its causes or to clarify certain obscure, hidden sides to it of which I have at least been given a glimpse. As for the occasion that, more than any other, unleashed the violent campaign of opinion against what Father Garrigou-Lagrange and others were to call (by a centuries-old expression): "the new theology", it was an article published by Father Jean Daniélou in *Etudes*, in the front of their April-May-June 1946 issue (79th year, vol. 249, pp. 5–21): "Les Orientations présentes de la pensée religieuse" [The current orientations of religious thought].

This very intelligent (and very innocent) article, although a little too journalistic in style (in the opinion of the author himself), made an appeal in its conclusion, in order to accomplish the tasks that were indispensable

for theology in the face of an invasive atheism, that "men add to a profound sense of the Christian tradition, to a life of contemplation that gives
them understanding of the mystery of Christ, an acute sense of the needs
of their times and a burning love of their brothers".

[3:15]

". . . Whatever might be the progress on which man prides himself or
from which he gathers the fruits, it remains and will always remain true
that every day, in our hands, 'the world is vanishing'. . . .

"It is the same for humanity, taken as a whole, as for each individual.
Let it develop thus indefinitely in its order, let it cross more and more
elevated thresholds: it cannot reach completion without a totally different
process—or rather a 'passion': a turning around of the whole being, a mysterious passage through death, a revival and a recasting that are nothing
other than the evangelical metanoia. Any external 'revolution' will never
dispense with this inner revolution. As it was necessary to consent to be
born, one now must consent to die. It is no longer simply a question
of self-control: it is self-renunciation. *Qui vult salvare animam suam, perdet
eam*. . . . [He who wants to save his life will lose it.] If no one is to escape
humanity for a solitary destiny, humanity as a whole must die to itself
in each of its members in order to live, transfigured in God. Such is the
first and the final word of Christian preaching. Such is the law imposed
on humanity in every man—for each is responsible for all, the bearer of
his share of the destiny of all; the law, if one accepts the expression, of
Christian humanism, which can only be a converted humanism. *Gloria
Dei, Vivens Homo*: the words of Saint Irenaeus express this truth well, but,
on the other hand, man has access to life, in the only total society that can
exist, only by saying quite by himself: *Soli Deo Gloria*. Whatever therefore
might be the natural progress gained, even in moral values, whatever might
be the new idea elaborated, something else must intervene in order to confer on all this its definitive value: a transfiguration, incommensurate with
all natural transformations. Something very different from a progress that
saves man even through human defeat. Neither an advance, a discovery, a
progress—and something without which all progress still leaves man his
misery. Nor merely an objective victory of freedom over the necessities
that impose themselves on the human animal; but in the innermost part
of the being, the passage from servitude to the kingdom.

"Now this passage is not at all within man's reach. It is not in fact a
question of some dialectical reversal, even the most incredible of all. Nor
is it a question of a new ascension, even the most audacious of all. It is

not a question of passing over into a new degree in the same order. The *supernatural* is not a higher, more beautiful, richer or more fruitful nature. It is not, as is sometimes said today through a poor neologism, an over-nature. It is the irruption of a totally different principle. A sudden opening of a kind of fourth dimension, without proportion of any kind with all the steps provided in natural dimensions. A 'new creation', the creation of a 'new heart'. Literally, a 'new birth'—the first benefit of which will be for the Christian the revival of a new childhood. Nature evolves and advances all through time: through the supernatural we pass endlessly from time to eternity. The first builds the earthly city: the second introduces the King-dom of God. And the latter is not a temple made by human hands. It is the 'Mountain of Sion', 'the City of the living God, the heavenly Jerusalem'. The bonds are real and close between nature and the supernatural, since it is the first that weaves, so to speak, the body of the second. . . . (Yet) no formation of a 'new man' will do away with the necessity of the passage to the 'New Man',[2] that New Man described by Saint Paul. . . . Any new stage into which man crosses in his history can only open it—or close it, for all natural progress is ambiguous—to the renewal of the Paschal Mystery. . . .

"Let man, therefore, confident of divine assistance, take responsibility once again for the work of the six days. Let him prolong it throughout the seventh day. Let him prove to be bold, victorious, inventive. 'What man can do, God does not rob him of it' (Msgr. Garrone). But the eighth day, on which alone everything is brought to completion and renewed, is the day of the Lord: man can only receive it. Let him pursue, as long as the world lasts, the activities of Prometheus: let him light in every cen-tury a new fire, the material basis for new human strides, new problems and new anguish. But at the same time, let him beg for the descent of the unique Fire without whose burning nothing could be purified, consumed, saved, eternalized: *Emitte Spiritum tuum et creabuntur, et renovabis faciem terrae* [Send forth your Spirit and they are created, and you renew the face of the earth]."

"La Recherche d'un homme nouveau", in *Affrontements mystiques*, 88–92.

Cf. even in *Catholicisme*, the conclusion: "There is no smooth transition from a natural to a supernatural love. . .", and so forth.

---

[2] The necessity will appear to be twofold, if we see in man, as we recalled above, not only nature but sin. . . .

APPENDIX IV

[4:1]

Hence the letter I was then led to write to my Provincial:

FOURVIÈRE, JULY 24, 1941, MY REVEREND FATHER PROVINCIAL, P.C.,

You have so often given evidence of so much kindness that I do not hesitate today to open my heart to you, for it is filled with a deep sorrow *that comes to it from the Society*, and the time for manifestation of conscience is still far off.

The last time I saw you, I asked if the Reverend Father Assistant had not made known several reproaches in my regard. Nothing of this had come to your attention. Since then, I have heard the same reproaches repeated, which were in particular expressed before the Rev. Father Rector of Fourvière. They are serious. I would have liked to be able to reassure the Rev. Father Assistant, but a request for an interview addressed twice in my name through the Rev. Father Rector met first with a desire for a delay and then with a refusal. This refusal was both a confirmation and a worsening of the reproaches. According to the Rev. Father Assistant, I am thus an "opponent", that is, as far as I can understand, I am supposedly in opposition both to the present political regime in France and to the general directives of the Society, especially as they have just been specified in his Letter to the Assistancy. The religious concerns I had shared with my Superiors in an impulse of confidence were supposedly only a screen, hiding a resentment of the political order; in reality, it is "democracy" for which I am presumably crying, and my actual attitude can be explained by the same motives that supposedly made me take the part of the "Reds" in Spain a few years ago! All that presumably proves that there is really something fundamentally wrong in my mind and spirit.

Such reproaches, which I hardly dare repeat, throw me into a state of true astonishment. I am very sure, my Reverend Father Provincial, that neither my words nor my conduct could under any circumstances have given grounds for them. On what contemptible reports has the Rev. Father Assistant really been able to base himself in order to entertain them? On the ill-considered and slanderous remarks of some fanatic? The pages of mine that he recently read could not have furnished him with the material for such an interpretation of my sentiments; so he must have thought those pages to be lies and hypocrisy. How is it then that, in *the paternal govern-ment* of the Society, misunderstandings of this magnitude can be produced between Superiors and subjects, living under the same roof, even though the subject asks only to make himself known to his Superior as he truly is and even though the Superior himself declares that he has lots of spare time?

What adds to my suffering is precisely finding once more that kind of a priori that, although I have never been able to determine why and although no one has ever consented to find fault with me directly and clearly, continues to reject me as though I were outside the Society. You have done much, my Reverend Father Provincial, to free me from so dis-tressing a feeling, but your personal kindness has not been able to trans-form such an intractable situation. If it were only a matter of a passing reproach with respect to some precise fact, I could without doubt simply ask God to grant me the humility necessary to accept it, even if it were unjustified. But a judgment so grave and so constant, which I feel hanging over my person and my entire activity, such an overall distrust, to put it more precisely, paralyzes me. I am aware that it has already restricted three-fourths of my action in the past—to say nothing of the part it has had in successive illnesses. I have too strong a sense of what the Society is, of what it demands of us in terms of union, cohesion, teamwork (as you reminded us again in your exhortation this spring), to resign myself, as some have done at times, to some individual action carried out more or less on the margin of obedience or, with even greater reason, to some little life avoiding troubles by avoiding responsibilities.

Since the Rev. Father Assistant has left without hearing me (I had hoped up to the last moment that he would have me called), allow me, then, my Reverend Father Provincial, to address you as the major Superior he has given me to contact and to declare to you that, in what concerns me, *there is absolutely no truth in the judgments the Rev. Father Assistant has repeated.* And since, at the moment, it is naturally with respect to the Letter he has just sent to the Assistancy that the question of our attitudes and our religious obedience arises, I am anxious to state precisely that two essential points in particular, in this Letter, correspond quite exactly to my spontaneous thoughts: a. It is not our duty to be involved in politics but to occupy ourselves with the Kingdom of God by always remaining on the most purely spiritual plane possible; b. We must know how to distinguish, fol-lowing Leo XIII and the whole of tradition, between the regime of the government and its legislation; our independence of judgment with regard to the latter (an independence that the Church could not surrender in any case) must not place our loyalty with respect to the former in question. It is precisely because our role is religious and not political, and because the religious situation in the world (a situation, moreover, with which we in France soon risk being very closely bound up) is of an exceptional gravity, that I have had the boldness to manifest, once more in total confidence and without the least insinuation, my uneasiness to my Superiors. If, contrary to the affirmations of principle contained in the Rev. Father Assistant's letter, a *wholly religious* action were, through the play of equivocations spread everywhere today, to be declared a political and subversive action; if everything a priest might say and do to place souls on guard against anti-Christian Hitlerism were to be interpreted automatically though absurdly as "an opposition to Marshal Pétain", I need to know that my Superiors would not consent to enter into such an equivocation and that if, on my side, I remain faithful to the line that they themselves have traced, I would not be in disagreement with them. For it is impossible for me, in conscience, to consent to what would today in my eyes be a very grave sin of omission, and in addition the things in question are so grave that I do not think it is enough, in order to be entirely covered by obedience, for me to act solely in accord with my immediate Superior.

I am, my Reverend Father Provincial, and I ask God to keep me, whatever happens, your very obedient child in Our Lord.

[4:2]

"In short, this *new theology* [underlined in the text], of which these two excellent Fathers have made themselves the knights-errant, while rudely demolishing the heretofore-classical system of our schools, does not present any reliable material or sound criteria for a reconstruction in harmony with the indefeasible demands of a perfect orthodoxy". The expression had some very ancient letters of nobility, or, if one prefers, of anti-nobility. On the other hand, in the bulletin that substituted for or prolonged for a while the *Cahiers* of "Jeunesse de l'Eglise" [Youth of the Church], edited by Father Montuclard, O.P., one could read: "We are not creating some new theology for the Youth of the Church". Around 1970, however, it was not unusual to see or hear a new theology demanded for a new Church. . . .

[4:3]

Here is that passage:

". . . Societatis Jesu igitur sodales . . . debent etiam accuratam perfectamque scientiam sibi adipisci et, praeclara sui Instituti vestigia secuti,

· doctrinarum progressus . . . sectari, id sibi persuasum habentes, se hoc itinere, quamvis aspero, plurimum ad majorem Dei gloriam et ad aedificationem Ecclesiae conferre posse. Insuper suae aetatis hominibus . . . debent ita loqui, ut intelligantur et libenter audiantur. Ex quo id infertur, ut in proponendis quaestionibus, in argumentationibus ducendis, in discendi quoque genere deligendo, oporteat sui saeculi ingenio et propensioni sapienter orationem suam accommodent. At quod immutabile est, nemo turbet et moveat. Plura dicta sunt, at non satis explorata ratione, 'de nova theologia' quae cum universis semper volventibus rebus, una volvatur, semper itura, numquam perventura. Si talis opinio amplectenda esse videatur, quid fiet de numquam immutandis catholicis dogmatibus, quid de fidei unitate et stabilitate? —Dum igitur inocciduam Veritatem vereri sanctum solemneque habetis, operam date problemata, quae labens fert tempus, studiose investigare et exsolvere, presertim si ea eruditis christifidelibus obstacula et difficultates progignere possint; quin etiam eadem illustrando, in auxilium convertentes impedimentum, illorum fidem inde confirmate. Verumtamen, cum novae vel liberae agitantur quaestiones, catholicae doctrinae principia semper mentibus praefulgeant; quod in re theologica omnino novum sonat, evigilanti cautione perpendatur; certum firmumque ab eo, quod conjectura ducitur, ab eo, quod labilis nec semper laudabilis mos etiam in theologiam et philosophiam introducere et invehere potest, secernatur; errantibus amica praebeatur manus, nihil autem indulgeatur opinionum erroribus."

[Therefore the members of the Society of Jesus must also achieve exact learning at the highest level and pursue advancement in learning according to the best traditions of their institute, confident that, following this path, hard though it may be, they can make the finest contribution to the greater glory of God and the advancement of the Church. Moreover, they must speak to their contemporaries in ways they can understand and enjoy. Therefore, it is clear how skillfully they must address the spirit and inclination of the times as they suggest lines of inquiry, marshal proofs, and select fields of study. But no one must upset and change what may not be changed.

There has been much talk, but not enough reasoning in depth about a "new theology", perpetually evolving as everything else evolves, perpetually on the move but never getting anywhere. If we suppose we ought to indulge that sort of thinking, what will become of our never changing Catholic dogmas, and the unity and stability of our Faith?

Therefore, while you hold it to be a holy and solemn duty to revere the unchanging Truth, take care also to study diligently and to solve the problems which time in its passage presents, especially if these can cause objections and difficulties for educated Christians. Rather should you shed light upon them, and by changing hindrance into help thereby strengthen men's faith.

However, in discussions about new or undecided matters, keep the principles of Catholic doctrine always before your minds. Utter novelties in theology must be evaluated with watchful care. Keep what is certain and solid distinct from what is conjecture—conjecture which it were unsafe and improper to drag and haul into theology and philosophy.

Offer a friendly hand to those who are in error, but give no welcome at all to the errors they espouse.]

Out of this mixture of encouragements and cautions, it was obviously the cautions that were noted and retained. As for the advice addressed at the end to the guardians of orthodoxy, it was an order for severity with respect to "error" more than that of a friendly hand extended to the "erring", as many made a point of applying it.

Among the numerous writings that orchestrated the Castelgandolfo address, I will quote these lines from an article by Father T. M. Bochenski, O.P., which appeared on February 8, 1947, in *La Liberté* from Fribourg (Switzerland), "The Directives of the Pope to Christian Thinkers":

". . . In two other recent speeches addressed by Pius XII to the General Chapters of the Jesuit Fathers and the Dominican Fathers (September 16 and 23), respectively, his thinking has been expressed with all desirable clarity. In speaking to the former, he gave a strong reminder that the Jesuit Fathers are bound by their own constitutions to follow Saint Thomas. . . ; with justifiable force, he branded as dangerous to the stability of religious faith the 'new theology', according to which the search for the true would always be en route without ever arriving. . . . We believe that these paternal warnings from the Head of Christianity are timely. For several years, a disturbing movement, strangely connected with modernism, has been developing in several countries, particularly in France, where a number of books, articles and mimeographed courses have come out, propagating an erroneous irrationalist doctrine. In certain circles, they have thought it possible to affirm that all ancient Catholic tradition has been irremediably transcended; they have gone so far as to compare theology to the out-of-date art of other times; they profess a radical and irrationalist evolutionism that returns to the negation of all objective truth. —These phenomena are only one repercussion in Catholic thought of a vague irrationalism that passed over Europe immediately after the war; they also proceed, undoubtedly, from certain remnants of modernism, insufficiently suppressed at the beginning of the century. . . ."

MEMORANDUM
(Excerpt from daily notes made from
September 9, 1946, to April 18, 1947)

SEPT. 9: In Rome, Father d'Ouince receives a letter from Father Daniélou (Jersey) warning us of criticisms formulated by Abbé Journet with respect to Teilhard, Daniélou and me.
Meeting with Erik Peterson at Saint Louis des Français.

SEPT. 11: At the General Congregation, report of the commission "Ad detrimenta" [Damage control committee]: attention is drawn to an "intoleranda aliqua sentiendi libertas" [an intolerable freedom of thought] to which is opposed: "secura et recepta doctrina" [safe and acceptable doctrine].
Father de Gorostarzu warns me that, since his arrival in Rome, he has noted an explicit opposition to the theological tendencies of the French, especially of Fourvière. One of the points of concern is original sin.

SEPT. 15: Election of Father John Janssens.
Arrival of *Surnaturel* at the Curia.

SEPT. 17: Castelgandolfo. Address of Pius XII. "Nova theologia". Presentation of each to the Pope: "I know your doctrine very well".

SEPT. 18: Saw the chairs of Saint Gregory at S. Gregorio and at S. Stefano Rotondo. The address of the Pope, which had been thought to be private, appears in *l'Osservatore*.

SEPT. 19: I learn that there would be formal denunciations against Montcheuil, Fessard, Daniélou. I receive the offprint of the article from the *Revue thomiste* (Nicolas-Labourdette).

SEPT. 22: Distribution of a circular on the Gregorian; among other things, a request for money. It is because of money that the professors of the Gregorian cannot publish scientific works.

SEPT. 23: Father Décisier, provincial from Lyons, was received by the Father General. The latter does not intend to judge our doctrines on the basis of rumors or outside reports. Good impression from Father Décisier.

SEPT. 24: Father Delos, O.P., canonical adviser to the ambassador, who had written to me of his desire to see me, receives me at Santa Sabina. He tells me that the significant passage from the Pope's address to our Congregation has been taken to be a reprimand to the French, that is, to Fourvière; for obviously, he adds, smiling: "it cannot refer to Father Boyer". He strongly advises two things: 1) a doctrinal counterattack; 2) a visit to Msgr. Montini. But the latter is away.

SEPT. 25: According to Father W. Klein, the Pope's address was composed by two German Fathers, Fathers Heindrick and Leiber, who supposedly consulted Father Bea in particular. The doctrinal part presumably expressed the reaction of these three Fathers to the progressive tendencies of the French Jesuits. The address being written about three weeks before the audience at Castelgandolfo.

SEPT. 26: Visit to Father de Boynes. I have known for a long time that he mistrusts me. Very friendly—but it is he who controls the conversation. He points out amicably that Father Maurice de la Taille, in his projected work on grace, was completely scrapping the idea of "pure nature".

OCT. 1: Visit to Msgr. Ottaviani, at the Holy Office. (This was recommended to me as well as to Father d'Ouince.) He tells me that the address of the Holy Father is not to discourage me in my work. In exchange for the volumes of *Sources chrétiennes* I offer him, he gives me his *Compendium juris publici ecclesiastici*, with an inscription.

OCT. 2: Students from the Angelicum come to see me. They reveal to me the menacing declarations made by Garrigou and Gagnebet against Bouillard, the "modernist".

OCT. 3: This morning, at the Gregorian, Father Delannoy, a Belgian, tells me that two things are certain about the Pope's address: the Pope wanted to say only things that would please the Society, and his address was prepared within the Society. He warns me of remarks being spread against Fourvière and against me.

Maritain has had me invited to come to see him at the Palais Taverna, where the embassy is headquartered. I come there this afternoon. The Gregorian seems intellectually miserable to him (although he does not say it quite so bluntly). He saw Father de Boynes a few months ago; the latter said to him: "I simply cannot stop those young French Fathers"; Maritain had the impression that he was repudiating us en bloc, *simpliciter*.

Maritain advises me to see both Montini and Pius XII. We exchange a few words on the subject of Teilhard.

At the Gregorian, Father Michel Ledrus, a Belgian, had said to me this morning that he was in complete agreement on the subject of *Surnaturel*.

OCT. 4:   Father Chamussy saw Father de Boynes yesterday. The latter confirmed to him that there were no specific complaints against his Fourvière house (except for some slight uneasiness with respect to Father Rondet on original sin). But his conversation showed well that he mistrusts several of us.

OCT. 7:   Alarmed letters received from Paris, England and Germany: they speak of my impending condemnation and that of "Fourvière". Long exchanges with Father Décisier, Provincial.

OCT. 8:   Father Chamussy recounts to me the conversation he has just had with Father Bea. The latter assured him that in his address at Castelgandolfo, Pius XII was not aiming at the Jesuits from France; this "théologia nova" of which he spoke was only a way of synthesizing a vague, unlocalized tendency. The Pope did not want to admonish the Society but, on the contrary, to say what the Society desired (Father Chamussy's understanding: the Pope read an address whose text he had left to the Society to work out). Responding to questions from Father Chamussy, Father Bea assured him that he had never heard anything bad said against Fourvière, except once, by Father de Boynes.

OCT. 9:   Saw Father René Arnou: he recently met Father Garrigou-Lagrange, qualificator at the Holy Office: "It was a declaration of war." I go next to see, at the Canadian College, M. Robin, P.S.S., whom I knew at the university seminary at Lyons. He tells me he hears daily talk of the impending condemnation of "Fourvière". Father Garrigou has sworn publicly to obtain it; his assistant Father Gagnebet repeats it. He said, scarcely a few days ago: "We will have them!" Father Garrigou-Lagrange is reportedly doing everything he can to disturb the conscience of the Pope in private conversations. Two men in particular in Rome are supposedly supporting his campaign: Father Monier, Superior of the French Seminary, and Dom de Saint-Avit, Benedictine from Saint Paul-Outside-the-Walls.

OCT. 11: It is reported in Rome that I have been summoned to the Holy Office, where Msgr. Ottaviani supposedly enumerated the blameworthy points of "my doctrine".

OCT. 12: Léon Bérard, former ambassador (of Vichy) to the Vatican, complains to Father d'Ouince about Father Daniélou and about me (who am, however, he says, "more cautious"). Bérard is on the best of terms with Garrigou.

OCT. 13: Yesterday and today, with Abbé Monchanin, who just arrived in Rome, accompanying his Indian bishop on his "ad limina" visit. Father Delos insists again that I see Msgr. Montini. Father Décisier has proposed writing a letter, signed by the four Provincials of France, in which they would ask the Father General for his judgment on and some clear directives for the doctrinal activity of our Provinces.

      According to the Provincial from Austria, the sentence in the papal address on "théologia nova" was added later.

OCT. 14: Saint Pudentiana. —Saw, at the Cancellaria, Msgr. Julien, P.S.S., Dean of the Rota. He thinks absolutely that I should see Msgr. Montini, whom he praised highly to me.

      From an outline by Father Bith, Provincial of Paris, Father Décisier drafted the letter from the Provincials to the Father General. Father Jeanuet ("Champagne" province) approves of it. They will decide tomorrow if they will send it or not.

OCT. 15: This morning, Father Décisier read me the definitive text of the letter from the Provincials, sent this day to the Father General. It gives me a great sense of security to know they are protecting us like this, without a word of reservation or doubt. Anyone who has read this text experiences a feeling of joyful gratitude. If the directives then requested turn out to be contrary or impose a few sacrifices, one will submit to it with a more cheerful heart.

OCT. 17: Father Parsons comes to see Father d'Ouince, in the name of all the American Fathers: they asked Father de Boynes if, yes or no, we were under suspicion. In front of them, he incriminated: Etudes, Fourvière, Teilhard; but without being specific. Which made a bad impression on them.

OCT. 18: Following the expression of some criticisms, the work by Father Bouillard, *Conversion et grâce*, was examined again here, on order of the Father Vicar General; the two special censors were entirely favorable. This information was given a few days ago to Father Chamussy by Father de Boynes himself.

In campaigning now against *Surnaturel*, they are seeking revenge for the refusal they encountered in condemning the book by Bouillard.

What risks giving a certain weight to the attacks of which we are the object is the fact that today we are in the process of losing the traditional idea, necessary to the very life of theology, of a freedom of theological schools within the same orthodoxy and the same submission to the Holy See. Under the shepherding of Father Boyer, the Gregorian is becoming the "brilliant second" of the Angelicum, where Father Garrigou reigns; that, contrary to the decisions of Pius XI obtained through Father Ledochowski. Whence the paradoxical sympathy of some old Suarezians of our Order for the "innovators" denounced today.

OCT. 19: Anxious letters received from Auguste Valensin, Mogenet, Fontoynont, Guillet, Abbé Beaudou. . . .

Father d'Ouince was received at Castelgandolfo; the Pope appeared kind, tired, concerned to him. He explained to him that in his address he intended to say nothing other than what the Society wanted. Letter received from M. Vincent, professor at the Theology Faculty of Strasbourg: "A Dominican from Rome, passing through Fribourg, has boasted in private circles that they would have you", that is, that the Holy Office would condemn "the Jesuits of Lyons, in particular Father de L."

OCT. 20: Negative response for Teilhard from the Father General to the French College.

OCT. 21: Saw Abbé Monchanin again; with him, the churches of the Coelius, etc. —At dinner in Saint Louis des Français, he heard Father Parra criticizing us and pushing for a condemnation.

Father Klein tells me that, considering all the information, it seems to him certain that something was added at the last moment to the Pope's address, coming from a source outside the Society.

OCT. 22: At 5 P.M., our Provincials, accompanied by Fathers d'Ouince and Chamussy, are received by the Father General. The audience lasts nearly an hour and a half. The Father General reassures them; no complaint against "Fourvière", complete confidence. Great joy and peace from that.

Oct. 23:   New information on the campaign led by Garrigou in conjunction with Boyer against Father de Montcheuil.

Father Rostoworoski, who was a close friend of Father Ledochowski, tells me at recreation that one should not question every word of pontifical speeches: "The addresses of the Holy See cannot turn out perfectly every day". He then speaks to me against the exclusivism of the Gregorian. Visit from Father Stanislaw Lyonnet, of the Biblical Institute. A few extended reflections have shown him that Father Boyer is hostile to "Fourvière". He is inclined to think that the famous phrase in the address at Castelgandolfo came from him.

Oct. 25:   Audience with the Father General, before my departure from Rome. It is he who had me called. He is anxious to tell me that, after having been informed with full particulars, he finds there is nothing, either as far as the Pope or he himself is concerned, against Fourvière or me. The Pope simply took the occasion of the General Congregation to say some things that do not concern the Society, and this is why his address was published. The Father General multiplies the most encouraging words, he assures me of his full confidence, he encourages me to "continue in the same line". He insists on the absolute certitude resulting from his inquiry. He himself authorizes me to repeat all that.

Oct. 28:   Return to Lyons. I find there a panic-stricken letter from Blondel. I reply to calm him down.

Oct. 31:   Letter from Father Jean Daniélou: (On his return from Rome) "Father d'Ouince told me many things. I am much delighted about what he told me with respect to you. And for my part, after excellent conversations with the Father Assistant and Father Bith, I am entirely reassured. It is a matter of avoiding certain points that are not understood beyond the Alps. But what is essential is that, in the presence of attacks that will certainly continue, our Superiors will support us openly".

Nov. 24:   Enthusiastic approval by Fathers Chamussy and Décisier of our Collective Response to the *Revue thomiste*, to appear in *Recherches*.

Nov. 30:   Father Rondet receives a letter from Father Boyer, in response to his book *Problèmes pour la réflexion chrétienne*. Father Boyer is pleased to tell him that everything in it is orthodox, but he goes back in an unpleasant way to the rumors that have circulated against Fourvière and insists on a warning by the Pope, which he hopes "some" will take into account.

Dec. 4:   Condolences, letters of sympathy, anxious questions from various quarters. . . .

Dec. 7:   Father Lebreton believes that, in the attacks aimed at us, it is the very conception of theology as the Society understands it that is at stake.

Dec. 12:   Brief visit by Father Assistant to Lyons. He insists on the confidence that the Society has in Fourvière. He foresees that there will be a battle to be endured against "integrist interference", but he says we should not let ourselves be intimidated.

Dec. 31:   Father Maurice Villain, S.M., has just read, at Nevers, a very long letter from Father Garrigou-Lagrange, who describes Blondel and several theologians as heterodox.

Jan. 2, 1947:   Letter from the Father Assistant: "With respect to your *Surnaturel*, I know nothing except that it is being read here and there attentively, as Father Boyer has told me again."

Jan. 3:   M. Augros, who is returning from Rome, saw Father Garrigou there, who was in a violent furor "against Fourvière and especially against Father de Lubac".

Feb. 5:   Letter from Father Rouquette, from Rome: "The Father Assistant asks me to tell you that there is no real danger and that the Father General desires that one continue working peacefully and in the same line."

Feb. 14:   Saw Msgr. Gardette yesterday, rector of our Catholic Faculties. He is returning from Rome. He asked Msgr. Ottaviani, at the Holy Office, if he had some directives or advice to transmit. The latter replied that, No, they were already doing what was necessary in Lyons and that, from the moment they worked there in union with the Hierarchy (an allusion to the Archbishop's Theological Commission), it was perfect.

APRIL 18: Letter from Canon Beaudou (Montauban): "I have heard an O.P. declaring, like one possessed, that they will go "the limit", which is to say to the Holy Office and to placing works on the Index, and that after having "had" le Saulchoir, they will have Fourvière. . . .

Such was, in a way, the raising of the curtain on the drama that has very improperly been called the "Fourvière affair", which evolved over the course of a number of years, which very deeply affected the life of the Society and of the whole Church, in the most unexpected directions, and the consequences of which, unknown to many, are still being felt today (1981).

[4:5]

In 1946, Father Lebreton had made known his desire to confide the *Revue* to me. Below is the report that I addressed at that time to the Provincials. It was followed around the end of the year, if I remember correctly, by a letter that was even more insistent. See also, below, the Note sent to the Provincials when my nomination was a *fait accompli*. (My memories as to precise dates are not clear.)

JUNE 7, 1946. MY REVEREND FATHER PROVINCIAL, P.C.,

You have asked me to tell you what I think about the editorship of the *Recherches de science religieuse*, which Father Lebreton would like to confide to me.

To my eyes, three reasons make the thing a bit difficult:

1. It is not very convenient to edit from Lyons (from which I cannot be absent during my periods of teaching) a journal whose vital center remains in Paris.

2. Although this editorial work does not represent, in itself, a heavy duty, it would not be good for me, in the present state of my strength, to add to a task that I already find it difficult to carry.

3. There is much debate about me in the Society, among the professionals for whom the *Recherches* should normally be the common organ.

These reasons seem to me to carry weight. If however, the Superiors do not judge them to be decisive, I would express the following two desires to them:

1. I would desire to obtain full latitude to introduce into the *Recherches* a few transformations—according to the desire manifested by Rev. Father

d'Ouince and after consultation with Father Lebreton—in view of making the journal, not less technical, but more living, better adapted to the intellectual needs of today, which are not completely those of the time when it was founded.

2. I would ask to be freed as soon as possible from what teaching I still do at the Theology Faculty and that I have already for several years now carried out only in miserable conditions. It would be very desirable if my Superiors would come to a precise understanding on this subject with the authorities of the Faculty; especially since the present situation is not regular, Father Ganne being accommodated among us, without official recognition and without salary, only as my personal substitute *ad tempus*. (I hasten to add that Father Ganne acquits himself perfectly of his task, that he would be very capable of replacing me completely; in his absence, and if the Faculty would allow the principle of two Jesuit professors, perhaps Father Coignet or someone else could be proposed.)

I am, my Reverend Father Provincial, in union with you in the Holy Sacrifice of the Mass, . . .

P.S. The suggestions I am permitting myself to make in what concerns the Theology Faculty are themselves only indicative of a temporary solution. In fact, the course in the history of religions demands a true specialist. This course (the only one I have kept up after Abbé Chavasse was introduced into our faculty and with which Father Ganne then came to assist me) was confided to me fifteen years ago, the very year it was instituted; without any preparation, I was at that time given only provisional charge of it, because they had not found the qualified specialist in the Church of France; since then, I have asked repeatedly, orally and in writing, both to my Superiors and to the Faculty authorities, that this matter be pursued with real attention; numerous assurances have been given me, without, as far as I know, any results having followed, even remote preparation. I have thus put out a great effort, always improvised, on the periphery of the normal work of my chair, in return for mediocre results, and this important part of the religious sciences still remains, in France, nearly entirely given over to irreligious scholars.

Once again this year, I have drawn the attention of my Dean to this regrettable situation (which I know was a question discussed, with regard to the whole of France, at the recent meeting of the Rectors of Catholic Institutes).

H. L.

When, despite my objections, the editorship of the *Recherches* was imposed on me, I sent the following text to my Superiors:

I do not think there is anything to change in the spirit of the *Recherches* —the very spirit of their founder, Father de Grandmaison, continued by Father Lebreton—or in their essential structure. The only evolution to be considered is the very evolution of problems, of centers of interest, of methods in the world of investigators and in the needs of the Church. It must always be a matter of research [*recherches*], covering in principle the entire field of the religious sciences; research whose freedom must not be shackled by any school of exclusivism. Orthodoxy and scientific value are the only absolute conditions of admission for the works presented.

An enlargement of the journal might have been conceived, following the amalgamation of various scientific journals of the Society in France. The intellectual effort of the Society could thereby have been more concentrated and more powerful. But this structure, which would have great advantages, seems unrealistic now. Consequently *Recherches* cannot leave entirely outside its perspectives the philosophical, social and spiritual aspects of religious problems.

The journal must preserve its technical character, which will avoid any competition with journals like the *Nouvelle revue théologique*. Neither should it enter into a competition with more specialized journals. The Bulletins cannot be systematic catalogues (on the model provided by the *Bulletin de Théologie ancienne et médiévale*, for instance) and must not be a catch-all. They must be distinguished by their variety, by the choice of works analyzed and problems discussed, by the quality of their criticism.

A serious effort must be made to give *Recherches* a new life, after an existence of thirty-six years now and the inevitable slowdown during the war and occupation years; an effort all the more necessary since similar organs have been founded or developed in the meantime that have neither its worth nor its possibilities but that have diverted a certain number of its subscriptions. Thanks to the support of *Etudes*, this effort will be possible; it will include, in particular, an increase in the number of pages, without anticipating more frequent publication.

[4:6]

Previously, in September 1947, the Father General had had *Surnaturel* examined by four censors and had communicated their censures to me:

First censure

De Lubac: Surnaturel. If I am not mistaken, this work has provoked two attacks: one bears on the conception of theological progress, a conception outlined (rather than really explained) by the author in his preface and on another page that I am not able to find again. This conception poses questions quite similar to those raised by reading Father Bouillard; only, since it does not form the subject of his book, it is understandable that the author limits himself to expressing it in a necessarily imprecise way; and there would probably not be any uneasiness in this regard if the ambiguous phrases of Father Bouillard had not suggested, with reference to Father de Lubac, the idea of a relationship in thought.

The other attack concerns the central thesis of the work, which is, roughly, the thesis of the concrete impossibility and inconceivability of an order of pure nature. From the point of view of orthodoxy, this thesis is defensible; it simply reproduces the doctrine of the Augustinians, Norti, Belleli, Berti; now it is certain that Benedict XV refused on various occasions to disqualify it in the least degree; a good many recent Scholastic theologians have a tendency to forget that. This is not to say that I would myself defend it; it does not seem to me intrinsically coherent, at least as Father de Lubac now expresses it and allowing for a possible development in his thought; consequently, the opposite thesis, that of the possibility of pure nature, despite its difficulties, still seems preferable to me at the moment; but are we not here in the province of free discussion between theologians, as long as the Magisterium has not pronounced?

Second censure

Father de Lubac's work on the supernatural, *Surnaturel*, seems to me, after a serious examination, to remain entirely within the limits of freely debated opinions. I do not accept his thesis. I see insurmountable objections to it; but I find nothing in it contrary to orthodoxy. It is the thesis of the Augustinians, who were never condemned and among whom there have been cardinals. My judgment coincides with the one laboriously justified by Father Malevez in *Nouvelle revue théologique*, which is negative, while recognizing the author's freedom of opinion.

Third censure

Although Father Bouillard's book appeared before the work *Surnaturel*, and although Father de Lubac more than once refers to Father Bouillard, I am giving my judgment on *Surnatural* first. After having studied the two works, it seems to me in fact that Father B. was more dependent upon Father de L. than the latter on Father B.

 1. *Surnaturel* is a work of more than ordinary richness: erudition that is extensive and well implemented, profound historico-theological views,

many surprising and liberating perspectives. I willingly recognize that I have learned much from it and am sincerely grateful to my learned colleague.

I cite two examples that strike me particularly: "the non-Augustinian character of Baius and Jansenius" and "the natural peccability of the created spirit" are magnificently brought out.

2. It goes without saying that there are in this work, which includes so many things, a few special questions where the proofs brought forward by the author do not satisfy me entirely. It would be outside our purpose to mention them here. For the specialists, they could be the occasion of historical or theological discussion of greater or lesser usefulness.

3. But I must make some serious reservations with respect to the "Conclusion, Divine Exigency and Natural Desire" (pp. 483–93), the ground for which was already prepared by the fourth part of the work and by various remarks made here and there in the preceding part of the book.

It is not therefore a question of the interpretation as such of Saint Thomas (Note C, pp. 449–65: Note D, pp. 467–71), although I do not regard that to be precise and although that may be in close relation to the author's "Conclusion"; nor is it a question of the rather harsh tone in which these notes are written and which might have been better avoided in this precarious question. Everyone will have to agree that the doctrine of Saint Thomas is not easy to grasp in this regard; and one must applaud any serious effort made to grasp it—and Father de L.'s effort *is* serious.

Neither is it principally a question of the historical examination of "the system of pure nature" (pp. 101–83) as such, although here and there this examination seems to me already too influenced by the personal opinions of the author.

It is a question above all of the author's personal conception, which is, in my opinion, not supportable from a theological point of view. I will try to demonstrate this in three ways (which are very closely related):

a. According to Father de L., "If there is in our nature a desire to see God, this can only be because God wants for us this supernatural end that consists in seeing him. . . . This desire is consequently nothing other than his call" (pp. 486–87). "Although there may be good reasons for calling this desire natural (since it is essentially in the nature and since it expresses the heart of it), it must be added that it is already in a sense something from God. . . . God himself is at its source, although still anonymous" (p. 487).

From this follows the in my opinion theologically inadmissible conclusion that, leaving aside the supernatural revelation we hold from the teaching of the Church, we can come to know our call to the supernatural life.[1] For this natural desire for the *visio beatifica* becomes conscious in every human act ("in Thomistic thought . . . the elicit desire has the role of manifesting the appetite of nature", Father de L. himself says very rightly, p. 433) and falls therefore under the analysis of our *ratio naturalis*. (N.B. I am using here the term *ratio naturalis* in the same sense as Father de L. when he speaks of the *desiderium naturale*; this *desiderium* is *naturale* not only because it is necessitated by nature—through opposition to *desiderium electivum*, pp. 432–34—but also because it is "essential to our nature", p. 487).

Father de L. indeed says in a note: "We do not wish to decide if this desire can be known by the sole lights of natural reason, or if those of revelation must be joined to it"; but he himself seems to feel that, strictly speaking, he should go farther and adds: "Perhaps however the antithesis has something artificial about it, if it is true that revelation has not been without effect on the reason itself" (p. 489, note 1). If it is true that "if there is in our nature a desire to see God, this can only be because God wants for us this supernatural end", it follows, in my opinion, that our reason does not need the external teaching of the Church to conclude with absolute certitude that we are called to the supernatural beatific vision; in other words, that this call to the *finis ultimus supernaturalis* [ultimate supernatural end] is no longer a *mysterium stricte dictum* [mystery in the strictest sense of the word], which is contrary to the express doctrine of the Church (Denz., 1669; 1786).

b. If human nature therefore desires essentially the *finis ultimus supernaturalis* (desires = requires, understanding the word according to the explanations given by Father de L.),[2] it follows that this human nature *is* already essentially a supernatural gift of God. ("We will understand without difficulty that our desire is not at all like a restraint of divine freedom, God putting it within us only because he freely wants to give himself to us": p. 488). But how could we then still safeguard the Catholic distinction between our nature and the grace of God? How can that be made to agree with "the true and full Christian idea of nature" (p. 437)? That escapes me totally.

c. If our human nature essentially *requires* grace ("exigency" again to be understood in the way in which Father de L. thinks to "excuse" it, p. 498, note 2),[3] I do not see how to place that in accord with the teaching of the Church (Denz. 2103) and with the very thesis of Father de L. himself: "The supernatural surpasses infinitely the *exigencies* of any nature whatever" (p. 248). Father de L. demonstrates excellently that in his con-

---

[1] This criticism is based on an error in reading.

[2] Same observation.

[3] My text says exactly the contrary.

ception it cannot be a question of an "exigency" with respect to God, and that one must speak rather of "expression of the right of God", the "divine exigency" (p. 489). But the fact remains that in following his conception there is indeed essentially in our nature an "exigency" with respect to *grace*, although this "exigency" comes from the free liberality of God. And a "germana verique nominis exigentia ordinis supernaturalis" [true and natural exigency for the supernatural order] has been quite justly condemned in the encyclical *Pascendi*.

Father de L. does not teach the conclusions I have drawn, but they flow directly from his doctrine.

In short, it seems to me that Father de L. should speak *with much more prudence* in his "conclusion" (and in the passages of his book that prepare the way for this conclusion). Above all, he must make clearly known what he himself understands by human *nature*, in relation to which grace is not absolutely due, and not merely be content to reject Saint Thomas' concept of "nature" (pp. 434–38).[4]

Fourth censure

H. de L. Surnaturel. This work defends the thesis of the impossibility of pure nature. The author thinks that there is an "absolute" (not merely conditional or conditioned) and innate desire for the beatific vision, which is due to the very essence of the created spirit. He thinks that God, who constantly places this desire in the spirit, could not refuse the grace by which one moves toward the divine vision. In this sense, one could speak of an exigency of the supernatural. But there is no exigency if one thereby understands a right that man could claim before God. There is rather a divine intention that is manifested in the desire and on which the desire is based.

This thesis resembles that of the "Augustinians", Noris, Berti and Belleli; particularly that of Belleli, who rejects the attenuations of Noris. Certain theologians speak quite severely of the negation of the possibility of pure nature. According to Father Rousselot, the opposite thesis would be *definibilis*. Msgr. Litt, in his thesis at the Gregorian, published in 1934, judges Belleli's positions to have been condemned by the constitution *Auctorem fidei*. I believe that to be an exaggeration. Father Boyer, in his *De Deo creante et elevante* (1940), 270–71, is more moderate: "Haec schola (Augustiniensium) numquam ab Ecclesia fuit damnata vel repressa. . . . Attamen non sufficienter differre videtur a sententia Baii" [This (Augustinian) school of thought was never condemned nor silenced by the Church . . .

---

[4] What the censor calls "Saint Thomas' concept of 'nature'" is not in reality that of Saint Thomas. Far from rejecting the latter, I made appeal to it.

yet it does not seem to differ much from Baius' opinion]. In my opinion, Father de L.'s thesis does not coincide with those that were condemned in the case of Baius, Quesnel and in the constitution *Auctorem fidei*. Nor do I believe that it is clearly rejected by an allusion in the encyclical *Pascendi* to those who seem to admit not only a "capacity" and a *convenientia* for the supernatural (which would be fine) but also a *veri nominis exigentia* (which would be blameworthy). (Denz. 2103). However, I do not see that it does much to safeguard the *gratuity* of the supernatural in the traditional sense of the latter; it seems to me also that it is not in as good an agreement with the doctrine of the essentially *mysterious* character of our elevation to a supernatural destiny. Finally, there is the agreement of theologians, which has become very general, about the possibility of pure nature. For these reasons, I would believe that Father de L.'s thesis (innate, absolute or unconditioned desire for the supernatural and consequently the impossibility of pure nature) can scarcely be considered as being a part of the "doctrina securior et magis approbata" that our professors must follow in their teaching (*Ratio studiorum*, 83; cf. *Constit.*, IV, 5,4).

Father de L. also seems to hold that only grace gives access to morally good activity (cf. pp. 219–20, 251, 254–55, 487). This is said in a less clear way and as if in passing; but I do not see how the whole of his affirmations can be understood otherwise. Father Rondet seems to express the same view (see "La Grâce libératrice", *Nouv. r. théol.* [February 1947], 121–22 and especially 132). I quote a line from this last page, where Father Rondet tries to return to the thesis of most theologians, according to which one can make certain good actions without grace. Here is his text (the emphasis is mine): "*without the grace of God, understood as without grace known to be such,* man can pose morally good acts." The affirmation that only grace gives access to morally good activity was defended by Baius and Jansenius, in unacceptable senses; these senses are assuredly not those of our authors. It was defended by the "Augustinians" in a sense that was not condemned. I am led to believe that the position of our authors approximates that of the "Augustinians". I therefore do not say that their opinion is heterodox; I doubt however that it is a part of the *doctrina securior*.

[4:7]

The Father General could not follow personally all the details of a complicated affair, which was pursued over long years and gave rise to all kinds of incidents. There was in Rome a lack of communication between himself, his own reviewers, the worlds of the Holy Office, Gregorian, Angelicum, etc. As a result, among other contradictions, he officially reproached me in

1950 for having opened wide the *Recherches de science religieuse* to writings that were not very sound or erroneous, for having persistently sunk into grave errors in matters of faith, for having thereby exercised a pernicious influence despite all warnings, for having gravely disobeyed him in matters of Catholic doctrine. The first of these reproaches was motivated by the acceptance of articles that he himself had had examined in Rome, that he had approved and encouraged and even practically imposed on the poor editor of the *Recherches* (an article, by Father Bouillard, had been drafted at his express request and had received warm approval from him). The reproaches of insubordination and personal error were motivated by the publication of my article on "The Mystery of the Supernatural", which he had himself encouraged; the letter by which he authorized its publication even specified that I could, if I wished, make a little booklet of it. —These incredible misunderstandings remained for a long time, and the accusations thus brought forward were echoed everywhere.

The two letters reproduced below make known the will of the Father General. A word of explanation about the "position" in which Father Bouillard had been placed. At the Father General's request, Father Bouillard had addressed him a letter concerning the criticisms made of him by Father Garrigou-Lagrange. Now this letter was very quickly known to Father Garrigou-Lagrange, provoking a new attack by him against Father Bouillard.

From the Rev. Father General to the Rev. Father Henri Bouillard, Lyons.

ROME, APRIL 11, 1948

MY REVEREND FATHER, P.C.,

Your letter of April 4 explains to me the position in which Father Garrigou-Lagrange's polemics have placed you. I not only permit, it is my desire that you respond publicly this time—in all serenity—as you deem necessary. Offer your work to me when it is ready.

YOUR SERVANT IN OUR LORD

From the Rev. Father General to the Rev. Father Henri Bouillard, Lyons.

ROME, MAY 17, 1948

MY REVEREND FATHER, P.C.,

I have had the article you sent me on the seventh reviewed. The reviewer advises that you suppress, on p. 20, the reference to the writings of Father

Le Blond and Msgr. de Solages and that you keep to what you yourself have said. In addition, I would ask you, out of charity for Father Garrigou-Lagrange, to make the ending more peaceable. It is indeed necessary to say the things you have said, but by themselves they are rather hard for the old professor.

I also authorize the letter to the Director of the Angelicum.

Asking, my Reverend Father, for a remembrance at Holy Mass.

YOUR SERVANT IN OUR LORD

[4:8]

I have kept in my notes this first part of the projected work, to which I gave the title "Réponses interdites". Five chapters try to respond peacefully, on the level of history and doctrine, to the criticisms raised by Fathers Jacques de Blic, Charles Boyer, Guy de Broglie, G. Frénaud, O.S.B. (of Solesmes), Réginald Garrigou-Lagrange, O.P. They are followed by several appendices. These discussions are obviously not of much interest today. I believe, however, that they contain many positive elements and that if they could have appeared at that time, they could have helped to clarify a situation that polemics had confused and perhaps to bring peace (except in a few minds) to a conflict that was not to be without grave consequences for the life of the Church.

I placed at the head of this work these words by Plato in his *Phaedra*: "Attacked unjustly, a writing always needs its father to come to its help, for it can neither resist nor help itself"—and these others from La Bruyère: "Some of those who have read a work refer to certain of its characteristics whose meaning they have not understood and which they alter still more by all that they place in it of their own; and these characteristics, thus corrupted and disfigured, which are nothing but their own thoughts and expressions, they lay open to censure, maintain that they are bad, and everybody maintains that they are bad; but the aspect of the work the critics think they are citing, and which in fact they are not citing, is not as bad."

[4:9]

Father Jean-Marie Tézé also wrote to me around the same time: ". . . This way of explaining the gratuity of grace from outside by supposing another, at least possible, end for man had always offended my sense of God. Your article in *Recherches* brings me, after reading *Surnaturel*, all the precise information desired and above all a great interior assent." And Father Marcel Régnier, of Heytrop College, on January 7, 1948: "I have just read *Gregorianum*. I will admit to you that Father B.'s attitude disappoints me very much. It seems to me that he has not even understood what you wanted to say and that the meaning of your book is precisely to get away from the dilemma that he brings back at the end of his article. . . ."

The approval backed by perhaps the most extensive justification would come to me later from Father Jean-Pierre Torrell, O.P. (in the *Revue thomiste* [1966], 1:93–107), which would in addition complement my own assertions with some very pertinent remarks.

On December 3, 1960, I had written to Father G. Van Ackeren, S.J., editor of the *Theology Digest*, with respect to an article that appeared in his journal:

". . . I believe it is very difficult, or on the contrary too easy, to reason on the basis of abstract hypotheses. Once one has recalled the absolute freedom of God, what is necessarily translated in our language by the expression: 'God could have . . .' says, I believe, in that line just about the only substantial thing that can be said. The rest is riskier. Yet, it seems to me as it does to you that, given the nature of the spirit as we know it (and how can we imagine it to be totally different without falling into a deadly empiricism of reason), it would be better to say that any spirit that God would not call to see Him would not have a properly 'natural' end either: simply, it would not attain its final (supernatural) end, and there would be something incomplete about its final equilibrium. It would not suffer from that, because God, in this hypothesis, would not have enlightened it about the final ground of its nature and its finality. —But, once again, I say that only to try to give some response to your question, without daring to speak of it with any confidence. That will explain for you, however, how, in my opinion, one can perfectly and logically admit what the Church (and in particular the encyclical H.G.) asks us to admit without entering into the modern complications of the hypothesis of a 'pure nature' with a 'purely natural' finality. It is very remarkable, besides, that the authority of the Church refuses to speak of this 'pure nature' as being a subject for explanation and theological discussion without immediate reference to the object of faith. As for me, I believe I insist as much and more than anyone on the absolute gratuity, on the absolute transcendence of the supernatural gift; and yet I would not like to part company too easily from the whole ancient patristic and medieval tradition (notably, from Saint Thomas), who never envisaged this kind of 'pure nature'. . . ."

In that year, 1947, I was led, at the request of my Superiors, to write various memoranda, one of which I will quote here:

EXAMINATION OF THEOLOGICAL CONSCIENCE
MARCH 6, 1947

1. I do not have the temperament of a reformer, still less of an innovator. Far from ever having had the idea of promoting a "new theology", I admit that I did not even know of this expression except through the use made of it by the Holy Father in his address of September 1946. I thought at the time, on the basis of some rumors, that it might have come from recent discussions among German theologians. Since then, I have learned that it appeared in the unofficial article commenting on the placing of the works of Fathers Chenu and Charlier, O.P., on the Index in 1942.

2. I have never been, except in passing, a professor of dogma. This is one of the reasons why my theological work has not taken the form of dogmatic treatises. In addition, often half brought to a standstill by health difficulties, I have done a lot of quick reading that has oriented my work in a rather historical direction, although I do not have any technical formation as an historian. This does not indicate a theoretic preference for history in relation to doctrine; still less, any sort of relativism disastrous for the idea of truth. These kinds of things have always been foreign to me.

3. Like (nearly) everyone else, I well perceive certain needs for renewal, even in theology. (I believe moreover that this is more or less true for all epochs.) But for my part, I have not undertaken such a task in any methodical way. I merely offer a little material and a few ideas drawn from the treasure of Tradition for whoever would like to make use of them (beginning by correcting them if need be) along with many other more important ones that other workers will contribute. I have neither plan nor program to propose. All the more reason for my not being the head of any school. I believe quite simply that if each one in the Church does his duty according to his own competence, following the indications of Providence, the work will be done, so to speak, by itself. It would be absurd and dangerous to dream here of some kind of revolution, even while wishing to insure the safety of all dogma. I will always be opposed to such ventures.

4. Those who truly read me, more even than those who know me through my teaching or my conversations, know that my tendencies are very traditional. I never cease reacting against the fixed prejudices of modernity, against being led astray by intellectual fashions, against ex-

cessive concern for adaptation or overly complacent theories about the progress of dogma. I always seek to bring back, and sometimes rather harshly, to the traditional sources and to the classical fundamental principles those who seem to me to be too enamored of "modern" thought. I love the Tradition of the Church, in its so varied unity. I love it in all its forms and not only in the forms that the accidents of existence have led me to emphasize. I am scarcely a theoretician, in the systematic sense of the word; but I do not hold theories and systems in contempt: on the contrary, I believe them to be necessary. As for me, I cling to all that has developed in the Church with her approval, for twenty centuries, in order to explore the unfathomable riches of Christ. What I have had the occasion to write is very far from being what I value most. These writings must be understood in a general, *assertive*, and not *exclusive*, way; for example, praise of a Greek Father is not directed against the Latins; a work of patristics is not directed against Scholasticism; a study on the spiritual sense of Scripture does not imply any disfavor toward scientific exegesis, and so forth. Nothing is more contrary to me than such oppositions. In a still more general way, no one should search for any "ulterior motive" in my writings.

5. Notably with respect to Saint Thomas and Scholasticism, I am anxious to specify this:

a. I am of a much more Thomistic formation than a number of the Fathers in the Society; I have a great admiration for Saint Thomas, the study of whom I am in the habit of recommending and whom I have myself studied with a deep sympathy on certain important points; I have thus never suffered from anti-Thomism; but the task I have received in obedience has led me to studies in which Saint Thomas in fact does not loom large: I am a professor of the history of religions and apologetics.

b. If it is a question of Scholasticism as a discipline of thought and means of forming the mind, I am concerned, like others, about the fact that, with the young generations, the least handling of this instrument is linked with a deficit in the precision of thought that is not without danger for theological rectitude. I do not believe that this evil, however, is without compensations, so I am not pessimistic with regard to these younger generations; I do note a deficit, nevertheless, with regret.

c. As requested of me by the Society through its rules and recommended to me by its whole tradition, I hold very much to a certain freedom in our adherence to the doctrine of Saint Thomas. I believe on the other hand that, except for the points that the Church herself fixes as necessary for the faith, it is a very serious distortion to seek to impose philosophical theses as an authority, like a kind of new Creed. I have not had to combat directly the demand some manifest, for example, with respect to the "twenty-four theses"; but my feelings on that must be rather well known, and in any case I have no wish to hide them.

6. I believe in addition that one whole contemporary Thomistic school —which is not the only one, thank God—is extremely far from the spirit of Saint Thomas (and often from his letter as well); that those who show the most intransigent zeal for Thomism are not the most legitimate heirs of the great Doctor; that Saint Thomas always proposes to us not only his doctrine but his example and that the one cannot be understood without the other. I believe that a certain narrow and sectarian Thomism, the principal factor responsible for the disaffection of many with respect to Saint Thomas and Scholasticism, is a considerable obstacle to the real knowledge of Catholic Tradition as well as to the action of the Church in the modern world. I insist on this very last point: a doctrine that closes minds and that proves to be anti-apostolic, no matter how "reliable" it claims to be, cannot be, even doctrinally, a sound doctrine.

7. I did not have any scientific formation, nor am I truly conversant with modern philosophy. So I can only do my best to encourage those who work in the Church and with the mind of the Church to examine the problems arising from the encounter between dogma, on the one side, and science and philosophy on the other—even if, in many ways, I do not feel in complete agreement with all their ways of seeing.

I will give two examples of this, which seem to me to be of capital importance.

a. *Science*. Father Teilhard de Chardin is, in the life sciences, a technician of the first rank. He is carrying out a work of great apologetic importance, and one that is indispensable today. Starting from the fundamental principles of science itself, through an original reflection that is more rigorous than some say, he leads his contemporaries, whose mentality is completely scientific, and often scientistic, to the recognition of the unique value of man in the universe, of the reality of the spirit, of the transcendence of God, of the necessity of the Church as the bearer of Christ and his charity. One can criticize in him certain rather overly bold views of the future; one can regret that he has not gone to greater lengths to explain his method, which obliges him to approach metaphysical and religious problems from a certain angle; one might also, I know, reproach him for one or two old essays that he has himself long since disavowed and passed beyond. Nonetheless the fact remains that his work is of an essential interest and at the same time of a profoundly Catholic inspiration and that it would be infinitely regrettable for the Church to be deprived of it. I am afraid that several of those who oppose him do so less by reason of a few debatable ideas (which he himself, as I know from experience, agrees to correct with docility when he is asked in a reasonable way) than by reason of their ignorance about the present state of science and of the problems resulting from it. Writings like that of Father Descoqs on "the crises of transformism" or like certain pages of *De Deo creante* by Father Boyer are, in this regard, significant.

b. *Philosophy.* Father Fessard is a specialist in Hegelian philosophy. Now, even if the latter is dead today as a system, all living thought is under its domination. The whole problematic of our era is affected by it. Most of the fundamental objections against faith, in all domains, practical as well as theoretical, are revived in it. Controversy borrows its dialectic. Contemporary atheism draws from it arguments that elude the grasp of our classical theodicy. A work like that of Father Fessard, which consists in stealing from the adversary his most effective weapon, is thus of a sovereign importance. I will add that it has always seemed to me to be conducted with a great soundness of views.

Such are the reasons for which I do not hesitate, even if I cannot follow all their processes, to support with all my strength undertakings like those of which I have just spoken.

[*4:11*]

Shortly before, on February 27, 1949, he had written to me this curious letter:

"I have finally been able to read *Surnaturel* (1946!). I had tried to lay my hands on it several times in 'Etudes': in vain! . . . I have gradually come back to life by reading you and then, after you, 'Kiki', *De fine ultimo vitae humanae*. . . .[5]

I admit that, at my first reading, I was carried away by the luminosity of your exposition of Baianism. But, when I had read Kiki, I perceived that this was not entirely so. And Kiki would have said to Father Joseph Lecler that your exposition of Baius was 'a caricature'! —Then Kiki, supported by Marrou and Gilson, demonstrates well, I find, that Saint Augustine was not very strong in 'philosophy' and that in the centuries that followed him, far from there having been a decadence, there was progress in 'philosophy' as such. Kiki strikes me as having a good knowledge of the history of Philosophy, Scholastic and other. His Appendix on the notion of natura in Saint Augustine is, to my mind, a magnificent Dictionary article. —All that he says about 'supernaturalia' and 'exigentiae' seems very just to me.

[5] G. de Broglie, *De fine ultimi vitae humanae*. Father G. de Broglie was a professor in Rome and Paris.

Perhaps I am mistaken, but I had the impression in several passages of your book that for you: once 'spirit' is in place, 'intuitive vision' immediately follows. . . . Hum!

I do not believe, as Kiki seems to, that you have, as they say in English, an axe to grind, that is, an idea in the back of your head, namely: to establish a 'Christian philosophy', expurgated of all the Greco-paganism of Scholasticism. But if you have such a plan, you would do well, I believe, in constructing this 'philosophia christiana', to take into consideration all the 'constructions' (= criticisms) that Kiki has made of your book.

As for myself, I believe that you are more (?) than Kiki thinks. You claimed simply to make observations. It only remains for certain observations to be revised or adjusted. This (?) appears particularly in the reflections that end the excursus on the history of the word 'supernatural'. Kiki was astonished that Father Lebreton did not react in some way to your manuscript. He accuses old age. I myself believe that Lebreton was won over by the supereminent place you give to the mystics. Their 'superessential' seduced him. And in fact, I believe that philosophy, even Scholasticism, would gain by studying the mystics a little more closely.

There, by fits and starts and in very brief, are my reactions. *Plura coram*."

L. Mariès, S.J.

[*4:12*]

See, as an example, this exchange of letters in March 1948.

Lyons, March 16, 1948. My Reverend Father Provincial, P.C.,

My book *Surnaturel* has been strongly criticized for the past year by Fathers Garrigou-Lagrange (Angelicum), Boyer (Gregorianum) and de Blic (*Mélanges de science religieuse*). Father de Broglie devotes long and very severe pages to it in his *De fine ultimo*, a recently published treatise, and I have been informed of a large work, which will surely be no less severe, by Father Gagnebet, O.P., a professor at the Angelicum.

Many tell me that if I leave all that without any reply, I will be theologically bankrupt. But, on the other hand, the Father General has given us instructions, according to which we are to abstain from all controversy, and I have willingly submitted to this.

I am therefore writing to ask you if these instructions apply in the present case of my *Surnaturel*, and to what degree. May I reply to the theologians named above? And can I do it freely, in the normal conditions of censure? I admit that if the permission to reply were coupled with the demands of

Roman censure, that would throw me into confusion again: for the theologians of the Gregorian, having taken a position against me, would in that discussion play the double role of critics and arbiters, they would be both judges and interested parties. Experience has shown me as well, more than once already, that reviews from Rome are not always objective. I would consequently be reluctant to put forth an arduous effort that would risk being rendered vain.

Such is the difficulty I find myself facing. Perhaps, my Reverend Father Provincial, you could bring me back a few directives from Rome. With God's help, I would do everything possible to follow them faithfully.

Rae vae in Christo servus et filius.

42, Montée St-Barthélémy
Lyons (5ᶜ), March 24, 1948

My very dear Father, P.C. I am passing on the reply of the V.R.F. General, whom I have informed of your letter.

I would like to keep this document. Yours truly in Xo.

A. Décisier, S.J.

Note from the V.R.F. General, communicated by the Rev. Father Provincial on his return from Rome, March 24, 1948.

I of course allow Father de Lubac to respond to the objections that have been made to him. Insofar as is possible, let him abstain from any personal polemics, seeking to win acceptance, objectively, for what seems to him to be the truth.

These responses, after review by the provincial censor, should all undergo supervision at Rome. Past experience proves that this is necessary.

The censor in Rome, like that of the Province, strives to be objective; he is not perfect. Neither is the one for the Province.

The censor in Rome has the advantage of knowing what the competent ecclesiastical Authorities want and do not want at this moment. We must follow the ecclesiastical Authorities. The direction to be given to theological teaching and even to research in the domain of theology is determined by the Authority. In the case of a disagreement between the diocesan Authorities and the Roman Authorities, it is the opinion of the latter that prevails. Thus prudence in matters of doctrine and a true Catholic spirit require it.

March 21, 1948.
J. Janssens, S.J.

MARCH 25, 1948. MY REVEREND FATHER PROVINCIAL, P.C.,

Thank you for having obtained this response, which I am returning to you after having made note of it.

It grieves me, for two reasons.

First, because of the insistent reminder of the principle of authority, which I do not believe I have ever contested in word or deed.

Next, because the exceptional rule to which it submits me (and which does not apply to any of my detractors) shows me clearly, despite the paternal assurances you have given me, that I am considered suspect.

So it only takes a few theologians, on their own impulse, to unleash an attack, even an unjust one, against another theologian to raise shortly a twofold fence of misunderstandings between him and his Superiors: suspicions about doctrine and suspicions about the spirit of obedience. . . . And these misunderstandings are impossible to dissipate because any try at explanation would be taken for a mark of obstinacy and a new attempt at insubordination.

You will not hold, my Reverend Father Provincial, this filial complaint against me, because you know well that I want nonetheless to make every effort to be faithful, in heart as much as in action, to the demands that are made known to me. If they were to lead me to a situation contrary to intellectual honesty, then I would ask you to be kind enough to relieve me from the task that is presently mine, and so it is always obedience that would have the last word.

Rae Vae in Xto serv. et filius.

HENRI DE LUBAC, S.J.

[4:13]

As early as 1947, I had written to him:

JANUARY 2, 1947, MY REVEREND FATHER ASSISTANT, P.C.,

You have been kind enough to say to us that we can always have recourse to you in our difficulties without fear of troubling you. Here I begin to take advantage of your paternal invitation.

You know that Father Garrigou-Lagrange has been talking a lot in Rome for some months against what he believes to be the doctrine of Fourvière and of several among us. He is not content simply to talk (as, for instance, to Father Arnou). He takes the initiative to send letters, just about everywhere. I have seen one of these letters, addressed to M. Blondel. I have been informed in detail about several others. Various rumors have reached me that seem very well to have had a similar origin. It is not a matter of assessments made in passing in private correspondence but of veritable little dissertations. According to what I know of it, the attacks are aimed especially at Father Bouillard, Father de Montcheuil, and a teaching on original sin (no proper name is given here, but those who think they know designate Father Rondet). These accusations claim to be founded on the discourse of the Holy Father of September 17, 1946. Now, to say nothing of behavior that is more than offensive, these accusations are clearly slanderous.

If I set these facts before you, it is not only because they foster in France a rather confused agitation in ecclesiastical circles. But I have just learned, on the other hand, that, according to Dom Lambert Beauduin, a Benedictine religious who lived for a long time in Rome and who still has many connections there, a kind of Syllabus is being prepared, one whole part of which is devoted to a certain "new theology". So it is quite natural to wonder if, in order to satisfy in some way the pressures exerted by Father Garrigou-Lagrange, without wanting to condemn any of us or to cite any name, they might not now be thinking of noting in an official catalogue a series of objectionable propositions. The latter might be very far from our thought and even without any real connection with our writings: but, if they mark the result of the campaign presently in process, they would necessarily be attributed to us, and we would find ourselves in the morally impossible situation of explaining ourselves without seeming to lack respect and even submission toward the Holy See.

Under these conditions, I recall what Father Delos had said to me in Rome, in September. If Father G.-Lagrange, he said to me, renews his attacks, why wouldn't your Superior General complain to us about it? That is therefore the idea, my Rev. Father, that I submit to your judgment. In my opinion, moreover, the fruit of such an intervention would be less to make Father G.-L. more cautious than to warn indirectly the responsible authorities of the limited confidence merited by his accusations. For the Holy Office would immediately know of the step if, for example, Father Creusen were informed. Thus, without any pressure, a dangerous decision could be averted.

Please excuse me, my Rev. Father, if this letter proposes anything indiscreet or inopportune. The idea I have just suggested to you is perhaps bad. In any case, it is not bad for you to be informed of this systematic offensive on the part of Father G.-L., who seeks to provoke scandal everywhere and who is succeeding to a certain degree. It is not that I want to overestimate the danger or to take anything too seriously. I hope, too, that our Response to the *Revue thomiste*, which is to appear in a few days, will have a good effect and will bring back to their senses some of those who have let themselves be carried away by their emotions these past few months. I believe that if by doing so we help to stop the kind of dictatorship that Father G.-L. is trying to exercise in the Church, our effort will not have been in vain. . . .

[4:14]

Father Fessard wrote to me, on October 7, 1945:

"You are a rigorous censor, but your rigor pleases me, and I do not ask you to be generous." Father Chaillet, who knew our habits of friendly collaboration well, asked me again, on December 9, to review first-hand the same work (which was mentioned previously on p. 65, note 10): "I have sent you two copies of the first edition, so that you can annotate them without fear of proposing corrections and suppressions. I expect much from this book in the way of a rectification in the face of communist temptations. You know what a drama that has produced with us. The affair has cleared up. . . . We need your help through regular collaboration."

[4:15]

At least I was able to get a brief review into *Etudes*, around the end of 1945:

"This fifth volume of the "Theology" series is an inquiry into the social function of authority. After having shown how authority is legitimate to the very degree in which it tends toward its end, in the dual sense of that word, in a fully realized common good, the author analyzes this idea of common good, distinguishing in it the idea of a 'good of the community' and a 'community of good', which must find their final unity in the 'good of communion'. Passing then to the examination of the present situation, he shows how political and social evolution, under the action of liberalism, has dissociated these two components of the common good, each of which is from then on at the basis of one of the two great conceptions between which the world has seemed to be divided: national socialism and communism. In order to overcome these fatal oppositions, he finally proposes Christianity to us as integrating what truth there is on both sides, the whole theory of authority and the common good constituting a kind of reflection of its dogmas in natural categories. —A short work, but of an extremely closely woven fabric; difficult, and yet of a wholly classical composition; Hegelian in style, but how different in spirit and doctrine! Entering in a rigorous way into the present texture of facts and thoughts, he proposes a renewed analysis in order to reestablish the most traditional notions in their rightful positions. Proceeding from the carefully considered conviction that the authentically spiritual must contain principles capable of overcoming the conflicts of this world, he unites through an original method, like that used by the same author in preceding works, the points of view of the sociologist, philosopher and theologian. A real model of incarnated and committed theology".

Here is the review I did not succeed in getting published:

Gaston Fessard: *Autorité et bien commun* ("Theology" series [Paris: Aubier, 1945]; 124 pages).

If it is true that the present evil of society comes for the most part from a crisis of authority—and not only or first of all, as those in command seem too often to believe, from a crisis of obedience—no work could be more opportune than this one, devoted to an examination of the foundation of authority and of its social function.

The first of the three chapters of which it is composed pays particular attention to defining the essence of authority from the standpoint of language, in order to determine its principle and end. A genetic analysis shows its concrete roots in the charismatic rise of the chief, the generative power of the father and the domination of the victor. But this would be pure, de facto power if some tendency toward a common good were not to initiate a process from which right could emerge. Thus authority appears as a mediatrix, a mediatrix of that common good before which, presuming it to be achieved, it then only fades away. Which is to say that it is legitimate in the very measure in which it has its own end in view: such as the father seeking to make his son into another himself or the scholar communicating to his disciple the truth that is to make him independent of him. For, even if the *fact* and the *right* are not opposed to each other in the way imagined by those who cling to abstractions of it, one still does not pass from one to the other by mere development: "Neither nature nor history is fruitful by itself; still less, egoism." Unless it opens itself to the universality of right, power remains that of force, and to the degree in which it positively rejects this appeal of the universal, it turns into tyranny. Much more, it must then transcend itself in order to aim beyond the temporal horizon at the reign of the concrete Universal, the source of all the particular common goods that it can attain. Having become the power of right, it must be accomplished in *value*, which reunites fact and right.

The will for its proper end, mediatrix of the common good: these two definitions of authority coincide: the one, more abstract, expresses the intention that must on principle animate all superiority; the second, more concrete, the result in which the movement inspired by the intention culminates. Whence the importance of this notion of the common good, said by Leo XIII to be the "creative principle and the preservative element of human society" and "after God, in society, the first and last law". What is it, then, more precisely? Like authority itself, it integrates three elements. The first two are in some ways antithetical: a "good of the community", which is not yet universal, and a "community of good", unlimited but abstract; when the first prevails, one has politics, the State, the relations of subordination; when the second does so, one has economics, society, the relations of coordination. These two aspects tend naturally to oppose each other; this is what permits the liberalism that, with its wholly rational and formal ideal, ignoring the Transcendent completely, opposing the individual to the city, dissolves the bonds of objective communities. There must therefore be a third element that reconciles them, as fact and right are reconciled in value: such is the "good of communion", a reciprocity of action between the good of the community and the community of good, which truly forms the soul, the vital knot, the substantial link of the common good. Thus we obtain the three categories of this common good, whose connections can be analyzed thanks to an original reworking of the Hegelian and Marxist dialectic of the master and slave. Completed by a dialectic of the family, it is to allow a fundamental resolution of the problem of the universal common good, the notion of which seemed contradictory at first.

At this end of the second chapter, we already see dawning the light that the Christian mystery is to project on the subject. For "if it is possible for the *master* to become the *father* in the Authority of his domination, as far as it extends, for the *slave* to become the *son* in the service of his obedience, as dearly as that costs him, for the one and the other to become *brothers* in the conjunction of their collaboration, whatever the object or occasion for it, then one should no longer despair of a universal communion being established between men where a love reigns that has the warmth and fruitfulness of that which unites the spouses of a family."

It was only in our time that the problem was capable of being posed to its full extent and that it assumed at the same time the acute character of an unprecedented crisis. The third chapter describes the genesis of this for us by applying in a more historical form the dialectic of the first two chapters. The stage of the French Revolution engenders the liberal State, which soon is dissolved in order to give birth to two antagonistic systems: communism, which advocates the ideal of a society without classes and without State; racism, which wants a people of masters organizing the world. But these two systems, despite the just critique they institute against liberalism, multiply the evil by their very opposition and by the partiality of their principles. The conflict breaks out between the will for power of the *homo politicus* and the appetite for pleasure of the *homo oeconomicus*. Thus the rational conquests of the modern age drive us to a social regression, which risks getting worse tomorrow. For more and more the common Good of humanity commands that of particular communities. "To determine what this universal common Good consists of and through what mediation the internal oppositions of humanity can be transcended, that is the primordial task."

In the final pages, Father Fessard applies himself to this task, showing in the mystery of the Man-God, universal Mediator and Reconciler, the sole principle capable of founding the universalism to which humanity aspires; in the Church, the sole milieu in which it can be achieved, or more precisely, the very type of its achievement. Finally, taking up the whole problem again in the light of the established solution, the conclusion makes us see how the dialectic of authority and the common good is none other, at base, than the very dialectic of Love, leading to the constitution of that "Body of Christ", the total and definitive common Good, "where all human authority, much more, all divine authority finds its end and its consummation."

It is surprising how much the author has been able to enclose within so short a text, a text of which the present summary can give only a vague idea. Not only are all the essential aspects of the problem of authority brought out in it but also the problems of the person and the community, those of the temporal and the spiritual; the two great phenomena of national socialism and communism are the object of an in-depth and solid explanation; critiques of Marxism, of the liberal society, of naturistic mystiques, of existentialism are outlined; new light is thrown in passing on various points of Hegelian philosophy and Christian dogma, and so forth. But all that—and this is where its strength lies—keeps to its precise place in a rigorously ordered whole. Nothing works to interrupt the dialectic process or to trouble its rhythm. Few works if any are of so tightly woven a fabric; few are so difficult, at least if one wants to penetrate to its core. Its composition is however as perfect in its way as that of a classic tragedy, and one has the feeling that all effort has been made in order to achieve the maximum of clarity. The author is in possession of an original method, which might disconcert some timid minds but which communicates to his thought a vigor and particularly a character of extremely rare fullness. The various points of view of the sociologist, the philosopher and the theologian are united and, as it were, fused together there; the most concrete analyses are inserted into the texture of a dialectic; a dramatic feeling of human progress pierces through the objectivity of the formulas; an uncompromising rationality does not prevent an opening out onto the highest mysteries of the faith. The thought is total here, because the human problem, whatever the bias from which it is approached, soon reveals itself to be total.

One thing, it seems to me, needs to be stressed. This theory that is so intellectualized is not an intellectualist theory. First of all because it makes provision for the irrational: not only in the concrete genesis of authority beginning from its biological roots but in its very reality, in which there always remains something sacred and gratuitous: "the dark and luminous faces of love". Next, because the recourse to Christian mystery, not from without and, as it were, to some *deus ex machina* but from within and, as it were, to a principle of understanding the use of which is carried quite far, nevertheless does not lead to any rationalization of dogma. It is only if God truly remains a personal and transcendent God, if Christ truly remains the incarnate Word of our Creed, if the Church truly remains the religious community in the womb of which we are recreated and united through the Spirit of Love, that there is a solution to the problem posed. Here we are very far from Hegel.

This is precisely what leads us to pose a question. If it is true, on the one hand, that the problem of authority and that of the common good coincide, the object of the former being to procure the latter and having to fade away before it, and if, on the other hand, this common good is achieved in the final analysis only in the "Body of Christ", how can the solution be other than eschatological? Once more, should we not note that the appeal to a transcendent factor resolves nothing in our immanence? Surely the author is not naïve enough to believe that authority might ever disappear in the human city or even be indefinitely dimmed. He knows besides that the Body of Christ will obtain the fullness of its stature only in a mysterious beyond. Does this "universal communion", the fruit of love, which he assigns as the end of our journey, not appear, therefore, within the limits of our temporal history, to be a wild dream? Must we nevertheless believe that the evolution of the world can tend toward it effectively without ever attaining it, so that only its consummation is es-chatological, or is it not more reasonable to think that it has nothing in common with the social accomplishments of a world given over to the devil or simply abandoned to its ever-unchanging misery? There, in other terms and from a different angle, we have the problem of the disparity or the tension between the ecclesiastical institution and the Body of Christ. It is the problem the author had already encountered when studying cer-tain surprising texts of Marx. It is the whole problem of the meaning of human history and of destiny. The general sense of the response is not in question. But we would have liked some further information, perhaps some complementary proofs on this subject.

We believe, in any case, that the author is precisely right in his carefully considered conviction that, without losing any of its transcendence, the authentically spiritual must contain the principles suited to overcome the conflicts of this world, and that Christianity, which has contributed more than any other force to making humanity become aware of itself, must also contribute more than any other to the solution of the problems to which this awareness has given birth. Does the tragedy of our age not consist precisely in the fact that humanity is beginning to reap the consequences of Christianity in vast domains at the very moment when it is turning away from it? The present work, if it finds the readers it deserves, could do much to remedy this evil. In any case, no one will deny that it searches out more deeply than has been done before a particularly difficult and particularly serious problem. Those who have read and admired the previous works by the same author, especially *Pax nostra* and *Le Dialogue catholique-communiste*, will recognize here the same thought and, as it were, the same stamp, with a simplicity of arrangement and an increased sobriety, which attest to a now-perfect mastery. Such a work should suffice to assure us that today more than ever Catholic thought is alive and present in the world.

HENRI DE LUBAC

[4:16]

Father Jean Daniélou and I were occupied with Origen at the same time. Our points of view about Origenian exegesis differed slightly—but a good understanding remained between us. I note here a few passages from his letters on the subject. February 5, 1948: "Thanks for your note and your very accurate remarks on my article. I have closely reexamined in this sense my *Origène*, whose first proofs I have just corrected." May 13th: "I am sending you my article on the typology of the week with all the corrections you had the kindness to suggest." June 29th: "I give you full freedom to edit my paper." August 3rd: "I hope you can go back to your Origen. I agree with you on what you say about the 'spiritual' sense. I believe that the word—and the thing—must be retained. But I believe it is useful at the same time to connect the exegesis of the Fathers to biblical theology. That is what I would like to do." From my side, I wrote to him on February 2, 1950: "I am happy that my 'Sens spirituel' [Spiritual sense] (in *Recherches*) has not displeased you. . . . The continuation of this text, in the conclusion of my book, will bring out some further details.

Even in places where I deviate from you in nuances, I think I have done it without marking any opposition, properly speaking, and I have, besides, made an effort to quote you in places where our agreement proved to be complete." And on May 30th: "I am happy to receive your book (*Sacramentum futuri*). It makes a very good impression. Your foreword defines its purpose clearly. The subject is well delimited, the plan is simple, so the work acquires more power. You tell me that you were not able to profit from my Origen. . . . That is mutual! Although I had known, in a general way, the first state of the work now published, I perceive many features that would have helped me to be more precise about more than one point. In particular, you show very well what the work of the prophets consisted in. Your conclusions, too, are presented in a limited and modest way that will discourage certain objections. If you will allow me to criticize one slight tendency, I would say that your title, which expresses the contents very accurately, seems to me in itself to be, not inaccurate, certainly, but a little narrow. For the prefiguration to which it refers is not only a prefiguration of a future but of a future that is at the same time something eternal, of a Fact to come that is a Mystery. A little like Cullmann and a few others, you have perhaps been too fearful of falling into some kind of Platonism. You are very right to be on guard! But there is a 'sursum', a movement from below to above, which is completely Christian and not Platonic; the two words *anagogy* and *eschatology* are not contradictory, and one of the two things must never make the other be forgotten. . . . It is obvious that we are very much in agreement about it; and, having worked in it myself, I would be very far from reproaching you for the stress you place on eschatology. I would only wish sometimes to see you emphasize the complementary aspect a little more. —But above all, your book is an historical work, of solid science, and I wonder how you have been able to finish it in the midst of so many other works."

[4:17]

Father Rideau would write in 1950 to his Provincial:

From Father Emile Rideau to the Father Provincial (of Paris)

ACTION POPULAIRE, JUNE 10, 1950

My Rev. Father, P.C. —You, like me and many others, must have been distressed by the note asking that Father Delaye's book, *Qu'est-ce qu'un catholique?* [What is a Catholic?], be withdrawn from sale.

I am extremely touched that you took the discreet initiative not to "notify" him officially. But public rumor did it for you: that is why I am taking the liberty to speak to you about this matter.

I consider there to be a grave and glaring injustice there both with regard to the truth and with regard to souls as well as an inopportune and dangerous measure of weakness.

This book, the importance of which must not have escaped the Rev. Father Provincial of Lyons, must have been reviewed with all possible seriousness and meticulousness by the competent censors, undoubtedly specialists in theology. It received the official approval of the Society, in the person of the Rev. Father Décisier, and that of the hierarchy.

The author, whom you know, is one of the most intelligent and profound theologians. The Society has given him its confidence, as a professor of our own members, and this confidence in him was renewed following the visit of Rev. Father Dhanis.

In my personal judgment, as in that of many other Fathers, Father Delaye's book, which I have read with critical attention, contains *nothing* that is theologically inaccurate. Quite the contrary, I find its form and its presentation classical.

The only review with which I am familiar is that in *L'Ami du clergé* (May 15, 1950): it is favorable, and the few criticisms from a "subscriber", reported in the issue, are without value or importance. One, at least, is based on an obvious misinterpretation that even a child could not miss.

Obviously it is always possible, for want of that benevolence recommended by Saint Ignatius, to interpret an expression unfavorably, particularly when it is taken out of context.

One could reasonably expect that many of the reviews that were being prepared, in particular that of *Etudes* and that of *Nouvelle revue théologique*, would have been very favorable.

The quickness of Rome's intervention is surprising when one thinks of the usual manner of the authorities in this domain: they proceed, so to speak, by "sounding out" and seeking to take their bearings according to the opinions given in journals.

It seems that one might voice the hypothesis here of a partisan pressure, insufficiently informed or malevolent.

It is eminently regrettable, in any case, that the decision made was not preceded by an invitation to the interested party, and, through him, to the responsible Society, to explain himself and, if need be, to defend himself. What we have here is an inhuman proceeding, contrary to the most elementary rights of man, to honor, to the natural law itself, resembling the tyranny of a dictator, employed by totalitarianism: man is there reduced to nothing.

I deem obedience, moreover, to have nothing in common with passivity and completeness; conscience makes it a grave duty to protest when truth and justice are obviously wronged.

I therefore implore you, my Reverend Father, not to consider the order received as definitive and without appeal and to act with all your power, in union with the other Father Provincials of France, to have it revoked as soon as possible. This, in my opinion, is one of those situations where, as happens sometimes in the State or in the army, it is the duty of the chief to take responsibility for his subordinates and to declare himself in solidarity with them. There are cases where the chief feels himself to be so involved in a common responsibility with his subordinate that he offers his resignation. In this case, Father Delaye cannot be disavowed by you, I mean by the joint authorities of the four provinces of France.

In addition, I, like many others, would feel personally uncomfortable and insecure in a Society that would refuse to demand justice for its unjustly attacked sons: it would no longer be a Mother.

I take the liberty to link this protest in favor of Father Delaye with that which I now address to you in favor of Father de Lubac, whose case is similar.

Gravely attacked, the latter has been forbidden to defend himself. That fact is unique in the history of the Church and, here again, contrary to the natural law. In the times when integrism prevailed, Father Lebreton did not hesitate to respond to Cardinal Billot, through an open discussion, in articles published in *Etudes*.

Now Father de Lubac, as you know, has been relieved of his position not only as editor of *Recherches* but as professor at Fourvière.

There is, as you also know, an integrist plot involved in that. The principal actors in it are two men, Father Garrigou-Lagrange and Father Boyer: they are not infallible.

It is not too late to intervene by all means possible against this injustice, increased twice over by a denial of justice.

These measures, finally, have the following disadvantages. Within the Society, they increase the discomfort of many young ones and favor those departures many of which are due less to desertion than to disillusionment. They cause a decline in our recruitment, in particular that of the most intelligent men, the ones most gifted in thought and character: they risk diminishing the quality of that recruitment. They also tend toward a devaluation of measures taken by those in authority and a loss of confidence.

Finally, on the apostolic level, they discredit us with the elite, especially in intellectual and university circles, provoking the sarcasm of unbelievers who militate for the rights of man. In short, they are a scandal for countless consciences, disconcerted by this attitude, to say nothing of that restless crowd that expects from us a message to match its thirst for truth, its appetite for God.

I beg you to accept, my Reverend Father, the expression of my very filial respect, *in Christo.*

E. RIDEAU

[*4:18*]

1. *Origène, Histoire et Esprit.* Father H. de L. a short time ago gave substantial *Introductions* to the translation of Origen's *Homilies* on *Genesis* and *Exodus* (*Sources chrétiennes*, 7 and 16). He returns to them and develops them considerably in order to give us an entirely new work on the *Intelligence de l'Ecriture d'après Origène* [Understanding of Scripture according to Origen]. Father de L. writes somewhere that Origen's exegesis is less the scientific study of a text than a theological meditation on Scripture (p. 414). One could say similarly that the present volume, coming after so many recent works, for example Father Daniélou's *Origène*, is less a further refinement or a *status quaestionis* than a rich mine of reflections proposed for our meditation. We encounter again here the author's own method and qualities: a knowledge of his subject that is both broad and specific, which allows him to work freely with an extraordinary accumulation of references and to cast unexpected beams of light through subtle comparisons. That, added to an extreme flexibility of thought and a delicate sense of nuances, makes one think of Origen himself.

Whatever might have been the "gropings" and "insufficiencies" of his thought (p. 39), Origen no longer has to be rehabilitated; but Father de L. recalls the incomprehension of which he was the victim up until our own times: the large monograph by E. de Faye is nothing but one long misinterpretation. Origen is neither the rationalist nor the extravagant mystic that some have wanted to see in him: he is a man of the Church, humbly and firmly attached to the "ecclesiastical rule" and full of a profound and tender affection for Jesus.

But it is with Origen's exegesis that we are concerned. There can be no question about the fact that he had no intention of "voiding" the letter. But in order to "save" the letter in places where it seems to him to offer a scandalous or inadmissible sense, he is often obliged to have recourse to "arbitrary" and "strange" methods that end only in "fantasies" that are "ingenious" and "evocative" but "without profit for sound knowledge" (p. 374). It cannot be emphasized enough that these were methods that were the product of culture and cannot be separated from the Alexandrian milieu in which the mind of Origen was formed (de Lubac goes so far as to speak of the "dangerous climate of Alexandrian Platonism", p. 377). It is in that way that this exegesis has become particularly outdated (p. 111). But these are only methods. Beyond that, there is the understanding of Scripture and the mystery of the unity of the two Testaments; Platonism is here transcended and transposed: "between Philo and Origen, there is the whole Christian mystery" (p. 164); "between Platonism and Origen, there is the whole Gospel" (p. 238). The spiritual sense, such as his commentator brings it out in Origen's allegories, is a theological view of the unity and progress of revelation far more than an exegesis in the modern sense of the word (p. 245). The "spirit" introduces *history*. It is there that we find the whole meaning of the book. To go from the letter to the spirit is to go from the past to the future (pp. 249, 257), and it is also to go "from history to the spirit" (p. 278), to discover the whole sense of history, polarized by Christ and his twofold parousia. The spiritual sense is the N.T. "[Lex] spiritualiter intellecta, Evangelius est" (Augustine). One must remark, however (does Father de L. do so sufficiently?), that this *historical* and properly Christian (past-future) perspective is blocked by another perspective that is Platonic (sensible-spiritual), and if our analysis distinguishes and brings them out, they are for Origen awkwardly tangled.

One understands also in this sense the relation between Scripture, Eucharist and Church (pp. 363–73). There are some excellent pages here, and Father de L. has no trouble demonstrating how an assertion such as the one made by Origen on the spiritual manducation of the Logos in Scripture does not impose a "symbolic", which is to say, unreal, interpretation of the eucharistic mystery. (One recalls how some, like Father Batiffol, for example, have toiled to explain these texts. . . . To the "dualism of meanings" that he perceived in Origen's language, we prefer the internal unity that Father de L. sees in it.)

The greatest service, it seems to us, that studies such as this can render is to show us how, beyond an exegesis that is in large part out of date, through these "allegorical poems" (p. 326) in which the homilist is enraptured, a *theology* is brought out, and a properly *biblical* theology. Certainly, being rocked in the "sweetness of allegory", thought risks being drowned in that "ocean of mysteries"; this theology does not yet have the precision and dialectical rigor from which it will benefit only later. But it is a true theology, based on Scripture, which, to use an expression of Father Lagrange, thereby seems, with the commentary of the Fathers, "like a new creation, completely full of Christian vigor" (quoted p. 274).

Toward the end of the book (pp. 395–400), Father de L. alludes to a fruitful distinction, which was formulated not long ago right here: if the purpose of exegesis is to make "the religious sense of the Bible" perceived, it is for biblical theology to bring out the "spiritual sense of Scripture", let us say the Christian sense of the history of revelation. In this distinction undoubtedly lies the solution to the problems that have been much debated, sometimes perhaps in vain, during these recent years.

(There are still many more excellent things to be noted in this fine book. Let us point out the pages devoted to eros and agapè. . . .)

T. CAMELOT, *Revue des sc. philos. et théol.* (1951), 316–17.

2. *Histoire et Esprit. L'Interprétation de l'Ecriture, d'après Origène,* by Father Henri de Lubac: a very good book, particularly opportune at the present time, when some rather lively and at times not very gracious quarrels often pit the historian-exegetes against the spiritualist-exegetes of Scripture. It was recently outlined in a remarkable chapter of *Catholicisme,* which had the same title, and progressively developed later in the introductions and notes with which the eminent theologian enriched the French translation made by his colleagues of Origen's Homilies on the Hexateuch. But since then the subject has been expanded. Since the Homilies were "only a vast repertoire of allegorical interpretations", Father de L. felt that in order to appreciate objectively Origen's attitude on the "letter" and "spirit" of Scripture it was necessary to know the whole of his work in depth: discourses addressed to the faithful, technical commentaries, special treatises such as the one on *Principles* and *Contra Celsius:* an immense task, the difficulty of which will be suspected by those who one day or other approach some aspect of it. Through Origen, reinserted "into the body of problems that were contemporaneous with him" and in understanding "his doctrine on the basis of the questions to which it was responding", the work has sought to grasp "Christianity itself . . . gaining a thoughtful self-awareness". The Introduction sets forth the methodological principles of the investigation. . . .

This conclusion is the masterpiece of the authoritative investigation, the study of which is fascinating from beginning to end. Heeding the wise old advice: "ne sutor ultra crepidam", I will not venture into a discussion of any particular detail of the investigation; I would like only to draw the attention of the readers of the RB to its conclusion, particularly those preoccupied in general with literal and historical exegesis and at times perhaps moved by certain exclusive and flashy exaltations of contemporaneous allegorizing exegesis. They will note clearly here, in Origen himself, that history and spirit, far from being opposed in some sterilizing antagonism, are, on the contrary, essentially ordered to each other in an integral exegesis in which the search for the literal sense is the basis of the argumentative value of the sacred text, while the spiritual sense develops the innumerable potentialities of the Word of God. Such was already the conviction of Father Lagrange when, in order to establish the necessity, which was more imperative than ever at the beginning of this century, of giving a firm basis for the interpretation of the Bible, especially with respect to the O.T., he briefly outlined the evolution of Christian exegesis. In reaction against the Jewish Midrash, it was first thrown "without restraint into the spiritual sense". . . . Tendentiously attacked by a harsh controversialist, who accused him of scorning the spiritual sense and of throwing overboard "five centuries of Catholic exegesis", Father Lagrange did not obtain permission to reestablish the facts with the necessary precision; but numerous parts of his work attest to the injustice of such an imputation. If the demands of the moment dictated that he undertake the especially arduous task of justifying and promoting the historical interpretation of the Bible, those who lived around him know how concerned he was to make the spiritual significance appreciated, how much he especially envied in his innermost heart the privilege of those to whom no other obligation falls but to sound the divine depths of it. (In my eyes, Father de L. deserves more than slight credit for having brought out this fact in many passages of his fine book.)

In his turn, and with the most successful expositions, Father de L. sets forth the principles of an exegesis whose spiritual efficacy has historical veracity as an indispensable foundation: a twofold modality of exposition that goes fully beyond the powers of the specialists themselves and requires a division of the task. Since, we are assured, contemporary aspirations, less affected than fifty years ago by attacks against the historicity of Scripture, proceed by preference to a savoring of the spirit, let us ardently hope that the exegetes of tomorrow will devote themselves increasingly to the satisfaction of them. They will do so all the more profitably if, instead of ill-advised repetitions about the opposition between the so-called "miserly milk" furnished by "the dry breasts of literal exegesis" and the generous milk flowing from certain swelling breasts of allegorical exegesis, they pursue the diligent application of the specifications formulated for their profit by Father de L., so that this copious milk may not be the exclusive and insipid product of the mimicry of patristic allegories deprived of their original creative vigor.

Histoire et Esprit is better than a fine book; it is good action.

VINCENT, Revue biblique, 57 (1950): 634–35.

3. Father de L.'s work on Origen is addressed to a more restricted audience, and it is more difficult reading, but we have no doubt that it too will enjoy a great success. Our readers have long been familiar with the emi-

nent Jesuit, professor at Lyons, whose writings figure among those who
have most given witness, even outside the Church, of the fine revival of
religious studies in the France of today. No one can contest his remarkable erudition, his talent as an author, the originality and the power of his
thought. Even if some of his views might be debatable or debated, one
can only encourage him in the pursuit of a work from which the Church
will be the very first to reap the fruit. May the impact of ideas bring forth,
according to the wishes of the Sovereign Pontiff, not sterile discussions or
petty rivalries or pernicious whispering, but more light and more clarity!

This is not the first time that the Father has applied himself to studying
and explaining Origen. The readers of our *Harmonies des Deux Testaments*
already know the essence of Father de L.'s thought concerning the work
of the great Alexandrian exegete. These views are taken up again here, but
greatly expanded, better supported, often nuanced with still more clearsightedness. This is not, moreover, the part of the work that we would
like to present here. Our attention is directed this time to the final chapter, where the author brings out, in part according to Origen, a synthetic
exposition of a doctrine that is dear to him, that of the *spiritual sense of the
Scriptures*.

We admit to having read these pages with a curiosity and an interest
that have not ceased to grow. . . .

J. COPPENS, *Ephemerides theol. lovan.* (1951), I–II:146–47.

To Hasso Jaeger, who was later surprised that no account had been taken
of *Histoire et Esprit* and that this book was never quoted, I replied, on May
2, 1960: "That is not surprising. The book did not sell well, and there
were few reviews. (The circumstances, moreover, were not favorable.)
This kind of problem is of little interest to theologians or to exegetes who
are each specialized in other directions. As for patrologists, most of them
like only those Fathers who pose problems of thought to them. There is
also, on the other hand, a rather well-established modern tradition of ignorant distrust with regard to Origen. Finally, the book is of the genre that is
today called "confessional"; authors with scientific pretensions, whether
believers or not, do not much like that."

(In August 1981, more than thirty years later, I received from the publisher a request for a new edition.)

[*4:19*]

Father Pierre Charles, who had come to Lyons for the *Semaine sociale*, said
to Father Décisier, my provincial, on July 31, 1948: "There is pressure

everywhere in Rome to condemn. Father Teilhard seems outside the question because they don't want to have a sort of new Galileo affair. The fires are concentrated on Father de Lubac".

[4:20]

Father René Arnou, Visitator of the Scholasticate, received from me at that time the text of this course and took it to Rome, where it was approved.

[4:21]

(Plan A). "Very Holy Father, the Society of Jesus has made obedience to the Sovereign Pontiff a special duty for its children. This submission is particularly close to its heart in doctrinal matters. In his rules for orthodoxy, our blessed Father Ignatius of Loyola invites us always to think in agreement with the Roman Catholic Church.

"Placed by divine Providence in a country and an era where scientific progress, the evolution of institutions and morals, the diversity and opposition of philosophical currents pose formidable problems and great and manifold dangers to the educated faithful, to apostles and even more to theologians, we are convinced that, without extraordinary vigilance, it is difficult to maintain the purity of the faith and to progress in the understanding of the revealed message.

"We are therefore anxious to express to Your Holiness our filial gratitude for the very sound teachings that he has given the world in his encyclical of August 12, 1950. We are happy to make this gesture on the eve of the first anniversary of the definition of the dogma of the Assumption of the Blessed Virgin Mary, a proclamation that has given us very special joy, charged as we are with studying and teaching the sacred sciences on the hill of Fourvière.

"We are not unaware that, on several points, the Encyclical *Humani generis* constituted a paternal warning for us. We had, according to pontifical directives, sought 'to express ourselves in our words and in our writings in such a way that men of our time might understand and willingly listen to us' (Discourse from Castelgand.). But in this apostolic effort, feeling the urgency of questions that had not until then been sufficiently discussed, wishing to express traditional truths in a more modern language, choosing among theses that seemed to them to be freely debatable, some of us have at times used forms of expression that were less fortunate, inadequate, or indeed theologically inaccurate. We have not all and always made a large enough distinction between the transmission of the common doctrine and scientific research, in which the theologian, like scholars, can advance hypotheses whose merits can be shown through discussion, while waiting for the Magisterium, if it judges necessary, to decide between the schools. We were therefore not above reproach, despite our intentions. But as soon as the text of the Encyclical was known, each of us has tried to verify, to clarify and, if called for, to correct his thinking and his teaching, in order to place them in agreement with the thinking of the Church and to prevent the abuse that otherwise well-intentioned students or apostolic works might make of certain expressions or certain tendencies.

"We are not the only ones who have had to do so, in the same concern for fidelity to the Roman and Catholic Church, our mother, to whom Christ Our Lord confided the words of eternal life. To distinguish between Christ and the Church, between the juridical Church and the body of Christ, would be an aberration against which we have always expressly warned those who come to us.

"We have not thought it necessary until now to express publicly to Your Holiness our submission to his directives, the obedience of a Jesuit to major superiors sufficing in itself to assure, in the doctrinal order as in the domain of the apostolate, that total and unconditional subjection to the orders of the Vicar of Christ. Desiring, however, to unite ourselves to the numerous testimonies that flow to the successor of Peter from all Catholic schools and universities, we are anxious to manifest to him today that deep attachment of our understanding and our heart.

"Today as yesterday, we join him in condemning Modernism, errors or tendencies, very particularly dogmatic relativism, the errors of irenicism, theological historicism. While thinking that 'through the study of the sources, the sacred sciences are ceaselessly rejuvenated', we strongly maintain that the living Magisterium is the supreme rule of interpretation of the Holy Scriptures and of Tradition. Despite our concern to gain a good understanding of the modern systems in order to criticize them better and to bring out the partial truths they might contain, we remain attached to the principles and the method of the Angelic Doctor, resolved to approach new problems only in the light of the Faith and of the doctrinal tradition of the Church, knowing that in this matter much prudence and humility are necessary.

"It is in this spirit that we prostrate ourselves at the feet of Your Holiness, asking him filially to encourage our efforts, to correct our errors if need be or to warn us paternally about our lack of prudence, and asking that he be kind enough to give his apostolic blessing to us, our students and our ministries." (August 19, 1951.)

There was also a second message, of which I still have the third (and undoubtedly the final) draft. It was sent on September 27:

"Very Holy Father, We have sent to your Holiness, through the Very Rev. Father General of the Society of Jesus, a message of gratitude for the teachings and paternal warnings of the Encyclical *Humani generis*.

"In this second letter, we believe we must explain to Your Holiness the delay in sending this message. We have in fact been painfully surprised to learn that our silence might have caused some doubt as to our immediate and total submission to the directives of the Apostolic See.

"We had all received the pontifical document as sons of Saint Ignatius, bound by a special vow of obedience to the Sovereign Pontiff. But, since our theology faculties do not have the same collective personality as others, we had thought that the spirit of our Institute did not authorize us to take the initiative of a message to the Holy See.

"If we had understood clearly that this particular gesture of gratitude and submission was expected of us, we would have made it immediately. When the Very Rev. Father General specified various points of doctrine for the Society, in execution of the Encyclical, we made known to him without delay our total submission to the Encyclical as well as to the specifications brought by his letter. We have always made it a point of honor to inspire in our students absolute respect for the decisions of the living Magisterium, the sole interpreter of divine revelation.

"If therefore our silence had been interpreted as the result of less docility, that would have been a great sorrow for us, but we would suffer still more to have thereby, against our intentions, grieved Your Holiness, and we would humbly beg his pardon.

"Prostrate at the feet of Your Holiness, we dare to ask him, as very respectful and very loving sons, to bless us again and to keep his very paternal affection for us."

[4:22]

In fact, the lightning had struck me a little before the professors of Fourvière. Through a letter from Rome addressed to my Provincial (then Father Rostan d'Ancezune), and which I have never had in hand, I was required to announce to the Cardinal Lord Chancellor that I had to leave the Theology Faculty. I wrote of this to Father Fessard, on May 4, 1950: "There is without doubt no precedent for this procedure: my Provincial, or I myself, must apply to the ecclesiastical authorities in order to persuade them, please, to throw me out." "All was coming from higher up": I believed this at the time.

This was in 1952. Again in 1954, Cardinal Feltin incurred a similar response from a "very high ecclesiastical personage" to whom he had pleaded my cause; as reported to me, the retort was even more brutal: "When the Father writes something orthodox, you can be sure it is not what he thinks." The article published in the *Gregorianum* already contained this little phrase, which had been very much noted: "(There is no supernatural;) let one say it, since one thinks it". —On May 14, 1951, I copied in a notebook this text by Newman in his *Apologia* (XVI): "What I insist upon here is . . . (the) plan . . . to cut the ground from under my feet;—to poison by anticipation the public mind against me, John Henry Newman, and to infuse into the imaginations of my readers, suspicion and mistrust of everything that I may say in reply to him. This I call *poisoning the wells.*" (But, unlike Newman, I was not able to make a public protest.) On July 4, 1951, Father Victor Fontoynont wrote to me: "Let us let the time of folly pass. . . . You are classified as *captious*; suspicion is regarded as the obligatory rule, and it is a suspicion that creates objects."

The same accusation of hypocrisy occurred again in a review, sent from Rome in 1951, of my *Connaissance de Dieu* (cf. my letter to Father Motte, Nice, March 1, 1951).

MY REVEREND FATHER PROVINCIAL, PAX CHRISTI!

"Since the beginning of this affair, of which it is increasingly impossible for me to understand anything, I believe I have placed myself, with the grace of God, in a disposition of entire and filial obedience, according to the mind of the Church and the Constitutions of the Society, without seeking to evade anything through some subjective interpretation. I am firmly determined, always with the grace of God, to persevere in this path, whatever happens!

"But here the Father General raises yet another problem, in another field. In a letter that the Father Rector of Fourvière has just received, he accuses me (conjointly with the other Fathers) of *pernicious errors on essential points of dogma*! Errors, he adds, in which I have been obstinate, despite the most authoritative warnings.

"Has the Father General considered the exceptional gravity of such an accusation? In any case, his office does not dispense him any more than any other Christian from having to justify it—and first of all to be specific about it. He is basing himself, he says, on the opinion of 'numerous theologians'. Who are these theologians? I have the right to know, to know with what I am being reproached, to obtain from them their reasons, to question them if necessary.

"All the filial respect that I have and that I wish to preserve intact toward my Superiors cannot remove all good sense and memory from me. I have in fact been attacked by several theologians (rather generally held in low esteem because of their notorious ignorance of Catholic Tradition and for several other reasons). From the very first day, through a measure without doubt unheard of in the history of the Society, the Father General has prevented me from answering them, or even simply from reestablishing, in the briefest and most objective terms, my odiously misrepresented thought in its true light. (An interdiction again renewed in explicit terms by the Rev. Father Dhanis, Visitator.) I have submitted to this measure—while other theologians and historians of theology either declared that I was entirely right, noted the inanity of the most important criticisms or declared that, in all of this, it was only a matter of open questions.

"Moreover, very far from reproaching me at the time for maintaining grave errors on essential points of dogma, the Father General said that if he imposed such a sacrifice on me, it was in order to be better able to defend me himself. Just after the attacks by Father Garrigou-Lagrange, he had someone write to me that he desired me to continue working peacefully, and in the same line. As to the words of the Holy Father at Castelgandolfo, to which he refers today, he assured us spontaneously, in the most precise manner, that they concerned us in nothing—after having received proof of it, he added, from the very mouth of the Holy Father. He authorized me, much rather he urged me, to repeat this. At the time when, under the growing pressure of the intrigue, he began to make a few concessions, he was nevertheless still speaking only of a few awkward expressions, with regard to which he assured besides that we had given entirely satisfactory explanations. Then, while continuing to reject my attempts to reply to some persistent criticisms still coming from the same little group in hot pursuit, he allowed me, after an examination by his personal theologian, to publish some pages that contained (as far as I can guess, since they refuse to enlighten me) the poison of error for which I am reproached today as being the effect of a bad, obstinate will.

"Those are the facts, my Reverend Father Provincial, facts that it is not within the power of anyone, neither the Father General nor God himself, to change retrospectively.

"As throughout the past, I remain ready to submit in everything not only to the decisions of the Holy Church but to the mere desires of my Superiors, from the moment that it is not a question of sin. I know also that an opinion that is at first free can be proscribed beginning at a certain date, for any reason at all, of which the authority is the sole judge, even if it does not have any direct relation to dogma. But such an act by authority does not legitimize in any way the accusations of those who, beforehand, suspect the faith or obedience of theologians holding such an opinion.

"During these recent times, it has happened that I have several times been slandered to the Father General. The latter has several times given a strangely zealous reception to these calumnies and taken grave measures in consequence, although it would have been extremely easy for him to inquire about the truth: for example, on the subject of the revision of my book *Surnaturel*; or even, still more recently, in a letter whose paternal tone had moved me with grateful joy, when he took responsibility for some untrue reports saying that I had 'opened wide the columns of *Recherches* to questionable authors'. I have always kept silence about these calumnies. But since today the Father General himself has become my accuser in the matter of faith, silence is no longer possible. I therefore dare to ask him first of all to make known to me in a precise way what he is reproaching me for and why he is reproaching me for it, then to allow me to present my defense to him. Although I am wounded to the depths of my soul by the one we call our Father, as being the representative of the Divine Paternity for us, I do not wish to despair of seeing my complaint awaken in him a truly paternal echo and arouse the desire for a more equitable evaluation. Moreover, in taking this step, I am sure of having with me our blessed Father Saint Ignatius, whose example I am only following. This is why, my Reverend Father Provincial, I earnestly ask you please to communicate to the Father General the subject of this letter, the simplest way being perhaps to forward the letter itself to him.

"Reverentiae Vestrae in Christo Servus et Filius."

[*4:25*]

Several excerpts from an article published in a theological journal will give the tone of what was said and published at that time:

". . . If any still doubt the gravity of the crisis, all they need do in order to be convinced of it is to note the tone of the document—the most solemn form of the ordinary Magisterium—and the seriousness of the orders given to the bishops and religious superiors. . . . What is deeply regrettable is the fact that some of their adherents (of the philosophico-theological renewal and of ecumenism) and at times the most visible ones are letting themselves be led into aberrations against which one must now deal severely.

". . . What the Holy Father is rising up against in particular is a certain current of 'dogmatic relativism', in more or less audacious manifestations, which minimizes the importance of the notions inserted into the human expression of the dogmas defined by the Church. A tendency to reduce as much as possible the essence of defined truth; a tendency to seek to translate this truth into new notions, whether one believes this makes them more accessible to the minds of our time or whether one declares them objectively more suitable than the old ones for expressing the supernatural reality. In that way, they have been led to make affirmations incompatible with the Catholic Faith; about the demonstration, for example, of the existence of a personal God, or again, on the divine foreknowledge, on the gratuity of the supernatural order, on the real presence of the Savior in the Eucharist, and so forth.

"[First cause: the irenicist tendency.] . . . On the other hand, and above all, the need for renewal in Catholic theology and philosophy, a need born from a reaction against the excessively rational and abstract character, at least in appearance, of Scholasticism during recent centuries, has engendered in some a mistrust, indeed contempt, with regard to Scholasticism itself. Instead of seeking the guiding principles of the necessary renewal in traditional thought, where they would have found them, these thinkers enamored of novelty have turned toward contemporary philosophies, philosophies in which part of the intelligence is much too reduced in favor of obscure intuitions of the emotions. From which comes a failure to appreciate the stability and exclusivism of intellectual certitudes and the notions they imply; and also an excessive preference for a more concrete and less technical expression of revealed truths, such as one finds in the Fathers, the Greek Fathers especially.

"These errors might have been avoided if they had known how to seek light in the instructions of the ecclesiastical Magisterium. But precisely —and the Pope deplores it vigorously—these same thinkers easily allow themselves to scorn the Magisterium, to consider it an obstacle to doctrinal renewal or to the unionist apostolate, even to claim to correct it in the name of teaching from Christian sources. With such dispositions, it is not surprising that they end up in the most lamentable consequences. . . ."[6]

Eugène Marcotte, O.M.I., professor at the Theology Faculty, *Revue de l'Université d'Ottawa*, col. 20, n. 4 (Oct.-Dec. 1950), 197–200: "L'Encyclique *Humani generis*".

[4:26]

Notwithstanding many of the rumors being spread, I noted, on September 22, 1950: "Folklore. The five Jesuits chased from Fourvière have gone

---

[6] Cf. letter from the Very Rev. Father General to the Assistancy in France, p. 15.

to find Pastor Boegner to ask him to join them in founding a 'French Church'; and, the supreme humiliation, Pastor Boegner showed them the door. That is what is being reported, and it continues to come to my ears." In this same month of September, the Jesuit Superiors of the Rome houses had to draft an official denial concerning my "apostasy". Around the same date, a professor from the University of Fribourg (Switzerland) designated me in a Polish journal as one of the principal heretics of the century, and so forth.

[4:27]

As early as the summer, he had composed this symbolic sonnet, entitled "Andante", to which he had added these words as a subtitle: "For the newly departed".

> J'ai perdu mon envolée
> Et j'ai perdu mon orgueil.
> Dans la maison désolée
> Les fenêtres sont en deuil.
>
> L'Unique s'en est allée
> Qui m'attendait sur le seuil.
> Sur la sable de l'allée
> On emporte son cercueil.
>
> Je suis seul avec moi-même,
> Sevré de tout ce que j'aime,
> Sans jeunesse et sans élan.
>
> — Quitte la maison déserte.
> Vois: la campagne est ouverte.
> Et puis chante en t'en allant.[7]

See also above, page 70.

[4:28]

Here, however, by way of example, is the checklist posted by the prefect of studies at the scholasticate of Weston College, USA, for the use of students in theology:

---

[7] I have lost my flight / And I have lost my pride. / In the desolate house / The windows are in mourning. / The Unique One who had been waiting for me on the threshold / has taken his departure. / On the sand of the lane / They are carrying his coffin. / I am alone with myself, / Cut off from all I love, / Without youth and without élan. / —Leave the deserted house. / See: the field is open. / And then sing as you depart.

Exercitatio on the New Theology
and the Recent Encyclical *Humani generis*

I

Origin of the term "new theology"; allocution of His Holiness to the Fathers of the last General Congregation of the Society of Jesus.

General trends and objectives: adaptation to modern times; exaltation of patristic theology, i.e., of history and symbolism over the Magisterium and Scholasticism.

Roots and affinities: the crisis of Modernism; Blondel, Bergson, evolution, existentialism, immanentism.

Chief adherents of the new theology: Daniélou, de Lubac, Bouillard, Theillard (sic) de Chardin, Durand, Rondet, etc. . . .

Chief opponents: Boyer, de Broglie, de Blic, Donnelly, Gagnebet, Garrigou-Lagrange, Gillon, Labourdette, Nicolas, Deman, Malevez, etc.

II

Topics for discussion and papers:

Manifestations of Gallicanism in the adherents of the New Theology; the place of Patristic and Scholastic theology in the development of dogma; the problem of adaptation with regard to modern philosophy, esp., Blondel and existentialism; the dogmatic value of Papal Encyclicals; Biblical interpretation of the O.T., esp. Genesis, spiritual versus literal sense, symbolic versus real, etc. . . . ; Evolution and Polygenism; the Supernatural of Father de Lubac: History of the controversy; Saint Thomas and the natural desire for God; possibility of a state of pure nature; de Lubac's theory and original sin; de Lubac's theory and Redemption.

The excellent author of this masterpiece, whom I later met in Rome, warmly embraced me.

[*4:29*]

Various suppositions have been made about which theologians may have contributed to the drafting of this encyclical. Father Pierre Charles wrote to Father Charles Baumgartner (then prefect of studies at the scholasticate of Enghien): "I can assure you, apart from any secret, as a simple honest man, that I did not have to be involved with *Humani generis* and that, if I had drafted it, it would be in better Latin. I am offended to have even a distant paternity for it attributed to me." According to Father Louis de Peretti (letter sent from Rome on March 5, 1951), three amalgamated drafts can be distinguished rather easily in the encyclical; a "malevolent" document was the original basis for it; a first reshaping gave a "more malevolent" document; the encyclical resulted from another reshaping, by "a man of very good will, with conciliatory desires", who might have been "some Benedictine from Saint Anselm's". . . .

[4:30]

Cf. my reply to a letter from my friend and colleague Heinrich Bacht, professor of theology at the Frankfurt scholasticate:

"Lyons, March 31, 1959. . . . Thanks, too, for what you said to me on the subject of Abbé Küng. He is a great worker, with a clear intelligence, and I had nothing but sympathy for him. But he has for some time now shown an *arrivism* [unscrupulous ambition], as we say in French, which has an unpleasant side to it. I knew him in Paris, when he was preparing his work on Karl Barth. I also often visited Father Bouillard, who gave him the benefit of his knowledge and who rendered him more than one service, even on the material order, with much graciousness. Father Bouillard was the examiner for his thesis; he proved to be very kind, more than the other examiners, and he did not want to manifest demands for corrections that would have greatly embarrassed the candidate. That is why, over and above the heart of the matter, the criticism published by Küng in *Dokumente* was truly improper.

"I cannot judge the German of my article. I relied entirely on Father von Galli for the translation. As for Küng's book, I had read it first-hand, twice, in the original, photocopied edition, which is in French. And, truly, it was not very difficult to see that there is a great difference in value between him and Bouillard.

"My wish for Küng is that he would work seriously, as he had begun to do in Paris, to give us mature works and to stop making publicity that is too noisy or steps that are too arrogant. . . ."

Another example.

NOVEMBER 1950

"[In the Encyclical *Humani generis*], most space has been given to the 'new theology' of the School of Jesuits in Lyons, led by Father de Lubac. This school has committed two errors by rejecting post-patristic tradition and by falsifying the theory of grace. . . . Father de Lubac . . . has unfortunately deviated in his difficult theological research. All these writers (T. de C., Desroche, Lubac) are linked by two characteristics: by a categorical rejection of Scholastic tradition and by temptations to compromise. . . . Why is it precisely in France that these dangerous misunderstandings appear? . . . I want to affirm one thing only: an inferiority complex and a lack of faith in the proper forms (forces?) of the Church have been striking in the French clergy for some time now. . . .

"In the force of the condemnation, the author sees how aware Rome is of the danger of heresy in France but also the fact that the Church does not count on the help of progressive democracies in the battle against bolshevism. . . . The Church no longer counts on anything but her own spiritual forces. . . .

". . . All conscious Catholics in Poland have had the impression that there is something unbalanced in Western Catholicism, that at the moment when men are suffering for the Faith in their country, eminent Western ecclesiastics are collapsing under the influence of a self-propaganda. A young Polish priest, returning to Poland after a two-month stay in France, said: 'I looked here for spiritual strength, and I found decay.' To those who think as he does, the Encyclical brings the assurance that the universal Church is unshakeable in her positions, that there will be neither wavering nor compromise. . . ."

"The Encyclical *Humani generis*", by Fr. Bochenski, O.P., professor at the University of Fribourg, in *Kulture*, November 1950 (summary, with passages of textual quotations).

[*4:31*]

The letters of Father Teilhard, published by Father Pierre Leroy, give a few indications about the rumors that were circulating before the publication of the Encyclical and about T.'s reactions in the months that followed.

Teilhard to Pierre Leroy: Paris, June 25, 1950. ". . . The decisions of the Holy Office concerning the 'new theology' are expected in July. (D'Ouince, still an optimist, indulges himself and me with the hope that the *imprimatur* will be given to me when it will be clear, after the lightning falls, that I am not included within the range of its action? . . .) While waiting, it is said openly that five professors at Fourvière have been discreetly dismissed . . . (p. 65).

Paris, July 6, 1950. "[According to Father Chaillet, returned from Rome.] In Rome they are talking about the 'Syllabus' as if it were a fact. And yet the rumor is beginning to circulate that this might have been only a bug-bear, which they will now withdraw since the result (the official dispersal of the 'new theology') has now been attained. Without any hesitation. —In the meantime, de L.'s withdrawal continues to create a certain stir; and he is circulating letters of protest. —The famous Syllabus (if it comes out) would be expected at the end of the month (or August): in any case, by vacation time" (pp. 66–67).

Paris, July 29, 1950. "Nothing from Rome (except a glass of holy water, from Gorostarzu). They are beginning to say the the famous 'Syllabus' will not come out in the end (either because they sensed anger rising in high places or because the dismissal from Fourvière is said to be a sufficient measure); and it is also thought that the dogma of the Assumption will remain in the drawer" (p. 69).

Les Moulins, August 29, 1950. ". . . I feel neither bitterness nor discouragement; and I have quite simply decided to continue openly along my way in a direction that seems to me to be accurately oriented toward the dogmatic realism that Rome desires and requests" (p. 74).

Paris, October 19, 1950. "Exasperated by the stupid things that were said (even here) on the question of monogenism, I decided to write a brief, purely objective note of clarification . . ., which I addressed to Father de Gorostarzu, with a very friendly but clear letter, in which I pointed out to him that, in contrast to the Encyclical *Pascendi* (whose target was those who were destroying Christ), the Encyclical *Humani generis* (in which one seeks in vain for anything 'human', in the sense of modern Humanism) was aimed at men who were seeking to increase and intensify the adorability of Christ: which amounts to Rome having just bombed its front lines" (p. 75).

Paris, December 7, 1950. "Finally (according to people returning from Rome), the entire avalanche was triggered by a report from Danis (sic) on the French scholasticates (1948 visit). The General supposedly found it so 'appalling' that he had to hand it over to the Pope(?!). Whence the execution of Fourvière and the Encyclical" (p. 79).

"Rather tragic as a misunderstanding" (p. 80).

"In the meantime, articles and books by de L. and Bouillard have been withdrawn from the trade and from the scholasticate libraries: which has the immediate effect of making the use and demand for them rise" (p. 80).

Paris, March 28, 1951. ". . . A 'super-Encyclical' by the General has been read to us, leaving everyone here bewildered . . . and unchanged" (p. 96).

In Pierre Leroy: *Lettres familières de Pierre Teilhard de Chardin mon ami,
1948–1955* (Paris: Le Centurion, 1976).

[4:32]

It may be that the initiative was less Lyonnese or Tunisian than Roman. I
had the impression at least that it came from Msgr. Ottaviani, undoubtedly
warned by several informers. A later letter from Msgr. Gounot led me to
understand that he had been discreetly invited, at the Holy Office, to take
me into his diocese. And when the Archbishop said to Msgr. Ottaviani
that he had heard me speak of the encyclical *Humani generis* "with much
edification", the latter was visibly surprised.

[4:33]

I take the liberty of reproducing here the letter addressed to me on July
29, 1951, by a Father in whom I have always had every reason to have
complete confidence: ". . . Oh, Father, how you must suffer from being
attacked in this way in what you hold closest to your heart, attachment to
the holy Church; from being attacked and accused on the precise point of
Truth that has always been the most sensitive for you. But I tell myself
that it is precisely because of that. I tell myself that there is no true love of
Jesus Christ without a sharing in his Cross, without persecutions ('Omnes
qui pie volunt. . .'). Father, I beg you, not to let yourself be overcome.
Do not let any of this, profiting from your exhaustion, alter any of the
profound Peace of your heart. Father, I assure you (how do I have the
right to speak in this way?) that you are in the Charity of Jesus Christ, that
all that attacks you only makes you, feature by feature, more conformed
to the dear, adorable Face. Of course, one must not stoop to base actions;
must not tell lies politically (they say: 'supernaturally') in order to gain a
false peace. You need only say that you disapprove of anything in your
books that Holy Church would judge going counter to her message and
that you are ready to discuss frankly the specific disputed points. (One
can make a profession of obedience but not, out of kindness, subscribe to
something that does not even exist.) But that being done, and given the
very 'persecuting' character of the polemics, there is really nothing to do
but submerge oneself in the Mystery of Christ. Oh Father, I know that
your life at present is a commentary on your last chapter, 'Mysterium Cru-
cis', in *Catholicisme. . . .*" One can see from this one example that spiritual
support was not lacking for me in the fifties.

[4:34]

On June 24, 1959, Father Le Blond wrote to me from Paris, by way of excuse for having asked me to write an article for *Etudes* on the *Recherches de science religieuse* (for their fiftieth anniversary): "It was the unanimous wish of the committee of *Recherches*, and I made it my own, without sufficiently measuring the difficulties that you are experiencing. I am sure, in truth, that the Holy Office would not find difficulties with it—and I have reported to you the words that Cardinal Ottaviani said to me about you —but I understand that, within the Society in Rome, some sensitivities would bristle. The new rejection of your article on Father Lebreton is a sign that these sensitivities remain; to tell the truth, I was expecting it, you know."

[4:35]

From a letter received in February 1974: "The other day, strolling around in the Catholic bookstore, I discovered among the remaindered books a copy of *Corpus mysticum*, second edition. The bookdealer asked me to take it as a gift and to lend it some day to Abbé X. As I have to prepare non-practicing children for private communion, I find in this work a wealth of teachings of which the new catechisms pretend to be unaware."

[4:36]

On Friday, October 1, 1965, on my arrival in the room in the Vatican where the Theological Commission had gathered, Father Gagnebet, O.P. (of the Angelicum and the Holy Office), approached me and, after an exchange of a few friendly words, warmly congratulated me for my *Corpus mysticum*. I responded by saying to him that this book was still banned today by a measure coming from the Holy Office. He was surprised at this. I replied, with a smile, that he was nevertheless in a good position to know. He then said to me that he would intervene in order to "settle the affair", that there must have been a misunderstanding about it. I answered that, in any case, I did not wish to ask for anything. "That is ancient history," I then noted, "which is no longer of any interest." I assume that Father Gagnebet had looked at my book that year on the occasion of a consultation that might have been requested of him in preparing the recent encyclical on the Eucharist.

I have discovered a copy of a letter sent to a young priest, who had just announced to me that he was leaving the Church, at the time when I was busy putting the papers for my *Méditation* in order.

L'OASIS, VERS-EN-MONTAGNE, JULY 25, 1951.
DEAR MONSIEUR L'ABBÉ,

. . . You were quite right in thinking that I would be very anxious to have accurate information about your present position and your state of mind. Be assured, it is with a very friendly heart that I have read these two pages. Yet, I cannot hide the fact from you that it is at the same time with a saddened heart. No, I do not doubt your loyalty or your ardent desire to be faithful to the Holy Spirit. But how can I fail to see—and how, seeing it, not tell you—that you are, for the moment, the victim of an illusion? Many others before you (each generation for centuries has numbered some) have made a similar gesture, discouraged as they were by similar, often all too real adversities. Where did they end up? The greatest among them, in rending the Church of Christ and in increasing her evils; most (and the merit of a good number of them was not mediocre), in losing their way in vain efforts and being lost for any great common effort.

What reassures me nonetheless and mixes a joy full of hope with my sadness is your total and pure faith in Christ Jesus, only Son of the living God; it is your hope in Him. You will not be able to fail to recognize, it seems to me, that it is his Church that maintains this Faith and this Hope intact and alive in the world, and that it is in the womb of his Church, in a submission that is at times crucifying but always all the more calming, that one finds Him, in security and in fullness. No human adversity can ever prevail against that.

Dear Monsieur l'Abbé, these are not just ready-made formulas coming from my pen. It is the expression of my innermost certitude, welling up, so to speak, from the heart of my soul. I do not want to put any shade of reproach in it; but, once again, my friendship is too strong to accommodate reticence. Yes, it is with all my heart that I will continue to pray for you, as you ask, and for those who are around you. I want to hope, I really do hope, that this spiritual venture will be for you all, in the final analysis, when you feel before God a "cor contritum et humiliatum" in forsaken distress, the mysterious point of departure for a very high ascent. What magnificent fruits would not then be promised you? In that perspective, I repeat, dear Monsieur l'Abbé, my faithful affection in Xto Jesu.

Preface to the 1985 reprinting.

This book has earned the author much praise and much criticism, one as unmerited as the other. Some have thought that it was written after the summer of 1950, following the encyclical *Humani generis*. Which explains the congratulations of some for an "exemplary submission", the reprobation of some others for a rather undignified "about-face". If, however, that encyclical had anything to do with the matter, it was not for having given rise to the work: on the contrary, as the foreword of the first edition and then the note to the second edition adequately indicated, it was for having delayed publication a bit. The book was written entirely between the years 1945 and 1950, with a view to rekindling, most especially in the souls of young priests, an authentic sense of the Church that, following the turbulent years of the Second World War, risked being blunted. Each of the nine chapters that comprise it had been given orally on priest's recollection days, and the whole of them, in the same order in which they were gathered together, had been the subject of conferences given several days in a row on the premises of one of our major seminaries. Of course—as M. Etienne Gilson has remarked—even if an author is unconcerned about stylistic niceties, he is incapable of rereading at a distance without making some little corrections: the delay thus gave rise to a few brief reflections here and there at the last minute. But if the author was unable to ignore one of those abrupt storms that come sometimes to shake the apparently restricted universe of theology, he has nonetheless never experienced for all that the need to change the course of his frail barque, nor has Holy Church, our mother in everything, ever asked him to do so, despite the legends that soon spread. Henri card. de Lubac, S.J., January 25, 1985, on the Feast of the Conversion of Saint Paul.

Review of Father Baumgartner (Enghien, June 23, 1952):

"In the Foreword, the author explains the nature of his work and the fruit he hopes from it, especially with regard to priests. The chapters of this work are not really scientifically established theses; they in no way intend to constitute a treatise *De Ecclesia* or even a summary of such a treatise. They are doctrinal meditations on several essential aspects of the mystery of the Church such as God created her and such too as she appears to us in the world of today. Reflections fully traditional, lucid, tirelessly leading the gaze of contemplation to the essential, nourishing and, in the Pauline sense of the word, edifying.

"The author's hope will not be disappointed. These pages will do much good for the priests who read them as well as for educated laypeople. Many, particularly among the young, are uneasy, troubled, anguished. What they lack is not faith but a certain fullness and depth of knowledge of the faith. Contact with the thought of the author will help them exceedingly to find or rediscover, in the midst of their difficulties, a healthy theology of the Church; their apostolic zeal will come away not only more ardent but purified. Even more, perhaps, readers will let themselves be won over by and drawn into the deep affection for the *Ecclesia Mater*, which is at once virile and delicate, as well as by the spirit of authentic obedience to which many of these pages give discreet witness. There will be many readers, priests or not, who will not resist this witness.

"To grasp the spirit in which this work was written, it is enough to read the beautiful chapter on the *Ecclesia Mater*. The author traces in it a portrait of the *homo ecclesiasticus*, the man of the Church. I confine myself to picking out a few characteristics of this description, remarkable for its fullness, equilibrium and fineness. Scripture, Tradition, Magisterium: that is the threefold and unique channel through which the Word of God comes to the man of the Church. His education is acquired in contact with his Fathers in the faith and with the great doctors of the Church; not for his own enjoyment, but in order to serve. No esoterism. The man of the Church is not only obedient, he loves obedience. And his filial piety, his gratitude and his love go to the hierarchical Church of today and, in the first place, to the Church of Rome. His heart overflows with praises for the *Ecclesia Mater*, at whose knees he has learned everything. —All these features are found from one end of the work to the other. It is the work of a man of the Church. —I do not see what could stand in the way of the publication of this writing. Everything, on the contrary, recommends that this witness, of so high and pure a quality, become the common good of all priests and educated laypeople. They will find in it an aid in overcoming their temptations with regard to the Church in the most ardent and pure filial attachment."

One gets the feeling that the reviewer wanted, so to speak, to wrench a positive opinion from the Roman censors. Yet he wrote the same day to my Provincial: "As I did not have any remark to make of any importance with respect to corrections to be made, and so forth, I did not do so; so my judgment is not only favorable but very laudatory, perhaps too much so. Not that I do not believe what I wrote or that I wanted to please the author, but I wonder if, in the end, it is very clever. (Given the mentality of the censors in Rome, are they not going to be dead-set, by way of reaction, to seek out some little thing?) I am thus disposed to modify or tone down my text, in view of the result to be obtained. For I consider it *absolutely* necessary that this book appear. I would be truly disappointed and irritated if its publication were prevented. . . . Everything is possible given that most of the time one makes the author say other things, even the contrary of what he asserts. . . ."

[*4:40*]

I have just discovered this letter: Milano, 18 aprile 1962.

Reverendissimo Padre, ricevo, con mio grande piacere, il suo nuovo libro, e Le sono molto grato d'avermene fatto omaggio con una dedica autografa, che ne accresce il valore per me. Legge sempre con molte interesse, e spero anche con profitto, i Suoi libri, sebbene gli obblighi del mio ministero non mi concedano molto tempo per la lettura e assai poco per lo studio. Vedro volontieri anche suo volume sul pensioro religioso del Padre Pierre Teilhard de Chardin, sul quale finora io ho sentito far più critiche, che elogi; penso tuttavia che sia uomo di grande talento e che meriti d'essere conosciuto e apprezzato negli aspetti positivi e moderni delle sue vedute scientifiche e delle sue aspiraziono religiose. La ringrazio pertanto dell' aiuto e del diletto, che certamente avro leggendo le Sue pagine.

Dio La benedica per il sapere e per l'esempio, ch'Ella dà alla Chiesa di Dio. —Accolga i miei auguri pasquali e mi creda—Suo devotissimo in Xto.

[Most Reverend Father, I receive with great delight your new book, and I am very grateful to you for having given me the honor of an autographed dedication, which increases the book's value for me. I always read with great interest, and I hope also with profit, your books, even if the obligations of my ministry don't concede me much time for reading and even less for study. I will also see gladly your volume on the religious thought of Fr. Pierre Teilhard de Chardin, about whom I have up to now heard far more criticism than praise; nevertheless I think he is a man of great talent who deserves to be known and appreciated in the positive and modern aspects of his scientific insights and of their religious concerns. I thank you again for the help and pleasure that I will certainly have reading your pages. God bless you for the wisdom and for the example that you give to the Church of God. Accept my Easter best wishes and believe me to be—Your most devoted in Christ.]

+ GB. CARD. MONTINI, ARCIVESCOVO

By this book, I cut myself off from a whole world of intellectuals who did not like to converse with a priest judged to be so precisely "clerical". I knew it and wanted it. I thereby, with one stroke, removed any ambiguities; but, by the same stroke, I shut myself off from some apostolic opportunities. Given the false situation to which I had been reduced, the good of the former of these two effects outweighed the evil of the latter. Those who had created (in good faith) this false situation could not feel any gratitude for my decision. But it was not for them that I acted. "If I wanted to please men. . . ." I love the Church of Christ, I believe in her divine mission, and I needed to say so. (1954).

In my *Méditation*, I wrote of the Church: "Clearsighted Mother, whatever the shadows the Adversary does his best to spread, she cannot fail to recognize one day as her own the children she has borne, she will have the power to rejoice in their love, and they will find security in her arms." Whoever in the Church has even marginal literacy cannot fail to recognize in this passage an allusion, though inverted, to the celebrated preoration of the sermon at Saint Mary's, in which Newman bade his sad farewell to the Anglican Church. Everyone, in any case, can easily discern in these words, beyond any flattery or sentimentality, my humble and confident supplication to my Mother, who declared me her secret enemy and about whom I proclaim with assurance that she will not persist in her judgment. —But no one, among those who for me represent her in a practical way, gave me the least sign that he had heard this appeal. Perhaps no one even noticed it, even read it—except here and there someone who might have been all the more irritated with me. I keep my basic confidence, but it is all infinitely sad. (1954).

A propos of the encyclical "Humani generis". It, like many other ecclesiastical documents, seems to me to be very unilateral; that did not surprise me: it is almost a law of the genre. But I read nothing in it that affected me. It is even curious to note that the only phrase that brings up the question of the supernatural and wishes to recall the true doctrine on this subject reproduced exactly what I had written about it two years earlier in "Le Mystère du surnaturel".[8] I could therefore presume with some likelihood that this sentence had been written or altered at the last moment by some-

[8] In *Recherches de science religieuse*, 35 (1949), 80–121.

one familiar with my article and favorable toward me; in any case, the encyclical keeps from pronouncing the words "pure nature", which was like the war-cry of my assailants.

I never received by name the least blame nor was I made the object of the least official measure, outside my Order, by any ecclesiastical authority whatever. My Superior General (the only official person with whom I discussed these things in Rome) assured me one day that, since my name in no way figured either in the Church documents or in his own, I was not obliged to take anything as concerning me (it is true that he had not always spoken or written thus). Later he even wrote to me that I had been the "victim" of "misunderstandings". I have never retracted anything, no one has ever demanded such a thing of me, and I have in fact always thought that I had nothing to retract. For some years I suspended my courses, because my Superior General ordered me to (later he was to specify that this had been on his part a simple "counsel of prudence"), but the Theology Faculty at Lyons said I was "on leave", and every year I was supposed to choose my "substitute". When, *motu proprio*, with the consent of my Superiors, I proposed to my dean that I resume teaching, the Congregation of Seminaries and Universities in Rome, when officially consulted, replied that I had no need of any authorization for that, considering the fact that I had never been the object of a measure to the contrary.

On the other hand, and as if by an irony of fate, two of the theologians who had done the most to obtain a condemnation were actually themselves affected by the encyclical (although without onerous consequences): the long treatise *De Deo creante*, by one of them, which was almost law in the teaching of many seminaries, was withdrawn. The other, perfectly aware of his misadventure, considered the passage aimed at his doctrine to be some kind of misappropriation, which he immediately strove to remedy (for which I could not blame him).

To a young American priest who had written to me of his confusion following all he had read and heard about this encyclical and its consequences, I replied on October 16, 1950: ". . . Remember this: from the day a text is published by the ecclesiastical authorities, it escapes from those who, in one way or another, may have contributed to its preparation; it escapes their particular mentality, their passions, their tendencies, their implications, their systematic views, in order to say no longer anything but what it says and to offer itself in that way to our filial adhesion."

APPENDIX V

[5:1]

The objections against the book were also inspired by the entirely mistaken but tenacious conviction that the establishment of *Sources chrétiennes* (falsely attributed, moreover, to my initiative) was an instrument of warfare against classical, more particularly Thomistic, philosophy and theology, under the pretext of a "return to the Fathers". —See, for example, the conclusion of an article by Father M. Corvez, in the *Revue thomiste* of 1948, p. 524: "We well understand that one might wish to lead us back to the Fathers if it is above all to nourish our spiritual life through them, but we refuse to find in this return to the sources any occasion for a renunciation, however discreet, of the definitive acquisitions of metaphysical science as it relates to God." Saint Anselm, Saint Thomas, Saint Bonaventure. . . , however, were cited with honor, but my critic seemed to have seen only Saint Gregory of Nyssa, Saint Hilary and Saint Augustine; and he reproached me for a mythical exclusivism, in the name of an inverse exclusivism that was all too real. Cf. the explanations given by my "Postface" to *Chemins de Dieu*, pp. 241–57.

Among other objections made to the little book *De la connaissance de Dieu*, I will note the accusation of "fideism", because it gave rise to a regular denunciation that had repercussions in our Lyons Faculty. The following letter, which I addressed to our Rector, on November 16, 1946, preserves the memory of this:

"Monsignor Rector, I owe an explanation to you and, through you, to His Eminence, our Cardinal Chancellor and to all the Bishop Protectors of our Catholic University. This explanation will be simple. It causes me no difficulty, thanks be to God.

"His Excellency, the Bishop of Annecy, shared the day before yesterday with the Assembly of our patron Bishops his uneasiness about my doctrine. (He himself recounted this in public shortly afterward.) The particular point that seemed reprehensible to him was the affirmation that 'in principle, the knowledge of God can only be *revealed*'.

"That is simply the question of a wholly material misapprehension. The immediate context of the page on which this affirmation is found (*De la connaissance de Dieu*, page 11) clearly proves that it has no connection at all with any 'fideism' or any 'ontologism' whatever. I will quote here only the sentence that immediately follows: 'Which is to say, there is in our humble reason something of the sacred'. And everything that follows, like everything that precedes, explains this with a clarity that it seems to me no reader will contest.

"Much more, this very affirmation is only a translation into French of what has been said many times, in Greek and in Latin, by the Fathers and the Doctors of the Church. If the truth that it expresses is sometimes left in shadows, it is nonetheless a traditional truth that could not be denied without going contrary to a teaching current in the Church from the earliest centuries.

"Certainly, I will not insult the Bishop of Annecy by believing him to be the author of the misconception that alone can motivate any uneasiness here. But perhaps he placed his trust too quickly in the religious who, he says, denounced me to him. And of course I do not claim infallibility any more than any other member of the faithful. But perhaps one could do me the honor of thinking that, if I should happen to be mistaken in a doctrinal matter, it will be through an error that is a little more subtle than the gross error attributed to me; or, if this is not accorded to me personally, it might be accorded at least to the theologians of my Order who were my censors.

"I am ready to offer further information, if you judge it useful, and am happy that this occasion allows me to express once again, Monsignor Rector, my feelings of profound and affectionate respect for you and my entire devotion to our Faculties."

[5:2]

"I have recently been accused of some sort of opposition to the acceptance of scientific exegesis in the Church and, by the same token, to the works of my colleagues and to the spirit of our Faculty. This rumor, although absurd, has become persistent, it has spread quite far, enough for me to see myself obliged to combat it. I thus find myself, as I am well aware, in the most ridiculous position: that of the man who must defend himself from having denigrated the very thing of which all those who know him well know that he was always the warmest supporter.

"In fact, without wishing to grant myself an award as a propagandist, I believe I can surely say that none of us has ever done more to proclaim, *urbi et orbi*, the praises of our Lyons school. For a long time now, for example, I have repeatedly said everywhere that M. Podechard, the glory of our Faculty, is not only the foremost exegete in France but probably in the entire Church; that the students who have a thorough knowledge of his courses have an inestimable treasure in their hands; that nothing would be more desirable than a change of atmosphere that would allow the integral publication of his works. I extol M. Vaganay, not as a master, but as *the* master of textual criticism; every year I strive to have my young fellow theologians read and put into practice his little introductory book. My feeling of friendship for M. Chaine is equaled by a great admiration for his courage in sustaining the cause of scientific work in the Church, and no one is more desirous than I to see his work on Genesis completed, particularly since the day I had the opportunity to attend a few of his lectures and after the occasions when I had to defend him ardently against certain rather poorly enlightened critics. Ever since M. Gelin began his teaching among us, I have always urged that he be discharged from any other obligation, stressing that he needed time in order to bring to a successful conclusion the works of exegesis from which I expected much and which would successfully carry on the biblical traditions of the Faculty. How many people would be able to testify to the praise I have given in front of them to all the works coming from Lyons and to recall the comparisons I had occasion to institute on that subject, comparisons that were not at all in favor of certain other centers . . .!

"In all that, my zeal was even a little naïve, a little excessive, perhaps, as happens with those who are not completely one of the group. It was not inspired solely by affection, personal admiration or esprit de corps. It was the fruit of decided conviction, one that has never varied. When, in my courses in apologetics, I had to treat questions relating somewhat at length to the Bible, I was anxious to get the opinion of one of my specialist colleagues and at times to submit to him the details of my text. Since the beginning of my theological studies, I have not ceased to educate myself through series such as the *Revue biblique* and the *Etudes bibliques*. Very often I have been heard to say that the Pope should make Father Lagrange a cardinal, that this gesture would have a great symbolic importance and would have a marvelous effect as a stimulus. My tendencies were so well known among us on this matter that, when it was a question, at the invitation of Cardinal Tisserant, of publishing the study of Father Condamin on Isaiah, it was naturally to me that they addressed themselves; I worked on it for several months, aided by the technical advice of Father Lyonnet, and if the publication was not accomplished, it was not my fault!

"Under these conditions, and since my feelings and my attitude have never changed, you can imagine how strange it seems to me to have to defend myself today for oppositions, denigrations or even simply for a lack of solidarity or an overly pronounced adverse tendency! Once again, I feel how ridiculous such a display of my sentiments is, and nothing less than my pressing desire to undeceive colleagues and masters whom I love and of whom I am proud would make me consent to this lack of modesty.

"I know besides that they themselves are the first not to want a kind of conformism that would be the death of all higher education and of all thought; that, committing themselves both to orthodoxy and to perfect courtesy among ourselves, they are anxious, as I am, that each one work and express himself in complete freedom, without that freedom ever being interpreted as an opposition made to anything whatever. It is in this spirit that I confide to them the additional explanations that follow.

"The occasion that gave shape to the absurd rumor of which I have spoken was an introduction that I published last year to Origen's homilies on Genesis. In that regard, I will simply note:

"1. That this is not a biblical study but a patristic one, in which my entire goal was to grasp the true thought of Origen, to show in particular that he neglected or denied the letter of the Scriptures much less than many historians say; a thesis for which I have the satisfaction of taking sides with Lagrange and Prat, who are, moreover, exegetes of some weight;

"2. that I do not at all accept responsibility for Origen's theories and processes; although this should be self-evident, I took care to warn the reader of it from the very first page and to come back to it once again at the end, in the most formal manner;

"3. that I have never treated this question of the 'spiritual sense' of Scripture personally, either in my courses or in writing.

"In addition, research into the spiritual sense seems to be perfectly compatible with the most strictly critical exegesis; the latter is the work of science, while the other is exercised from within the faith and through all other ways. There are many ways of understanding it, not all of which are equally successful; those are questions of theology that are debatable and that theologians have perhaps abandoned too much. But no more than one would be right, in the name of an interest taken in the 'spiritual sense', in denigrating or systematically neglecting scientific exegesis is there reason in the name of the latter to set oneself in opposition to the former. It is a fact that some very expert critics are sometimes also profoundly spiritual; it is equally a fact that the circles (Catholic or Protestant) least willing to accept criticism are often also the least open, the most opposed to any spiritual interpretation.

"I am perfectly well aware, moreover, that certain partisans of this 'spiritual sense' have said some silly things about me; but I do not see why I should be made answerable for it in the least; I am responsible only for what I say and write. Many theologians have also said silly things: are we going to condemn all theology? Many so-called critical exegetes have created a false science, some have lost their faith in it; are we, for all that, going to reject all exegesis, all criticism, and suspect our scholars?

"I believe that the silly things in question are in part at least the fruit of deficiency, not in exegetes as such, but rather in theologians. In the younger generations there is evidence of a more ardent taste for the Bible, considered as nourishment for the soul; but there is also some naïveté, lack of moderation, indeed, some deviations. If we understand the new aspirations and if we strive to sympathize with what is right in them, we will be better able to direct them and to straighten them out when necessary. I do not pretend to have done it, but this simple acknowledgment prevents me from adopting a simplistic attitude of sulkiness, condemnation or scorn toward anyone feeling his way today in this domain. I believe that there are serious studies to be made there. Instead of opposing, I would like to work, however little I can, to unite. It seems to me that in this, I am only conforming to what has been asked of us by Leo XII, Benedict XV, Pius XI and also Pius XII."

[5:3]

On December 6, 1954, I wrote from Nice to Father Charles Nicolet: "Abbé Steinmann has sent me a long letter; he tells me that he along with the whole Port-Royal party felt that the choice of Father Daniélou, a Jesuit, to celebrate Easter at Saint-Etienne du Mont was an offense. His letter was hard for the Society. I replied to him with a defense that is going to set me at odds with him, without of course earning me any gratitude from the Society. . . ." Abbé Steinmann did not hold it against me.

[5:4]

In 1975 Father André Ravier gave me some more detailed information on this old history. In the course of his proceedings in Rome, when he was the Provincial of Lyons, he was forced to acknowledge the impossibility of any exchange of view with regard to me with Father Janssens, who seemed "blocked". Out of conscience, he therefore decided to address the supreme authority directly. But those most inclined to introduce him hesitated, either from fear of compromising themselves, fear of antagonizing Pius XII through an untimely step and of provoking a conflict with the Society of Jesus, or the conviction that they would fail because the Pope would ascertain that the Father General, the normal intermediary, had refused to intervene and must have had his reasons for that. At the

Secretariate of State, Msgr. Veuillot hesitated to introduce Father Ravier to Msgr. Montini. Finally approached and at first favorable, the latter hesitated to deliver to the Pope the copies (bound in white) that Father Ravier had had delivered to him for that purpose and in the end backed out, having been assured that the General Curia refused to support this initiative of my Provincial. Father Bea, the Pope's confessor, was then approached. He too hesitated, then promised, then delayed, then drew back: he did not think he could take so unusual a step, especially since there was a personal opposition, known in Rome, and much despite themselves, between himself and Father Janssens, since the election of the latter to the Generalate when Pius XII had discreetly let it be known that Father Bea was his desired candidate. Pius XII, moreover, obviously had to be aware that there was some relentless opposition to me in the Holy Office and in the Society, and how could he disregard that? If Father Bea's action failed, my situation would be worse. —Finally, Father Ravier's tenacity won out. Prompted by his great kindness, Father Bea at last let himself be convinced. —But it all came down to a private action that changed nothing about the situation; the Pope did not want to send an official letter in thanks for an homage that had not come to him "through official channels", and the Society declared that it wished to know nothing about it.

[*5:5*]

MAY 27, 1959, MY VERY REVEREND FATHER GENERAL, P. XTI!

I do not wish to overburden Your Paternity with correspondence, but there is a serious case of conscience that obliges me to write to you again.

The Dean of my Faculty needs to have before June 8 my final instructions for the course that I should teach beginning in October. Your Paternity knows that the authorities of the Church place no restrictions on my activity as a professor. Yet, the letters and censures received from Your Paternity for nine years continue to impede me. How am I to commit myself to my Faculty unless I know that it will simply be possible for me to face the responsibilities of my charge in conformity with the demands of the Society. Now I would be reluctant to hand on a doctrine that Your Paternity judged bad: not because I would be troubled in my faith about it, but because I would not feel myself to be entirely in obedience; nor could I devote myself to teaching or respond to consultations when I knew in advance that the public expression of this would be forbidden me, for that would place me under the reproach of esoterism.

This is why I have recourse to Your Paternity to ask you if you still consider me as afflicted with an incurable heterodoxy, if you still judge that it would be better for me to leave aside all question of theology, and if I must not understand the numerous censures coming from Rome, with their grounds, to be a desire to discourage me from all publication in matters of doctrine.

I do not mean this simple question to be either a complaint or a request for a change. I merely seek some light to guide me in the reply I must make to my Dean, and whatever the decision of Your Paternity in my regard, I can assure you, as in the past, of my filial obedience.

I am, my Very Reverend Father General, in union with you at Holy Mass,

ADM. REV. VESTRAE SERVUS ET FILIUS IN CHRISTO

P.S. Your Paternity spoke to me recently of a "misunderstanding" between us. For my part, I have always opened my soul to Y.P., addressing myself to you as to a father, according to the spirit of the Institute. In the entire measure allowed me by obedience and respect, I have endeavored to tell you the precise truth, and I have not hidden from you that fact that, for me, a lie remains a lie, whatever success it might obtain. If an investigation had ever been made, the verifications on the essential points, moreover, would have been easy.

[5:6]

For a little more accuracy, here are a few rediscovered dates. December 21, 1956, Cardinal Gerlier received from Rome a letter authorizing him to let me give *ad experimentum* a few discreet conferences, outside the body of the Theology Faculty, on "Hinduism or Buddhism". In March 1958, the Father General received me in Rome with kindness but remained inflexible about his interdictions. In June, Msgr. Jouassard, Dean, wrote to me on return from a trip to Rome that he had found a very "complex" situation there and that the intransigence in my regard came from within the Society. In December, Cardinal Gerlier reported from Rome a verbal approval of the resumption of my courses. But new complications arose. My Faculty could rightly fear some problems if it did not receive an official approval, and it judged, not without reason, that it was not up to it but to the authority of the Society to seek the approval. From which arose a series of exchanges and discussions, of which I heard rumors from one side and another. In fact, it was only in the first semester of the 1959–1960 year that I resumed a few hours of classes. On March 1, 1960, the final class. I am passing over many details, for this is not the place to recount them.

From the Gregorian, at Rome, Father Chaillet wrote to me on May 16, 1937: "Thank Father Fontoynont very much. . . . But I would be happy to know if he is considering the publication of the *Greek text*; in this case, by whom will it be established? . . . I am waiting for additional information before setting sail from here." And from Istanbul, July 10: "I am taking advantage of these very interesting voyages to study the situation of the separated Churches a little. . . . I told Father Fontoynont that the Hausherr feeler was very encouraging." The main thing Father Chaillet, in 1938, expected from his study of Moehler was "the knowledge and love of the Fathers of the early Church". —A provisional statute for the *Sources* series was adopted on July 21, 1941, which ended in this way: "A definitive statute will be drafted according to the direction of Superiors and will be presented to them when the conditions of life have become more normal." —These *Sources chrétiennes* were not exactly what their founders had at first dreamed of: books done by good specialists but always conscious of belonging to one and the same Tradition, in order to nourish the faith of new generations: books that were easy to use, of an accessible price; something similar but more critical than the "Library of the Fathers" that Pusey completed with Newman's *Lives of the English Saints*. But the evolution was inevitable and undoubtedly should not be regretted.

I had the opportunity to express my feelings about the study of the Fathers of the Church in a preface to the collection of texts published by Father Quéré-Jaulmes and A. Hamman, *Les Chemins vers Dieu* (Centurion, 1967):

The surprising fecundity of the Fathers of the Church! The surprising timeliness! More than one reader will undoubtedly be surprised by this last statement; he will object that these old authors have become unreadable; that the world in which they lived is no longer ours; that if they once brilliantly held the role that earned them their beautiful title of Fathers, it is attempting the impossible to try to make them live again today. . . . But perhaps one is in too much of a hurry to make a judgment of that kind. The timeliness of the Fathers of the Church is not a superficial timeliness, and it is true that it does not blaze forth or will ever blaze forth before all eyes. But it is a *fructifying* timeliness.

Every time, in our West, that Christian renewal has flourished, in the order of thought as in that of life (and the two orders are always connected), it has flourished under the sign of the Fathers. All centuries give witness to it—the history of it would be a long one to retrace—and the law is again verified in our own. Someone like Moehler or Newman is perhaps already too old a witness; but how many others since then! Claudel, one will say, is only a poet: let us admit that, although there is in this poet, thanks to his knowledge of the Fathers, much more doctrinal substance than one might think; but let one look into the work of theologians such as Karl Rahner or Hans Urs von Balthasar. They cannot be denied technical character, depth of thought or penetration of the most lively problems of our age. Now they were nourished on the Fathers of the Church. It is impossible to separate Karl Rahner from Hugo, the great specialist in patristics, whose younger brother rendered their collaboration the most touching homage. As for von Balthasar, none of his numerous, very diverse writings fails to show him to have been formed in the school of the great ancients. It was more than a familiarity that he acquired with them: it was a kind of connaturality, and without any archaism, through the freest processes; it was in their way that he sought to tap all the contributions of our culture in order to convert them and make them bear fruit in Christ.

The Fathers of the Church: a whole universe, and how much variety! Let us not evoke here those of the earliest Christian generations, those first links that bind us forever to the testimony of the Apostles of Christ. For this reason, they are particularly dear to us—but their fruitfulness is more hidden: "We rarely speculate," they seem to say to us through the voice of one of them, "but we live!" They show us "the power of the Gospel" at work. Nor let us say anything of Saint Augustine: better and better explored by the professionals, this giant suffers an eclipse today in a certain average opinion; only one aspect, and even that deformed, of his exceptionally rich personality is any longer considered, and then only in order to reject it. But here are the Greek Fathers of the great era. They are more present to us than it seems. Directly or through intermediaries, someone like Teilhard de Chardin owes them much. And from the pen of Abbé Monchanin, that contemplative apostle for penetrating understanding, who is ahead of his contemporaries in his questioning rather than in need of making their questioning his own, we also read, in a letter coming from the depths of Tamil, India, with respect to Origen and Gregory of Nyssa: "This theology, this philosophy, this mysticism is so congenital to me that it seems to me that it comes from myself. It is the only form (except for the details) in which I can think of Christianity. I cannot manage to persuade myself that the Indian form of Christian thought (that at least for which I have been able to begin a formulation) might differ essentially from it. . . ."

But rather than multiply examples, it would be better to cast a glance at the great conciliar *aggiornamento*: the true one, the one whose roots are at the basis of the promulgated texts, the one that is accomplished at first in depth, in a renewed faith—not the foam that is splashing around all over. In a very large part, in all the sectors touched by the Council, this *aggiornamento* was made possible by the patristic renewal of the last fifty years. So it was not at all an artificial or secondary subject that was treated, in December 1965, in Rome itself, just at the end of the Council, by Msgr. Pellegrino, the new Archbishop of Turin, in a conference at Saint-Louis-des-Français: "Vatican II and the Fathers of the Church".

Rather than multiply texts and give us "extracts" cut to excess, the authors of this collection were right to retain only a limited number of passages, long enough to allow us to follow, with some of our Fathers, the progress of the mind in search of God. So, for example, with his customary meandering, Clement of Alexandria leads us, starting with the sages of Greece and through the believers of Israel, up to the revelation of the Gospel. Commenting on the march of the Hebrews across the desert, Origen describes for us the interior stages that we must pass through in order to arrive at the threshold of the Promised Land. Gregory of Nyssa takes us by the hand to lead us, like the betrothed in the Song of Songs, to the encounter with the Bridegroom. John Chrysostom reminds us vigorously of the doctrine of the incomprehensible God in order to show us his manifestation in Jesus. The Pseudo-Marcarius, that extraordinary spiritual man, teaches us to seek God with fervor, to wait for him with patience. Hilary of Poitiers shares his own itinerary with candor. Augustine, harassed by that question posed to him by the pagan: "Where is your God?" and burning like the deer with thirst for running waters, leads us with him on his incessant course. Gregory the Great, so misunderstood, so truly great, comments with subtle depth, as if in a painting by an intimist master, on the Emmaus account and unfolds before us like an immense Oriental carpet the magnificent things concealed in the inaugural vision of Ezekiel.

None of these masters dispenses us from seeking and, in the full measure in which we think we have found, to seek again. All, on the contrary, like Origen exploiting the marvelous symbol of the wells of the Patriarchs, which the Philistines never ceased to obstruct, all teach us to hollow out new depths in ourselves, to dig ever deeper and to "drink the water from our wells". They do not dictate our solutions to us. They do not dispense us from reflecting: they stimulate us. They prepare in us the movement that must not be stopped. They initiate us to a faith that frees us as much as it engages us. We said it in the beginning: "Their timeliness is a fructifying timeliness".

APPENDIX VI

[6:1]

I made (I no longer remember where) this brief review of these two works:

All Parisian intellectuals—and many others—are well familiar with the CCIF (Centre Catholique des Intellectuels Français [Catholic Center of French Intellectuals]) and its manifold activities. In its early years, it was called the University Catholic Center. Father de Montcheuil was one of its founders in 1941. He gave there, during the last three winters of the German occupation, three series of lectures, on Christ, on the Church and on the Sacraments. The first two series are finally appearing here in published form. These two little works are not popular works: if their language is always simple, avoiding technicalities, theologians themselves will nevertheless find material in them for reflection. They are *elementary* works, which is to say, *essential*. They contain lofty, strong doctrine. There is nothing in these lessons that seeks to shine or to please but rather a fine, personal touch that is vigorous and ardent. Nor is there any effort toward a surface adaptation that would already be out of date. Father de Montcheuil quite simply hands on, as a believer and a thinker, the truth received from Christ and transmitted by his Church, about Christ and about his Church. A twofold subject that is but one. A subject about which we need ever and again to be taught. Once again, there is nothing more essential. And in that, nothing of greater timeliness. Something of Father de Montcheuil's great soul passes again through these two little books. They will continue his work among us. May they enlighten, restore peace of mind, reaffirm in their faith, in their love of Christ and in their confidence toward his Church those who, today, might have need of it! May they establish us all a little more in this Mystery of Christ, outside of which there are only shadows and death for us!

[6:2]

March 10, 1948, Maurice Blondel would write to me from Aix: "How many times I have wanted to thank you for the fine discoveries I have made in the posthumous works of the admirable Father de Montcheuil! How grateful I am to you for having acquainted me with the penetration and the tenacity of his commentaries on my thought, on which he reflected with so much perseverance and progressive understanding. I am happy to tell you that his first interpretations have in the end helped me to understand more myself about the philosophy of action and also with the two books on which I am trying to work in the moments when I can still dictate."

And on November 19: "I have been extremely encouraged by the rereading I have done of Father de Montcheuil."

See also below (Appendix 9:5, pp. 377–78) the letter he wrote to me on December 19, 1946, after having examined, in the posthumous *Mélanges théologiques* of Father de Montcheuil, the study on "Les Problèmes du *Vinculum* leibnizien d'après M. Blondel", which appeared first in February 1931 in *Revue apologétique*.

[*6:3*]

I wrote from Nice to Father Charles Nicolet, on February 16, 1955:

". . . Poor Auguste suffered, in all ways, more than I would have believed. He was so much more deeply 'committed' at the time than those who, knowing nothing, speak of his aestheticism! A strength of will and supernatural courage of the first order were necessary for him in order to begin again, on several occasions, a life unbearably broken. And he knew what it was to practice obedience heroically. . . . There are human documents there of immense value—but permission will never be given for them to be publicly known. . . ."

And again, on March 3: ". . . The figure of Father Auguste is still my principal subject of meditation. I am very afraid that I will never be able to publish the biography-collection about him that would be indispensable. Times are hard in the Church, definitively hard, for whoever has concern for the truth, at however slight a depth. Even the most virtuous, the most loving dispositions cannot, I suppose, take away the bitter taste in that. . . ."

Father Teilhard de Chardin had written on October 12, 1921:

"We have exchanged many ideas, Auguste Valensin and I. We have spoken with an absolute frankness, and it has been a true comfort to me to be able to be completely natural with someone I know to be perfectly believing. In the long run, if forced to remain in contact with people with whom one must continually transpose one's thought, one ends by having the impression of being a stranger in one's own religion. Conversations like those I had in Lyons dispelled that impression."

". . . Father Auguste Valensin had, as we know, a singularly acute mind. People will gradually become aware of the place he held in the course of the last half-century. But it would be a great mistake to see in him only the intellectual. He was just as much, perhaps even more, a volunteer, a man who acted spontaneously, and this was the secret of the power that radiated from him. Now, with a great burst of will, he had given himself, as a young man, to Jesus Christ, and this love of Jesus Christ was the soul of his life. There was no other source for this love than a precise perception of the Christian faith and life. But if one wants to seek more particular influences, one will find three principal ones: that of his father, a converted Jew, that of Pascal, and finally that of Saint Ignatius and his *Exercises*.

"Father Valensin did not wonder how to understand Christ, how to represent him to himself, how to preach about him. Like all Christian generations have done, he quite simply loved him, he contemplated him in a spirit of faith, such as the Gospel shows him to us, such as the Church gives him to us. . . .

". . . The originality here is only in the depth of the lived sincerity. . . . And if someone is tempted to say that there is much anthropomorphism, sentimentality, subjectivism here? Father Valensin would have shrugged his shoulders. He did not have the scruples of the semi-philosophers or the pretensions of the semi-clever. He was too intelligent not to be simple, beyond subtleties and gnoses; too much a believer not to understand, with Augustine, Bernard and all the Catholic doctors, the benefit of the Incarnation, which confirms the use of human sentiments in the exercise of faith while laying the foundations for this use. He also knew, from Christian and Pascalian science, that the order of persons is infinitely above the order of ideas. —Will one at least say that despite everything there is some individualism here, and that it would be better to learn to find Jesus Christ in the Church and to serve him in our brothers? . . . He would certainly have acquiesced to all that is positive in this twofold remark; he himself said and endeavored (more than once heroically) to practice it. No one will be surprised at not perceiving in him all the human harmonics to which we are generally more sensitive today; each generation has its own, each personality too. That does not prevent the essence of common being. But if one had seemed to want to place personal love addressed to the person of Jesus in competition with insertion into the Church or devotion to men, then, frankly, he would have seen an illusion in this. Of course, he would have replied, all Christians see Christ in the Church and in the neighbor, that is the necessary sign of the authenticity of his love.

But why seem to set one thing up against the other? Am I going to wait to become a hero of charity before having the right to love my Savior? In order to love him in others, is it not beneficial to contemplate him in himself, and precisely in his love of men? What is the Church, finally, if not the Church of Jesus Christ? What would she be to me, if she did not give me Jesus Christ? What example does she give me, if not to love Jesus Christ? So the spiritual dialectic that leads me from Jesus Christ to the Church, then guides me from the Church to Jesus Christ. And if I ever lose the person of Jesus Christ from view, if I cease to have a personal love for Jesus Christ, I would lose everything.

"In the Christian life as in doctrinal reflection, the accents can be varied. There is no need to set up one truth against another, one attitude against another. In his love of Jesus Christ, which I discover in him as in Léonce de Grandmaison, Joseph Huby, Yves de Montcheuil, Pierre Lyonnet—and so many others—Father Auguste Valensin reminds us forcefully of this first truth, that Jesus is the All of Christianity and that there can be no truly lived Christianity without a love for the person of Jesus. His voice can be understood by all. Simple, ardent and pure, it adds to the uninterrupted concert of twenty centuries: *Quantae animae, hodie renovatae, dilexerunt te, Domine Jesus!*"

[6:5]

From a letter I addressed to Father Gaston Fessard on July 23, 1961:

"Publications by or about Blondel produce a predictable effect: from the *Revue thomiste* or "Garrigou"-genre side, they are more or less irritated at not finding justification for so many accusations of modernism; from the other side, a Blondel discovered to be orthodox, whose name can no longer be brandished about as the authority for all sorts of misrepresentations, becomes a contemptible being. . . . So we have gossip and lies, which are at times malicious and for which I end up paying the price. Men will be men. . . ." But it was not a matter of only two extremes. On the whole, these publications of correspondence were well received and considered instructive.

[6:6]

This was the subject of my letter to Msgr. Bruno de Solages, July 15, 1960:

"The Teilhard question preoccupies me more and more. The growing success is becoming dangerous. The group of people who speak of Teilhard is composed almost solely of those who are too worldly, political, incompetent, dogmatic and short-sighted; and they will soon end in imposing a profoundly distorted interpretation on everything. A voice, authoritative from every point of view, should be raised, and strongly. I say 'should' rather than 'must' because I do not want to put indiscreet pressure on you, but you know my desire."

In September, on the advice of Father Stanislas Lyonnet, I wrote to Father René Arnou, in Rome, to ask him if I could try to write a little work about the *Milieu divin*, taking advantage of the offer that Daniel-Rops had made me to publish it in his new series. But the project was premature. The request presented by Father Arnou was rejected, and he indicated that the matter should not be pushed.

[6:7]

Actually, as I see from a letter I recently discovered but of which I had had no memory at all, the Roman reversal was a little less abrupt. Based on the desires manifested by Father Arminjon, I had in fact written, on May 5, 1961, to Father Swain, Vicar General for Father Janssens in Rome, who had already received a request from our French Provincials:

Saint Gervais les Bains, May 5, 1961. To Rev. Father Vicar General of the Society of Jesus:

. . . I cannot be considered a disciple of Father Teilhard, although I owe him a debt of gratitude, and this is undoubtedly why the Provincials have proposed my name. The sole passion of my life is the defense of our faith: those around me knew this well before 1950, and they continue to know it—and that has caused and still causes me to be much ostracized. In the present case, it happens too that I am one of the very rare men who have a good knowledge of both the life and writings of Father Teilhard. That creates an obligation of conscience in me. For—you know this, I think, but perhaps not the degree to which it is true—some adversaries of the Christian faith, after having feared for some years the action exercised by Father T.'s work—the only work that effectively makes inroads into unbelief today—noting the hostility declared by some men of the Church and the silence of others, have decided to adopt it themselves by means of transforming it, through a clever exploitation, into a weapon of war against the Church.

Now, whatever judgment one may make about this work, provided one has some slight knowledge of it as well as a little moderation, one cannot fail to see that such an enterprise (which progresses with far-reaching means) falsifies and distorts it completely. Some polemicists on our side unfortunately encourage this blindly. A work that, properly explained, completed, corrected when necessary, freely and loyally discussed, could be an apologetic weapon of great importance, thereby risks being turned to the profit of unbelief. The confusion in minds, especially in France, is such that the danger is infinitely great.

Aware of this tragic situation, and placed in the circumstances I have described, I have a pressing obligation to try everything possible. I do not know the precise reasons why *Milieu divin* and then *Phénomène humain* were kept from being published earlier; for neither Father Teilhard nor anyone else since his death communicated to me the censures regarding them. But I have enough respect for the government of the Society for one thing to be evident to me: that those reasons, whether to do with timeliness or doctrine, are not identical with the objections—or the praises—that are doing holy Church and souls an immense harm today. Here as in all things, I desire only to act in full accord with the Society. If its government has an incurable distrust of my orthodoxy or of my filial spirit, I have nothing to add. But if it is not completely so, I would dare to ask Your Reverence if the reasons adduced by the Roman censors concerning Father Teilhard could be communicated to me, at least in summary. If I felt unable to accept the essence of it, I would loyally advise your Reverence of this and would renounce the projected work; if the contrary were true, I would undertake that work, though of course submitting it afterward to the regular censors. —Even if the Society thinks it has cause for grievance about something from one of its children, I am sure it cannot consent of its own free will to having the truth in his regard ridiculed and to seeing, as a result of an abstention that would be regarded as encouragement, serious damage done to the Faith.

I am, my Very Reverend Father Vicar, in union with you at Holy Mass, Rev. Vestrae infimus in Christo servus et filius.

The reply, after some delay, asked for explanations, which I supplied. On September 4, I had the two provincial reviews of my book; around the end of January 1962, I was still waiting for the review by the special censor from Rome.

[6:8]

On return from a lightning trip to Rome, on July 9th, the Father Provincial confided to me that the Father General, irritated by this *Monitum*, nevertheless attributed little importance to it; as for the article in *l'Osservatore*, he treated it as "cowardly". Both nonetheless caused a considerable stir (and were to be abusively exploited for a long time by integrist groups). The rumor circulated in Rome that a special issue of the journal *Divinitas* had been prepared against Teilhard and that the Pope, warned, had stopped it. —The Holy Office had wanted to impose secrecy on me; but I was forced either to betray it or to refuse to obey; how, for example, could I break the six contracts already signed with six foreign publishers and make them believe it was because of some purely personal fancy?

[6:9]

Here is the text of these remarks, which my Provincial and Father René Arnou had encouraged me to address to the Father General:

A few remarks on an anonymous article in *l'Osservatore romano* (July 1, 1962):

1. I am not speaking here of the *Monitum* from the Holy Office, an act of the ecclesiastical authority that I accept without discussion. I am, moreover, aware of having succeeded, in my book on Father Teilhard, in giving a first "warning" on many fundamental points, in the very spirit of the *Monitum*—without, for all that, giving over to the adversaries of our Faith (which would be to betray it) a work that might be fruitful for its defense, elucidation and propagation. —I am speaking solely of the anonymous article that appeared in *l'Osservatore*.

2. This article quotes a certain number of Father Teilhard's texts. I do not claim to redeem all of them; I have myself criticized many others.

But the method employed in the article seems to me to lead inevitably to a misapprehension. Father Teilhard's work extends over forty years; it contains numerous essays that correct each other and many that were not intended for publication; it claims to be research and not definitive expression. That makes it easy to undertake any needed correction of it. But the author of the article extracts about fifteen or so sentences from it, without any concern about the context, and, placing them one right after the other, he thinks he is thereby reconstituting an entire thought "sul piano filosofico e religioso", summing up "il 'sistema' scientifico-religioso del Teilhard". Now, even if these sentences, correctly understood, were all blameworthy, that would not signify that Teilhard's contribution as a whole "on the philosophical and religious level" should simply be rejected.

On the other hand, from the beginning, the author of the article rejects on principle what he calls "an unwarranted transposition on the metaphysical and theological level of the terms and concepts of his evolutionist theory". He sees in that a "grave and fundamental" methodological deficiency. It is one thing, however, to criticize mishandling or misuse of a method, and something else entirely to oppose the method in principle; as if that method of transposition were not the very law of thought just as of language, and as if Saint Thomas, in particular, had not constantly practiced it! Now this automatic rejection is in part the cause of the errors of interpretation that follow.

3. On the subject of creation, the author does not give an accurate summary of Father Teilhard's thought. The analysis that we have given of it (pp. 281–89) is more complete and more faithful. Father Teilhard professed explicitly not only the self-sufficiency of God and the full freedom of the creative act but the fact of the creation *ex nihilo*. Now the article gives the contrary impression and places Father Teilhard in formal opposition to the First Vatican Council. —It would have been good, moreover, to point out that Father himself recognized, along with the difficulty of the problem, the insufficiency of some of his explanations.

4. The author quotes one sentence from *Esquisse d'un univers personnel* (*Energie humaine*, p. 86): "God is definable only as a Center of centers. In this complexity lies the perfection of his unity".

He has not seen that, in this paragraph, at this precise moment of a demonstration that proceeds by stages, Father Teilhard is opposed to the pantheistic conception according to which the evolution of the world would culminate in a God conceived as undifferentiated Unity: at the "Summit of the World", he explains, personal beings will on the contrary constitute so many distinct centers, bound together in a personal Center. Having reached this point of his argumentation, Father has still not established the nature and properties of such a Center; he has not even shown if it must be conceived as still virtual or already real. This is what he is going to do, beginning on page 87, where he announces quite clearly: "And now, a final—essential—point remains to be determined so that the End of which Life consists in order to bring us closer together might be entirely defined, in its position and in its nature. . . ." Now, while refraining from bringing forward, through the "limited" process of "Ultraphysics" to which he restricts himself, all the precisions of Metaphysics, he strives to prove at least, with the personality of God, the independent, incomparable consistency of his Being.

The article thus gives as a definitive conclusion, which would be directed more or less against our classical theodicy, what was only a still provisional result, given the factual reality of this world, and directed against an unmistakable error.

5. If one is shocked by these words: "The Christ of Revelation is none

other than the Omega of Evolution", it is undoubtedly because one does not understand them. It would, on the contrary, be shocking if these two realities were said to be "other": as if Christ were not the final cause of the Universe, or as if God had not ordained everything in the world in view of his Son, and so forth.

It is in the same way that we say, for instance: "The trinitarian God is none other than the God who is the Prime Mover" or: "The God of Abraham and Jacob is none other than the God of the philosophers and the learned", and so forth. Which does not signify that there is not more in the idea of the first than in the idea of the second. There is more in our idea of Christ (received by faith) than in the idea of the Omega formed by the sole resources of science and natural reflection: as Father Teilhard himself said many times, without ambiguity.

It is also very difficult to figure out how one might have understood the following sentence in order to judge it to be reprehensible: "In a universe that revealed itself for me as a state of convergence, You have taken by right of Resurrection the master position of the total Center where everything is gathered together". I see in that only the expression of a thought of faith that is not only legitimate but imperative (whether the universe is conceived as evolutionary or not).

6. There is another passage that apparently shocked the author, though he does not tell us why. It is a prayer:

"Jesus, Center toward which everything is moving, deign to make for all of us, if possible, a place among the chosen monads and saints who, redeemed from the present chaos by Your solicitude, are slowly joining You in the unity of the New Earth."

I see nothing that is not in conformity with all dogmatics in this humble and conditional prayer, similar to those made by numerous saints. It presupposes faith in human freedom, in the divine initiative, in the necessity of the grace of Christ, in the eventuality of perdition, in the definitive reality of human persons, in that of the "mystical body", and so forth —all things, moreover, that are also very often called to mind by Father Teilhard.

7. The author again writes: "In *Christique*, there is question quite simply and 'in a true sense' of a 'third nature' of Christ, neither human nor divine, but 'cosmic'."

Certainly, taken literally, this paradoxical expression would be "a veritable heresy". The way in which Father Teilhard introduces it seems sufficient to show that it is not at all to be taken literally. If he says that it entails "a true sense", it is because he recognizes that it could have a false sense. He began by speaking rather of a "third aspect, or function"; then, fearing that these words might be a bit pale, he adds: "or even, in a true sense. . . ."

The phrase is unfortunate, it is useful to challenge it; I am in agreement with the author of the article. But let us recognize, nevertheless, that for Father Teilhard this was merely a striking way of drawing attention to "the dominant place Saint Paul gives to Christ in his vision of the world", a truth he considers too often neglected, even forgotten, despite the vigorous affirmations of Scripture. It does not do him justice only to accuse him of having, at the minimum, "increased the confusion of ideas". And one can wonder which is more serious: to use a forced expression, once and in passing, in order to call an unquestionable truth to mind, or to omit that truth.

Non omnia possumus omnes. Even if he did it awkwardly, Father Teilhard reminded theologians of the ideal of a doctrinal fullness that they must rediscover, and it is their task to work out the exact, clear and precise expression of it.

8. The author quotes a sentence drawn from a rough draft of 1918, which we do not believe Father Teilhard had even had typed, and which many subsequent writings explained and refined:

"Are not Creation, Incarnation, Redemption each marking one more degree in the gratuity of the divine operation, three acts indissolubly bound together in the apparition of participated being?"

One could argue about the second part of this sentence (which, we should remember, was quickly jotted down on paper, at the front, during the 1914 war and was undoubtedly never reread). But in any case one cannot understand it in a way that would ignore the existence of the first part, and this first part absolutely prevents one from suspecting some heterodox meaning in the second.

The same is true for another sentence quoted afterward: "The three fundamental mysteries of Christianity no longer seem anything but, as it were, the three faces of a single mystery, that of the Pleromization"; there is nothing scandalous in that. It is even rather close to the theology of Saint Paul. And the First Vatican Council invites us to seek the link between the mysteries in order to put some unity into the understanding of our faith. Father Teilhard fulfills this task by making use of Saint Paul, in a way that is not imperative (nor indisputable in places); but the author of the article does not demonstrate in what way the principle of the undertaking, such as it is affirmed in this sentence, would be reprehensible.

If one is slightly accustomed to Father Teilhard's language, he will find hardly anything to be corrected in the fact that he once calls the Incarnation "a prodigious biological operation" (cf. my explanations, pp. 227–28).

9. Because Father Teilhard says, for example: "There is not, concretely, matter *and* spirit"; or because he rejects a Spirit "incomprehensibly jux-

taposed with Matter", this does not at all mean that we should conclude that he confuses matter and spirit. In reality, he never ceases to distinguish them. Thus, in *Union créatrice*: "All is held together from above; this principle consecrates above all the royalty of the Spirit . . .", and so forth. He only rejects, and with good reason, a dualism of two concrete principles juxtaposed like two things. A similar misunderstanding would cause one to reproach Thomism for confusing the soul and the body because he speaks of a unique "human composite". Several other expressions of Father Teilhard would be more debatable if they had to be taken in a metaphysical sense; but he warns us of the contrary and, remaining on a phenomenological level, he uses some very strong expressions in order to indicate the originality of the spirit (notably by speaking of a difference "of nature"; cf. the various texts cited in my chapter 8).

It is because he has not taken note of this essential distinction of levels that the author again criticizes this other sentence: "The spiritual phenomenon is not a kind of quick flash of lightning in the night, it reveals a gradual and systematic passage from the unconscious to the conscious, and from the conscious to the self-conscious. It is a change of cosmic state." What the author seems here to take for materialism is, on the contrary, the express refutation of it (or rather, it is the conclusion of a refutation that was first developed in long analyses).[1] And how has he failed to notice that Father Teilhard's thought is moving here on the level of phenomena when the very word figures throughout the whole of it?

10. With respect to original sin, we certainly agree that Father Teilhard has not provided completely satisfactory explanations. But when he writes that in humanity "the collective bonds are revealed to be more real and more profound than any strictly and linearly hereditary connection", it would be a distortion of his thought to conclude from this that he is showing himself to be "opposed to hereditary transmission" and thereby to place him in opposition to the Council of Trent.

11. The text that seems to make the author of the article most indignant is drawn from the first paragraph of an apologetic writing entitled *Comment je crois*. Returned to its proper context, this passage reveals a very natural sense, which could only be approved. Here it is:

"If, as a result of some interior reversal, I came to lose successively my faith in Christ, my faith in a personal God, my faith in the Spirit, it seems to me that I would continue to believe in the World. The World (the value, the infallibility and the goodness of the World) is, in the last

---

[1] It is likewise the same with matter and life. Cf. the summary of Jean Piveteau, preface to *Groupe zoologique humain*, p. XII: "Life is not at all a fortuitous combination of material elements, an accident of world history, but the form that matter takes on a certain level of complexity. It introduces us into a new order. . . ."

analysis, the first and the only thing in which I believe. It is by this faith that I live, and I feel it is to this faith that, at the moment of death, over all the doubts, I will abandon myself. . . . To an obscure faith in a world that is One and infallible, I abandon myself, wherever it may lead me".

We will not deny that the turn of thought printed here by Father Teilhard does not present something subtle and paradoxical. But, once again, *read in their proper place*, these words are very well explained. Under the general title: "*The individual stages of my Faith*" they constitute the first and final words of the first paragraph, entitled: *Faith in the World*. Creating a completely unreal hypothesis ("If, as a result of some interior reversal, I came to lose successively. . ."), and bringing about a movement in the opposite direction from the positive movement he will later achieve through the whole of his work, the apologist begins, so to speak, by making a clean sweep: he thereby places himself on the level of the unbeliever whom he wishes to lead to the Christian faith. He indicates in advance, by enumerating them first in reverse order, the four successive stages of the demonstration he is undertaking to furnish. What he thereby proclaims, from his own perspective, is the most classical process of our natural philosophy and of our apologetic.

In other words, like any honest and serious apologist, Father Teilhard knows very well not to presuppose the very thing he wants to establish. So, in order to begin, he is going to retrace his steps, by leaving out of consideration "successively", through a just concern for method, his faith in Christ—his faith in a personal God—his faith in the Spirit (that is, in the irreversibility, or again, in the immortality of the soul). For none of these three objects is evident by itself. He will therefore ask the unbeliever to grant him only one thing, the most elementary, the most immediate thing, which will serve as a common springboard, in view of the stages he hopes to make him pass through. Then, on the basis of this "fundamental adherence", he will endeavor to reconstruct, before the eyes of this unbeliever, the complete edifice of his own faith. Such a basis seems to him well chosen because, unlike the three other faiths he has distinguished, a certain faith in the World seems imperative to everyone from the beginning; at the very least he discerns it in a number of his contemporaries as also in himself: "Matter could sooner escape gravity than a soul could the presence of the Universe."

Continuing to address himself to his unbelieving reader, he says to him: To this faith in the World, to this first faith that is also yours—faith that is not only elementary but "obscure", faith about which we still do not know what it bears in its womb, so to speak—"I abandon myself, wherever it may lead me". It is an invitation made to his reader to abandon himself to it as he does. Now, where is it going to lead him, "successively"? To faith in the Spirit—to faith in a personal God—finally, to the threshold of faith in God revealing himself in Christ. That, let us repeat, is the whole object of the work. It is solely for that purpose that Father Teilhard took up his pen. These are the essential stages of his apologetical demonstration —which begins immediately.

As we see, the process is very classical—of a classicism underlined by the titles of the successive paragraphs: faith in the Spirit—in Immortality —in Personality, and so forth. (Faith in Christ will be the subject of a second part, conducted differently, because faith in Christ is not generated simply by a rational step taken from the World as its starting point.) It is, in essence, the process Saint Thomas Aquinas uses, going, in the *Summa contra Gentiles*, from truths recognized as natural by the "Gentiles" of his time (in fact, by the Muslim understanding) to those professed by the Christian faith; or, in the *Summa theologica*, going from the world to God (for he rejects the thesis of those who say the existence of God *per se nota*; and consequently he too, in an "interior reversal" of method, begins by leaving out of consideration his own faith in God). It is the process followed by our present teaching. It is that which the Church recommends to us, at least as a general outline.

Of course, following this process, or within its framework, Father Teilhard changes the points of view, and one is free to debate the value of his argumentation: but that is another matter. He proceeds by a process whose more "scientific" character is also, in another respect, more "existential", as one would say today. Where others would speak of a "chain of reason", for example, he speaks of a "psychological axis of spiritual progression toward God". Although, moreover, the personal accent of his writing is undeniable, it would be wrong to believe it to be a kind of subjective confidence. If he speaks there in the first person, it is in the conviction, as he specifies, that "man is essentially the same in everyone". He seeks to cause in some way an experience in the other. That permits him, for example, in recalling the "obscurities", the "shadows of the faith", to communicate the "certitudes" with more warmth. But that also accounts for certain expressions, in the passage quoted, that could at first seem too strong. Does Father Teilhard not say there that the World is, "in the final analysis, the first and the only thing" in which he believes?

There is in fact a certain—but necessary—ambiguity in this passage. It is the ambiguity inherent in all thought that is in motion. For what Father Teilhard is preparing to show the unbeliever is that this World, in which they both believe even before setting out, presupposes many more things than he, the unbeliever, yet sees. He is going to strive to show him that, in good logic, this faith in the world presupposes, in order to appear definitively founded, first of all faith in the Spirit—then faith in a personal

God—and perhaps, finally, even faith in Christ. And this is why he can say already, in language that is necessarily ambiguous because he cannot yet name at this precise moment the realities whose existence he has not yet established, that the World is, "in the final analysis", the first and the only thing in which he believes: "the first", inasmuch as it constitutes the natural basis, the point of departure for all the rest; the only, inasmuch as he discerns all the rest as being implied in it. This is at the same time why he can, at the outset, agree with the unbeliever, for whom this faith in the World is in fact very much, in a more strict sense, in a more restrictive sense, the only one—although he hopes indeed to show him that, as the "first", it is to be followed progressively by three others.

In other words, within this context of "existential" appearance, his basic affirmation returns to the conclusion that the World is intelligible. But he already sees in it all the conditions of its intelligibility, conditions he is waiting to reveal, step by step, to his reader.

Our apologist is perfectly well aware of this inevitable ambiguity in his language. He sees very clearly that "the primordial intuition" that "founds the entire edifice of *his* belief" is at once one and diverse; one in itself, diverse in its considered explanation. It cannot therefore be taken as a pure point of departure from which one does not even yet know if it will be possible to advance farther, or as already pregnant with all that reflection might extract from it. Thus he speaks very justly, with respect to this first faith, of an "obscure" faith, and his very idea of faith, which he defines generically as an "act of intellectual synthesis", is itself analogical. —But one must not stop reading at that point! One must not take the point of departure (very clearly designated as such) to be the point of arrival! It is starting from this that all that is implied by the first "intellectual synthesis" is going to unfold. It is now that everything begins. It is thus everything that follows that will give the key to these first sentences.

Under these conditions, the grieved commentary made about these sentences by the author of the article seems pointless: "Tuttavia leggiamo con vera pena queste righe. . . . Sono parole del 1934, ma quanto sarebbe meglio che non fossero mai state scritte!" [Nevertheless we read with true pain these lines. . . . They are words of 1934, but how much better had they not been written!]

How could one interpret as a confession of quasi-defection, of semi-apostasy, the methodological declaration made at the threshold of a writing completely devoted to leading minds to Christ and one that proves at the very least the apostolic ardor of its author? How did the anonymous author not see that the apologist was expressing himself in the hypothesis of an "interior reversal" as total as it was unreal? And how, finally, did he not sense that such an interpretation, forbidden by the immediate context,

was contradicted besides by countless texts of all periods, in which Father
Teilhard obviously manifests the absolute firmness of his Catholic faith?

12. Please allow me to add a personal word. In indicating, toward the
beginning of his article, certain criticisms that my book addresses to Father Teilhard, the author omits many others and is silent about the most
important. He thus gives a false idea of the book. On the other hand, in
quoting, toward the end, one sentence from this book, he mutilates it in
such a way that the reader might believe I had given my approval almost
without reservation. If one has recourse to the book itself (pp. 293–95,
and many other passages), one will see that this is not so.

LYONS-FOURVIÈRE, JULY 26, 1962

On July 31, I wrote to Father Fessard:

. . . As for me, it is always the Teilhard affair, and I am at the center of the
cyclone. The Holy Office intended to impose secrecy on me, but I was
obliged either to refuse to obey or to betray the secret. How, for example,
could I break six contracts already signed with six foreign publishers and
make them believe that it was because of some purely personal fantasy?

I have received piles of letters; many people have thought me to be much
more upset than I am. (That is because they have absolutely no suspicion
of what I have had to endure for seven or eight years running; next to
that, today is not even a trifle.) I have written down some remarks on the
anonymous article in *l'Osservatore* (which is the visiting card addressed to
me by some of my former colleagues from the theological fire commission) and, on the advice of the Provincial, I have addressed some Remarks
to the Father General (and to Father Arnou). . . .

[*6:10*]

This letter was in no way confidential, and the Father General would certainly not have written in that way if he had not known that the *Monitum*
in question did not correspond to the thinking of the Pope. Only a basic principle of discretion kept me from bringing it forward. There is no
longer anything improper about quoting it today.

[*6:11*]

On April 1, 1968, Abbé Louis Cognet wrote me the following letter in
this regard:

"My very dear Father, . . . Your commentary on the text of Father Teilhard, *l'Eternel Féminin*, is excellent, and, as far as I am concerned, nothing in Fr.'s ideas on this point disturbs me, although the lyrical form of his text is a bit disconcerting for me. I imagine you wanted to reply indirectly to the attacks that have been made on Father's memory in this regard for the last few months. I had a very modest share in it. At the end of vacation, Régis Teilhard de Chardin had sent me an issue of a publication entitled *Le Monde et la vie*, which I hardly knew, which contained a vile article on this subject, in which Father was accused of having been the lover of Léontine Zanta—which, for me, who knew him, is simply ludicrous. Since Régis asked me to send a protest in the name of the family to which I am besides related through the Chazelles, I did so through a letter of which I kept the copy I am sending you, but which that paper has never, I think, published. You can either destroy this copy or do whatever you like with it, there is nothing confidential in it!

"The second part of your book interested me quite particularly. It is very closely connected with my present preoccupations, which, in fact, bring me nearer and nearer to Father Teilhard: the necessity of formulating the eternal principles of Christian spirituality in a way that is valid for a world that knows itself to be in a process of evolution. I am going to try to devote my course next winter to the problem, and your pages will be a great help to me. It seems to me that the wind of insanity that was shaking so many minds in the Church is letting up, but the problems are rather complicated than clarified by all these fantasies against which you have very good reason to protest."[2]

[6:12]

The Father General (Pedro Arrupe) wrote to me, on March 22, 1968:

"I am sure that this book will be received with gratitude by all those who wonder about and desire to be enlightened about some of Father's more difficult writings, like those you present here. —So I thank you for

---

[2] Here is that letter he sent to the editor of *Le Monde et la vie*:
"Juilly, September 18, 1967. Monsieur, the August-September issue of your periodical has been sent on to me by a member of the Teilhard de Chardin family, a family to which my own is related. The book I published in 1952 on Father Teilhard de Chardin, when he was alive, scarcely allows me to be considered one of his partisans. I am therefore all the more free to protest against the article about him that appeared in the issue mentioned above. Whatever judgment one may make of his ideas, there are at least two indisputable things for all those who came close to him: the sincerity of his faith and the purity of his life. The text you have had published amounts to slander, and I insist on expressing the painful feeling of disgust with which the use of that kind of behavior fills me. Please accept, Monsieur, my greetings."

this new contribution to the defense of Father's memory. —Let us have confidence: in spite of the systematic opposition of some minds, the truth will indeed win out in the end. . . ."

[6:13]

Between 1958 and 1966, at five different times, my correspondence with Msgr. Journet consisted particularly of a series of discussions on the thought of Father Teilhard de Chardin, relating to articles appearing in *Nova et vetera*. In 1960, we corresponded through the agency of Msgr. André Baron, then rector of St.-Louis-des-Français in Rome. After 1966, my relations with Cardinal Journet were never again troubled by a painful discussion. No more than with Maritain do I claim here to bring some overall judgment to bear about Cardinal Journet's work. Particularly since, with the internal situation in the Church for some dozen years, he gave proof of a magnanimity far removed from any petty quarrels. And during the two convalescent stays I had to make in Fribourg, in 1971 and 1973, we had some extremely cordial conversations, which left me with a moving memory. (Shortly after these lines were written, I learned of his death.)

[6:14]

On the principle of his Indian missionary vocation, these two reflections: "As long as all mankind has not been gathered into the Church, the Church will only be adolescent: she must grow"; "From the Christian graft in India, I am expecting a more profound submersion of the Church in the depths of the trinitarian Mystery, of this divine *co-esse* that must command from above the progress of our spirit and our life." In a letter from 1952, he revealed one of the key ideas of his theology. He wonders there "if the *gens theologica*, too eager for analysis and insufficiently respectful of mystery, has not so dissected the Sacral that its profound unity has become invisible. Christ is The Sacrament: *ut per visibilia ad invisibilium amorem rapiamur*. The Church, his Body, is—from Pentecost to the Parousia—the place where the spiritual is incarnated, where the historical becomes porous to the eternal. With points of condensation, *the* Sacraments, which, like stars, gravitate around *The Sacrament*: his Resurrected Body in its inadmissible, transbiological and transhistorical mode, no longer an element of the universe but transcending the universe and ordering it, by conferring its meaning upon it. Such is at least *my* theology of the Eucharistic Sign, so real that it is *reifying the world*. . . ." Quoted by Claire Lucques, "L'Abbé Monchanin", in *Choisir* (Geneva), June 1979, p. 16.

I want to quote here an old poem by Father Fontoynont, written during a trip to Athens in 1917, when he was a soldier in the French expeditionary corps of Salonika. A witness to his Hellenic education, this poem gives us as it were the flower of Christian humanism from his youth:

ATHÈNES, 1917, CIMETIÈRE ANTIQUE.

De la terre légère où reposent ses os,
La beauté monte encore aux veines de ce marbre
Comme jaillit du sol l'élan des jeunes arbres,
Ou l'appel musical et paisible des eaux.

Aussi, puisque le poids du jour lourdement tombe,
Seul, hors du camp vautré dans un brutal sommeil,
Par l'antique faubourg embrasé de soleil
Je suis parti, cherchant l'harmonieuse tombe.

Je viens me reposer, fille de Proxénos,
Simplement, et non pas comme font les artistes,
Mais je veux contempler parce que je suis triste
La ligne d'un beau corps aux plis d'un long peplos.

Puisque pèse sur moi la guerre inexorable,
Son hautain esclavage et sa vulgarité,
Peut-être n'est-ce pas tout à fait vanité
Et même ta beauté peut m'être secourable.

Pauvre enfant, tu peux bien m'entrouvrir tes trésors:
J'ai parcouru ta ville et j'en sais le langage,
Son âme m'appartient plus que son paysage,
Et puis je viens aussi du pays de la mort.

La vie qu'on mène là m'a sevré du mensonge:
Hier soir dans le musée où j'errais au hasard
Le vrai passé vers moi montait de toute part
Et quand je t'évoquais, c'était bien plus qu'un songe,

Puisque j'ai regardé dans l'argent des miroirs
Où vous vous admiriez, ô jeune Athénienne,
Vos gemmes ciselées, vos bagues anciennes
Les voici, et l'amphore au dessin rose et noir;

Et puis te voici, toi, cans ce grand cimetière
Pareil avec son sol défoncé, ses débris,
Aux champs silencieux que la guerre a meurtris,
Et ta tombe, Hégéso, presque seule est entière.

Le marbre avec nos corps à son tour périra.
Mais j'ai pris ta beauté dans mon âme immortelle
Et la sérénité qui tombe de ta stèle
Sur mes renoncements à jamais sourira:

L'esclave indifférente entre ses mains dociles
Tient ouvert le coffret des joyaux précieux.
Déjà tes doigts ont pris le plus beau, et tes yeux
Le contemplent encore en ton adieu tranquille. . . .

Et pourtant tu pleuras, petite fille vaine.
Mais l'artiste, pour nous du moins n'a pas menti,
Puisque dans la beauté la mort s'anéantit
Et que la joie fleurit de la souffrance humaine.

Mais tu ne comprends plus, ô petite païenne.[3]

---

[3] Athens, 1917, Ancient cemetery:
From the light earth where its bones rest, / Beauty again rises to the veins of this marble / Just as the vigor of young trees springs from the sun, / Or the musical and peaceful call of waters.

So, since the weight of day falls heavily, / Alone, outside the camp sprawled in a brutal sleep, / Through an old district set afire by the sun / I left, seeking the harmonious tomb.

I am coming to take my rest, daughter of Proxénos, / Simply, and not as artists do, / But because I am sad I want to contemplate / The line of the beautiful body in the folds of a long peplos.

Since the inexorable war weighs on me, / Its proud slavery and its vulgarity, / Perhaps it is not complete futility / And even your beauty can be helpful to me.

Poor child, you can well open your treasures to me a little: / I have traveled through your city and I know its language, / Its soul is more my concern than its landscape, / And then I am coming too from the land of death.

The life that is led there has deprived me of delusion: / Last night in the museum where I had strolled by chance / The true past rose toward me on all sides / And when I evoked you, it was far more than a dream,

Since I looked in the silver of the mirrors / In which you admired yourself, O young Athenian, / Your carved jewels, your ancient rings / Are here, and the jar with its design in red and black;

And then you are here, you, in this great cemetery / Similar, with its broken earth, its debris, / To the silent fields that the war has ravaged, / And your tomb, Hégéso, is almost the only one that is whole.

The marble along with our bodies will in its turn be destroyed. / But I have taken your beauty into my immortal soul / And the serenity that falls from your stele / Will always smile on my renunciations:

The indifferent slave between his docile hands / Holds open the coffer of precious jewels. / Your fingers have already taken the most beautiful, and your eyes / Contemplate it again in your tranquil adieu. . . .

And yet you cried, vain little girl. / But the artist, for us at least, has not lied, / Since in beauty, death is humbled / And since joy flowers from human suffering.

But you no longer understand, O little pagan.

Lyons, September 12, 1950. To the Reverend Father Décisier, delegate from the Province of Lyons to the Congregation of Procurators.

MY REVEREND FATHER, P.C.,

The document issuing from the Magisterium of the Church that has just specified a certain number of points of doctrine that must no longer be the subject of discussion and that has not judged it appropriate to draw attention to any single work or to quote a single name among the theologians must not make us forget that there have been on several occasions in recent years some publications in which the thought of certain theologians of our Province, and in particular that of Father de Lubac, has been distorted in an outrageous manner.

To cite only one example, Father Garrigou-Lagrange, in an article in the *Angelicum* of July-September 1950, implies in an insidious way that Father de Lubac would accord to human nature, open to indefinite progress, the power of raising itself by its own powers to the level of the supernatural realities (pp. 220–21). Moreover, that whole article entitled "Le Relativisme et l'immutabilité du dogme", in which only the name of Father de Lubac is mentioned explicitly, tends to imply that the thought of Father de Lubac is identified with dogmatic relativism. Now, in reality, not one text of his work authorizes such an insinuation or allows one to suppose him to have such a conception of the supernatural.

Since Father de Lubac has not been given the authorization to defend himself, I believe it to be a matter of conscience for his Superior to assume the responsibility of demanding the rectifications that are imperative.

I therefore ask, my Reverend Father, that you would please intervene, as the delegate of the Congregation of Procurators, with the Very Rev. Father General that this flagrant injustice might be rectified. It is not at all a question of defending Father's personal ideas about the supernatural, it is simply a question of reestablishing his actual thought, which has been outrageously distorted.

In addressing this request to you, I believe I am representing more than a mere concern for probity on the part of most of the Fathers in the Residence of Lyons where I am Superior.

Please accept, my Reverend Father, the assurance of my most respectful sentiments,

CHARLES NICOLET, S.J.

APPENDIX VII

[7:1]

During this same year 1964, I also wrote the following letter to a Cardinal
—and I communicated to several Council members or experts the brief
note on "Doctrine" and "Pastoral" that follow it.

ROME, OCTOBER 18, 1964. EMINENCE,

Would you please allow me to draw your attention, filially and confiden-
tially, to a problem that certainly must already preoccupy you and whose
seriousness has worried me for a long time?

Here in Rome, the bishops are obliged every day to be careful to prevent
the maneuvers of a tiny but powerful minority (or, to be more precise, of
a small anticonciliar faction) from wrecking the Council. But the desired
and hoped-for success is itself not without a formidable danger. According
to all I have had the opportunity to observe during the course of these
past two years, the best decisions often risk being taken in the wrong way.

Reform, *aggiornamento*, openness to the world, ecumenism, religious
freedom, and so on: that is all to be understood within the faith, as a
present requirement of the purified and deepened Christian spirit. Now
all that, distorted, is nearly equivalent in the mind of many to careless-
ness, indifference, amorphous liberalism, concessions to the "spirit of the
world" and almost an abandonment of the faith and of morals.

I well know that this is in part the effect of propaganda coming from
opposition that is bent on presenting things that way. But doesn't the language of many of the partisans of *aggiornamento* also contribute to it? They
speak, for example, of "conservatives" and "progressives"; greater emphasis on a return to traditional positions (on the Church, on Revelation,
and so forth) is presented as the victory of new ideas; few serious efforts
are made to explain in the press the principal subjects treated or to justify
the orientations adopted: even all the Catholic journalists whom I had
occasion to read declared, on the day the discussion of *de Revelatione* was
opened, that the Council was entering into "ultra-technical questions",
thereby discouraging readers from taking an interest in it, even though
this subject is the source and center of our faith. On the contrary, what
would have been simpler, or more necessary, than to remind everyone

of the proclamation of the Good News through the revelation of God in Jesus Christ, the essential subject of this schema.

But that is not the most serious of the issues. From the necessity of having to combat an obstinate resistance, the Council has long been held fast, as though hypnotized, by the question of the agreement between the primacy of the pope and episcopal collegiality. This has led to a discussion in juridical terms, claims of authority, outside the spirit that was at first affirmed in numerous interventions. This unilateral perspective has extended to other subjects. Old schemes of thought, certain theological deficiencies and still other causes, notably the difficulty of expressing the realities of the spiritual life in exact terms, have acted in the same way. With the exception of a few passages, the texts adopted or studied so far on the whole lack spiritual density. The mystery of the Cross does not appear there in full relief. Nor does one feel enough of the great breath of Christian hope in them.

The famous "schema 13", which is so necessary (but which has been discussed perhaps too much in advance for rather publicity-oriented purposes), in particular risks increasing the confusion if care is not taken. A strange doctrine has been spreading for a couple of decades: everything about the Christian faith is some sort of "abstract theology"; it should usually be spoken of only among specialists or, at the very least, among believers; when addressing "the world", one should speak only about what is of interest to it, that is, keep exclusively to problems of the temporal order, which alone would be the "real problems". Some justify this attitude of weakness by appealing to the idea of "pre-evangelization", magnified beyond measure. Others, going farther, construct theories according to which there would no longer even be any true evangelization in view for the future, the so-called "profane" world being already Christian in reality, independent of any evangelical revelation.

I know of course that this is not at all the spirit of the Fathers who are preparing or who are getting ready to vote on schema 13. But I also believe that if they are not alert to the real danger of this distortion, they will not avoid giving rise to it. Silence or timidity in the schema about the eternal vocation of man would be exploited as an encouragement to turn away from the realities of the faith.

It is in order to prevent this that, according to the small measure of my powers and after having often reflected about it before God, I have written this letter. It is because of the very clear and direct attitude adopted by Your Eminence in favor of true *aggiornamento* that I chose to send it to you. If I seem to judge the situation with too much audacity, I hope Your Eminence will have the goodness to forgive me, out of regard for my intentions and for the trust I place in that goodness.

Please accept, Your Eminence, the expression of my very devoted respect in Our Lord.

P.S. I am attaching two appendices to this letter: 1. an excerpt from a letter I had addressed to several bishops last June to accompany some remarks on the plan for schema 13; and 2. an excerpt from a letter I have just received from a French priest.

Excerpt from a letter containing some remarks on the plan for schema 13. Rome, June 5, 1964:

. . . Today many of the faithful, and even priests (including religious), are tempted to "open themselves to the world" in such a way as to allow themselves to be invaded by it; they are tempted to abandon little by little the perspectives of the Christian faith in order to interest themselves only in this present and temporal world. (I am thinking especially of France, whose religious situation is better known to me, but I note this elsewhere as well.) Now it is to be feared that they might be encouraged in this, although through a misunderstanding, by certain ways of speaking or certain reticences in the schema in its present form.

As for unbelievers, some will not fail to say: So here the Church is abandoning her dogmas little by little; she is becoming vaguely aware that her role is finished; then she comes to us in order to survive, without daring to abandon her religious phraseology yet. . . .

In consequence, and in order to avoid these fatal equivocations more surely, it seems to me that it would be good to speak from the beginning (if one began with a theoretical exposition) in such a way that the Christian faith might be proclaimed in its entirety. A few words would suffice. The eternal and divine vocation of man would be emphasized well. The Council would show the world not only its faith but its confidence in its faith. The problems of the temporal order would be considered in this complete light, with all the desired distinctions.

Without that, the great, intelligent and authentic charity that has reigned in working out this schema would be taken to be a concession rooted in weakness, the expression of an inferiority complex with respect to the "world"—and a "sign of the times", the Catholic Church beginning to doubt her mission of eternity.

The danger of placing too much emphasis on a distinction between "doctrine" and "pastoral".

1. The partisans of "doctrine" always respond that this is the first pastoral duty.

2. They take advantage of it in order to give themselves a monopoly on "sound doctrine", which is very often only an abstract Scholasticism and much less traditional than they imagine.

3. They thereby end in a deadly separation. Which is profoundly anti-Christian. This has already led, on the part of some, to a strange proposition of schemas in two parts: on the one hand, a "doctrinal" text, for the scholars, and, on the other hand, a vague "pastoral" exhortation: thus, Msgr. Lefèvre. And also Cardinals Bacci and Ruffini. . . . This amounts to canonizing a theology put in the place of dogma, to sliding down a slope to esoterism, to an offense against the non-pedants—and it is contrary to the practice of the Church, especially in her Councils. (1964)

[7:2]

Shortly after the interventions to which I have just referred, a booklet began to circulate secretly, which a strange blunder happened to place in my hands. The title of it was significant: "Aggiornamento or Change?" The first of these two terms, according to the booklet, was the vain work of a Council without importance; the second alone designated something serious. Aggiornamento concerned only the transformation of sociological structures of the Church, while change implied the modification of the mental structures of Christians. "We understand by change the adoption by the Church . . . of a new Humanism [that] would coordinate within a single, open synthesis all the original contributions of the great religious and metaphysical wisdom of the East and West and all the advances of the sciences of nature and man. . . . A revolution as radical as that which transformed a Galilean sect . . . into a Church [is necessary today]. . . . —The principal object of a philosophical revolution . . . is a radical calling into question of notions that were until now indisputable. . . . All our approaches to the infinite or the transcendent pass through particular expressions that participate in a thought that is always in progress. . . . We note today the appearance of a new type of man, in the process of change. . . . [These new men] distrust above all the paranoid rigidity of a certain dogmatic spirit. . . . They are ready to open themselves to dialogue if the Church, herself in the process of change, truly becomes a universal Church."

With these revolutionary but still general formulas (the subtitle of the booklet was "Planetary Perspectives of the Council"), they were urging a program not only bolder but quite different from that of the Council, and the experience of the years that followed show well enough how it was applied. —In June 1965, an article in *Etudes* indicated the direction taken with as much clearsightedness as decisiveness, although it too was still in rather general terms and not without caricatures: "Atheism is part of current language. . . . Marx, Engels, Lenin, Nietzsche, Freud . . . have passed through it. Now, some contemporary idealists, a bit too attached to obsolete forms of Christianity and taking a bit too quickly for granted slogans that have scarcely been analyzed, speak thoughtlessly of the immense drift that for 150 years has supposedly carried the West toward the shoals where it would risk getting sunk forever. . . . We must return one good and last time to atheism so as to discern beneath this word, which is terribly equivocal, the true attitudes that it masks. . . . Fideism has today become a cancer that works its ravages more or less within all doctrines, as opposed as they might be *in appearance*. . . .

"[According to Henri Raynal, *L'Oeil magique*, Seuil, 1963] 'Mystery is the surreality. . . . God is the surreality of this world, no more, no less, its total surreality. . . . The lesson of the great mystics remains infinitely precious, even after the categorical rejection of all deism. It is only that we must sift out the significance of their prodigious experience'. [This author, and two others quoted first] are in agreement in their affirmation that Christianity is not only in decline but reaching its final days, its attempts at renewal being only the convulsions of an obvious agony. . . .

"For some, the end of Christianity is a fact that is henceforth not even debatable. . . . But others retort with a tone of equal certainty: 'If there is to be a religion in the future, we can be at peace: it is Christianity' (K. Rahner). It is true that another question hovers over this debate: Will there be a religion in the future? And still another: We have arrived at a point 'where we no longer know precisely what Christianity is' (Kierkegaard).

"This is why . . . we must from now on deal with the crucial question: What relation does Christianity maintain with Truth? But do we love the Truth enough to devote ourselves to this radical question?" (end).

("Chemin spirituel de notre temps" [The spiritual path of our time], 755-71.)

[7:3]

Letter sent from Rome to Lyons, December 1, 1965, after reading the disturbing program distributed for the study of the Council in the Society during the summer of 1966. This program was an attempt to distort the work of the Council (and it was to be, although with various precautions, systematically applied).

"In the coming months and years, it will be necessary to study seriously the overall work of the Council. One must know how to take the dogmatic constitutions as the center of perspective, for they are in fact at the center of everything. To do so, it will be necessary to break away from the propaganda and tendentious attempts that are already arising and that will soon be in danger of aborting the undertaking of reform and of compromising the very foundations of the faith. The Society will have a salutary role to play here; this will demand a great effort of faith and abnegation from it. —Will the Superiors in France be able to see the cynicism of the program that is already circulating, a program that ignores the existence of all the doctrinal, spiritual and apostolic aspects of the Council and that commits us to the ways of a miserable secularization?"

I will note again here that, after having agreed, on the advice of my Provincial, to become a part of the governing committee of the *Concilium* journal, I was not long in resigning (November 1965), having observed that the orientation of the Review did not correspond to what its title had led me to expect.

Some time later, I wrote the following letter to Father Wenger, editor of *La Croix*:

To Father Wenger, Editor of *La Croix*.

Lyons, July 26, 1966

Very dear Father and Friend,

It is with all friendly trust and in confidence that I write you today.

I have just read in *La Croix* of the 26th the very interesting review that Father Ehlinger gives us of the conference by Dr. Joseph Ratzinger to the *Katholikentag*. I must congratulate you for having given a report of it in this way.

And, if you will permit me, I would add the following: This text by Dr. Ratzinger gives the model for a vigorous orientation, for an urgent rectification to be carried out in the authentic sense of the Council and of true aggiornamento. Our bishops as a whole scarcely seem to dare commit their authority to it; the Catholic press as a whole scarcely seems to care about it. There is an increasingly pronounced split between a so-called active element, that gives the impression of making Christian faith and life more worldly, of evaporating them, of dissolving the bonds of Catholicity —and a so-called "integrist" mass, which many excellent Christians have been tempted to join, Christians who value the whole of the faith and the uprightness of Christian life. Yet desires for true renewal abound; it is necessary to help them overcome the scandal; and it is necessary to unite them.

So, I turn to *La Croix*—to you. And I wonder if it would not be possible for you to enter more resolutely into the path indicated by this conference of Dr. Ratzinger. The Holy Father (about whom so little is presently reported in France—to say nothing more) and our bishops would surely be grateful to you for doing so. You would be helping the religious orders, whose influence in many cases can be a determining factor, to follow faithfully the straight path of the Gospel. You would be dissipating the temptation toward integrism on the part of many Christians, troubled by the present disorder. You would be protecting the efforts for renewal from the quagmire of a "progressivism" that is leading us to spiritual disintegration.

This is in fact what you are already doing, and this is precisely why I am addressing you. But a firmer decision and increased vigor, communicated also to your principal collaborators, are necessary. For the situation is getting worse. I have seen many signs of it, first-hand, during the course of recent months.

Many Catholics of merit today in France cannot express themselves: Why does *La Croix* not take the initiative to make a larger appeal to them? But above all, it is your team, it is you yourself, who can do much to enlighten us, to comfort us, to guide us, to inspire courage in us.

Yours always, with best wishes, *in Xto Jesu.*

[7:4]

DE OPINIONIBUS PERICULOSIS HODIERNIS
NECNON DE ATHEISMO
[*Dangerous modern opinions and atheism*]

On the whole, these pages have been well written; their author shows himself to be well informed about the present doctrinal situation. The judgments are both sound and moderate; the opinions he gives are wise. In brief, it is an excellent "status quaestionis", which seems very well suited to serve as the basis for the works and decisions of the Synod.

Nevertheless, for a text coming from the Magisterium, the form in which it is presented does not seem entirely suitable. That is due to a twofold reason:

1) Because of its very title, and the large amount of space given (as was necessary) to dangers and errors, it would be too negative in tone.

2) Its very even balance is not appropriate for arousing an awakening of faith or for giving the desired impulse to the effort for renewal.

The Synod certainly does have to show that it understands well the errors and the dangers of the present time and to place itself on guard against them; but without getting weighed down by it. It is much more desirable that it show its confidence in the Spirit of God; that it invite all the faithful to share in that confidence; that it remind us that the more danger there is and the more need there is for searching, the more the faithful of Christ must feel their complete solidarity, united around their Pastors in the Church. The Church and the Spirit are bound together.

Neither in its masses nor (still far less, undoubtedly) in its intellectual elites do the Christian people expect from the Magisterium of the Church on such an occasion deep philosophical dissertations or long historic-social considerations, any more than they do massive condemnations, which would do more harm than good. They would be equally disappointed by decisions that were wise but monotonous, by "middle-of-the-road" texts, in which the Breath of the Spirit of God could not be felt.

What is needed first of all in such circumstances is on the part of the representatives of the entire episcopate gathered around the chief Shepherd:

— a lively witness of Christian faith and of Catholic unity;
— a message of hope;
— accompanied by several clear directives with a view to clarifying the progress of the Christian people through the difficulties of the present time.

In fact, for various reasons, many of the faithful are troubled today. Some, overly sensitive to a few noisy deviations, imagine that the Council has overthrown everything and are tempted to think themselves betrayed in their faith by their religious leaders. Others, on the contrary, dream only of changing everything without discernment, of reinventing everything. A certain number have become dizzy in the face of criticisms of every kind and negations coming from a world to which they have "opened" themselves. A more solid group seems to be becoming dissatisfied, without much reflection, with all that the Church represents and maintains among us. Thank God, we also have the faithful who have entered with clearsightedness and generosity into the paths opened by the Council or who would commit themselves more deeply if they felt better understood and supported. All need to be either reassured or reaffirmed or encouraged. All need to be enlightened and guided by Pastors filled with the Spirit of Christ.

It is true that the present crisis is serious: taking note of this does not mean giving in to alarmist tendencies; the dangers of it are manifest. But the bishops as a whole can effectively contribute to transforming it more quickly into a fortunate crisis of growth. (It is not necessary to dream of a false pacification, which would only increase the delay caused by long years of excessive repression or stifling.) It is true that, through a nearly unexpected explosion, all questions are posed at once, everything seems to be placed in question, from the smallest usages up to fundamental dogmas: but those in authority will not answer the needs by losing themselves in a multiplicity of details. The most "scandalous" of the things published or produced within the Church for some time is most often of rather mediocre intellectual quality and scarcely finds any credit except by reason of the "mood of the times". If the bishops were to succeed in establishing a climate of confidence, many things could be restored. This is why the necessary reminder of the truth on principal points where it has been compromised today must, it seems to me, be accompanied by words of encouragement.

Fundamenta

The two principal foundations of the present doctrinal crisis are well indicated. In reality, they even coincide.

In the first (with respect to biblical revelation), it is a question less of particular difficulties of exegesis than of a total aversion to admitting a divine revelation; and this aversion itself stems from an inability on principle to think of a transcendent order of truth. This is the reason for that "fascination", so well noted here, that the Bultmannian idea of "demythologization", in its most general sense, exercises over many. (Bultmann's exegesis depends in considerable part on his previous philosophy.)

Anthropologia

1. It is appropriate to note both the great progress achieved by the "human sciences"—and the disintegration of man that results from it in many cases when these sciences are not considered in a metaphysical or religious synthesis. As with the natural sciences, it is then that abusive conclusions are drawn from it. Just as Marx was an atheist before applying himself to social problems, so, for example, Freud was so before his discoveries in psychoanalysis.

2. Should the formula used here: "creatio immediata humani spiritus"[1] be preserved? It has long been traditional; but it has more than once been criticized, and not without reason; for it seems to state that a spirit (a soul) was created first, separately, and entirely constituted, then "infused" into

---

[1] "Animae humanae" is usually said. But this term "soul" is today quite wrongly the object of a true phobia.

a body; which is a bit mythical and does not really take into account the individual characteristics of each person.

3. The page devoted to original sin has some very carefully considered formulas. But it deals only with *peccatum originans* and says nothing of *peccatum originatum*, which should be, in a complete exposition, the first thing considered, for it is essential, and it is that which has a direct relation to the mystery of redemption. It is possible to be very literalistic about *peccatum originans* and still minimize that evil in which humanity finds itself plunged and from which it cannot get out without the Redeemer.

Ecclesiologia

1. The connection indicated between "institution" and "charism" is just. It responds well to the preoccupations of today. Representatives of the institution must take care not to "stifle the Spirit": their role is to govern, discern, rectify, approve, direct. As for those who think they enjoy charisms, they must be convinced that the Spirit does not lead to demands and criticism but to initiatives of self-sacrifice. It is a Spirit of renewal rather than of reform, a fortiori of contestation.

2. With respect to the Magisterium, it would be better for the Magisterium itself, to whatever degree possible, not to dwell on this subject too long. In the long run, insistence on this subject produces an effect contrary to that expected. It is by inspiring confidence that the Magisterium best restores its authority if it has been shaken—by avoiding a tone of annoyance but by placing very high the demand of faith and the ideal of the Christian life.

3. It is extremely important that there be an exchange and regular communication between the center and the periphery, just as between the particular workers and the hierarchy. That must be extended in both directions. Authority has the right to demand the same confidence that it manifests. It would be very good to stop that a priori of criticism, mistrust, irony or even of veritable anticlericalism that, in large part under influence from outside the Church, governs a certain number of Catholic consciences today.

Similarly, the intellectuals have to remember that they are part of a Church that is made for all; the particular schools, the local Churches, must remember that they are part of the universal Church, of the one People of God.

De Atheismo

The formulation of this section suggests several remarks:

1. It is accurate to say that, in its origin as in its motives, atheism often

seems to be, first of all, the will to affirm man rather than the negation of God. That is why it is important to say and to show that the negation of God is, on the contrary, what places man in danger.

2. There is equal reason to point out the present spread of certain expressions that are at least paradoxical ("death of God", and so forth) and that contribute to shaking faith in God, even when that is not the intention of their authors or their disseminators.

3. It is very important to explain how faith in God, such as professed by the Christian tradition considered in its authentic representatives, is in no way that superstitious belief that science and technology would clear away, nor is it that childish abandonment that would tear man away from his responsibilities, and so forth. It is even more important to show the unhappiness of man "cut off from the Eternal" and closed to the mystery of Love.

4. No. 2 (page 79) repeats the old schema of philosophical history according to which the origin of atheism would be sought in the subjectivism of Descartes, who supposedly engendered the immanentism of Kant, and so on. Such an outline is overly simplified; it would be better to *reject* it. It only adds to the disastrous impression that an irresistible movement of thought, marked out by the names of all the great philosophers, uninterrupted for nearly four centuries, *leads inevitably to atheism*. Whatever certain direct relationships might be, many other things can be found in Descartes, and even in Kant, than what is said here.

5. The purpose of the program distributed to the members of the Synod was not to dictate nor even to indicate the measures to be taken. Nevertheless it does seem possible to suggest two principal things:

a. After having recalled, as the Council already has, that the causes that have favored the *spread* of atheism are not all of the intellectual order, one could address a new appeal to all members of the Church in order to remind them of the duty to give witness to their faith by a better, deeply committed practice of social justice and charity.

b. But we must not stop there—for, on the one hand, the *roots* of atheism are deeper; they penetrate an intellectual and spiritual ground well beyond social realities. On the other hand, if man is made for God, our duty of fraternal charity, if not always the most urgent, at least the most specific and the most serious, is to make him know this God for whom he is made. Our duty is to reveal to him this mysterious Love that has been revealed to us. That is the true witness of faith, a witness given above all by a sincere and deep spiritual life, the source of joy and of charity, a witness given by the Christian community as such and by each member of it; a witness expressed, as far as possible, with authority by the leaders of the community.

The "eternal Life" manifested in Jesus Christ (cf. 1 John and *Dei Verbum*, intro.) must be manifested again to men through the faithful of Christ. Each man is called to participate in it here on earth—and if it does not recognize this, the earthly society itself will only succeed in organizing itself in an inhuman fashion. (A word is said about that, page 73, with respect to social morality.)

6. There is one thing not mentioned in the *Argumentum* that is nevertheless of great importance: it is that, for about a century and a half, atheism has often been presented as being, not a negation properly speaking, but a development of Christianity; it has wanted to transform "nonviolently" the Christian into an atheist; it calls itself the legitimate heir of the message given by Jesus. It borrows as needed the Christian vocabulary ("religion of the Son", "action of the Spirit", and so forth) and declares that literalist believers are mentally retarded. It says, for example, in an ambiguous way: "God become man has only revealed man become God", and so forth. So well that the adoration of man is coming to take over the adoration of God. The Christians who today are giving into "secularism" do not always perceive that they are the victims of these equivocations.

H. L.

(About the preparatory text of the 1967 Synod.)

[7:5]

The only thing really new in the book with respect to the old article is a preface, in which I endeavored to show that the traditional doctrine, such as I was trying to bring it to life once again, responds to the theological situation of the sixties just as it responded to the opposite theological situation of the forties and earlier years.

The 1949 article (see above, p. 62) had elicited, among others, a rather long, very favorable review by Hans P. Ehrenberg, a Lutheran theologian, in the journal *Evangelische Theologie*, 9 (1949–1950), 497–502—a study only recently pointed out to me (1976) by Father Karl H. Neufeld. The author judged that my article put an end to an unthinkable Scholastic dualism, restored the best of Augustinianism, set the bases for a true Christian anthropology, furnished Lutheran thought with the ontology it lacked and was thereby opening the way for a serious dialogue between Rome and the other Christian confessions.

Henri de Lubac—*Augustinisme et Théologie moderne*. Theology series, 63 (Aubier, 1965), 340 p.

Henri de Lubac—*Le Mystère du surnaturel*. Theology series, 64 (Aubier, 1965), 302 p.

The two works form a diptych and are linked, at some twenty years' distance, with no. 8 of the same series, *Surnaturel. Etudes historiques*. In the meantime, the discussions and clarifications, indeed the polemics, have confirmed the soundness, the validity of this celebrated book. The theological sky having cleared, Father de Lubac, who had never ceased to accumulate notes with as much abnegation as perseverance, has been able to pick up once again and considerably develop several chapters of *Surnaturel*. They have become in their new form *Augustinisme et Théologie moderne*. Then he has recast, reorganized and amplified, to the dimensions of a whole volume, the theoretical conclusions formerly sketched only briefly, more like the article from the RSR of 1949, which is also entitled *Le Mystère du Surnaturel*.

In their historical parts and in their constructive explanations, these rejuvenated writings, quite like the former ones, invite us to revise the notion and the system of "pure nature". This system, whether belated or recent, however one wishes, has hindered the elucidation of the mystery of our supernatural destiny, or rather it is the fruit of an obliteration of the great Christian tradition, Augustinian as well as Thomist. Such as it is, within the context that saw it arise, with the Baianist and Jansenist controversies (Baius and Jansenius were misguided Augustinians), it undoubtedly was a useful thing; it was inevitable, perhaps even indispensable for attending to the most urgent matters, for avoiding glaring deviations. But, proceeding from a system of theological and philosophical separatism, handled by second-rate theologians, this hypothesis represents a degradation, a type of theological regression, and it seems superfluous to many today. It can be dismissed without shame. Father de Lubac, nevertheless, does not condemn it without qualification. He does not argue the fact that it might be legitimate and, for some, invaluable and necessary: they would not be without danger in rejecting it.

But the traditional faith is not aware of pure nature. It is inscribed in the sublime exclamation: *Fecisti nos ad Te. . .*, of which the whole of Father de Lubac's work constitutes a magnificent commentary. This is because it rests on the paradox of our destination at the divine resemblance, itself grafted—there is a correlation but not a necessary dependence—on the paradox of our being an "image", of our created spirit: the vocation *to* the infinite, which is a call *from* the infinite, in our finite nature. A "perfect gift", absolutely gratuitous and prevenient, and yet one which is to complete the being to which it is offered, to which it offers itself. A Love that arouses and measures the desire to which it responds. It is the "Christian paradox of man", "unknown to the Gentiles", "denied by good sense", "overcome in faith". Saint Thomas, not always well served by his interpreters, called it the natural desire for beatitude, "desire of his nature", not elicited but incapable of being frustrated. In fact, on the natural order, Saint Thomas knows only the natural ends of human activity. Augustine, Thomas, the great mystics are but one, single voice. And it is at bottom a very simple but inexhaustible idea that, following them, Father de Lubac, who is too modest when he speaks of his own contribution, endeavors to inculcate.

His deep intention, indefectible in all his writings, is to lead back to the vivid sources of the living faith, to supply theology with something to drink from the waters of Siloam. We know his way, characterized by transparency, by sober lyricism and by masterful, prodigious erudition. Through ancient texts and references, the idea that guides him inserts its thread of light. May its clarity be projected ahead of us! For Father de Lubac is thinking of the men of our time, his readers. Another danger, graver than the quarrels between schools, threatens the undying vitality of Christianity: that to which the preface of *Mystère du surnaturel* alludes (p. 15), a disastrous sequel of dualism: laicization, secularization, which seduces the Christians themselves, and naturalization of the supernatural, immanentism. There, too, alas!, new theologians have arisen to make man the common measure and the illusory place of encounter between the believer and the atheist.

Xavier Tilliette

[7:7]

Nevertheless, "Esprit et liberté dans la tradition théologique" was to be taken up again much later, without change but with a slightly more abundant documentation, in an Italian edition (*Opera*, Ed. Jaca Book; vol. 13, 1980).

[7:8]

On the other hand, the private testimony of several people allowed me to believe that the spiritual importance of the subject had not been destroyed by the confusion that had occurred since then in the intellectual, philo-sophical and theological situation. I will quote something quite recent, taken from a letter of 1975: "This news [of your departure from Lyons] has reawakened in me the memory of the days I once spent in Fourvière, particularly of my reading of *Mystère du surnaturel* on that far distant night. There are moments in which that memory attains an intensity that has its equal only in hope. . . . That desire for the supernatural has perhaps never been as acute as in the present period of my existence, which is rich in unexpected spiritual discoveries, . . ."

Another more recent letter, from November 21, 1975: ". . . May I say to you that reading *Surnaturel* was, even then, on the benches of the Faculty, decisive in the orientation of my studies and research? When, much later, I considered devoting a doctoral thesis to Pascal, I discovered the four senses of Scripture, Augustinianism and modern theology, the mystery of the supernatural. Should I speak of those Paradoxes that have always been among my bedside books? Nourished by your thought and your knowl-edge, I no longer know today how to distinguish between what I have borrowed from you and the use I have been able to make of it. May I at least have remained faithful to the inspiration received and in no way betrayed or distorted it! May these pages . . . be the proof to your eyes that here and there are hidden disciples of your teaching who continue to be nourished by it and who endeavor to prolong the echo of it according to their means! . . ."

[7:9]

In *Revue thomiste* of 1966: pp. 93 to 107, Father Jean-Pierre Torrell, O.P., gave a long review, under the title "Nature et surnaturel", of my "twins" of 1965, by relating them to the 1946 *Surnaturel*. He confirms the accuracy of the historical analyses of these three works, of their interpretation of the texts of Saint Thomas Aquinas, and finally, at base, even of their doctrine. In addition, he considers that the problem treated "continues to be of an incontestable timeliness for Catholic theology", notably for an elucidation "of the relation between the Church and the world". See also the article published by Dom Illtyd Trethowan, the same year, in *The Downside Re-view*: "The Supernatural End: Father de Lubac's new volumes".

[7:10]

This work earned me the following letter from Rev. Father Arrupe:
    "Warm thanks for the filial gift of your book on the 'crisis of the Church' (sic). I had read with great interest your article that appeared in the *Nou-*

velle revue théologique, to which you return here in substance. You need not fear being disavowed by the Society, dear Father de Lubac! Of course, the ferment of ideas and the calling into question that stirs the Church today also includes positive aspects, and it is normal that some, in the Society as elsewhere, see these aspects in particular; but the deviations and the dangers—especially for the faith, and this is why they are extremely serious and call for an attentive vigilance—are, alas!, only too real, and this is a very timely work that you have done in writing these pages. A very beautiful work as well: you wrote there in particular about the love of Jesus Christ and about the love and concern for the unity of the Church, pages that will endure.

(P.S.) *Avanti*, dear Father! The Church expects much from your theological knowledge!"

[7:11]

With respect to this second part, one reader wrote to me: "This *maternal* Church that you defend, I feel that she is indeed mine. How right you are to insist on a proper character for her, *sui generis*, in opposition to those who would like to model her on civil societies. To call for a parliamentarist Church, after having so criticized the monarchical Church of former times, is, it seems to me, to succumb to the same error that one is denouncing (and I am not sure that this 'democratic' Church would not be more tyrannical than the other). . . ."

About the same time, in *Le Temps de l'angoisse et de la recherche* (1971), 89–91, Joseph Folliet wrote: "Bureaucracy is invading the structures of the Church. . . . I am alarmed by the proliferation of these staff officers, by the countenance of the Church that a number of bureaucratic priests think they reflect. . . . When she seems to be confused with a bureaucracy, I no longer find the face of my mother."

[7:12]

". . . An Episcopacy Has Been Constituted. What Have the Bishops Become?"

. . . Within the episcopal conference, the diocesan bishop has always had the right to make his voice heard. . . . Experience nevertheless shows that a good number of bishops have difficulty in taking the floor in the plenary

Assembly, either because the presence in that Assembly of some nonepisco-pal member hinders them or because experience has made them sceptical about the Assembly's taking into consideration an opinion that is not the feeling of the majority. . . . There is no lack of backstage conversations to give evidence of this disappointment, as do certain letters addressed to the permanent Council after the closing of the Assembly. . . .

Powerful structures: the permanent Council, Commissions, Secretari-ates, bring [to the bishop] invaluable information. . ., but he is defenseless before them. . . . Before the Commissions, the bishop feels inferior. He participates only in one of them. Even then, he does so more as a specialist than as a diocesan pastor. . . . But there are all the other commissions of which he is not a part. If he wants to intervene in some domain, he has the impression that he is moving into territory that is not his own and he fears giving voice to an opinion contrary to that which rules in the Commission. So there is the temptation to seek refuge in silence, even if he has the dim sense that he is not in agreement.

The Commissions themselves do not always have absolute freedom of movement. —Middle-level commissions have to reckon with the Catho-lic Action movements whose members declare themselves to be the most important. . . . At times these movements . . . have become . . . a force of formidable pressure. . . . In these negotiations, the bishops cannot always count on the unconditional support of the chaplains, who seem today, in certain cases, to be the representatives of the movements to the bishops rather than representatives of the bishops to the movements. . . .

As for Commissions that run the technical machinery of the apostolate, they are assisted by national secretariates that have not ceased to further their own development by taking greater and greater authority. . . . The bishops do not have the time to follow in detail the questions that are sub-mitted to them in commission. The commission meets for one or two days, two or three times a year. The corresponding Secretariate is permanent and has to fulfill only the specialized task assigned to it. One sometimes has the impression that the Secretariate inspires, perhaps even orients in fact, the Commission, although it is not possible for a Secretariate to have that over-all pastoral view that diocesan responsibility gives, in all directions. . . . Moreover, faced with the difficulty of finding capable responsible people, the secretariates themselves indicate to the Commissions the priests they deem the best equipped to undertake subsequent action. The difficulty of releasing priests of real ability . . . leads sometimes to a kind of cooptation. It facilitates the maintenance of chosen options that the bishops who do not share them find themselves powerless to counter. Through the bias of the recognized authority at the Commissions—although this authority may not be defined—these options in fact become imperatives, and the best the bishop can do, when he considers them inadvisable or dangerous, is to ignore them.

Since their origin, the Secretariates have, little by little, grown and increased their strength, in spite of the lack of clergy. The minor secretariates all aspire to be recognized nationally. We see their number grow; we do not see any of them being suppressed. The logistical apparatus has not ceased to be inflated although the body of clerics, which does not have, it is true, a monopoly on the apostolate, has not ceased to diminish. . . .

Isn't the increasing authority of the permanent Council going to diminish in turn the freedom of each bishop? . . . The general Secretariate never ceases to furnish the bishops with invaluable information in the form of printed files and mimeographed circulars on the most diverse questions. . . . But the very abundance of this documentation and its technical quality often overwhelm the bishop. . . .

Where then can the bishop find supportive points to affirm his conviction? . . . —In fact, the bishop will intervene if the question concerns a particular event in his diocese: local scandal, unjust social situation, a public calamity that affects the members of his diocese. Beyond that, he will fear to go outside his own responsibilities and, through a sense of the general interest, a lack of self-confidence, a fear of the reactions that he would arouse even in his own diocese, where in our times his situation is often difficult, he will postpone his intervention in the hope that a better-advised Commission or a better-placed colleague will speak with more effect and more success. . . .

. . . Is it an exaggeration to note that, with respect to what we knew at the beginning of the century, the situation has been nearly reversed. At that time, there were bishops, there was not an episcopacy. Today there is a strongly structured episcopacy. But the freedom of the bishops seems narrower than before. . . .

We may well think that it would be advisable to make it possible for the bishops to free themselves of the pressure that at times threatens to reduce them to silence. . . .

His Emin. Cardinal Gouyon, Archbishop of Rennes: "Les Relations entre le diocèse et la Conférence Episcopale" [The relations between the diocese and the Episcopal Conference] *L'Année canonique*, vol. 22 (Paris, 1978), 1–23.

[7:13]

The work was well received by more than one specialist, even in Italy. It was the subject of a very sympathetic article by Father Mario Fois, S.J., in *Civilta Cattolica* (?): "Il Pico della Mirandola di Henri de Lubac. Un modello di metodo storiografico" (1976?), 572–80; as well as a review by the same author in *Gregorianum* (1976), 393–95. Italy did me the honor of a translation, by Editions Jaca Book (Milan, 1977): *L'Alba incomputia del Rinascimento, Pico della Mirandola*. I returned to Giovanni Pico in a preface to a work by Father Henri Crouzel, *Une Controverse sur Origène à la Renaissance: Jean Pic de la Mirandole et Pierre Garcia* (Vrin, 1977).

The Protestant author of a review of my *Pic*, having misread one page, thought he saw a diatribe against Luther. I addressed the following letter to him, which brought a pacified reply back from him.

Chantilly, July 8, 1976. Monsieur le Professeur, In the rest home where I am being cared for at present in my old age, I have just seen the most recent issue of the very interesting *Etudes théologiques et religieuses*, in which I had the surprise of finding a review, by you, of my work on Pico della Mirandola. If I permit myself to write to you, it is first of all to thank you, and then it is to reassure you. In the text you quote, there is in fact nothing aimed at Luther, either directly or indirectly. As you yourself say, this text is speaking of Erasmus. It is summing up a series of interpretations that were proposed by him (not all, moreover, as "accusations" but often as praise), and which I believe to be inaccurate. The thought never entered my mind to "shove" Luther into any of these "bags". If you would take a closer look at the pages from which you excerpted this kind of section about Erasmus, you would see quite simply (at the end of an historical study that wishes only to be objective) a wholly peaceful idea, expressed in the form of a "dream" or regret: if, on the side of the Catholic Church, Luther had encountered interlocutors of greater breadth, in their intelligence as well as in their Christian depths and their spirit of conciliation, perhaps the rupture could have been avoided. . . . I well know there is something naïve in that, and I made that observation; but I do not believe there was anything offensive, as you seem to believe, for a disciple of Luther. On my part, in any case, not only was there no doubledealing, which you think to recognize, there was not any "dealing" at all. For these words were dictated to me by the sadness of a situation in which, along with many others in each of the Christian confessions, I do not take my part lightly. My letter is in no way intended as one of recrimination; but I would be grieved if your misunderstanding of my intentions were to persist. I do not believe that the rather numerous Protestants whom I have met in the course of my life have ever been able to mistake them. Pastor Hébert Roux, who collaborated on that very issue of your journal, will be able to testify to this if necessary.

Please accept, Monsieur le Professeur, the expression of my Christian sympathy and all my respect.

APPENDIX VIII

[8:1]

Mme. Renée Bédarida, who knew Father Chaillet well from 1941 on, agreed to write his biography (1981).

[8:2]

(With respect to the notice by Herbert Vorgrimler, published in *Bilans der Theologie im 20. Jahrhundert* (vol. 4), Bahnbrechende Theologen [Herder, 1970], 199–214, and reproduced in the French translation of the work.)

While grateful to the author for his extreme kindness and for the care with which he wrote as complete a notice as possible, I must still warn the reader of two things.

1. As is nearly inevitable, in addition to various inaccuracies of interpretation, a certain number of factual errors have slipped into the text. I will point out only two. I was never incarcerated by the Germans (p. 812). When the Theology Faculty of Lyons declared me to be "on leave", it was to show that it still considered me one of its members, and this expression was deleted as soon as I resumed my teaching.

2. Without contesting in any way the author's freedom in his judgments, I have the strict duty to declare that I do not always share them. I have never confused what I thought to be unjustified criticism coming from men I respect and revere with "stupid", "malicious" or "cruel" attacks; I owe it to the memory of my Superior General to say that he was, insofar as he could be, of great kindness to me; finally, the idea, stated without restrictions and in language lacking any moderation, that it would be appropriate to resist any "repression" in the Church and that the latter should "never inflict suffering or punishment" is so far from my unchanging opinion that it seems to me contrary to the nature of the Church and to her whole tradition, made manifest from the earliest times and testified to in the writings of the New Testament.

H.L., 1975

From a letter to Hubert Schnackers, a student in theology at Regensburg:

". . . I do not much like it when people talk of 'new theology', referring to me; I have never used the expression, and I detest the thing. I have always sought, on the contrary, to make the Tradition of the Church known, in what it offers that is most universal and least subject to the variations of time. 'New theology' is a polemical term, whose use through the centuries it would be amusing to follow and which most of the time signifies nothing, serving only to throw suspicion on the author in the mind of those who do not take a closer look at it (unless some today, on the contrary, take pride in it). —As for my theology being based *solely* on the Fathers and Scripture, that does not please me at all either. I don't even think I have ever used the banal expression (which might be understood in a good sense, if it were not exclusive) "return to the sources". It would be enough, moreover, merely to open one of my books, for example, *Surnaturel*, to see that I in no way scorn the effort of Scholasticism, and in particular that of Saint Thomas, who is the author I have most often read and studied for a long time. But it is quite certain, on the other hand, that in less technical, less strictly theological works, one is naturally led to quote texts of concrete style, coming from the Fathers of the Church, spiritual authors or contemporaries, more often than Scholastic theologians or philosophers of the Schools.

"It would be very difficult to explain my attitude on the ecumenical problem to you in a few words. I was very early and rather actively interested in it in Lyons, beginning in 1929–1930. But I had little occasion to write *ex professo* on the subject. As happens to all those who took part in some nascent (or renascent) movement in their youth, I have not failed to be disappointed at times at seeing what became of it, here and there, to the degree that it was popularized—while delighting in the successes achieved. I believe that we have developed many illusions about the conditions of union and on the ease of arriving at it; for the moment, I believe that the weakening of the Catholic spirit within the Church is, not a promise, but an obstacle to the ecumenical cause. That was even said to me very clearly, and with sadness, by an Orthodox bishop. I—along with many other observers—seem to note that the ecumenical openness, for which the Council gave the signal and of which the Catholic Church continues to set the example, does not exist to the same degree in the Reformed Churches or in most of Orthodoxy. We must not, for all that, feel sorry for ourselves, but rather persevere in patience. There is no lack of good minds, moreover, among the Protestants of various confessions as among the Orthodox, to recognize the strength of the Catholic position, especially in what concerns the papacy, either from the point of view of its New Testament foundation or from that of its necessity for the unity of the Church.

"My role in the Council? It was not considerable, although I followed it closely and (except for an absence at the beginning of the second session) was regularly present at the meetings of the doctrinal commission. Many private conversations with bishops from nearly everywhere; a few written or oral interventions; no important role in the actual drafting of the texts (except for certain details). A good number of "extra-conciliar" conferences to groups of bishops in the course of the four years; notably, the first year, I was in a good position to give them information because I had participated during the two preceding years in the (not very happy, as you know) work of the preparatory theological commission. (I do not believe that the enormous amount of literature published for ten years concerning the Council always made it well understood, far from it.)

"You ask me, too, if my thinking in the course of the years has not shifted. Perhaps I am not in a very good position to judge. I believe nevertheless that there has not been a very clear evolution nor, for all the more reason, any true change. But the situations over some fifty years have been so different! Never having remained locked into pure speculation, I have tried to respond as well as possible to the demands addressed to me, in order to face the needs of the hour as well as the duties of my charge. When it was necessary, for example, to try to show the resources of a living Christian thought, coming up against a Scholasticism at once modern and obsolete—or when it was necessary to fight (with the weapons of the spirit and mind) nazi neopaganism, etc., the situation was quite different from today, when a work of disintegration is operating within the Church. —And then, most of the time, these were the circumstances that dictated not only the orientation but the very subject of my books: this was the case with Buddhism and with Teilhard de Chardin. On the other hand, one cannot say everything at once: to speak of *Catholicisme* or of *Surnaturel* or of *Humanisme athée* is not to speak of *Exégèse médiévale* or of *La Structure du symbole des apôtres* or of *Eglises particulières*. Finally, it happens very often that what is closest to your heart you cannot say in your books: because the more you desire it, the more you fear to speak too poorly about it. . . ."

[8:4]

With respect to the school of Jacques Maritain, I will cite here two articles that appeared on the subject of *Paysan de la Garonne* (1966); they seem

very illuminating to me, even with respect to the present situation: 1)
Jean Aucagne, S.J., in *Travaux et jours* (Beyrouth), 1967, 111–16: "Revue
des livres, *Le Paysan de la Garonne*". 2) Father Jean-Mohammed Abd-el-
Jalil, O.F.M., "Countryman of Oued-Fès and consultor to the Secretariate
in Rome for Non-Christian (believers)": "Témoignage d'un tard-venu à
l'Eglise; no e poi no!", in *Evangile aujourd'hui, Cahiers de vie franciscaine*, 54,
2d trimester (1967), 63–73.

While giving warm homage to the essential values with which "Maritain's book is wholly penetrated", Father Aucagne wrote, p. 114: "If
Maritain had nothing to do with the crisis of the fifties, which cut off
theological thought in France, first from its strict non-Thomist leaders,
then even from the Thomists on the left, the theologians he cites in his
book had much to do with it. That deprived generations of students for
fifteen years (generations of students pass quickly) of the person and the
works of dear masters, whom we forced to keep silent after having criticized themselves. How can we be surprised that these students, handed over
to imitators who were much less orthodox—even if they were Thomists
—than those who had been driven away, are now particularly disarmed
before a neomodernist virus that turns from hay-fever into a pernicious
fever, to use one of Maritain's expressions? . . ." Father Aucagne particularly stressed the perspicacity of Father Fessard's analyses in *De l'actualité
historique* (1960) and compared it to the "misadventures of the Thomist
school confronted with communism".

In the book on Claudel and Péguy, I tried to bring back to a more equitable judgment those who look with excessive and poorly informed severity on Maritain's attitude toward Péguy, notably with respect to *Mystère de
la charité de Jeanne d'Arc*. Yet, since then, I have had to defend the memory
of Father Teilhard against the unjust accusations in *Paysan de la Garonne*.

Blondel wrote to his friend J. Wehrlé, on October 21, 1917: "The more
I've studied Saint Thomas, the more I've become aware of the prodigious
and tendentious distortion to which he has been submitted by our neo-
Thomists, who have excerpted from him only what can end in a theo-
cracy and an exclusive monophorism. . . ." Blondel-Wehrlé, *Correspondance*, vol. 2 (Aubier, 1969), 531. The judgments made by Etienne Gilson
are no less severe.

We also read in the Journal of Charles Du Bos, on November 20, 1929
(vol. 5, p. 223), that the "Thomism" that some have made it a sacred duty
to profess was "the equivalent of what one calls a doctrine of State".

I wrote to Father Bouillard in 1959: Some of our current "Thomists"
"are making themselves a very extraordinary idea of eternal beatitude,
which is to be, according to them, the triumph of their 'speculative theology'. Nothing is less in conformity with the thought of their Doctor.

Rousselot was a hundred times right about this. But one doesn't dare to speak of Rousselot without affecting an air of disdain. Gilson, who is becoming more independent in his language in his old age and who has had time to reflect, has just spoken quite differently". And, to the same, on October 31, 1960: "See the next to the last *Ami du Clergé*, it's worth the trouble. Father C. explains there that for twelve centuries, they were content in the Church to ensure Christian life; but that Christian thought began in the thirteenth century. Much more, he says (it is his first sentence, his stroke of the bow): 'Theology properly speaking, as revealed wisdom, as the object of scientific study, was born in the Middle Ages.' That sentence gives a wonderful material representation of a diffuse tendency evident today in a whole little theological world."

On August 28, 1965, I had occasion to address M. Kalinowski the following reflections:

"Editions internationales have sent me the book you have just published with M. Swiezawski on 'La Philosophie à l'heure du concile'. I have read it with much interest. Although I have never had to occupy myself *ex professo* with philosophy in the course of my life, you are right in thinking that I can well understand the great importance of such a subject. This dialogic style, or two-voice choir, that you have adopted allows you to show well, here and there, the two complementary aspects of the questions broached. You are quite right to point out in the process the dangers or possible bad implications of a theology that chooses to be purely 'positive' (27); and to criticize that opposition set up by some between 'pastoral' and 'doctrinal', an opposition whose effects are disastrous (72); and again, to warn the 'laity' discreetly that it must overcome an adolescent crisis (116), etc., etc.

"But it is not just numerous details that I appreciate in your pages. Yet it would be pointless to tell you at length how close your essential theses are to mine; how I too esteem the authors you most often quote as authorities. To mention only the 'laymen', I myself often refer to the work of Etienne Gilson; and I much admire the overall work of Jacques Maritain—although his Thomism still perhaps feels the effects of having been adopted too quickly in an act of excessive docility to Dominican masters who had a better knowledge of commentators than of Saint Thomas himself (and who linked the cause of Thomism to that of *l'Action française*).

"Permit me to submit two reflections to you that in no way place me in disagreement with you but that the experience of an already long life, in our French situation, suggest to me.

"In the first place: in addition to the various dangers you very justly point out, there is another that seems particularly serious to me today. It is what I would call the danger of 'philosophism'. Some, in fact, who have a strong hold on young minds affect to call a man a 'fideist' if he lives in faith, even if that faith is solidly founded: they claim to pass beyond this simple believer by an intelligence declared to be superior; and this is one of the indirect means, no doubt the principal one, by which atheism tries to infiltrate the Church, or by which, at least, faith in Jesus Christ is relativized.

"The second thing is the following: you have shown very well that certain excesses or deviations of a modern 'Thomism' have contributed in some circles to the discredit of Thomism itself. There is a bit more to be said on this subject. Throughout my youth, the most official 'Thomists', and the ones most in favor, presented us with 'Thomism' as linked with traditionalism and Maurrasism; then, they linked it to Christian democracy; finally, after the last war, it was again under the banner of 'Thomism' that a communistic 'progressivism' developed that has been devastating in its effects. At the same, many highly placed men, very little concerned with any philosophical reflection at all, made this 'Thomism' into pure ecclesiastical conformity; to such a degree that it no longer referred to anything but a kind of etiquette, a certain hardening of the mind, a certain negative attitude of universal condemnation. It is a fact that this would-be (or overly simplistic) Thomism has in many cases stifled the serious study of Saint Thomas and discouraged several men of the Church, who certainly were actually more Thomists than those who were shouting their Thomistic conformity so loudly. —Now those who today set themselves in opposition to the conciliar majority like to use Thomism as their reference, and yet some of them would be much embarrassed to have to give us any analysis whatever of the thought of Saint Thomas. This explains the reactions of some bishops. Having learned from experience, they are afraid that formulas that put too much stress on Saint Thomas might in the future be a pretext for renewing such abuses.

"May your voice, always very wise and which I second in agreement, be heard. You are much thanked, dear Monsieur Kalinowski, and please, when you have a chance, thank M. Swiezawski too, whom I will doubtless soon have the pleasure of meeting again at Saint-Pierre. Although this letter is not worth the trouble, you can send it on to him if you wish, so that he will at least know the interest I took in reading it. And always believe in my feelings of friendly respect."

[8:5]

"Even a few years ago, a certain number of theologians still followed the theological trend of Lyons-Fourvière in specialized circles. . . . But that theological trend is today lost from sight. It did not bring forward anything very new for speculative research, or then it did not go beyond the body of neo-Scholastic thought. And current theological research does not get anything out of it. . . . It is a tragic fact that several theologians, respected for years because of their participation in the theology of Fourvière, are rising up strongly in opposition to the new theological orientations. A tragic fact, truly, for one must not forget that it is to this theological trend that the honor is due for having made possible the breakthrough effected by Vatican II."

E. Schillebeeckx, O.P., in *Les Catholiques hollandais, rencontres et dialogues* présentés par H. Hillenaar et H. Peters, trans. by J. Alzin (DDB, 1963), 9. (The preface, p. X, speaks of "rediscovery of the Gospel", "blossoming of a new Church life", "renewal", "breakthrough". . . .)

On the way in which the author tried to justify what he calls "new theological orientations" by the teachings of Vatican II, I have offered some additional information in my *Petite catéchèse sur nature et grâce* (Fayard, 1980) [*A Brief Catechesis on Nature and Grace* (San Francisco: Ignatius Press, 1984)], Appendix II.

[*8:6*]

On December 5, 1968, I refused to be associated with a "Declaration" issued by the theologians of the "Concilium" group; it seemed to me completely improper and demagogic and, in addition, without purpose (for these theologians were in reality enjoying full freedom of expression and were seeking in fact to impose their own dictatorship). Here is my text:

1. I have always been hesitant with respect to manifestations made by means of the press. [This declaration was destined for publicity.] One thereby makes appeal to the most incompetent, easily impassioned and in large part non-Christian opinion. I have more than once noted the improprieties of such proceedings.

2. In the present context, the proceeding seems to be doubly inopportune:

a. It risks increasing the trouble and agitation that are presently a sign, not of vitality, but of disintegration.

b. All the remaining chances for a true renewal in the Church depend on a sustained or reestablished awareness, affirmed in deeds, of Catholic unity. Before demanding for themselves additional freedoms and guarantees, even legitimate ones, theologians in the present circumstances have the incumbent and urgent duty to defend and promote this unity. That is an essential part of their "duty to preach the Word, in season and out". Otherwise, proceeding in a unilateral way, they enter into the round of demands, nothing more.

3. To express my entire thought: too many facts show as well that the plurality of theological schools is today really threatened by all sorts of pressures, propaganda, intimidations, exclusivisms, which come from sources other than the legitimate authority. And seeing all that is or is not done, I have acquired the firm conviction that the freedom of action of the Magisterium of the Church is more seriously hindered than the freedom of speech of the theologians who are making the demands.

Finally, one question: Before having recourse to this path of collective declaration and manifesto, has one or another of these theologians proposed to the competent authorities, with the required deference and freedom, a plan of reform or reorganization on the points close to his heart?

[8:7]

Review of Georges Chantraine, S.J., *Vraie et fausse liberté du théologien*.

Theology is in the headlines today. Yes, but what theology? Some theologians are demanding greater freedom in the Church. Yes, but what freedom? By the sole fact of posing this twofold question, Georges Chantraine is provoking a debate. Let us say rather that he is deepening the research, a pivotal research. The occasion for doing so was provided by a manifesto issued last December with some sensation by a group of editors of the *Concilium* journal—but that is not the only such occasion. This essay does not intend to hold the reader either by pungent anecdotes or by the witty eloquence of a pamphlet. In the midst of the most living timeliness, it provokes reflection. Whoever will agree to pose the previous twofold question with him will be unable to put it down: he will be led right to the end, in a single stroke. Employing once again a very necessary word of Maurice Blondel, the author first institutes a close critique of the *extrinsicism* that characterized a certain theology of yesterday and that is found again, trait by trait, in a certain theology of today. Opposites share one and the same genre! Here they clothe, although in opposite senses, the same false opposition between Magisterium and theologian, as if between two rival powers, where what is granted to one would be as though wrenched from the other. Recalling then the proper object of theology and the proper mission of the theologian, he reestablishes the inner bonds, from which are seen the true nature and the true demands of Christian freedom.

HENRI DE LUBAC. *Le Monde*, SEPTEMBER 29, 1969.

[8:8]

Among other similar texts, cf. this warning from Paul VI, from even before the end of the Council, in May 1965: "Whoever would see in the Council a weakening of the interior commitments of the Church toward her faith, her tradition, her asceticism, her charity, her spirit of sacrifice, her adherence to the Word and to the Cross of Christ, or even an indulgent concession to the fragile and changeable relativist mentality of a world without principles and without a transcendent end, or a kind of Christianity that is more permissive and less demanding, would be mistaken" (Speech to the General Chapter of the Salesians). In July, a new appeal by Paul VI for true renewal, a new denunciation of misinterpretations that were spreading on conciliar aggiornamento. (*La Croix* of July 9 gave an excerpt of this speech on page 4—but I do not believe that our bishops or religious superiors took it up.) On August 2, during a long conversation, Georges Villepelet, P.S.S., with a remarkably open and clearsighted mind, shared the same concerns with me: the apparent unawareness of our bishops, the political deviations of their dear "Catholic Action", uncontrolled liturgical disorder, internal decadence in the seminaries, the privileged position given to former priests, scorn for tradition, lack of constraint in doctrinal (eucharistic) and moral (marriage, etc.) matters, the heavy responsibility of certain journals. . . .

[8:9]

In 1976 I gave to Rev. Father André Costes, Provincial of France, the following manifestation of conscience to read:

For seven or eight years, paralyzed by the fear of confronting head-on, in a concrete way, the essential problems in their present burning state. Was this wisdom or weakness? Was I right or wrong? Would a frank discussion, which obliged me to cite texts and proper names, have been understood as anything but polemics? Would it not have run the risk of increasing fraternal discord? (But, to be deaf, isn't it already known by all, and, in certain cases, can it still be called fraternal?) Nevertheless, would it not have been the only way possible to achieve some positive, truly clear and firm statements? I don't know. I have in any case lost much time in thinking about it. My stray impulses have stopped short. My interventions, which were too allusive, too occasional, too general, too "academic" at times (I am told), were unable to serve any purpose. But would I have obtained permission to print? Would I have found a publisher? Would I not have been thrown back despite myself, ostensibly, into the integrist clan I loathe? I know so well the processes shamelessly used by those in power to discredit the least show of independence in their regard. . . . Would I have had the strength to pursue the discussion? —Despite everything, it seems to me that in my silence, in the refuge I have taken in a few little historical works, there was much timidity, false pride, fear of blows, at least as much as there was a desire for peace and a reluctance to criticize the writings of men some of whom were my brothers and one or two my friends. (1974).

Am I not a *Pilatus redivivus*? (1975).

[*8:10*]

In his book on *La Foi* (1973), Cardinal G.-M. Garrone pointed this out, taking one major point as an example: "More than from any other cause, the Church suffers today from the fact that the directives of the Council are neither understood nor respected as they should be, when they are not totally misunderstood. At the center of the Church, the heroic will of Paul VI is striving to put them into operation without any weakening. How things would change, for example, if the chapter of the Constitution of the Church concerning the successor of Peter were considered and followed by those who have the duty to do so with the same awareness and the same rigorous fidelity with which the successor of Peter respects and puts into practice the conciliar orientations on collegiality!"

[*8:11*]

I have quoted above [8:6] the note by which I replied, on December 5, 1968, to the Declaration issued by *Concilium*, which I had been urged to sign. A wholly private reply, whose text I communicated only to a small number of friends. As some of them were of an opinion contrary to mine (they were not aware of the reality of the situation), and as, even within the Society, this subject was being debated rather strongly, I decided to send my text to the Very Rev. Father Arrupe. The latter replied to me, on

February 2, 1969: "My dear Father, Pax Xti. —I have received your letter of January 25 along with the accompanying document. Many thanks! I will not hide from you the comfort and even the joy I felt at seeing the attitude, as clear as it is loyal, that you have adopted with respect to the declaration. Courage was needed to take it. You have acted as a very good son of Saint Ignatius. You are well aware, I think, that other theologians of the Society have replied in the same way. Thanking you for your letter, I ask for a remembrance at Holy Mass. Very fraternally in Xto."

Resourceful in its publicity initiatives, *Concilium* was later on to circulate all over the world a leaflet written in English in which I was presented, several years after my resignation, as a member of the editorial committee of the journal. *Concilium* had also organized a large international theological congress, which was held in Brussels. The conclusions of this strange congress had been prefabricated. The majority of the participants, apart from a little inner circle, were not allowed to discuss them. One of the fully privileged members, known in the past to be better inspired, explained to the press that the theologians who had not come to Brussels were no longer worthy of the name.

[*8:12*]

When he had to renounce making his profession in the Society of Jesus in order to carry out the foundation of a secular institute, a task to which he felt God was calling him, Father von Balthasar wrote the following letter to his colleagues in Switzerland, in March 1950:

DEAR FATHERS AND BROTHERS OF THE SOCIETY OF JESUS,

In parting from your community to do the will of God, I do not want to leave the house through a secret door but much rather to look you in the face in saying goodbye to you, you who for dozens of years have been those closest to me and who, as far as I am concerned, will still remain so spiritually. The reasons for my departure are not usual, the case should not be confused with others. So a little explanation seems to me to be indicated.

I would like first of all to repeat one part of what I stated to the Father General, John Janssens, on April 20, 1948: "After some years of prayer and meditation before God and our Holy Father Ignatius, I have arrived at the conclusion, which I have shared with you in two oral conversations, that God has set aside a personal, particular task for me, that I cannot turn over to others: to shirk it or to turn a deaf ear to it would amount to betraying the love of God in the deepest part of myself. I am far from thinking to place my unworthy person next to the great and pure in the kingdom of God: yet, I can't keep from comparing the certitude granted to me, in that respect, with that which someone like Brother Nicolas received, when he had to leave his family, or John Eudes, when he left the Oratory, or Charles de Foucauld, or any other to whom a mission was made known by God. And if today I ask your Paternity to release me from my vow of entering the Society of Jesus to live there in poverty, chastity and obedience, this is certainly not in order to escape the cross of religious life, to avoid submitting my mind and my will and to follow a personal plan, but with the clear awareness of binding myself to God and to our Father Ignatius by a still more strict obedience, which strips me still more severely of my liberty, in accordance with what [Jesus] said: When you have grown old, you will be led where you do not wish to go.

"If I leave, it is thus both voluntarily and involuntarily at one and the same time. Voluntarily, for my request for a leave of absence has no other purpose than my desire to obey God. Not any estrangement, any quarrel, on my part, with the Society, which is dear to me above all things, and, as I have been assured, not any dissatisfaction on the part of my superiors. Both before and after, the work of our Father Ignatius appears to me to be the finest on earth, and to live in his house, the most desirable of all fates. And despite all that could be found to complain about in the present Society, particularly in our German countries, the criticism of these facts would never have been able to lead me to choose another path. But I also leave involuntarily, forced by a chain of circumstances in which I cannot recognize an inescapable necessity. That your Paternity, in his position as responsible guide, ought to follow the traditional, most sure path; that it will clearly remind me that God prefers to lead by ordinary ways rather than extraordinary ways and that obedience with regard to superiors is always a guarantee of security, while personal certitudes can easily fail: How could I see in all that anything but the expression of your experience and your prudence, of your solicitude for the whole and of your paternal love for me in particular? But it became equally clear that, from the moment my business in Rome took the form of one alternative, either/or, it was lost, for me, within the Society. That form could have been avoided only if others besides me had recognized that the obedience owed to God and its founder by the Society does not have to contradict the obedience that one particular person may have to furnish God and Saint Ignatius, even if this obedience were once to become completely personal."

It was obviously necessary, if I wanted to be taken seriously, to present some verifiable data for the interior certitude obtained in prayer. This is what I did, first with the Provincial of that time and then, when the question was brought to Rome, with the Father General, in all frankness. But, given the fact that ecclesiastical testing in this way usually requires years, while God can ask immediate obedience from a particular person, a completely possible, legitimate and foreseen situation can arise in which two opinions oppose each other with the best of intentions, in such a way that, here, clarity appears and a resolution is imperative, while on the other side the nature of the things does not yet allow a solution to be reached. I refer to Thomas, *de Veritate* q 17, a 5, or to what Father de Lugo, S.J., develops in his *tractatus de virtute fidei divinae*, in disp. I. n. 226–29.

"Sententia communior jam docet, omnem revelationem sufficienter propositam pertinere ad objectum formale fidei nostrae, sive privata sit, sive publice ab Ecclesia proposita; nam licet privatam non teneantur fideles omnes communiter credere, tenetur tamen credere ille, cui fit et sufficienter proponitur, eodem habitu fidei quo credit et alia fidei mysteria. Hanc tenet. . . . Catherinus in Apologia contra Sotum de certitudine gratiae, cap. ult., ubi testis oculatus testatur, hanc sententiam, quam P. Lainez Generalis nostrae Societatis contra Sotum acriter in Tridentino probavit, communi Concilii approbatione fuisse acceptam. Eandem tenet Suarez. . . . Quam defendunt jam communiter nostri recentiores.

"Dubium esse potest, an revelatio privata possit obligare sub peccato gravi infidelitatis ad credendum objectum sic revelatum, antequam ab Ecclesia acceptatur. In hoc puncto distinguendum videtur. Possumus loqui vel de ipsomet, cui immediate fit revelatio, vel de aliis, ad quos postea notitia ejus derivatur. Loquendo de aliis, credo communiter loquendo nunquam aut rarissime obligari ad credendum, quamdiu non proponitur ab Ecclesia. Non est sermo nunc de revelatione alicui immediate facta ad hoc ut id ex parte Dei alteri etiam privatim nuntiaret; tunc enim occurentibus motivis sufficientibus, credere teneretur positive is etiam, ad quem mandatum vel nuntium illud deferretur. Si vero loquamur de eo, cui fit revelatio privata immediate, non videtur negari posse, quod aliquando et non raro teneatur illam et objectum revelatum credere. Si adsint motiva talia, ut non possint prudenter dubitari, debet positive credere, alioquin erit gravis irreverentia in Deum, cui loquenti et sufficienter suam locutionem proponenti ad exigendam hominis fidem, illam non possumus negare. Et equidem cum adsit motivum divinae auctoritatis sufficienter propositae, cui summus cultus intellectualis debetur, erit etiam obligatio assentiendi non utcumque sed super omnia, sicut in rebus fidei assentiri debemus. Ceterum non est dubium quod possit revelatio privata proponi cum tantis credibilitatis motivis et cui fit, cum quantis proponitur revelatio publica."

[At present, the more common opinion is that every revelation that is sufficiently promulgated belongs to the formal object of our faith, whether it is a private revelation or one publicly promulgated by the Church. For although Catholics in general are not bound to believe a private revelation, anyone who receives such a revelation and to whom it is sufficiently promulgated is bound to believe it with the same virtue of faith with which he believes the other mysteries of the Faith. This is the view of Catherinus in his Apologia against Soto on the Certitude of Grace, in the last chapter. There, he testifies as an eyewitness[1] that this view, which Father Lainez, the General of our Society, vigorously proved against Soto at the Council of Trent was unanimously adopted by the Council. All our recent theologians defend it now.

One may doubt whether a private revelation may oblige one to believe something as revealed under pain of a mortal sin of infidelity before it is accepted by the Church. There is need here for a distinction. We can talk either about the person to whom the revelation is immediately directed, or about others who come to know of it later. I believe, generally speaking, that these others are never or very rarely obliged to believe as long as the revelation is not proposed by the Church. We are not talking here about a revelation made immediately to one person with a view to his relating it, even privately, to another person on God's behalf. For in that case, in the presence of sufficient motives, the one to whom the command or message would be delivered would be positively obliged to obey. But if we are talking about the person to whom the private revelation is immediately directed, undeniably sometimes and even quite often he is obliged to believe in the fact and content of the revelation. In the presence of motives such as cannot prudently be doubted, he must positively believe; otherwise he will commit a serious irreverence toward God. We cannot withhold faith when God speaks and establishes his word sufficiently to demand man's faith. Indeed, in the presence of a motive of divine authority adequately proposed, to which supreme intellectual worship is owed, there will be the duty of giving no ordinary assent, but the supreme assent we owe in matters of faith. Doubtless, moreover, a private revelation can be made with motives of credibility just as weighty for its recipient as those with which public revelation is proposed.]

So one cannot allege that the good solution to the conflict is found, in principle and for each case, in obedience to the Order. It is found in principle and for each case in obedience to God. The superior who will never confuse himself with God is the ordinary way for the manifestation of the divine will. He is not the exclusive way. God remains free with respect to man—especially if it is a question of someone who has wished to place himself entirely at God's disposition in the way of life of the counsels—he is free to make use of him according to his good pleasure,

---

[1] [Or "there an eyewitness testifies" —Ed.]

as he wishes. The religious life does not consist in seeking refuge in a safe harbor but in valuing and remaining faithful to the "go from your country" (Gen 12:1) and to the "leave everything"; and religious obedience is not a blindspot where the breath of the Spirit can no longer reach us, unless in an indirect way, unless obedience removes from us the final responsibility of ourselves before God. What order knows better or preaches more about instrumentality and availability with respect to God (not only for its members but for itself) than the order of the Jesuits? Unless it is simply a matter of empty phrases, the Jesuit must be, in principle, always ready to hear and follow a new call, even an unexpected one, which will make him leave the forms to which he is accustomed and attached. Any other point of view than that of simple and real obedience is not then taken into consideration: whether it be easy or laborious, whether one be understood or not, whether the chances of succeeding stand out as consoling or somber, whether the night of obedience be deeper in staying than in leaving: what does it matter to one who seeks the will of the Lord. And if what the Exercises foresee (no. 167) then comes true almost of necessity, he will accept it with an inner recognition, but once again: What does it matter? God himself takes care that such an obedience, given with the simplicity of a child, without heroism or exaltation, does not run aground but culminates in the foundation of the Catholic Church.

Some members of the Society have thought it good—I do not wish to examine for what reasons—to have all kinds of anecdotes spread about me. With respect to those that have reached me, I can only say that they are either fabricated or very distorted, to the point of making the context unrecognizable, which I am in every instance prepared to prove and confirm. Anyone concerned with the truth will do well to abstain for the moment from judging rather than listening to (or even spreading) the gossip of people who claim to know things that in truth they do not.

A special problem is comprised of the arguments drawn from my conduct and example, within the Society, which are summoned up to refute the validity of my affirmations. This objection places me in the paradoxical situation of accusing myself here in all truth while I must nevertheless justify myself. In this respect, one point should have priority over the rest: great personal faults can indeed prejudice the execution of a task but not render impossible a delegation on the part of God. Taking that for granted, I take advantage with gratitude of the opportunity to ask pardon sincerely from my confreres for having much scandalized them. I feel myself most particularly guilty of a continual lack of active charity. The fact of having lacked an understanding consideration of the concerns of others, of having been sparing with my time and my sympathy; of having been too independent in my plans for work, negligent in my expenses: that must be pointed out. In that and in many other things, I have failed, and I pray God might prevent anyone from suffering lasting harm through my fault. On the other hand, I do not know what to think when I am today accused of having been absolutely false, disloyal, arrogant and disobedient. I have not managed to discover these fundamental attitudes in myself. In particular, I sincerely think that I "have always judged each in my heart as above myself". I must leave the judgment about these things to God and beg him to enlighten me. Yet, the more one of my old confreres discovers faults in me, the more I will have the right to count on his prayers.

All that I owe the Society, and the reason for which I will always remain grateful to God for it, is, in a word, nearly everything. I can only praise God for this wealth and beg him to share it with a great many. One more point that I would like to stress: the edification I received from the humility of some of the coadjutor brothers, which will remain unforgettable for me.

Full of gratitude, I say goodbye, and the light that is behind me and accompanies me will illumine the obscurity of the near or still distant future. One would have to be blind not to see that the fulfillment of my mission will be much more laborious outside than it could have been inside. But what joy and what peace on earth is greater than the awareness acquired in prayer that one has obeyed as well as one was able to understand. There is also the joy of being able to give joy to my Father Ignatius, who is dearer to me than all else: To the glory of God and perhaps as well, I hope, for a revival of our Father Ignatius on earth. No saint is perhaps today more timely, more alive, more active than he; capable of exploding anew, and especially this time again, the incrustations of centuries. Who knows, perhaps he hides in his heart a beautiful, still invisible secret: that the detour that must be accomplished will later be revealed, when we are long since gone, as the path of a new and deeper unity.

There is no truth except in prayer. I recommend myself to your prayers and ask for a remembrance at Holy Mass, and promise to remember you in my prayers.

HANS URS VON BALTHASAR

APPENDIX IX

[9:1]

"The entire contemporary culture, from philosophy to the cinema, is a critical culture, which rests only upon what it can submit to its disintegrating inquisition. It has given itself the task of exposing the hidden springs of the social conscience and the individual conscience, to dissipate all illusions, to denounce all beliefs, to destroy all traces of the sacred, to make man a stranger to himself, to reduce what had seemed to him to be profound mysteries to the play of impulses or of words or genes or productive forces or of structures and, finally, of numbers. . . ."

"Prospective et utopie", *Revue générale belge* (1960); excerpt, 13–15.

[9:2]

Shortly before, the Protestant exegete Philippe H. Menoud had similarly recalled: "The apostles were certainly the first to baptize and to celebrate the Eucharist. . . . Announcing the word of God and presiding over the eucharistic service are only two complementary aspects of one and the same ministry. . . . The 'presider' (cf. 1 Th 5:12; Rom 12:8) is at once the minister of the word and of the Eucharist, like the bishop (and deacons) at Antioch and like the elder-overseers at the time of Clement of Rome. . . . They grasped by instinct that the Church lives by the word of God and by the Eucharist, together forming a single unity that does not allow itself to be broken. . . ." *Jésus-Christ et le foi* (1975), 351–54.

[9:3]

In September 1955, at Aix, I read in a letter from Blondel to Father Joseph Maréchal, from Louvain: "Father H. de L. has recently sent me a very remarkable article on the problem of Christian philosophy, and I am very happy to be spontaneously in agreement with him on all points."

[9:4]

Rejected by our intelligentsia, this modest catechesis had its usefulness (at least in a few individual cases). So I am told in a recent letter from someone unknown to me: ". . . You have just passed the systematic examination of the Protestant Theology Faculty of X. I will explain myself. On my program, among other things, was grace. . . . I was completely at sea with it. . . . Well, fifteen days before the exam, a friend loaned me your book. I read and reread it with much joy, a new light was given to me. So, on the exam, I chose the subject of grace, . . . and it went very well. I hope that you, or other theologians, will always make a point of writing in a comprehensible and serious way for their brother Christians, so as to bring them true nourishment for the understanding of the Christian mysteries, the knowledge of God, from the approach of faith more than of intellectual satisfaction."

[9:5]

Since Father de Montcheuil has been very unjustly discredited by some with respect to his interpretations of Blondel, I will quote here two letters from Blondel himself, concerning *l'Action* and *Vinculum*. (The first was addressed to me, the second to Father Auguste Valensin.)

AIX, DECEMBER 19, 1946

VERY DEAR AND VENERATED FATHER,

. . . On the other hand, your "Theology" series with Aubier is still growing richer: the admirable book I have just received through your kindness relieves me of a great weight. Undoubtedly I feel some remorse for my anonymous protest against the attitude of the heroes of Vercors toward me and for the criticism I formulated against the insufficiency of participation as a definition of the life of grace. But nothing of that remains in the splendid posthumous work of the Rev. Father de Montcheuil that I have just had read to me. I am infinitely grateful for the penetration and the accuracy with which the dear Father discerned, specified and clarified the effort I had made to establish the human part in the work of grace. What he showed in my intention and in my development about *Vinculum* has won my admiration: no one up to this had brought out my fundamental thought and my intention to substitute for participation and for consubstantiation the truly Catholic doctrine, which even Leibniz maintained, of Father des Bosses, S.J., faithful to the dogma of transubstantiation. I feel as though a great weight had been lifted from me in learning that, thanks to your holy friend and the publication of his works (of which I had known nothing despite my desires to know a little about his efforts and his apostolic successes), I am free of a misunderstanding that was very painful to me and which I had not been able to dissipate.

AIX, NOVEMBER 3, 1948

. . . Your book of excerpts from *l'Action* has born fruit, for which I cannot thank you enough. Then, you devoted the second volume to Father de Montcheuil, the introduction of which I had read to me: I had not remembered that it was so penetrating and in sum so favorable! And in the volume of *Mélanges théologiques*, he gives a very remarkable study that goes far beyond the occasional review of a publication. If you have read these pages, you have been able to note the depth of his agreement in my regard. This testimony is all the more important and timely as much lack of understanding still exists. —I have not been able yet to have very much of Abbé Duméry's book read to me; what I heard of it seems a little cursory, and I fear that his lively intelligence and his haste are too quickly satisfied with the better intentions of the world. . . . It is good, I think, that you can straighten out, as needed, the rather hasty judgments of this young mind, which promises much but risks misusing his facility. I don't need to cover up insidious deviations with a preface. . . .

[9:6]

Some good specialists remarked on this chapter. Cf. Bernard McGinn, of the University of Chicago, "Apocalypticism in the Middle Ages: An historiographical sketch", in *Mediaeval Studies*, 37 (Toronto, 1975), 275:

"Henri de Lubac has devoted attention to Joachim in his *Exégèse médiévale* (2,1, Paris, chap. 6, pp. 437–558), and has also briefly discussed aspects of the earlier twelfth-century apocalyptic thinkers. De Lubac's analysis of Joachim is one of the most comprehensive and perceptive in recent literature, though many of the needless oppositions of earlier Joachim scholarship with an admirable insight, showing the Abbot's originality in terms of his theory of exegesis, as well as the radical implications of this originality, despite his orthodox intentions. Perhaps it is the sympathy that de Lubac has for the authentic religious genius of the Calabrian Abbot that helps to make this such an excellent introduction. Altogether, Grundmann, Kamlah, and de Lubac have given us some sense of the genius of Joachim in the area of exegesis at least; we still await the studies that will do the same for the more difficult areas of this theory of history and his views of the Trinity."

In 1981, Father Henri Crouzel, having become the editor of the *Bulletin de littérature ecclésiastique de Toulouse*, asked me to come to his aid: he lacked copy, he said. This is why "La Controverse sur le salut d'Origène à l'époque moderne" appeared in two articles in the Bulletin of 1982—a subject of pure curiosity following upon a passage from *Exégèse médiévale*, I:257–74.

The various journal reviews of *La Postérité de Joachim de Flore* allowed me to verify how little effort reviewers devote to a thorough reading of the work they are discussing. All, or nearly all, whatever their judgment of my work, had me placing (among others) Buchez, Mickiewicz and Soloviev among the "Joachimites", although I had devoted long pages to each one of them in order to demonstrate that they were not.

I replied to Paul VI: "Very Holy Father, the extreme kindness of which Your Holiness has long since given me so many indications surely authorizes me to thank him with simplicity. If the praises received are very poorly deserved, I at least accept without hesitation the mention of my attachment to the Vicar of Christ. Certainly the deepest reasons for it are not of a personal order: they are dictated by history and by faith, as well as by the observation of the present times, which render the mission of the Apostolic See more urgent than ever. But Your Holiness will allow me to express to him, too, since he gives me the occasion to do so without taking an indiscreet initiative, my affectionate veneration for him personally; it is all the more lively as I see or imagine the heavy trials that weigh on his shoulders but which he carries with such magnanimity. —From the servant and son of Your Holiness in Our Lord."

Here is this letter, a typical model of a time-worn genre that had obviously passed through the hands of a pompous Latinist:

DILECTO FILIO
HENRICO DE LUBAC
SOCIETATIS JESU SODALI.

DILECTE FILI,

a.d. XI Kal. Mart. hoc anno, diem tuum ages, annos natus octoginta; qua occasione iam non solum amici atque Sodales Societatis Jesu, cui tanto es ornamento, circum te saepient, sed omnis prope Gallia et docti quam plurimi totius orbis catholici. Has vero Litteras Nostras idcirco ad te dari voluimus, ut simul Nostra patris gaudia ostenderemus, simul egregiam, in qua sumus, tui opinionem patefaceremus, simul justas ac debitas gratias tibi ageremus, Nostro scilicet Ecclesiaeque nomine.

Atque primum id tene, gaudia Nostra haec ab ipsa consideratione fluere ac manare donorum, quibus amplissimis a Deo cumulatus es atque sapientissime usus: acerrimo ingenio, dicimus, sacerdotio, vita religiosa, fide sancta ac singulari, studio praeterea atque amore rerum indagandarum, quae interdum in adorationem ac pietatem vertunt.

Natum est inde, dilecte Fili, id vitae genus, ut numquam ab inquisitione veri aut quiesceres aut cessares; fuitque investigatio tua illa copiosa, subtilis, acris, ardens, cum naturam interrogans, tum etiam historiam rerum gestarum, christianam religionem, Ecclesiam, sacras Litteras, philosophiam, varias populorum religiones, atheismum ipsum, viros denique virtute, doctrina, sapientia per hominum aetates insignes.

Unde mirabilis illa librorum series profecta est, —haud sine labore et incommodo tuo, neque interdum sine quibusdam difficultatibus—in quibus semper tibi sacrum ac solemne fuit, ut et veritatem diligentissime quaereres, et Patrum vestigia veneranda premeres, et probatas maiorum traditiones amplectereris, et tractanda argumenta in suo quodque tempore, loco, momento collocares, quam plurimis semper allatis testimoniis; et rectum animi sensum in iudicando sequereris, aeque ad analysim, quam dicunt, aeque ad synthesim aptus. Nimirum hae scriptorum tuorum dotes ac quasi leges, sunt etiam causae virioitatis ac perennitatis eorum.

Verum et hoc in tua laude ponendum est, quod inter rerum peritos celebrati Concilii Vaticani II fuisti, cui operam navasti egregiam, et quod sodalem Commissionis Theologicae internationalis uberi cum fructu egisti. —Neque est praetereundum nonnulla librorum edendorum corpora de tuo etiam labore nomen sibi comparasse et famam.

Egregiis his ceterisque igenii tui operibus, *monumentum* exegisti, dilecte Fili, *aere perennius* (Horat. Carm., 3, 30, 1), in doctorum omnium admirationem atque utilitatem. Quae quidem cause fuit, cur nonnullae Studiorum Universitates te Sodalem honoris gratia delegerint, atque *Academia Scientiarum moralium atque politicarum* Parisiensis in membris suis te annumeraverit.

Attamen haec, de quibus hactenus, merita tua omnia non exhauriunt, cum omnis vita tua reliqua tibi et Ecclesiae honori cedat. Qui profecto per annos ferme triginta in Instituto Catholico Lugdunensi professus es, eo quidem modo, ut tum inquirendi via, tum tua magistri auctoritas, tum cotidie a te discipulis tradita veritas his et lucro fuerint, et gaudio. Insuper, et id commemorare placet, tua pietas, verbo Dei alita, casibus vitae confirmata, flamma fuit semper lucida calida iis omnibus, quos vitae consuetudo vel officiorum societas tecum coniungeret.

Haec praecipua, dilecte Fili, merita tua erga Ecclesiam et patriam; de quibus sane gaudemus. Quin et gratias agimus pro beneficiis, quae e scriptis tuis in sacram religionem, in theologiam, in disciplinas varias manarunt, simul exoptantes, ut quam diutissime limpidae ingenii et pietatis tuae aquae de tuo fonte dissiliant.

Tandem decet Nos esse tibi animo gratissimos ob istam erga Christi Vicarium venerationem; quod et spes alit in Nobis, et cor haud leviter tangit.

Ceterum, dilecte Fili, Benedictionem Nostram Apostolicam cum tibi, tum etiam Sodalibus Societatis Jesu omnibusque quos caros habes, quam aequissimo animo impertimus, benevolentiae Nostrae signum, caelestium donorum auspicium.

Ex aedibus Vaticanis, die I mensis Februarii, anno MCMLXXVI, Pontificatus Nostri tertio decimo.

PAULUS PP. VI

[TO OUR BELOVED SON, HENRI DE LUBAC, MEMBER OF THE SOCIETY OF JESUS.

BELOVED SON,

On February 20 this year you will celebrate your 80th birthday. On that occasion, you will be surrounded not only by your friends and members of the Society of Jesus, whose ornament you are, but by almost all of France and by scholars from all over the Catholic world. We wanted to send you this letter to express our fatherly joy, to display the high opinion we have of you, and to thank you as you well deserve, in our name and that of the Church.

Know first of all that the source of our joy is the contemplation of the impressive gifts God has heaped upon you and you have wisely used: to wit, your keen intellect, the priesthood, the religious life, the outstanding and holy faith, the zeal and love for research which sometimes becomes a religious worship. Beloved son, these were the sources of a life of unwearied, increasing search for truth. Your research has been abundant yet precise, keen and enthusiastic. You have questioned nature, history, Christianity, Church, Scripture, philosophy, world religions, even atheism, men too of every age outstanding for their virtue, learning and wisdom.

These, too, were the sources of your remarkable output of publications. These cost you hard work, pain, and some hardships. In them your holy and awesome task was ever to seek the truth with utmost care, to follow the venerable footsteps of the Fathers, and to embrace the established traditions of our forbears. The subjects you treated were ever in their proper time, place, and moment, each provided with abundant critical apparatus. In them you showed a faultless critical faculty, gifted both in analysis and synthesis. The gifts you brought to your writing and the principles you followed are the sources of their enduring freshness.

Greatly to your credit, you were among the consultants at the Second Vatican Council and performed outstanding work there. You were also a valuable member of the International Theological Commission. We must mention also your work as editor of several noteworthy collections of books.

With these and other works of genius, beloved son, you have built a monument more enduring than bronze (Horace's Odes, 3, 30, 1) for every teacher to appreciate and use. For this reason, many universities conferred honorary degrees on you, and the Academy of Ethics and Politics in Paris made you a fellow.

But we have not yet described the full extent of your attainments. Everything else in your life reflects honor upon you and the Church. For almost thirty years you have been a professor at the Catholic Institute of Lyons. There your research, your teaching, and your availability to students in their search for truth have made you their helper and joy. We want to mention also your religious practice, sustained by God's Word and strengthened by the sufferings you have undergone. This has been a flame of light and warmth for all your fellow Catholics and professional colleagues.

Beloved son, these are but the highest of your services to the Church and to your country, and they fill us with joy. We are grateful, too, for the blessings which flow from your writings upon holy religion, theology, and other fields of study. We greatly desire that the clear waters of talent and devotion may flow from your spring for the longest possible time.

Finally, we must feel grateful for your devotion toward the Vicar of Christ. This fills us with hope and deeply moves our heart.

Beloved son, as a sign of our good will and with a prayer that heaven will bless you, we give most lovingly our apostolic blessing to you and also to the members of the Society of Jesus and to all whom you hold dear.

From the Vatican, February 1, 1976, the thirteenth year of our pontificate.

POPE PAUL VI]

On October 10, 1980, welcoming the participants to the congress on "evangelization and atheism" and speaking to them of the "spiritual drama of our times", John Paul II insisted on quoting integrally and adopting as his own this very keenly contested passage.

In June 1978, I published in *l'Osservatore romano* an article commemorating the fifteenth anniversary of the election of Paul VI. (It was known that the Pope would die shortly thereafter.)

June 1963. Barely out of the thick fog in which I was kept following a twofold surgical intervention, here, as in a dream, I see before me an indistinct shadow bending over my hospital bed, and I make out these two words: "Montini . . . Paul VI. . . ." At that moment, the long nightmare was dissipated. Contact with the real world was reestablished. It was the return to light, life rising once again in me.

Coincidence? Yes, but much more. A great hope had just rushed into me. It would not be disappointed.

Heir of John XXIII, Paul VI had brought the Council to a successful conclusion. Day after day he obtained the application of it. The Church, once more, is being renewed. At the life-giving breath of Pentecost, the tree of the Cross always grows green again and promises new fruit.

But at the same time, once more, the tempest rages. Those who accuse the Council for having given rise to it do not know what they are saying. One did not need to be a prophet to discern the symptoms of it long ago. Yet the jolt would not have been so strong without a more immediate cause, which it is too early to trace but which historians careful to gather the documents will not have much trouble elucidating. The Church invited her children to a great collective effort in an atmosphere of freedom. Not all were able to hear that, or did not care to understand. In many cases—although it is not popular to dare to say it—the Council has been betrayed. Not only through the effect of an all-too-natural inclination but through the action of what I may be permitted to call a paracouncil, which was no less an anticouncil with respect to the truth than a declared opposition, and how much more effective. It is the same with respect to the Council as to the Gospel: I suspect that many keep from rereading it so as not to blush at what they are preaching in its name.

Yet for fifteen years Pope Paul has been at the helm. Without knowing him, I had learned enough about him to be assured that it would be in good hands. With a methodical and persistent firmness that does not cease to give the lie to an equally persistent myth, he steers the ship. Out of all that his detractors put forward, one single trait should be retained: the sorrow that grips him at times and which he cannot suppress, although it never breaks or even lessens his momentum. In truth, we would regret it if this sign of humanity, among so many others, were lacking in him —this trait that shows a resemblance to Jesus. And what makes it more precious to us is precisely the outrageous misunderstanding to which he is subject, not so much on the part of the "world"—and not, of course, on the part of Christians, Catholic or not, in general—as on the part of those from whom he had the right to expect support.

We used to speak (must we say only "used to") of "court theologians", that breed of intellectuals who are never lacking around princes of every sort. If they were still with us today, anyone with open eyes would know well that it is not around the See of Peter that we must look for them. The all-powerful queen who distributes her favors is elsewhere. But Christ is closer than ever to Peter in the insults.

A situation that is paradoxical three times over! In the wake of the last Council, at the very hour when the papacy, having shed the last effects that still recalled, like cumbersome witnesses, an out-of-date past, proves to be in the forefront of evangelic renewal and increases the appropriate actions to encourage it, acrimonious voices of protest are raised from the most opposite horizons, then to give way to the silence of a contemptuous estrangement. On the other hand, it is not so much from quarters foreign to the Church or by those who, through traditional prejudices, are ill-prepared to understand; it is much closer, it is by some of her sons, unfaithful to their own vocation, that she is publicly ridiculed in the person of her chief pastor. It is not here a question of initiatives requested or of preferences manifested, whose advisability each, according to his competence and his responsibility, always has the right to evaluate; rather it is a question of the very foundations of the faith, of Catholic morality and discipline, which the body of bishops united to the Pope has the mission to maintain. Finally, the third paradox: the dispute with the papacy is increasing in Catholicism at the time when, among Christians of other confessions, the awareness of an urgent need for unity is awakening or deepening. I will never forget what one of them, who exercised an eminent role in his Church, confided to me at the end of a long conversation: "Unity must be accomplished. Despite the obstacles still piled up, many signs show that the time is ripe. Now, it is obvious that unity can only be achieved around the bishop of Rome; various arrangements should insure respect for traditions that have developed in diverging directions since the time of separation, but that is not impossible to achieve. But", he added, and his voice then took on tones of an uneasy sadness, "we note that the Pope is today disputed from within the Catholic Church herself. That is the great obstacle that risks delaying our union very much."

My interlocutor was not mistaken. If the person of the Pope is thus disputed, it is often in reality because of what is most incontestable about him (if I may speak in this way). Throughout, it is the principle of the papacy, the very function of Peter that is the object of the dispute. It thereby receives the supreme homage. Everyone senses it or has a presentiment of it: insofar as this function is assured, whatever the tides of history, the light of Christian revelation remains intact and what one rightly calls, in a unique sense, the Christian revolution preserves its inexhaustible power. That is the rock against which break the efforts of perversion, of rupture or "radical change" that can always find, in troubled circumstances, so much unconscious complicity.

In the choir of Santa Maria dell'anima, at the center of old papal Rome, one can read, beneath the tomb of Adrian VI an epitaph of melancholy beauty before which I have meditated more than once. It evokes the situation of the Church at the beginning of the seventh century and what might have been her renewal if so many adverse forces had not paralyzed the action of this Pope who disappeared too early. The Lord has not spared Paul VI the trial any more than the others; it has not been moderate; on the other hand, more time was given him (and, we hope, will still be given to him) than to Pope Adrian to go forward, against the winds and tides, in the accomplishment of the program announced already by the encyclical *Ecclesiam suam* and the inaugural discourse of the last session of the Council. One day, when a serious historian undertakes to discover the real life of the Church in the course of these past fifteen years, then, with all pointless agitation reduced to dust, it will undoubtedly be apparent that in complete Christian fidelity, under the impulse of Paul VI, everything was being prepared so that the salutary action of the Church of Christ might be pursued in the midst of a profoundly transformed world.

H. L.

(*Osservatore romano*, JUNE 20–21, 1978.)

[*9:12*]

"One need not blush or excuse oneself for being tender: it is an honor for which one must be proud, it is a grace that one must spread, for where there is no tenderness, neither is there joy given nor joy received. I know of course that one can misuse one's heart, one can wither one's body and soul in debilitating and sterile tenderness. It is the path that is opened wide to those entering into life. . . . It is the same with human tenderness as with all beautiful things: it must gain mastery over itself and free itself from its masks, just like the morning sun, leaving the mists of dawn. . . . But one would be wrong to laugh at this word and this thing called affection. Do you think that the hearts of the great apostles did not overflow with this tenderness? Look again at the epistles of Saint Paul or at that wonderful passage from Acts that recounts the farewell of the Saint to his faithful at Ephesus: tears stream on all sides from these eyes that will never see each other again here below. Meditate especially on the profound tones, the ardent rhythm of Paul, writing to his faithful, whom he has engendered in Christ and who are his children. . . . Affection has its dangers, but the way to guard against them is not to hound it: one must educate it. Rather than destroy the sympathies, one must strive to universalize them. . . . If there is no love without tenderness, there is no tenderness without strength and purity. Wine that is watered down loses its quality, its vigor and its aroma, but wine that is cloudy is no longer wine. Water is better."

[9:13]

ON ABJECTION

[In Matthew 11:2–3], we see John tried to the utmost. His life at the end is the opposite of a life filled with honors, decorations, presidencies, academies, and so forth. It ends in abjection. Father de Foucauld had often remarked that, like the life of the Lord, so ends the life of the Lord's disciples. Far from receiving the human reward for what he has done, John sinks into total poverty, total privation. . . . We do not find here merely an anecdotal biography from the past but, rather, certain aspects of the ways of God, of his manner of leading his own and of introducing them deeply into the very reality of the spiritual life.

Jean Daniélou, *Jean-Baptiste, témoin de l'Agneau* (Paris: Ed. du Seuil, 1964), 144.

. . . Jesus, who deserved the adoration of the Angels, "in whom are all the treasures of wisdom and knowledge", in order to learn humility, willed to be unknown, then misunderstood, excommunicated by the State and by the Church, submitted to the chastisements of the law, ranked with criminals, without having deserved it. . . . To accept, even to desire, for love of Him, to be dishonored, even in the eyes of those I love, if He allows. . . . Or at least to accept the thousand little dishonors, desertions, contempt with which my life is going to be filled to the degree that others discover better by experience what little foundation I have. . . . To accept the great abjections, of which I am not worthy, in order to be ready at least to accept the small ones.

. . . Jesus, I have understood that you do not want me to distinguish between my sins and other sins, but rather that I enter more profoundly into your heart and that, as you take on the sins of the world, I take on the sins of the world: that I consider myself responsible for the sins of those you wish. . . : so that in this way any affront, any suffering will seem entirely just to me since it punishes in me faults that are mine, that I have willed for my own. . . . You make me feel today, Jesus, that it is necessary . . . to take upon myself the sins of others, to accept as a result all the punishments that they will draw down upon me from your justice and in particular the contempt of those for whom I offer myself. Then, Jesus, my charity will resemble in some small way the charity with which you have loved me.

Jean Daniélou. *Carnets spirituels*. Long retreat from the Third Year (November 1940).

[*9:14*]

In this same year, 1978, Etienne Gilson died, at age 94. As early as the thirties, I had attended, with enthusiasm, some of his lectures. We had begun to have contact with each other at the end of 1945, with respect to my *Proudhon*, which he declared having read "with the most consistent interest" and considered "the best introduction we possess in French on Proudhon's work". When the encyclical *Humani generis* appeared in 1950, he had bluntly criticized the "Scholasticism" of the so-called "Thomistic" theologians whose campaign had culminated in this encyclical (which in their eyes, moreover, was too benign). In a conference given in the United States, at Marquette University (Milwaukee), he had declared, according to what Father Gerard Smith, S.J., wrote me: "I am waiting for the promised commentary. . . . I cannot comment on the Encyclical itself without difficulty, but the commentary!, I will comment on that commentary!" Nevertheless, he had written nothing to me about it. It was between 1956 and 1968 that he addressed a series of important letters to me, from some of which I have quoted above. His lively approval of *Chemins de Dieu*, and still more of *Surnaturel* as well as of subsequent writings on that subject, were a great encouragement for me. In our private conversations, he let his witty eloquence flow even more freely. With regard to Blondel and Teilhard de Chardin, he nourished an antipathy at least equal to my sympathy for them, but that in no way bothered our friendship. He did not take the least offense at my outspokenness, when I wrote to him, for example: "I am persuaded that if you had read more of Teilhard and ignored all that has been recounted about him, your impression would not be so bad." One day I even obtained from him, certainly not a retraction, but some rather noteworthy concessions. It was in 1967. He had just published, in his little book of *Tribulations de Sophie* (1967), a conference requested of him by Msgr. Dino Staffa in which he attacked a pseudo-quotation from Teilhard found in a work by Garaudy. I had pointed out his error to him, not without a little caution. "Of course," he replied to me, "you can write what you think to me! What would friendship be otherwise? Besides, it's quite possible, all too possible, that you are right. . . . Furthermore, I am hoping to get out of these verbal battles, in which I got involved without exercising much caution, I admit. Sometimes one assumes responsibilities that are none of one's business."

I will quote here still one more passage from a long letter he wrote me on September 3, 1968, with respect to Paul VI:

"I have always been extremely timid with my great men. I would never have dared to take a half-hour of Bergson's life for myself alone; the only time I had anything but a chance conversation with him, in Strasbourg, it was he who summoned me. I never went to see Claudel, that unique phenomenon in the history of our literature. I often ran into him, and for me our meetings were unforgettable, but I myself never presumed to occupy five minutes of his life. The idea of going to see Paul VI would never enter my mind, and that is perhaps a mistake, for this man of God, animated by a prophetic spirit, as you say with perfect justice, could well be in great need of both comfort and simple human affection, if only in compensation for the indignities heaped on him, which some of his sons heap on him. This is why I think that you, who are a priest, and a priest twice over since you belong to the Society of Jesus, should not hesitate to let him know how you feel. You have never had more than one adversary in the Vatican (to my knowledge), and that was a Jesuit. Msgr. Montini held you in the highest esteem, and I am certain that it has only increased with the passing years. A priest, a theologian as well known as you are and as universally esteemed(!) has no reason at all to feel the timidity that restrains me, too often perhaps, from expressing my admiration to those I admire the most. —After all, our beloved Christ himself was not content to be loved, he wanted to be told of it: 'Peter, do you love me?'. . . Yes, we do have a prophetic Pope, whose gift of prophecy is so obviously a gift from God that he is bowed down beneath its weight. Everything we can do to help him bear it, let us do."

The last letter I received from him was dated July 1, 1975. He was already frail and was forced to dictate it. "Do not think", he said to me, "I have ever failed to recognize, much less been indifferent to, your affection. . . . Affection like yours, and the prayers it inspires in you, are very precious to me." I am happy that I was able, however slightly, to help console this faithful Catholic, whose last years were clouded by the crisis he noted in the Church of France.

[*9:15*]

Some of his letters throw light on his spiritual life. I will quote only one passage. He wrote to me from the college of Poitiers, on December 29, 1931: ". . . I have received a letter from my Father Provincial, on the subject of my 'admission to the celebration of next February 2nd':

" 'You surely understand what a delicate point this is to resolve. In the questionnaires[1] for profession, the questions are posed with such precision that the recent difficulties during your theology cannot be overlooked. Now, if everyone is agreed in recognizing that on many of the detailed points of this inquiry you have attained—and even at times surpassed— what is required of a candidate whom the Society admits to this degree of profession, it nevertheless remains true, unfortunately, that some of your words—I said this to you last year, and it grieved you very much—could make one believe that you do not find in the Society and in the Institute what you believe to be the ideal of your religious life. You affirmed to me with tears, in an hour I will never forget, that you see no other providential path of salvation and perfection but the Church, and, for you, the Church through the Society. Nevertheless, words and actions that could really be interpreted as severely critical of the methods of the Society, of its scholastic processes and of its ideas have succeeded in slipping into your words and your attitude in the scholasticate. One could believe that you held in phil. or theol. positions that are not the "communis modus" of which No. 7 of the above-mentioned inquiry speaks.

" 'I know that you love the Society with a very filial love and that if some words have escaped you that might make you be judged severely, you regret them, and that in all that you have been motivated only by the desire to give better service to souls and to the providential means provided by the Society. But "sub specie boni", there may have been illusion and excess there.

[1] [Questionnaires sent to a certain number of one's fellow Jesuits regarding one's suitability for profession—TRANS.]

" 'Once again, I want to thank you for the very comforting example of generosity, obedience and abnegation you have given by accepting with simplicity and by fulfilling with zeal—which Providence is rewarding with a success unknown by your predecessor—a position that is particularly difficult for you.

" 'The precise point that motivates your non-admission this year to Profession is that which I have pointed out to you above. I know you well enough to know what pain . . . and that I can rely on you. . . .'

"I was anxious to quote this whole document to you, very dear friend. It seems to me that the awkwardness of the one writing it in the face of such a task is clearly evident, and I acknowledge that if the 'precise point' with which I am reproached is very accurate through the events to which he alludes, it seems to me much less so through the words, gestures or attitudes that earn me so serious a suspicion; but that has very little importance!

"This news has not, on the whole, surprised me very much. Knowing all that you and I know of the events of two years ago, we will find it rather logical. I said to my Rector, in explaining the matter as best I could —the good man couldn't get over it: the session for the 2nd is in preparation!—as prefect, I have occasion every day to take measures like this and to punish students who are perhaps not very guilty simply because the punishment is necessary for good order. It is a consequence of original sin that the government is obliged to take such measures. Since I am in a position where I oblige others to submit to such measures, it would be bad form for me not to recognize the justification of that which affects me.

"And in my situation, this little added trial is not very important and will weigh very little once I am caught up again in the whirlwind of the *admittatur* and the little internal quarrels to be resolved by Solomon with justice and peace; obviously, this proves that in Rome they are intent on taking things seriously and on showing me that they do not forget quickly; but what does it matter! let us have faith in Providence, which directs everything. For two years we have been living in a kind of overturning of what we can humanly hope to accomplish for the glory of God, this delay is a very little episode that, I assure you, does not shake my confidence at all. Of course, I am grieved to see the atmosphere of suspicion, which has already been such a heavy weight for me, affirmed once again and receive, as it were, an official and public consecration and consequently the further distancing and diminishment, if possible, of the possibility of ever accomplishing or at least making any rough draft at all of the dreams we have made together. But, after all, what does it matter! Religious philosophy or a better adapted theology are of little importance, and if the Lord needs it, he will know very well how to manage things to make them arise when and as he wishes. So let us rest in peace and distribute our *admittatur!"*

I have kept the outline of a reply to one of these attacks, which appeared in a journal whose title escapes me. This page could not be published, but Father Fessard had kept it:

We do not like polemics. But we cannot allow the best workers in our spiritual Resistance to be slandered publicly without saying anything.

The *Cahiers du Témoignage chrétien*, to which we are heirs, owes a debt of gratitude to the Rev. Father Fessard. He was involved at their very beginning. One of the very first, at a time when others, who speak so loudly today, still gave no sign of their prodigious development, he sounded the alarm on nazism. He denounced the danger of the death of the French soul. He awakened the benumbed Christian conscience of many. Let those who have not read, during the Occupation, that first *Cahier: France, prends garde de perdre ton âme,* read it today at least in reprint. It will be an historical text from now on. One can only admire, along with his courage, the perfect clearsightedness of his diagnosis. Even before the war, in *Epreuve de force,* Father Fessard had signaled the rise of the danger. From one end of those terrible years to the other, he remained faithful to himself.

Because, in the necessary fight, he did not abdicate the rights of reflection; because he endeavored to understand historically a situation that was terribly equivocal instead of thoughtlessly casting anathemas at all those who were less clearsighted than he; because he preserved the sense of justice and because the horror of nazism did not become for him as for some others, unfortunately, the cover for similar abuses, here he is, attacked in the basest fashion.

The quarrel that some seek to pick with him can only be formulated on the basis of lies.

To cut out a few pieces of a sentence from his writings, whose meaning is then distorted; to mix up dates in order to apply these texts to situations totally different from the one at which the texts were aimed; even to present what was an objection or a presentation of an adverse point of view as expressing the thought of the author himself: these are—unless it is a question of unprecedented thoughtlessness—actions of bad faith.

We know all too well that, in the drive of political passions, such excesses are not rare. But here, by his serene studies, the Rev. Father Fessard has furnished, no motive, no beginning of an excuse for such a drive. The bad faith seems really to work systematically and without emotion. One is ashamed on behalf of French thought to note that the attack is led in a journal that shields itself with a few great names and presents itself as the work of thinkers. *Le Témoignage chrétien* would be denying itself if it did not protest against such proceedings.

[*9:17*]

See for example *De l'actualité historique*, vol. I, pp. 52, 113–15, 160–62, 204–9, 270. Cf. "Dialogue théologique avec Hegel" (1970), in *Stuttgarter Hegel-Tage* (1970), hersg. v. Hans-Georg Gadamer (Bonn, 1974), 231–48, etc. Hegel, Kierkegaard and Marx: "Father Fessard has come face to face every day for half a century with the reflection of these three masters of modern thought so as to show in the speculative deepening of the Catholic Faith and Theology the solution to the problems they have posed and, simultaneously, the resolution of the contradictions that can be noted between them as well as within their own thought." (Michel Sales)

[*9:18*]

Already in 1947, Father Fessard had written in a memorandum destined for the Father General, J. Janssens, who had requested it from him: "By comparing our period to that of Günther and by brandishing Hegelianism as a bugbear that must lead to modernism, Father Garrigou makes us fear that his philosophical and historical sense might not be completely awake. In fact, if it is true that a hundred years ago, in the time of Günther, Hegelianism was alive, it is nonetheless true that today it is dead and well dead. What is alive and what Father Garrigou seems not to have perceived are some systems derived from Hegel but quite distinct from him, Marxism, racist neo-paganism, existentialism. Why does he not attack these real errors instead of pursuing with his anathemas those who are fighting against them? . . . Father Garrigou does not seem to have a very deep knowledge of this situation, to judge not only from this historical comparison but also from his refutation of Hegel in his large work on God.

"Assuredly he gives there a classic refutation and one that can suffice for 'schoolboys' in philosophy. But it will make the least student smile who has understood today the true problems posed by Hegel and the systems born from him because it passes them by completely."

One can apply to him the beautiful maxim of Saint Thomas Aquinas, Job 13:1, 2: "Cum aliquis veritatem loquitur, vinci non potest, cum quocumque disputat." [When anyone speaks the truth, he cannot be refuted no matter who his opponent.]

Here is the rejected clarification:

Monsieur le Directeur, The two articles on Father Gaston Fessard published by [your journal] on November 9 and 16, 1979, call for a few remarks. I make them in all friendship, for their author.

1. Toward the end of the first article it is said that "the unpublished writings by the author will not shed any essential light for the understanding of his work, because they are limited to results drawn from principles. . . ." This is a manifest error. It is enough to read the two works published after his death (one, whose final proofs he had reviewed completely, appeared a few days later, the other, which he had left entirely finished, came out a few months later) to see that they are not at all comprised of results drawn from abstract principles; the fruit of a very deep knowledge of Marxism and from a very concrete observation of its current *praxis*. Father Fessard did not write them in order to bring out an application of his own "principles" but because of his Catholic faith and his love of the Church of Christ, like a "good and faithful servant".

It is also a manifest contradiction, since the second article speaks of "decisive essays", several of which remain unpublished. And, on the other hand, it is curious to see two works that give witness to the most courageous commitment in our spiritual combats brushed aside with disdain (without so much as naming them) by someone who says he dreads thoughts remaining "pure academicism".

2. In the same sentence, the author adds that the "principles" of Father Fessard, "as principles of a thought that is above all theological, need to be rooted in a *new reading of Scripture*". Farther on, he warns us against "the illusions and dangers of intellectual research that would apply intellectual categories and abstract models directly to the understanding of the concrete. . . ."

The reader might believe that such was also the method of Father Fessard. It was precisely the opposite. It was a long meditation on Christian reality in its concrete singularity that led Father Fessard either to universalize (using Saint Paul particularly as guide) the categories of "Jew" and "pagan" or to bring a judgment to bear on the Marxist contaminations that are threatening the Christian consciousness today.

The author speaks in the name of a "biblical and theological culture" freed from the "handicaps" that still cripple the work of Father Fessard. He provides no light on the subject of the "new reading of Scripture", without which this work would lack a foundation. He merely warns us that one cannot venture such works without "an act (of reading) that produces a full coherence. . ., that, from one Testament to the other, makes us intimate friends of Jesus in the face of his life and his death", without "a very rigorous study of the texts", without "providing oneself with the means and taking the time for a new study of Scripture", without "a long period of gestation", without "the strictness and flexibility that rarely go together", without "an utmost familiarity with the terrain from which the traces of past history are extracted and where the tools of thought that decipher and interpret are worked out". . . . We see very well that these instructions are addressed directly to those who would wish to continue the work of Father Fessard, but they are just as much a criticism of his work, for "his personal reading of Scripture was old". We really wish to believe that the author has all the necessary competence in this domain, but we do not see in what respect Father Fessard, failing to possess as much competence as the author, apparently was unable to understand anything at all of Scripture or to propose anything but a worthless theology. Let us observe merely that if his "reading" was "old", it was always direct and minute. He had been initiated in it from the time of his novitiate by his companion Father Marcel Jousse, according to the most precise methods that could then be practiced; he pursued his reading throughout his life, and, in his last years, he was more in touch with the new methods than some might believe, as the documents in his archives testify.

3. The author then develops some personal views, which we will not go into in detail. They seem to imply to us, at the very least through his emphases, on the one hand, and through his silences, on the other, a certain lack of understanding of Father Fessard's thought, which is not without consequence. What the latter said of the newness in Christ, he seems to hear with respect to a newness to be achieved in the future; what Father Fessard showed as the divine work accomplished in the conversion of man, he speaks of, according to his fashion, as an "invention" resulting from an historical process. "The surprising Fessardian analysis", according to him, would thus contain "a seed", "but still chilled by the cold of a long winter", of the newness that it is possible for us finally to "invent". "The societies of the past up to our own days, notably in Europe", have maintained "the Master-Man and Woman-Slave relationship"; but "today we men and even more the women, our companions, in whom the great-

est developments are being accomplished, announcing the world to come, feel that something very different is in gestation".

We are there far from Father Fessard and from his "theological" work.

4. We will not dwell on the method of insinuation, so foreign to the uprightness of Father Fessard, which it is painful to see used in an article coming, nevertheless, from one of his admirers. But we must point out in closing that a study entitled "Une Oeuvre qui est une vie [A work that is a life]" is in error both through omission and through a lack of information.

Through omission: the author fails to mention (except for one very general phrase about "the problems first treated, on the contemporary level, with respect to the great anthropological options that consisted of nazism, on the one hand, and Marxism, on the other") everything to which Father Fessard committed his life and which earned him much disfavor, in the Church, in his order and in public opinion, disfavor always endured with a peaceful heart.

Lack of information: besides the revealing choice of books mentioned or brushed aside, the author does not seem to be familiar with the principal places where Father Fessard explains this dialectic of Jew and pagan of which he speaks. He seems not to know that the work *Chrétiens marxistes et théologie de la libération*[2] contains, among other fundamental reflections, a development that, in "its conciseness" deserves, like *Autorité et bien commun*, to remain a "classic". For better information, he should have at least consulted the copious bibliography (171 titles) compiled by Father Michel Sales, a well-informed expert and sound interpreter, which appears at the end of the second posthumous work: *Eglise de France, prends garde de perdre la foi!*[3]

HENRI DE LUBAC, S.J., NOVEMBER 16, 1979

The appropriate superior of Father Fessard (in Chantilly) to whom I had communicated this clarification replied to me on December 6: ". . . I thank you very warmly for sending this. . . . Some notable errors have been made in these articles on the subject of Father Fessard. And these kinds of errors risk being passed on to posterity, especially since [X] could be thought a faithful interpreter and expert on the thought of Father Fessard. As is proper, I have communicated your text to the community."

Father Michel Sales wrote on December 28 to the representative of the journal in question:

". . . More than a month ago, I told you of my hope to see published

[2] "Le Sycomore" series, Lethielleux, 1978.
[3] Julliard, 1979.

in [your journal] the corrections by Father de Lubac. . . . I have many objective reasons to deplore the fact that your journal has not proceeded with this publication. But one that seems to me to take precedence over all the others is expressed best by S. Weil in a text on which I have often meditated: 'There are men who work eight hours a day and who make a great effort to read at night in order to instruct themselves. They cannot devote themselves to verifications in large libraries. They take the book (or journal) at its word. One does not have the right to give them mistakes to eat. What sense is there in alleging that the authors are of good faith? They do not work physically eight hours. Society [the Church] feeds them so that they have the time and can take the trouble to avoid error. A railway switchman who causes a derailment would not be well received if he alleged that he was in good faith'. . . ."

[*9:21*]

See in *Eglise de France*. . ., pp. 277–83, the postface by Father Michel Sales: "Défense d'un mort et de la vérité"; similarly, the appendix, pp. 285–98: "Bio-bibliography of Father Gaston Fessard" (extract from the journal *Plamia*, 51 [Christmas 1978]), and pp. 299–314: "Bibliographie". Also, in the journal *Choisir* (Geneva), May 1979: "Gaston Fessard: Une Philosophie chrétienne de l'histoire". Father Sales is preparing at this time the edition of vol. 3 of *Dialectique des Exercices spirituels* (III, Symbolisme et historicité. Le Sycomore [P. Lethielleux, 1984]). Also foreseen, among others, is a collection of Hegelian studies.

[*9:22*]

Excerpts from letters from Father Bouillard.

July 15, 1957: "The meeting organized by *Recherches* aimed at treating a theological subject in a way that was as little theological as possible. Rather than seek to bring out the essence of the priesthood, they endeavored officially to emphasize the 'contestations'. Fortunately, Pastor Leuba was there to recall, with the authority of the 'heretic', a few fundamental truths. . . . Father Morel set before us, without the least critical judgment, the thinking of Nietzsche on Christianity and Western civilization. Father Beirnaert invited us to take seriously the 'questions' posed by Freud to Christianity (Pastor Leuba said, quite to the point, that he was more interested in the 'replies'). Father Moingt said some things that were very interesting and others that were debatable. We parted company not really knowing what the Priesthood is. But that was not, it seems, the point of the meeting. . . .

Many of the participants, fortunately, realized the defects of the project, and even their intentional character."

June 29, 1961: "I have read . . . the letters of Teilhard to Valensin. They are fascinating and deeply moving. Teilhard had an admirable loftiness of vision and grandeur of soul."

August 3 and September 5, 1962: "A surprise: Father Fessard sent to Chantilly. I deeply regret his being forced to leave Paris, where he found the necessary stimulus for his work and where he had a profound influence. No reason was given him for it. But he simply obeyed, and looked at the bright side of the thing."

September 5, 1962: "I have reread for the fourth time the entire works of Saint John of the Cross. . . . I have also reread for the fourth time the major part of the three volumes by Morel. Much more than before, the book appears to me to be of poor quality, despite some interesting contributions. Not only is he completely unfaithful to Saint John of the Cross; but the thinking that is expressed in it is poorly managed and confuses everything. It is the work of a self-taught man who does not know or understand any of the works of analysis done before him."

December 22, 1963: "Have you read the book by F. Jeanson: *La Foi d'un incroyant* [The faith of an unbeliever]? It has made me sick to see a number of Jesuits and Dominicans admire this inconsistent text. . . . I said to Father Provincial, at table in the refectory, that, not being an atheist, despite my good relations with atheists, I was henceforth going to feel myself to be in an inferior position when I had to teach our scholastics. . . ."

December 29, 1968: "I, too, have received the Declaration by *Concilium* on the freedom of theologians, along with an invitation to sign it. This invitation has posed me a true problem of conscience. Having been the victim of proceedings at the Holy Office and not having received like you a public reparation, living always in the fear of new troubles, I would feel inclined to sign it because of that. But I have nonetheless abstained, . . . because the tone of this declaration, the context, the procedure of having recourse to the press, seem inappropriate to me. . . ."

December 23, 1972: "I have read with some surprise the preparatory papers for the future General Congregation, in particular what concerns the concept of the Church. What an obsession with caricaturing the old things in order to substitute hazy propositions for them! And why this desire to call into question the fundamental principles on which the Jesuits were precisely gathered together? . . ."

October 20, 1973: "Girardi moved heaven and earth against my decision.[4] I receive new complaints every day. . . . But my decision, firmly

[4] Decision not to renew an annual invitation (as "invited professor") to lectures at the

approved by the Rector, will not be changed. Among the complaints I have received is a mimeographed paper, signed by a group of teachers from our Philosophy Faculty. It demands, among other things, freedom for Marxist options among Christians. That is what is clear and disheartening." —And, April 25, 1974: "I am having difficulties with a few colleagues, led by X. . . . On the other hand, I note, in the overall religious and philosophical sections of the I.C., such divergences that one wonders if a real unity in faith and in affection for the Church still exists. Finally, the present evolution of the Society disturbs me. . . ."

July 23, 1975: "I have calculated, with a smile, the close relationship between Garaudy's *Parole d'homme* and a number of ecclesiastical resolutions, including certain texts from our General Congregation: the same vague and confused idealism. . . . X arrived last night; he said he deplored the articles by Father Moingt on the ministries: they trouble a clergy already too carried away by fantastic innovations."

[*9:23*]

Here is the text of this article, which appeared in *La Croix* in 1965:

Faith in Search of Understanding

I remember the day I found myself with some time on my hands in the library of a Dominican monastery, and what better place is there than a monastic library? My eyes chanced to fall upon a book that had lost its binding, worn out from having been read over and over again, entitled *Surnaturel* and bearing the name of the Rev. Father Henri de Lubac, S.J. I picked it up out of curiosity, for I had never read it, but I had often heard it discussed in that tone theologians take when advising a prospective reader that he will do well to exercise caution. In short, something like the Censors' film catalogues, a book "for adults only". How could it be that this rather disquieting book had such well-thumbed pages?

Years have gone by. Father de Lubac's book has become two books: *Augustinisme et Théologie moderne* and *Le Mystère du surnaturel.*[5] Here they are on my table, I have just read them, I have been invited to inform the

---

Institut de science des religions, under the Institut Catholique de Paris, lectures Girardi had transformed into Marxist propaganda.

[5] Two octavo volumes of 333 and 300 pages; "Theology" series, no. 63 and 64 (Paris: Aubier, 1965).

public of their existence, and I think so highly of them that something inside of me tells me it is my duty to accept that invitation. Not without scruples, however, for how am I to go about it?

Their two titles alone give some information about the author and his way of thinking. We are inundated with books carrying flashy titles that promise much but do not keep their promises. Here, on the contrary, two austere titles to introduce a fascinating work that includes all of the substance of *Surnaturel*, but enriched, matured, brought right up to the moment, and topped off with a refreshing touch of that discreet satisfaction that any right mind experiences in noting that, all in all, *it was he who was right*!

The subject of this work, which is at once twofold and one, is at the very heart of the Christian religion!, the relationship between nature and grace, and then also the mystery of man's supernatural vocation and the economy of revelation, of redemption, and, in short, of salvation. Some believe that we should not be concerned with speculation in these matters and that piety can do very well without it. I would feel tempted to say they were right, as long as they kept quiet and didn't start speculating themselves. It is alarming to see what can happen to a sound religion when it cannot come to an agreement on what its own piety is. One primary merit of these two volumes will be in making it clear to many people how impossible it is for just anyone at all to pass himself off as a theologian.

Father de Lubac's extraordinary erudition, so often demonstrated in other fields, is here placed at the service of controversies that, from Saint Augustine and Saint Thomas down to our own time, have set so many good minds in opposition on a problem that really ought to be quite simple, since the personal life of every Christian presupposes it to be practically resolved. But no, the theses and the men oppose each other endlessly like a kind of seesaw, falling now on the side of nature, now on that of grace, and each accusing the other either of misunderstanding the just rights of nature or of encroaching on those of God.

Father de Lubac undoubtedly thinks they are forgetting that all their disputes are doing battle with a mystery. Creation is a mystery. For us, the first of mysteries and the seed of all the others is that God freely created finite being, unable to exist without him; yet, he can subsist, himself, without it, as indeed he did from all eternity before creation. Nature is not grace, but God's free gift of existence is a mystery that human reason immediately perceives to be impenetrable. Why this gift? Why this act? Could not God foresee man's sin, or even prevent it? Now that the evil has been done, where do we stand with God? What I have called Father de Lubac's erudition astounds me less in its extent than it does in its nature. He does not muster up theologies for us, but theologians, men like us, whose problems are the same as ours, men we can identify with even in their failures.

Because the problem is that of our destiny, it carries the same urgency today as ever it did, but those who read these two fine books will soon see that their author would not have written them if he did not experience the feeling that our own time offers a promising opportunity to move the discussion forward. For anyone who has studied history, nineteen centuries of arguing create a distance that ought to make it easier to discern the true stakes in the debate.

I do not want to distort Father de Lubac's thought by presenting as the guiding principle of his work the dominant impression I gained from the thrill of reading it, but I do see in it two great figures that stand out, two great saints who were at the same time two great theologians, Saint Augustine and Saint Thomas Aquinas. Neither of them is primarily concerned with theology, but rather with the unfathomable mystery of man, of God, and of the relationship of man to God. Real theologians build their doctrines as explanations of the highest reality, that is, divine reality. Since divine reality is so far beyond them, they do not leave a finished interpretation of it, frozen once and for all in definitive formulae. Their disciples use these great theologies themselves as the object of their reflections rather than the divine reality that was the object of these great theologies. Clinging to their formulae rather than to reality, the disciples are amazed to discover that their formulae are not in perfect accord, they try to make them agree, sacrificing, if they have to, certain essential aspects of the doctrine in order to force it into consistency with itself, as if the important thing about doctrine were not that it must first agree with reality. Thus the object is lost from sight, drowned in its own explanation.

Schools of thought in theology, along with their interminable disputes, come into being in this fashion. Father de Lubac's firm, and in my opinion justifiable, conviction is that the closer one gets to the source of the great theological movements, the more one notices their convergence, for the simple reason that they come into contact with theological reality itself, a reality that is one, as opposed to the multiplicity of its expressions.

In recommending this return to the sources, and by standing outside the "falsifying" interpretations that turned Augustinianism into a Jansenism hostile to nature and Thomism into an Aristotelian naturalism suspicious of grace, Father de Lubac is not unaware that the very premise of the problematics renews itself: "The naturalist deviation symbolized by the name of Baius, which has taken so many other forms since the sixteenth century, obliges us to make theological progress. It beckons us to a new effort at reflection. Now, more than ever, the gratuity of the supernatural must be clearly drawn and fully explained; we must gain a more distinct

awareness of it and give a more rational account of it." The great lesson
this book teaches, a lesson as true as it is fascinating, is that if theological
progress is sometimes necessary, it is never possible unless you begin from
the source. Father de Lubac's two volumes will be a priceless help to those
of us who are doing our best to go back there.

ETIENNE GILSON, OF L'ACADÉMIE FRANÇAISE

[9:24]

Here is that correction:

ON THE SUBJECT OF "TEILHARDISM"

While thanking René Pascal for the very interesting article he gave to
La Croix in the September 17 issue ("Le Teilhardisme a-t-il un avenir?
[Does Teilhardism have any future?]"), I think it opportune to offer some
additional information (or, for one part, a correction) on a point about
which the author has allowed himself to be taken in by a popular but
erroneous opinion. "This evolutionism", we read, "without any hazard,
without any risk, to linear and irresistible development—which is the
weakness of Teilhardism just as of Marxism—is surely—and fortunately
—impossible in the new scientific mind. The latter knows that it can no
longer be promised paradise; . . ." Teilhard knew it, and he never stopped
saying it. He rejected "the religion of Science", the "religion of Progress",
"evolutionary Humanism". He knew that there is a progress of the species
but also that this progress is "the most dangerous of forces", since it always "coincides with the greatest battles, the greatest evils, the greatest
risks", and since "the more humanity is refined and complicated, the more
the chances for disorder are multiplied and their gravity increased"; "The
more man becomes man, the more the problem of Evil, of understanding
evil and suffering evil, becomes imbedded and is increased (in his flesh, in
his nerves, in his mind)." He said and repeated many times that "all energy
is equally powerful for Good and for Evil". Scorning all dreams of easy
happiness and pleasure, he proclaimed that "the highest life is attained by
a death."[6] According to him, on the other hand, "the hope to dominate
the future scientifically, if one pushes it to the extreme, presupposes a . . .
static and materialistic concept of nature". Besides, as invaluable as it may
be, science "sees only the crust of things"; it is incapable of saving our

---

[6] *Le Christique* (1955). *Escrits du temps de la guerre. La Mystique de la Science* (1939). *Analyse et
synthèse* (1921). *Mon Univers* (1924). *Note sur le Progrès* (1920). *L'Energie spirituelle de la souffrance*
(1950). *L'Hominisation* (1923), etc.

race from the *taedium vitae.* "There is not a single one of the 'religions' arising up until now from science in which the universe does not become desperately frozen and desperately closed. Which is to say, in the end, uninhabitable. There is the truth!" The "social mystics" rush toward "the conquest of the future"; but "no precise summit and, what is more serious, no *lovable* object is presented for their adoration. And that is why, at bottom, the enthusiasm and devotions they arouse are hard, dry, cold, sad, disturbing for those who observe them." This is because, "in order to give oneself completely, one must know how to love. Now, how can one love a collective, impersonal—in some respects, monstrous—reality, such as the world, or even humanity?" The world? Even supposing it to be conquered, possessed, it is "a prison in which the soul suffocates". Humanity? "Fixed on the collective, humanity, so exalted for centuries, is a frightful Moloch."[7]

In the full sense of the word, there is no other "optimism" in Teilhard than that of Christian hope and prayer. But it is not my purpose to speak of that in this brief Note.

HENRI DE LUBAC, S.J.

[9:25]

I would like to close by quoting a letter addressed to me on January 6, 1962, shortly before his death, by Father Eugène Hains, who was my spiritual guide during my youth, from 1909 to 1913 (he was spiritual father and rector of the College of Mongré at that time), to whom I owe the birth of my religious vocation:

". . . Providence brought us together at the moment when you were searching for your path, and that is not forgotten. I faithfully say, every day, the *Veni sancte Spiritus* for you, as you know; and I am delighted at the good your books and teaching do. Who would have said, a few years ago, that you would be one of the theologians of the Council? . . . I hope that you can work for a long time yet for the good of the Church. —As for me, I think that growing old is a great grace; one has time to recollect oneself, to go over one's life again, . . . to get a better sense of the infinite divine goodness. . . . Imagine, I am just now discovering the beauty of the Psalms: they speak to us only of the mercy of God."

---

[7] *Le Christique* (1955). *Réflexions sur le bonheur* (1945). *La Grande Monade* (1918). *L'Atomisme de l'Esprit* (1941), etc. Still more quotations and various references will be found in H. de Lubac, *Teilhard posthume* (Fayard, 1977).

No authority in the Society (General, Assistant, Rector, Visitator, mandated theologian or anyone else) ever questioned me ex officio about my doctrine (oral or written, published or not, publicly or in private . . .).

Nor any authority in the Church (Pope, Holy Office, Congregation for Education, or any other . . .).

Not once in my life.

∼

On the other hand, numerous accusations of all kinds. . . . No legitimate authority adopted them.

One apparent belated exception: the speech read by the Very Rev. Father General Janssens, S.J., in 1950 to the Congregation of Procurators, in Rome. He did not write this speech; it is full of obviously untrue statements. The Very Rev. Father General subsequently gave me numerous oral and written signs to the contrary.

INDEX OF PERSONS

Abd-el-Jalil, Jean-Mohammed, 363

Allmen, J. J. von, 133

Anselm, 140, 144, 154, 216

Aquinas, Thomas, 25, 35ff., 42, 63, 65, 81f., 97, 123–30, 140, 144, 184, 196, 200f., 204ff., 209, 214–18, 221f., 223, 239, 249, 261, 263, 267, 269, 327, 332, 364f., 372, 393

Aristotle, 214, 216f.

Arminjon, Blaise, 89, 91f., 102, 104f., 107, 131, 324

Arnauld, Antoine, 36

Arnou, René, 62, 252, 274, 290, 324, 326

Aron, Robert, 50

Arrupe, Pedro, 107, 335, 354f., 369

Aubier, Fernand, 30, 100, 122

Aucagne, Jean, 363

Augros, M., 256

Augustine, 35ff., 64f., 97, 125f., 144, 147, 184, 196, 208, 214f., 217f., 221, 271, 286, 318, 322

Bagnoli, Sante, 157

Baius, Michael, 35ff., 124, 184, 205, 208–10, 214f., 217f., 220f., 263f.

Balic, Carolo, 126

Balthasar, Hans Urs von, 7, 20, 38, 47, 76, 81, 109, 123, 134, 150f., 194, 318, 370–75

Bañez, Domingo, 125, 214, 218, 222

Barbier (Abbé), 18

Barth, Karl, 70, 118, 131, 163

Baruzi, Jean, 112

Bastaire, Jean, 137

Baumgartner, Charles, 70, 75, 92, 141, 198, 298, 305

Bea, Augustin, 88ff., 251f., 315

Beaudou (Abbé), 254, 257

Beauduin, Lambert, 275

Beauregard, Jean-Baptiste Costa de, 15

Bédarida, François, 53

Bédarida, Renée, 53, 232, 360

Begouën, Marc, 112

Béguin, Albert, 39f.

Belleli, 260, 263

Benedict XV, 260

Bérard, Léon, 194, 253

Bergson, Henri, 32, 65

Bernanos, Georges, 170

Bernard of Clairvaux, 216, 322

Berti, 260, 263

Beuve-Méry, Hubert, 49

Billot, Louis (Cardinal), 284

Bith, 196, 253, 255

Blondel, Maurice, 18–20, 24, 29, 35, 46, 58f., 65, 94, 99, 101ff., 108, 110, 146, 149, 165, 177–80, 183–88, 209, 213, 255f., 274, 320, 363, 376ff.

Blum, Léon, 55

Bochenski, T. M., 249, 299–300

Boegner, Marc, 92, 297

Boisard, 196

Bollaërt, M., 18

Bonaventure, 35, 81, 125f., 205

Bonneville, Cristophe de, 28, 48

Bonsirven, Joseph, 57, 75

Borne, Etienne, 111, 150, 183

Bossuet, Jacques-Bénigne, 191

Bottereau, 105

Bouchet, Joseph du, 198, 232

Bouillard, Henri, 30f., 33, 62, 68, 70f., 81, 109, 167f., 194–97, 199, 251, 253f., 260, 265, 267, 275, 299, 301, 396, 396–98

Bouyer, Louis, 113

Bovelles, Charles de, 139f.

Boyer, Charles, 30, 63, 108, 125ff., 167, 170, 194f., 254ff., 266, 271f., 284

Boynes, Norbert de, 60, 245ff., 251, 254
Bremond, Henri, 85
Bro, Bernard, 121
Broglie, Guy de, 35, 213, 266, 271f.
Bruaire, Claude, 81, 150
Bruckberger, Raymond, 195
Brunschwicg, Léon, 24, 58, 165
Buchez, Philippe, 156f.
Bulot, Auguste, 15, 21
Bultmann, Rudolph Karl, 140, 348

Cajetan, 82, 125, 214, 223
Calvez, Jean Yves, 109
Camelot, T., 66, 238, 285ff.
Cappuyns, Maieul, 30, 128, 130, 213–17
Castro, Fidel, 158
Catherine of Siena, 206
Catherinet (Bishop), 23
Cavallera, Ferdinand, 48, 227
Cayré, Fulbert, 195
Chaillet, Pierre, 30, 41, 50f., 53, 55, 57, 95, 141f., 160, 165, 230, 276, 317, 360
Chaine, Joseph, 23f., 57, 312
Chamussy, Charles, 53, 252, 254f.
Chantraine, Georges, 139, 367f.
Chardin, Pierre Teilhard de, 20f., 30, 33, 46, 49, 65, 71, 99, 101, 103f., 105f., 108–11, 117, 121f., 153, 160, 170f., 182, 250, 254, 290, 300, 318, 321, 323–36, 401–2
Chardin, Régis Teilhard de, 335
Charlier (Father), O.P., 268
Châtillon, François, 50
Charles, Pierre, 21, 289, 298
Chavasse, A., 141, 210–12, 258
Chelini, Jean, 231
Chenu, M.D., 30, 58, 77, 112, 141f., 231, 268
Chevallier, Paul, 72
Chevrot, Georges, 92
Chifflot (Father), O.P., 95
Chouraqui, André, 50
Chrysostom, John, 153, 319
Claudel, Pierre, 47ff., 137f., 207, 228f., 318

Clement of Alexandria, 319
Cognet, Louis, 334
Combes, André, 105, 107
Comte, Auguste, 32, 40
Congar, Yves, 28, 69, 116, 141f., 203, 231
Coppens, M.J., 66, 288–89
Couénot, Claude, 104
Couillé (Cardinal), 16
Creusen (Father), 200
Croix-Laval, Armand de la, 35
Crouzel, Henri, 139f., 358, 379
Cruvillier, Louis, 53
Cuttat, Jacques-Albert, 34

d'Alès, Adhémar, 36
Daly, Cathal, 118
d'Ancezune, Rostan, 292
Daniélou, Jean, 30, 47, 53, 64, 95, 150, 160–64, 194, 242, 250, 253, 255, 281, 285, 314, 386f.
Daniel-Rops, Henri, 324
Daujat, J., 170
Debeauvais, 65
de Biran, Maine, 65
de Blic, Joseph, 63, 266, 272
Décisier, Auguste, 51, 115, 195, 232, 250, 252f., 255, 272f., 282, 289, 339
de Faye, E., 285
Delannoy, 251
Delaye, Emile, 15f., 46, 68, 282ff.
Delhaye, Philippe, 128
Dell'Acqua, A., 88
Delmont, Théodore, 18
Delos (Father), O.P., 250, 253, 275
Demaux-Lagrange, 48
Denat, Antoine, 26, 32, 111
Desbuquois, Gustave, 30, 40
Deschamps (Cardinal), 209
Descoqs, Pedro, 21, 42, 164, 271
Desroche, 300
de Vaux, (Father), O.P., 95
Dhanis (Father), 283, 294
Dillard, Victor, 57
Dockx, S., 130
d'Oncieu, Eugène, 104, 109
Doncoeur (Father), 49f., 230

Dondeyne, 141
Dostoyevsky, Fyodor, 40
Drey, Johann Sebastian van, 142
Dubillard (Cardinal), 16
Duns Scotus, 126, 184, 205, 219
Dupanloup, Felix, 17
Duperray, Edouard, 45f., 113
Dupuy, (Father), O.P., 122
Duss, Sr. Benedict, O.S.B., 113
Duquesne, Jacques, 112
Durand, Alexandre 68

Eckhart, Johannes (Meister), 48f., 216
Ehrenberg, Hans P., 351
Eliade, Mircea, 110
Emmanuel, Pierre, 197
Erasmus, Desiderius, 139
Erigena, Johannes Scotus, 216

Fabrègues, Jean de, 239
Feltin (Cardinal), 293
Fénelon, François, 97, 112
Fessard, Gaston, 33, 46, 51, 65, 85,
    160, 164ff., 192, 194, 232, 239,
    250, 271, 277ff., 292, 323, 363,
    389–96
Festugière (Father), 230
Feuerbach, Ludwig, 41
Finance, Joseph de, 80
Flory, Charles, 58
Fois, Mario, 357
Folliet, Joseph, 355
Fontoynont, Victor, 29f., 46, 67f., 94,
    114f., 198, 228, 254, 293, 337f.
Forest, Aimé, 25, 188
Forestier (Father), 49
Foucauld, Charles de, 371, 386
Frénaud, G., 266
Freud, Sigmund, 348
Frings (Cardinal), 107
Frossard, André, 48
Fumet, Stanislas, 41, 48, 51

Gabail, Madame, 122
Gagnebet (Father), O.P., 128, 251f.,
    272, 303
Galtier, Paul, 75
Gandillac, Maurice de, 140

Ganne, Pierre, 47, 68
Gardette (Monsignor), 256
Garric, Robert, 44, 93
Garrigou-Lagrange, Réginald P., 22,
    33, 60, 66, 125, 242, 251f., 253–
    56, 265f., 272, 274ff., 284, 286,
    294, 339
Garrone (Cardinal), 161, 163, 244,
    369
Gauthier, R. A., 128, 202
Gélin, Albert, 24, 312
Gerbet, O., 27
Gerlier (Cardinal), 50, 68, 88, 91, 105,
    232, 235, 316
Germain, Gabriel, 33
Ghellinck, Joseph de, 21
Gillon, L. B., 128
Gilson, Etienne, 19, 24, 37, 65, 76f.,
    81f., 123, 125–28, 138, 169, 305,
    387–89, 398–401
Girardi, 397f.
Gorostarzu, B. de, 64, 250, 301
Gouhier, Henri, 93
Gounot, M.C., 48, 71, 226ff., 302
Goussault (Father), 74
Gouyon (Cardinal), 133, 357
Grammont (Dom), 83
Grandmaison, Léonce de, 20, 64f., 73,
    259, 323
Gregory the Great, 319
Gregory of Nyssa, 47, 318f.
Guardini, Romano, 197
Guénon, René, 141
Gueroult, Martial, 92
Guillet, Jacques, 31, 92, 254
Guimet, Fernand, 146
Gundlach, 59
Gut, H., 150

Hains, Eugène, 402
Hamel, Robert, 19, 65, 160
Hamelin, 65
Harcourt, Robert d', 48
Haubtmann, Pierre, 39, 223
Hausherr, Irenee, 64
Hébert, Marcel, 182
Heckel, Roger, 161
Hegel, Georg, 41, 280, 392

Heindrick (Father), 251
Henry, Paul, 105, 201
Hilary of Poitiers, 319
Hildebrand, Dietrich von, 111, 202
Hocedez, Edgard, 21
Holstein, Henri, 141
Hommes (Professor), 59, 238f.
Höpfl (Father), 226
Houang, François, 46
Huby, Joseph, 16, 20f., 34f., 63, 195,
    198, 204–7, 323
Hugh of Saint Victor, 211

Ignatius, St., 167, 290, 322
Irenaeus, St., 65, 194, 243
Isaac, Jules, 50
Isidore of Pelusia, 216, 222
Ivanka, von, 64

Jaeger, Hasso, 289
Janier, Emile, 44
Jansenius, 35f., 208, 210, 213ff., 217,
    221, 264
Janssens, 20f., 37, 60–64, 66f., 70, 72–
    75, 88, 90f., 104, 106f., 250, 254,
    259, 265, 272f., 292, 295, 301,
    309, 314ff., 324f., 334, 339, 370,
    392, 403
Jarlot, Georges, 59
Jeanuet, 253
Joachim of Flora, 155ff.
John Damascene, 193
John of Saint Thomas, 214
John Paul II, 119, 159, 168, 171f., 383
John XXIII, 106, 116, 195
Jordy, M., 225
Jouassard, Georges, 22f., 91, 316
Jossua, Jean-Pierre, 203
Journet, Charles, 25f., 94, 111, 178ff.,
    200, 250, 336
Jouve, Raymond, 46
Julien (Monsignor), 253
Jugie, Martin, 23
Justinian, 66

Keble, John, 83
Kierkegaard, Søren, 48f., 87, 239, 344

Kiki, 271f.
Klein, W., 251, 254
Kojévnikoff., Alexandre, 165
Küng, Hans, 70, 299
Kunz, E., 20, 182

Laberthonnière, 16, 20, 102, 177, 180f.
Labourdette, 30, 194
La Bruyère, 266
Lachièze-Rey, 19, 42
Lacroix, Jean, 59
Ladrière, Jean, 153
Lahitton, M., 47, 226, 228
Lainez, Diego, 373
Lang, F., 194
Lanversin, de, 98
Laurent, P. M., 149
Lauriers, Guérard des, 196f.
Lavallée, Fleury, 16ff.
Le Blond, J. M., 62, 73, 266
Le Bras, G., 212
Lebreton, Jules, 29, 72f., 140, 192f.,
    198, 200, 256f., 259
Lecler, Joseph, 70, 271
Ledochowski, Wladimir, 60, 143, 254f.
Ledré, Charles, 69
Ledrus, Michel, 252
Lefèvre, Luc, 70, 107, 343
Leiber (Father), 251
Leibniz, Gottfried Wilhelm, 65, 377
Lennerz, Heinrich, 213
Lenz-Médoc, Paulus, 48, 116, 190
Leo XIII, 278
Leroy, Pierre, 300ff.
Levassor-Berrus, 195
Lévi-Strauss, Claude, 86
Litt (Monsignor), 263
Loisy, Alfred, 32
Lyonnet, Pierre, 323
Lyonnet, Stanislaw, 255, 324

Madelin (Father), 155, 171
Malebranche, Nicholas, 65, 97
Malevez, Léopold, 21, 128, 141, 190–
    92, 260
Mandonnet, 178
Marcel, Gabriel, 25, 48, 92, 111, 149,
    165, 180

Marcotte, Eugène, 296
Maréchal, Joseph, 19, 21, 35, 144, 376
Marella, Paolo, 34, 83
Marie of the Incarnation, 79
Mariès, Louis, 64, 271f.
Maritain, Jacques, 24, 26, 111, 122,
    127, 169, 178, 251, 336, 362, 363
Marlé, René, 102f.
Marrou, Henri I., 50, 95, 149
Martelet, Gustave, 92
Marx, Karl, 39ff., 239, 280, 348
Massaut, J.-P., 139
Massignon, Louis, 45
Matagne (Father), 132
Mathieu, Clément, 48, 225, 227
Maublanc, R., 212
Mauriès, 33
Maurras, Charles, 41
Maydieu (Father), 231
McCormick, J. F., 125
McDermotte, John M., 182
McGinn, Bernard, 378
Medina, Jorge, 118f.
Mejía (Father), 119
Menoud, Philippe H., 376
Mersch, Emile, 193f.
Michel, A., 30
Michelin, Alfred, 49, 58
Mickiewicz, Adam, 156
Misset, Jacques, 92
Mirandola, Pico della, 138f., 151, 358
Moehler, 148, 318
Mogenet, Henri, 47, 92, 254
Molina, Luis de, 125
Mollat, Donatien, 31, 47
Monchanin, Jules, 22, 45, 61, 113,
    253f., 318, 336
Mondésert, Claude, 65, 79, 95, 99f.,
    153
Monier, 252
Montcheuil, Yves de, 46, 53ff., 97ff.,
    103, 142, 155, 163, 165, 194, 213,
    232, 250, 254, 275, 320f., 323
Montini, Giovanni (see Paul VI)
Montuclard, 68, 247
Morel, Georges, 168
Mother Saint John, 78
Mounier, Emmanuel, 27, 38, 50, 230

Mouroux, Jean, 31, 64, 141
Mulla (Bishop), 102

Nédoncelle, Maurice, 103, 182
Nemeck, Francis, 109
Nemoz, Adrien, 51, 53
Neufeld, Karl H., 15, 142, 351
Newman, John Henry, 10, 64, 81, 83,
    170, 182, 293
Nicolas, M. J., 30, 194
Nicolet, Charles, 15, 35, 65, 92, 115,
    155, 314, 321, 339
Nietzche, Friedrich, 41
Noël, Léon, 93
Noris, 260, 263

Olichon, 27
O'Neill, Cobman E., 28
Orcibal, Jean, 112
Origen, 64, 66, 83, 140, 154, 281f.,
    285–89, 313, 318f.
d'Ormisson, Wladimir, 48, 75, 137
Ottaviani (Cardinal), 61, 117f., 195,
    251, 253, 256, 302f.
d'Ouince, René, 46, 61, 97, 109, 111,
    160, 165, 196, 250f., 253f., 258,
    300

Pardes, M., 225, 227f.
Parra, 254
Paquier, M., 226
Parente, Pietro, 20, 60, 106
Paul, St., 136, 162, 164, 329, 386
Paul VI, 75f., 108, 119ff., 149, 157–
    60, 168, 172, 251, 307, 315, 368f.,
    379–85
Pegis, Anton, 123, 125, 128
Pègues, 47
Péguy, Charles-Pierre, 41, 55, 137f.,
    145, 162, 229f.
Pelagius, 208, 221
Périer, M., 226
Perrin, M.-T., 72, 177, 182
Pétain, Marshal, 247
Petit, Paul, 48f.
Philips, Gérard, 37, 56, 128, 207–10
Philo, 286
Picard, 164

Picarda, Gabriel, 20
Pierre, Gonzague, 53
Pignedoli (Cardinal), 132
Pius X, 72f., 77
Pius XI, 28, 48, 254
Pius XII, 60f., 68f., 89, 116, 169, 250, 252, 254ff., 291, 294f., 314f., 326, 334
Piveteau, Jean, 330
Plaquet, Clément, 92
Plato, 183
Podechard, Emmanuel, 22
Poupard (Monsignor), 133
Pressoir, 196
Proudhon, P.J., 39, 223f.
Puech, Henri-Charles, 112

Quesnel, Pasquier, 264

Rahner, Hugo, 318
Rahner, Karl, 62, 169, 318, 344
Rambaud, Henri, 108
Rambaud, Joseph (see Trinité, Philippe de la)
Ratzinger, Joseph, 107, 122, 150, 345f.
Ravier, André, 43, 72, 88f., 91, 102, 109, 112, 314f.
Raynal, Henri, 344
Refoulé, F., 121f.
Régnier, Marcel, 108, 153, 267
Régnon, de (Father), 56
Renouvin, Pierre, 93
Renwart, 128
Ribes, Bruno, 108
Ribière, Germaine, 51
Richard, Louis, 54, 232, 235
Ricouer, Paul, 86
Rideau, Emile, 47, 282–85
Ripalda, 208, 214, 222
Riquet, Michel, 53
Rivau, du (Father), 70
Rivière, Jean, 25
Roncalli (see John XXIII)
Rondet, Henri, 30, 46, 67, 70, 95, 128, 195, 252, 256, 275
Rougier, Marie, 99f., 109, 165
Roullet, André, 27

Rousselot, M., 19f., 35, 144, 181f., 213, 263
Rousseaux, André, 38
Roux, Hébert, 358
Ruffini (Monsignor), 47, 228, 343
Russell, William, 119
Ruysbroeck, William, 209, 216

Saint-Avit, Dom de, 252
Salaville, Severien, 24
Sales, Michel, 131, 142, 155, 165ff., 392, 395f.
Saliège (Cardinal), 48, 50f., 98, 230
Savonarola, Girolamo, 180
Schellenbaum, Peter, 109
Scheur (Father), S.J., 42
Schillebeeckx, E., 154, 366
Schlier, Heinrich, 119
Schumann, Maurice, 137
Schuon, Frithjof, 33
Schutz, Roger, 45
Seconsac, Dunoyer de, 49
Segond, Joseph, 46
Sertillanges, 80ff., 226
Siauve, Suzanne, 114
Siri (Cardinal), 168f.
Smith, Gerard, 123, 125, 128, 202, 387
Smulders, Pieter Frans, 122
Solages, Bruno de, 27, 32, 54, 103, 105, 108f., 128, 141, 177, 195, 228, 232, 235ff., 266, 323
Soloviev, Vladimir, 156
Sommet, Jacques, 53
Soras, Alfred de, 46
Soto, 125, 129, 373
Soulages, Gérard, 149
Spinoza, Baruch, 140
Steinmann, Jean, 86f., 314
Stern, Philippe, 32
Suarez, Francisco, 214, 223
Subilia, Vittorio, 199
Suhard (Cardinal), 58, 195
Swain, Jean L., 105, 324
Sylvester of Ferrara, 214f.

Taille, Maurice de la, 251
Tapié, Victor-L., 93

Tauler, Johannes, 216
Tézé, Jean-Marie, 266
Thibon, Gustave, 239
Thurian, Max, 45
Tillich, Paul, 71
Tilliette, Xavier, 101, 130, 165, 352
Torney, Hilaire, 138
Torrell, Jean-Pierre, 267, 354
Trethowan, Illtyd, 36, 354
Trinité, Philippe de la (Joseph Rambaud), 106, 128
Tromp, Sébastien, 37, 117
Turner, Vincent, 212f.

Vaganay, Léon, 23, 312
Valensin, Albert, 15f., 27
Valensin, Auguste, 16–21, 46, 94, 99ff., 103, 105, 108ff., 165, 254, 321f., 323
Valéry, Paul, 100
Van Esbroeck, 85
Van Hove, A., 221ff.

Varillon, François, 47, 112
Vernet, Félix, 22
Veuillot, Pierre, 75, 315
Vialatoux, Joseph, 27, 209
Vigneaux, Paul, 56, 217–19
Villain, Maurice, 195f., 256
Villepelet, Georges, 88, 368
Villot, Jean, 24
Vincent (Father), 66, 86, 122, 254, 287f.

Wehrlé, J., 102, 177, 363
Weil, S., 396
Wenger, A., 345f.
Wetter, P. G., 190
White, Victor, 128
Winling, Raymond, 223
Wojtyla, Karl (see John Paul II)
Wright, John J., 118
Wulf., J. de, 182

Zupan, Jean, 32, 46, 154